Have you got questions?

answers:

ANY QUESTIONS?

QUICKEN 4 for WINDOWS MADE EASY

David Campbell, CPA
and Mary Campbell

Osborne **McGraw-Hill**

Berkeley New York St. Louis San Francisco
Auckland Bogotá Hamburg London Madrid
Mexico City Milan Montreal New Delhi Panama City
Paris São Paulo Singapore Sydney
Tokyo Toronto

Osborne **McGraw-Hill**
2600 Tenth Street
Berkeley, California 94710
U.S.A.

For information on translations or book distributors outside of the U.S.A., please write to Osborne **McGraw-Hill** at the above address.

Quicken 4 for Windows Made Easy

Copyright © 1995 by McGraw-Hill. All rights reserved. Printed in the United States of America. Except as permitted under the Copyright Act of 1976, no part of this publication may be reproduced or distributed in any form or by any means, or stored in a database or retrieval system, without the prior written permission of the publisher, with the exception that the program listings may be entered, stored, and executed in a computer system, but they may not be reproduced for publication.

1234567890 DOC 998765

ISBN 0-07-881734-X

Publisher
Lawrence Levitsky

Acquisitions Editor
Joanne Cuthbertson

Technical Editor
John Heilborn

Copy Editors
Marc Polonsky
Kimberly Torgerson

Proofreader
Patricia Mannion

Computer Designer
Roberta Steele

Quality Control Specialist
Joe Scuderi

Illustrators
Marla Shelasky
Lance Ravella

Cover Design
Compass Marketing

Information has been obtained by Osborne **McGraw-Hill** from sources believed to be reliable. However, because of the possibility of human or mechanical error by our sources, Osborne **McGraw-Hill**, or others, Osborne **McGraw-Hill** does not guarantee the accuracy, adequacy, or completeness of any information and is not responsible for any errors or omissions or the results obtained from use of such information.

About the Authors:

David Campbell, co-author of the previous best-selling editions of *Quicken Made Easy* and *Quicken for Windows Made Easy,* is a certified Public Accountant and widely published author on accounting system methods. He is chairman of the Accounting Department at Case Western Reserve University, where he is also a professor of accounting. He holds a Ph.D. in Accounting from the University of Georgia.

Software and training expert Mary Campbell co-authored the previous best-selling editions of *Quicken Made Easy* and *Quicken for Windows Made Easy*. She is the author of numerous widely acclaimed books on Excel, Lotus 1-2-3, Microsoft Access, and WordPerfect. She is also one of the authors writing for Osborne's new series of *Certified Tech Support* books. As an experienced corporate trainer and president of her own computer training company, she has taught thousands of people how to use these and many other popular software programs.

TABLE of CONTENTS

INTRODUCTION

Whether you are trying to manage your personal finances or those of your business, Quicken for Windows can end your financial hassles. The package contains all the features necessary for organizing your finances, yet because the features are jargon-free, you can focus on your financial needs without becoming an accountant or a financial planner.

If you use the program for your personal finances, you will find that you can easily determine your financial worth or create a report with the information you need for your tax forms. You can also create budget reports or a list of all your cash, check, or credit card transactions. Everything you do will be with the benefit of menus and easy-to-use quick-key combinations. You will soon wonder how you managed your finances without Quicken.

If you are trying to manage a small business and deal with all the financial issues, Quicken can make the task seem manageable. Whether your business is a part-time venture or employs several people, Quicken provides all the capabilities you need to look at your profit and loss picture, analyze your cash flows, or put together a budget. Quicken's ability to handle the recording of payroll information makes it easy to monitor what you owe for federal and state income tax withholding, FICA, and other payroll-related costs such as workers' compensation and federal and state unemployment taxes. Although it is not quite the same as having an accountant on your payroll, Quicken can make an otherwise unmanageable task possible.

About This Book

Quicken 4 for Windows Made Easy is designed to help you master Quicken's features so you can apply them to your financial situation. Even if you are a complete novice with the computer, you will find that you can learn from the step-by-step exercises in each chapter. As you work through the exercises you will feel as though you have a seasoned computer pro guiding you each step of the way.

This book offers more than just instruction for using Quicken's features. The exercises throughout the book are based on the authors' personal and business transactions. Although names of the banks, suppliers, and employees as well as dollar amounts have all been changed, all of what you read is based on factual illustrations much like the ones you will need to record your own transactions.

Throughout the book we have included financial tips. When we started our business 14 years ago, we had to invest a considerable amount of time in finding answers to even the simplest questions, such as federal and state agency filing requirements. We have tried to include some of this information to simplify what you are facing if your business is new.

How This Book Is Organized

This book is divided into four parts to make it easy for you to focus on Quicken basics, personal applications, business applications, and the supplementary information provided in the Appendixes. Part I, Quick Start, includes the first six chapters. This section covers all the basic skills needed to use Quicken, even if you are a new Windows user. You will find that the exercises within these chapters will make you productive with Quicken in a short period of time.

Chapter 1 provides an overview of Quicken's features. You will see examples of reports and windows that you can use for your own applications. Chapter 2 introduces HomeBase, a new graphical approach to using Quicken. Chapter 3 introduces the Quicken account register where you record all Quicken information. In this chapter you will learn the skills needed to record your basic financial transactions. Chapter 4 teaches you how to create and print several Quicken reports. You learn to select the correct printer settings to print all the reports you will be preparing in the book. Chapter 5 illustrates how easy it is to balance your checkbook (the account register) with Quicken. The exercise actually takes you through the reconciliation steps. Chapter 6, the conclusion of Part I of the book, teaches you how to create Quicken checks. With one set of entries on a check, you can print the check and update your records.

Part II focuses on personal financial applications. It shows you how to create accounts for checking, credit cards, savings, and investments. You will learn how to determine your net worth and find the information you need to complete your tax returns. Chapter 7 shows you how to set up accounts and categories for personal finances. You will learn how to enter individual transactions as well as how to memorize them and automate their entry through transaction groups. Chapter 8 introduces the concept of budgeting in Quicken and discusses the Quicken 4 for Windows graphs. You will learn how to enter your budget estimates by category and how to monitor actual amounts against budgeted amounts. Chapter 9 illustrates how Quicken can be used to help complete your personal tax return. The example used demonstrates how to record your tax-related financial transactions and how Quicken can be used to summarize your tax-related transactions for the entire year. Chapter 10 shows you how to determine what you are worth financially. You will learn how to keep records on stocks and other investments and how to revalue these holdings to market values. Chapter 11, the final chapter in Part II, provides a look at Snapshots, additional Quicken reports, and the customizing options that you can add.

Part III covers business applications of Quicken. You will learn how to use the package to manage your business finances, including payroll record-keeping. Chapter 12 shows you how to create a chart of accounts for your business. You will also look at entering transactions for basic business expenses and revenues. Chapter 13 teaches you about payroll entries with Quicken, which not only prints your employees' paychecks, but can handle all your other payroll-related record keeping. Chapter 14 teaches you how to prepare a business budget with Quicken. You can enter the same value for each month or budget a different amount for each month. The budget reports that Quicken produces can provide an early warning of potential budget trouble spots. Chapter 15 discusses the forms you will need to file for business taxes. It also covers the income statement (the profit and loss statement) that tells you whether or not your business is profitable. Chapter 16 continues with coverage of another important financial report, as you have an opportunity to prepare a balance sheet that shows your assets, liabilities, and your equity (or investment) in the business.

Part IV includes three appendixes which provide installation and startup instructions, a glossary of financial terms, and a guide to all the options available for customizing Quicken 4.

New Features and Improvements in Quicken 4 for Windows

There are many new features in Quicken 4 for Windows that make it easier to use. The following is a list of some of the most important improvements:

- Snapshots, which provide an instant overview of your finances
- HomeBase's graphical alternative to making selections from Quicken's menu bar
- Supercategories, which group standard categories to simplify budgeting.
- The Tax Planner, which can help you determine whether your withholdings have been appropriate
- Progress bars to provide a quick gauge of how you are doing
- Savings goals to help you squirrel away money so you won't spend it
- A Global Find and Replace feature

Conventions Used

There are step-by-step examples for you to follow throughout the book. Every entry that you need to type is shown in boldface to make these exercises easy to follow. In addition, the names of menus, windows, and reports are shown with the same capitalization used in Quicken.

The names of keys such as ALT, E, and T are shown in small capitals. In situations where two keys must be pressed at the same time, the keycaps are joined with a hyphen, as in CTRL-E. If you use the keyboard rather than the mouse to make menu selections, you will find it convenient that this book underlines the letter needed to make each selection. In the menu at the top of the screens, use the ALT key in combination with the underlined letter to activate the menu and define your selection. In the pull-down menus, pressing the underlined letter alone is sufficient.

In cases where there are two ways to perform the same task, we have shown you the most efficient approach. As you learn more about Quicken, you can feel free to use whichever approach you prefer.

Quicken can provide the help you need to organize your personal finances. It will enable you to establish accounts for monitoring checking and savings accounts, credits cards, and investments. You will learn how to record and organize your financial information with Quicken's easy-to-use features. You will also learn how to prepare reports for taxes, budgeting, and computing your net worth.

PART 1

QUICK START

CHAPTER

An OVERVIEW of QUICKEN and YOUR COMPUTER COMPONENTS

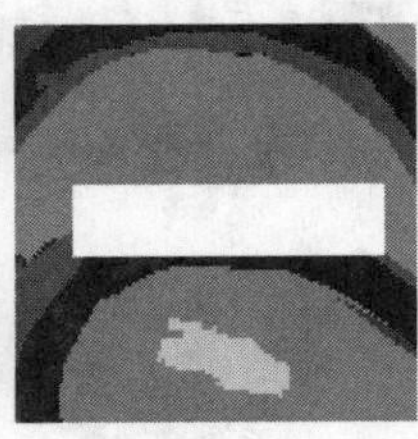

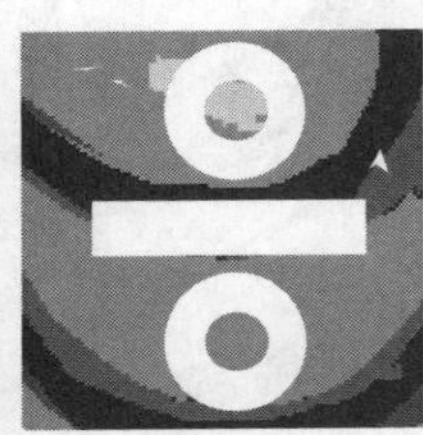

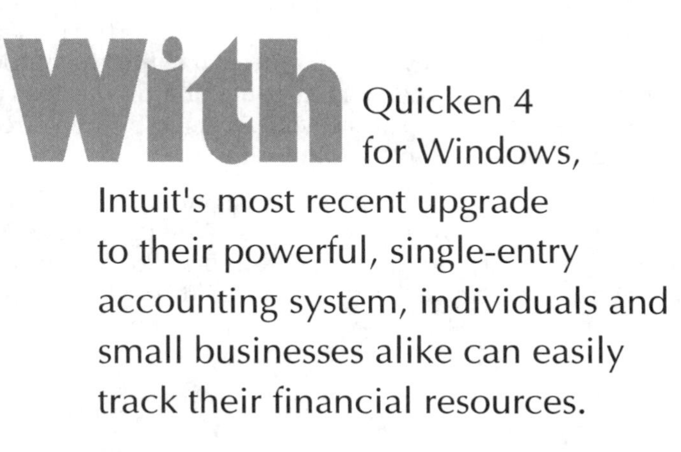

With Quicken 4 for Windows, Intuit's most recent upgrade to their powerful, single-entry accounting system, individuals and small businesses alike can easily track their financial resources.

Quicken is an *integrated* system, which means that it accumulates the information you enter, then provides a variety of methods to group and present that information.

Quicken is as easy to use as your current manual recording methods—but it is much faster. You will be surprised at how automatic using the application can become. It can memorize and record your regular transactions or write a check for your signature. It also organizes your information for you. This chapter's overview shows you the components of the package, examples of windows and dialog boxes used to enter data, and the output that is produced. You do not need to sit at your computer to read and understand this chapter. Later chapters, however, give step-by-step directions for using Quicken, and you will want to follow along.

This chapter also introduces the various components of your computer system and their relationship to Quicken. You learn how Quicken uses your computer system, disk space, memory, and keyboard. Some important mouse techniques and keys are introduced through a series of visual examples. In later chapters, you'll use what you learn here to enter and review Quicken data.

An Overview of Quicken

Quicken can assist you in meeting all your personal and business financial planning and reporting needs.

Quicken can handle all aspects of your financial management: everything from the initial recording and maintenance of information through organizing and reporting. Quicken provides features for recording your financial transactions easily. You can make a direct entry in a register that is an accounts journal or have Quicken write a check and record the information in the register automatically. Once your information has been recorded, you can have it presented in a variety of standard and customized reports.

Quicken 4 for Windows offers many exciting features that were not present in earlier versions. The redesigned screen makes it easy to use Windows graphical elements as you select from an icon bar, button bars, and other screen buttons. The Windows version provides support for the features in the current Quicken for DOS and can directly read these files, making it easy to switch from the DOS to the Windows version of the product.

Recording Financial Transactions

If you are tired of entering financial transactions in a handwritten journal, you will appreciate the recording abilities of Quicken. Entries are always neat—even if you have corrected several errors in the recording process—and there is no need to worry about math errors, since Quicken does the arithmetic for you.

Accounts are the major organizational units in Quicken. Each piece of information you record affects the balance in a Quicken account. You can establish checking and saving accounts for both personal and business purposes. In addition, you can establish credit card accounts, asset accounts (stocks and real estate), and liability accounts (mortgage and other payable loans). You can also transfer funds among these accounts with the Transfer feature—for example, move funds from savings to checking. You can store all of your accounts in a single file on your computer. Later, as your experience grows, you might want to create additional accounts in your Quicken file.

Quicken helps you track your investment activities.

Quicken 4 for Windows supports specialized investment accounts to allow you to track a collection of investments. You can enter information for stocks, bonds, mutual funds, and other investments. You can use the Portfolio View window, shown in Figure 1-1, to update the market prices of your investments and determine your gain or loss. Quicken 4 for Windows even lets you handle lots, to let you identify which group of shares have been sold if you own several lots.

Quicken can record the details of your financial transactions—both money you earn (income) and money you spend (expenses). Quicken can differentiate between income from a number of sources, such as salary and dividend income. It also supports entry of all types of expenses, from mortgage payments to clothing purchases. If you use Quicken to record business finances, you can keep track of freight charges, payroll costs, and so on. You can also customize Quicken to handle additional sources of income or expenses.

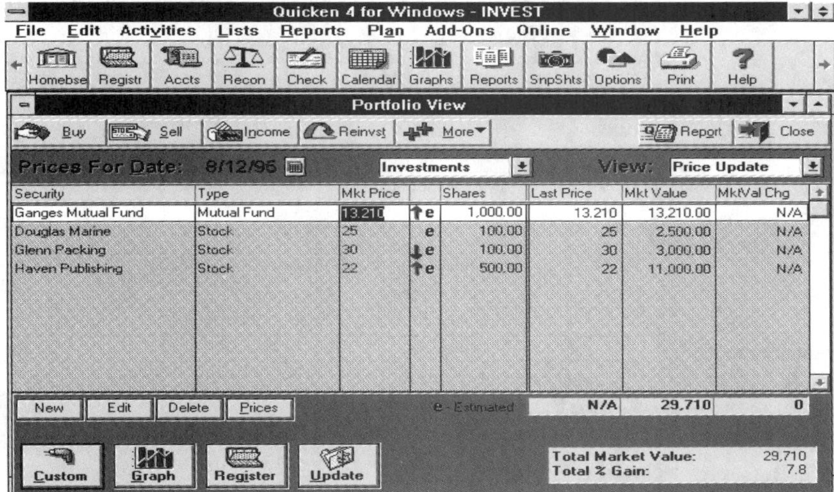

Updating the market prices for your investments
Figure 1-1.

The information recorded on a financial event is called a *transaction*. Purchasing an asset such as a car, or making a payment for services or goods such as groceries, is considered a transaction. In Quicken, you must record your transactions in order to have the correct balance in your accounts. This is accomplished by using a *register*, which is similar to a notebook or journal for record keeping. This serves the same purpose as your checkbook register, but with Quicken's advanced capabilities, you can generate powerful reports that help you manage your finances. Thus, one of the major components of the system is the register that you establish for each of your accounts (checking, savings, and other assets and liabilities). Figure 1-2 provides an example of entries in a Quicken register using a single line display mode, available by selecting the 1-Line Display check box at the bottom of the register window.

The account register is the center of your recording activities with Quicken.

With any checking account, reconciling the balance is tedious. Quicken reduces the time needed to reconcile the difference between the bank's balance and yours. Through the reconciliation process, you can accurately maintain the balance of your checking account and avoid the embarrassment of overdrawing your account. Quicken adjusts your register for service charges and interest earned on your checking account balance.

Quicken can also automate all your check writing activities. Figure 1-3 shows a check entry form enhanced with an optional graphic. You can buy checking supplies directly from Intuit (the company that developed and markets Quicken) or other check printers that allow you to write checks directly from the register and print them on your printer. While this option

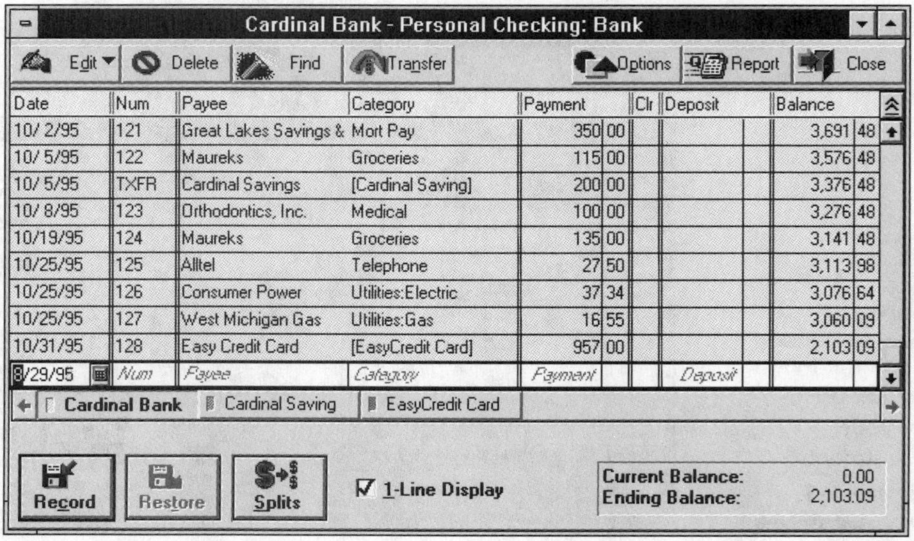

Cardinal Bank - Personal Checking: Bank

Edit | Delete | Find | Transfer | Options | Report | Close

Date	Num	Payee	Category	Payment	Clr	Deposit	Balance
10/ 2/95	121	Great Lakes Savings &	Mort Pay	350 00			3,691 48
10/ 5/95	122	Maureks	Groceries	115 00			3,576 48
10/ 5/95	TXFR	Cardinal Savings	[Cardinal Saving]	200 00			3,376 48
10/ 8/95	123	Orthodontics, Inc.	Medical	100 00			3,276 48
10/19/95	124	Maureks	Groceries	135 00			3,141 48
10/25/95	125	Alltel	Telephone	27 50			3,113 98
10/25/95	126	Consumer Power	Utilities:Electric	37 34			3,076 64
10/25/95	127	West Michigan Gas	Utilities:Gas	16 55			3,060 09
10/31/95	128	Easy Credit Card	[EasyCredit Card]	957 00			2,103 09
8/29/95	*Num*	*Payee*	*Category*	*Payment*		*Deposit*	

Cardinal Bank | Cardinal Saving | EasyCredit Card

Record | Restore | Splits | ☑ 1-Line Display

Current Balance: 0.00
Ending Balance: 2,103.09

A Quicken register window
Figure 1-2.

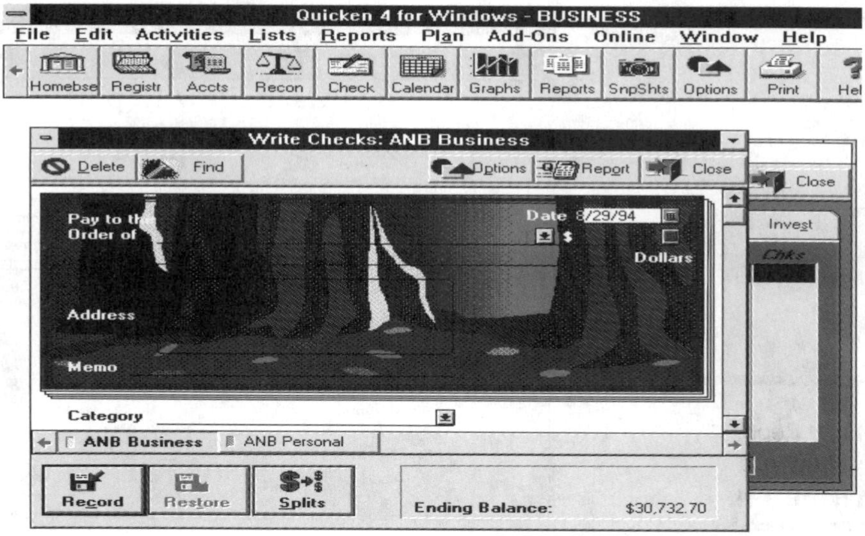

The Write Checks window
Figure 1-3.

is particularly attractive for business activities, it can be useful for your personal checking account as well. Even if you write your checks by hand, you can benefit from maintaining your transactions in Quicken.

Quicken Reports

Quicken's reports let you monitor your financial condition easily.

The value of any accounting system lies in its ability to generate useful, informative reports that assist you in making financial decisions. With Quicken, you can prepare personal, business, and investment reports, and preview them on the screen before printing.

You can choose to print an entire report after viewing it, or you can print a range of pages. You can access the detail behind a summary report while viewing the report with the QuickZoom feature. You can also customize a report displayed on your screen. Figure 1-4 shows an onscreen personal Cash Flow report.

If you'd rather look at an overview of your financial picture, you can start with Quicken 4's new Snapshot summary. The six reports and graphs shown in Figure 1-5 let you look at various aspects of your finances. You can zoom in for a closer look at any one area or define another snapshot that would be more useful to you.

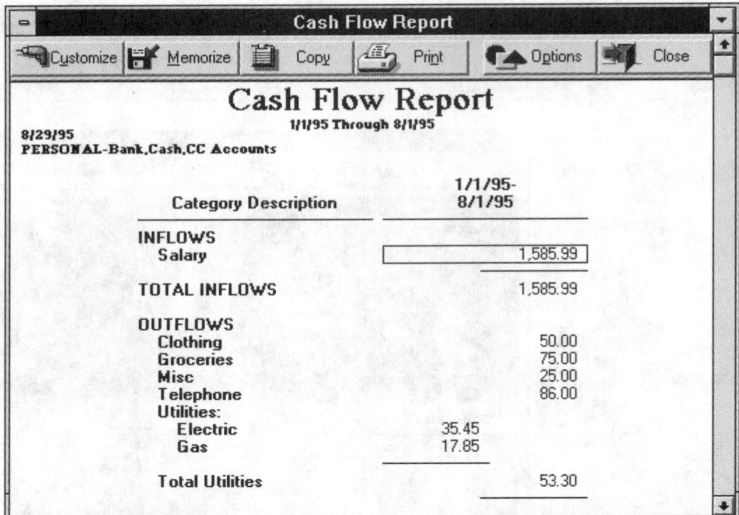

The Cash Flow Report window
Figure 1-4.

Home or Personal Reports

Besides providing you with a printout of your check register, Quicken can generate other reports tailored for personal financial management. They will become valuable as the year progresses, showing how you spent your money and how much you have. You can create personal reports that summarize cash inflow and outflow, monitor your budget, summarize tax activities, and look at an overall measure of how well you are doing.

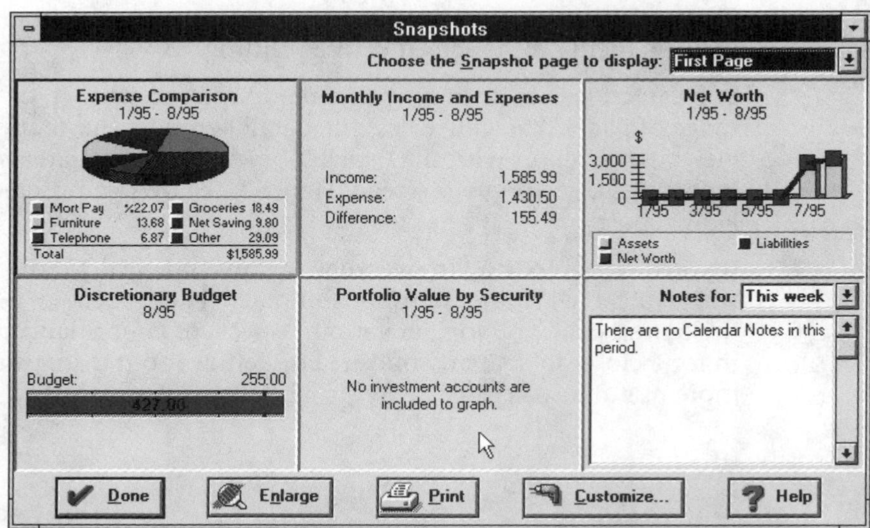

Quicken 4's new Financial Snapshots
Figure 1-5.

Business Reports

Quicken handles accounting transactions for businesses as well as for individuals. Because small business reports differ from those of an individual, the package provides a separate list of standard business reports. Some of the business reports that you can create are a profit and loss report, an analysis of cash flow, a balance sheet, accounts payable, and a payroll report. Quicken also allows you to create customized reports for home or business use.

Investment Reports

With Quicken's investment accounts, you can record and track all of your investments. The five standard investment reports provide information on portfolio value, investment performance, capital gains, investment income, and investment transactions.

Creating Graphs

Reports can provide extremely useful summaries or detailed records of transactions. Graphs, on the other hand, are much more effective at giving a quick overview of a financial situation. Quicken 4 for Windows provides four basic graph types, and you can further customize them by deciding what data to include. You can use the QuickZoom feature to show more detail. If this detail is not sufficient, you can use QuickZoom again to look at a report more closely. You also can use graphs to look at trends and other comparison information as shown in Figure 1-6, which compares budget and actual figures. Figure 1-7 provides another example showing the monthly portfolio value by security.

Financial Planning

Quicken 4 for Windows provides many tools to assist you with financial planning. A loan calculator and four other financial planners let you perform what-if analysis in areas such as retirement or college planning, investments, and refinancing.

Quicken 4's budgeting features allow you to plan and monitor expenditures at a detailed or summary level. The new budget supercategories let you establish groups of categories so that you can see an overview of your budgeting, or set budget amounts for sets of categories rather than each individual one.

The new Quicken 4 Savings Goal feature lets you earmark funds for planned expenses. It effectively hides these funds so you won't be tempted to spend them for other purposes. Savings goals are designed for letting you track

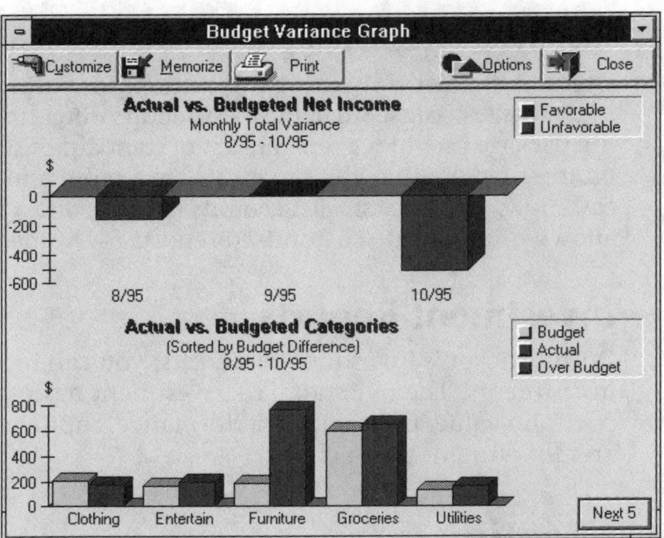

A Budget Variance graph
Figure 1-6.

savings that are part of an existing account, rather than being deposited into a new account.

You can use the new Progress Bar on screen to monitor your progress toward your savings or budgetary goals. The Progress Bar displays your current progress in meeting budgeted amounts or savings goals using "gas gauge" type graphs.

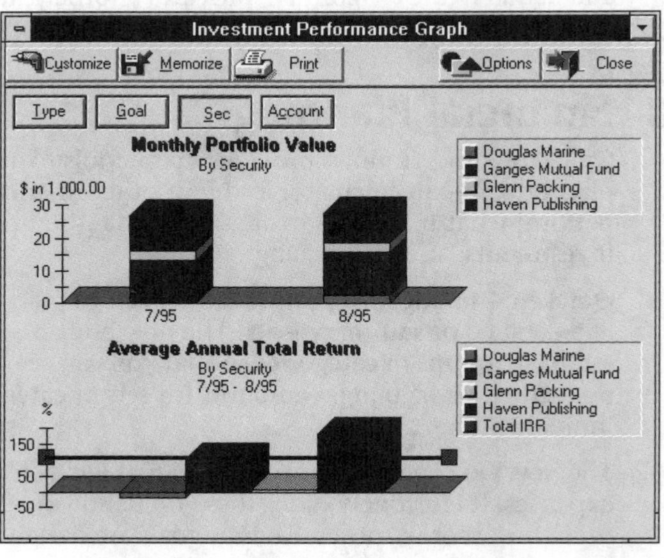

An Investment Performance graph
Figure 1-7.

The Quicken 4's Tax Planner can zero in on the taxes you'll owe at the year's end. With this planner, you can determine whether you need to adjust your withholdings or file quarterly tax estimates.

Changing Preference Settings

Quicken's customization features let you fine-tune the application to meet your needs. This means you can make changes to fit your exact reporting requirements or to work properly with the computer equipment you have selected. You can make these changes by selecting the options button from the icon bar or Preferences from the Edit menu, opening a dialog box that contains icons you can choose from to make the changes you need, as shown here:

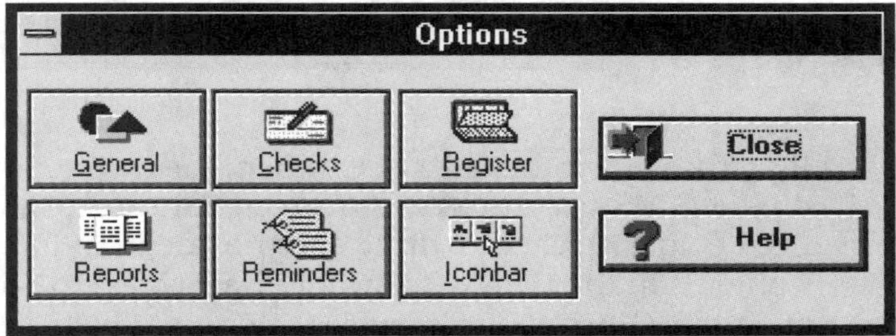

You can set customization preferences for individual features of Quicken, such as the register or budget window by selecting the Options button in the window's button bar.

Quicken's Help Features

Quicken's onscreen help features make the package easy to use.

Onscreen help is at your fingertips. All you ever need to do is press F1 (Help) or click the Help button in the icon bar. Quicken assesses the type of help you need and displays a Help window that contains information about the feature you are using or the problem you have encountered. Quicken's ability to assess your situation and choose a relevant help topic is called *context-sensitive help*. Figure 1-8 shows the Help window that Quicken displays if you select the Help icon while in an investment account register window. The highlighted or colored text in the Help window is called *hypertext*. When you select hypertext, you switch to a new window of information on that topic. You can select hypertext by moving the insertion point to it with the TAB key and pressing ENTER. In the section "The Keyboard, Mouse, and Screen Display" later in this chapter, you learn how to use a mouse to make selections.

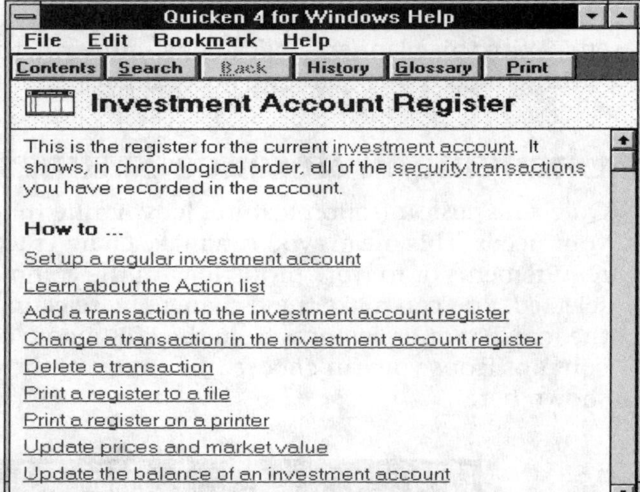

The Help screen for the Investment Account Register window
Figure 1-8.

If you are in another area of Quicken, the help topic presented may be very different. With a check on the screen, for example, Quicken assumes you need help with check writing and provides that information. You can select Contents in the Help window for direct access to the Quicken Help Index at any time. Quicken also provides tutorials to help get you started through the Help menu.

Quicken provides additional help through Qcards, which provide hints to walk you through the completion of some more complicated tasks such as reconciling an account, creating a new account, and using the investment register. The default setting is to display Qcards for tasks on which they give guidance. To turn them off, choose Show Qcards from the Help menu to clear the check mark in front of it.

Quicken and Your Computer System

If you're a novice computer user, read the rest of this chapter carefully. It will eliminate much of the confusion experienced by new users trying to figure out what is in memory, what is on disk, and exactly how their computer makes it possible for a program like Quicken to do so much work so quickly. If you are already knowledgeable about your system, you may want to skim the rest of the chapter just to see how Quicken works with the computer. If you are using Quicken, it is assumed that you are using Windows 3.1 or higher and are running the DOS operating system on an IBM PC or compatible computer.

Memory

There are two kinds of memory in your computer: RAM and ROM. *ROM* is read-only memory—you cannot affect its contents, so it's of little concern here. *RAM* is random-access memory—temporary storage inside your computer. RAM contains the program you are running (for example Quicken, 1-2-3, or dBASE) and the data you are currently working with in the program.

If you lose the power to your machine, you lose the contents of RAM. This is why permanent storage media such as disks are an essential component of your computer system. If your data is saved to disk, you can always load it into memory again after turning off your system or after a power failure.

The amount of RAM in your system is determined by the computer you have purchased and any additional memory you may have added to the system. Memory is measured in kilobytes (K) or megabytes (MB). 1K is the space required to store approximately a thousand characters of information, and 1 MB is the space required to store approximately one million characters. Some systems have as little as 2 MB of memory, while others may have 8 MB or even 64 MB of memory. To run both Windows and Quicken you need at least 2 MB of memory. The amount of memory your system has determines the number of other Windows programs you can run and the performance of your system. A system with 4 MB of RAM is required if you want to run Quicken with other programs.

The more memory your system has available, the better your Windows applications will operate. With enough memory, your applications won't need to keep swapping information as they operate, since everything needed by each application can remain in memory. When it comes to computer memory, more is always better.

Disk Storage

Disk storage on your system may consist of one or more hard disks and floppy disks in either 3 1/2-inch or 5 1/4-inch sizes. Quicken requires a hard disk with more than 7 MB of free space in which to install the program files and store your data. Like RAM, disk space is measured in either kilobytes or megabytes.

Most hard disks have from 120 to 340 MB of storage capacity. This means you will have room for Quicken as well as other software packages such as dBASE, WordPerfect, or 1-2-3.

Your computer uses a letter to represent each disk drive. Typically, hard disks are called drives C or D, while floppy drives are called A or B.

You can organize the files on your hard disk into *directories*. Directories are like file folders that contain individual documents so that you can find them easily later. All the program files you need for Quicken are stored in a single directory on your hard disk. The following illustration shows a possible configuration of the directories on a hard disk.

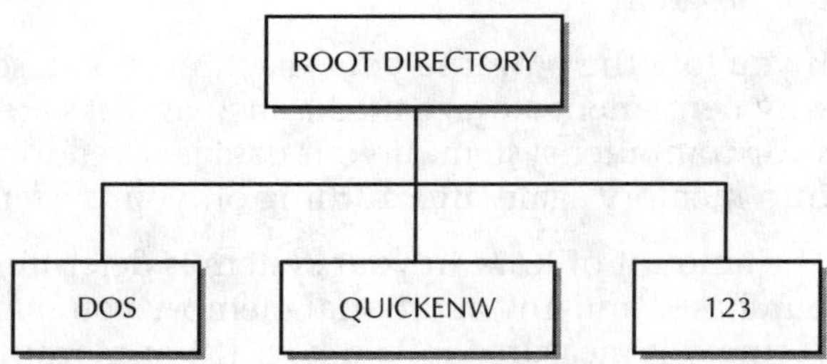

In this illustration, the root, or main, directory on your hard disk would contain batch files, which contain DOS instructions. Separate subdirectories are created to maintain the program files for DOS, Windows, and any other programs. When you install Quicken on your hard disk, it creates its own subdirectory, called QUICKENW.

When you run Quicken for Windows, you need free space on your hard disk to store your Quicken data. You also need free space for Windows to use as temporary storage space as it swaps data between memory and a temporary file on your hard disk. If you do not have sufficient free disk space, you will degrade the performance of Quicken and other Windows applications.

The Keyboard, Mouse, and Screen Display

Throughout this book, you will be using your mouse as well as the keyboard to communicate with Quicken.

The screen and the mouse or keyboard serve as the central communication points between you and Quicken. Everything you want to tell Quicken must be selected with a mouse or entered through the keyboard. If you are using a keyboard, you are already familiar with many of the keys; they are used to enter data regardless of the type of program you are using. Although a few key combinations issue standard commands in all Windows applications, other key combinations have special meanings in Quicken. Even if you have used the same key combinations in other programs, you may find that they issue different commands in each program.

The mouse lets you make selections and perform tasks without using the keyboard. You will learn new terms and new ways of doing things as you click, double-click, and drag with a mouse to accomplish activities. You will learn about each of these new options in this section.

Quicken uses the screen to present information to you. Quicken supports both monochrome (one color) and color monitors. Your computer must have a graphics card to view Windows or Quicken for Windows.

Keyboard Styles

Not all keyboards are alike, although virtually all of them provide all of the keys you need to use Quicken. However, you may have to look around to find the keys you need, especially if you are getting used to a new keyboard. On all the older model PCs and compatibles, the arrow keys move the insertion point or highlight around on your screen. These keys are located on the *numeric keypad* at the far right side of the keyboard. They can also enter numbers, when the NUM LOCK key is depressed to activate this feature. With NUM LOCK off, the arrow keys move the insertion point in the direction indicated at the top of the key. If these keys aren't set properly for your use, just press NUM LOCK and they assume their alternate function.

On newer keyboards, called IBM *enhanced keyboards*, there are separate arrow keys to the left of the numeric keypad that move the insertion point. This lets you to leave the NUM LOCK feature on for data entry because you can use these arrow keys to move around on the screen.

Mouse Devices

Quicken 4 for Windows supports all Microsoft-compatible mouse devices. Quicken automatically recognizes a compatible mouse and displays a mouse pointer that looks like a small arrow on the screen. As you roll the mouse over your desktop, the mouse pointer arrow moves to different locations on your screen and sometimes changes its appearance. Your mouse device will have either two or three buttons on top.

Mouse Actions

A mouse button can be used to perform a variety of actions. You can *click* the button by pressing it and quickly releasing it. You can *double-click* by completing two clicks in rapid succession. You can *drag* with the mouse by continuing to hold down the mouse button while rolling the mouse across the desktop. Mouse actions require you to position the mouse pointer on the desired screen element before proceeding.

Left Mouse Button Tasks

The left mouse button is used for most Quicken tasks. With this button, you can accomplish the following actions:

- Select a command from the pull-down menus or Quicken 4's new HomeBase feature.
- Select an action by clicking a button on the icon bar.
- Finalize a record by clicking on Record.
- Select a register transaction.
- Display a Split Transaction window by clicking the Splits button.
- Scroll through transactions by clicking the vertical scroll bar arrows.
- Page up or down with a click to that side of the scroll box on the scroll bar.

Double-clicking is not used as often as the click action. You can use a double-click to select any item in a list. Dragging moves you to a different location in a list as you drag the scroll box vertically. Holding down the mouse button with the mouse pointer in a list or register scrolls up or down the list or register.

Menu Selections

Quicken provides pull-down menus to simplify your features and command selections. These menus lead to all major tasks or activities the program performs.

The menus display either an ellipsis (...) immediately following the selection to indicate that additional information must be supplied in a dialog box, or an arrow pointing to the right to indicate that further menu selections are required for carrying out an action. Some menu choices will display a key combination that can be used to activate the feature in lieu of making a menu selection. You can see each of these elements in the File menu, shown here:

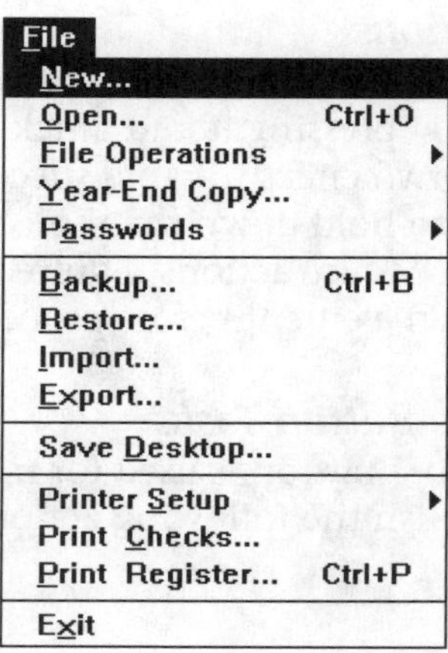

You will notice that each of the options in a menu has an underlined letter just as the menu names themselves do. You will learn to use these letters in making selections if you prefer to use the keyboard instead of the mouse.

Making Menu Selections with the Mouse

You can select a menu name by moving the mouse pointer to the desired name and pressing the left mouse button. This is referred to as clicking the menu name. The menu options will appear in a pull-down menu. You can move the mouse pointer to the desired option in this menu and click again to select it.

Making Menu Selections with the Keyboard

Working in the Windows environment encourages using the mouse, since there are many graphical elements that can be selected easily. This approach is often easier than using the keyboard for the same selections. If you are not quite ready to make the transition to the mouse, Quicken still supports the keyboard. You can select a menu by pressing the ALT key in combination with the underlined letter in the menu. This will display the options in the pull-down menu, and you can type the letter of the desired menu item to select it.

Effects of Menu Selections

Some selections result in the appearance of a *window* or *dialog box* on the screen. Windows and dialog boxes differ from menus in that there are several pieces of information for you to complete, as well as buttons to select. If you want to use the option already chosen (the *default*), there is no need to make a change. You can simply press TAB to accept that choice and move to the next *field*, where you will supply information. If you do not understand what is expected in a field, you can press F1 (Help) for an explanation.

Dialog boxes and windows look very similar. Here, however, are some differences:

- Windows always have sizing buttons in the upper-right corner. Dialog boxes do not, since they cannot be sized.
- When you are in a dialog box, you must complete it or cancel your request before switching to another task. You can switch between windows as often as you want using either the Windows menu or your mouse to change the active window.
- Dialog boxes almost always offer buttons for actions or confirmation such as Done, Save, OK, and Cancel.

QuickFill Saves Entry Time

Quicken's QuickFill feature speeds up the transaction entry process and helps reduce errors.

No matter how proficient you are with the keyboard, the quickest way to enter data is to have Quicken do it for you. Quicken 4 for Windows' QuickFill feature is designed to do just that. If you are typing a check number, category, payee, security, or action, Quicken checks its list of entries as soon as you type a character and displays the first match its finds. As you type additional letters, Quicken is able to refine the match. You can press TAB to accept the entry. Alternatively, you can select an entry from a drop-down list box of possible options. Use DOWN ARROW to advance through options in the list, and press ENTER to select the currently highlighted one.

If you prefer not to use the drop-down list boxes, you can stop Quicken from displaying them automatically. To do this, select Options in a register window. Switch to the QuickFill tab, and clear the Drop Down List Automatically check box before selecting OK. When you are in the payee field of a register, Quicken checks for payees in any of your memorized transactions. When you accept the payee, Quicken copies the entire transaction, which you can edit if you choose.

Quick Keys

Quick Keys provide access to commands. You can use these key combinations throughout Quicken to speed up transaction entries in the register, check writing, and report printing. All Quick Keys involve pressing the CTRL key in combination with another key. When you pull down a menu, you see "Ctrl+" and a letter next to the menu items that can be activated with a Quick Key combination. The more you use the Quick Keys, the easier it will be to remember the combination needed for each activity.

As you become familiar with Quicken, you will find that these keys help you reduce time spent on financial record keeping. If you wish to use the keyboard to activate menu options, review the Quick Keys listed here:

Quick Key	Equivalent Menu Selection
CTRL-O	File ¦ Open
CTRL-B	File ¦ Backup
CTRL-P	File ¦ Print
ALT-BACKSPACE	Edit ¦ Undo
SHIFT-DEL	Edit ¦ Cut
CTRL-INS	Edit ¦ Copy
SHIFT-INS	Edit ¦ Paste

CTRL-N	Edit¦New Transaction
CTRL-E	Edit¦Edit
CTRL-D	Edit¦Delete Transaction
CTRL-V	Edit¦Void Transaction
CTRL-I	Edit¦Insert Transaction
CTRL-M	Edit¦Memorize Transaction
CTRL-F	Edit¦Find
CTRL-X	Edit¦Go To Transfer
CTRL-W	Activities¦Write Checks
CTRL-R	Activities¦Use Register
CTRL-K	Activities¦Financial Calendar
CTRL-H	Activities¦Loans
CTRL-U	Activities¦Portfolio View
CTRL-A	Lists¦Account
CTRL-C	Lists¦Category & Transfer
CTRL-L	Lists¦Class
CTRL-T	Lists¦Memorized Transaction
CTRL-J	Lists¦Scheduled Transaction
CTRL-Y	Lists¦Security
F1	Help¦Quicken Help

Special Keys

If you've already used other Windows applications on your computer, you'll find that many of the special keys work the same in Quicken as in those other applications. For example, the ESC key is used to cancel your most recent menu selection. The SPACEBAR, at the bottom of the keyboard, is used to add blank spaces when making entries. The BACKSPACE key deletes the last character you typed, the character to the left of the insertion point. DEL deletes the current selection if an item is selected. It deletes the character to the right of the insertion point when text is not selected and the insertion point appears as a vertical bar.

The SHIFT key is used to enter capital letters and the special symbols at the top of non-letter keys. The CAPS LOCK key is used to enter all letters in capitals, but it does not affect the entry of special symbols, which always require the SHIFT key. To enter a lowercase letter with CAPS LOCK on, hold down the SHIFT key. To turn CAPS LOCK off, just press it a second time.

The TAB key usually moves you from field to field. Pressing SHIFT and TAB together moves the insertion backward through the fields on the screen. CTRL-END moves the insertion point to the bottom of the display; CTRL-HOME moves you to the top of the display.

The PAGE UP and PAGE DOWN keys move up and down screens and menus.

Quicken uses the + and - keys on the numeric keypad to quickly increase and decrease numbers such as the date and the check number. When these keys are pressed once, the number increases or decreases by one. However, since the keys all repeat when held down, holding down either of these keys can rapidly effect a major change. The + and - keys perform their functions in appropriate fields whether NUM LOCK is on or off.

The Icon Bar

The icon bar provides a shortcut for performing many common Quicken tasks.

The icon bar is the band of icons that appears immediately under the menu bar in the Quicken window. It is also a useful shortcut for Quicken. You can use the icon bar to simplify various activities you carry out in Quicken. You can use either the default icon bar, or you can modify it to include the icons most useful to you.

When you select an icon, an action is carried out. You select an action by pointing the mouse at the icon and clicking the left mouse button. For example, when you point the mouse at the Accts icon and click it, the Accounts List window appears in the Quicken window. Icons have both pictures and text associated with them. You can choose to display both, as is the default, or to display only the picture or the text.

You can also change the icons that appear on the icon bar. You can create a whole new icon bar, or modify the current one. You can use a selection of graphic images, and create text to go with them.

Button Bars

Button bars are icon bars located at the top of various windows, such as the register, budget, and report windows. Each windows' button bar presents a variety of buttons for performing common tasks for the type of information displayed in the window. You can click a button or press ALT and its underlined letter to have the desired action performed. Buttons can be used to copy or paste a transaction with a simple click, or to create an automatic report.

The Calculator

Quicken's calculator lets you perform basic computations on the screen, using the mathematical operators such as + for addition, - for subtraction, * for multiplication, and / for division. Simple calculations or more complex formulas are possible.

A significant feature of Quicken's calculator is its ability to compute a payment amount or other figure needed in the *current transaction entry* (the one in use) and then place, or *paste*, the result onto the screen. When you select Use Calculator from the Activities menu, you get the following calculator:

You might use the calculator to compute the total of nine invoices so that one check can be written to cover all nine. You can also compute discounts or interest on a loan. Once Quicken computes an amount, you can click the Paste button to paste the amount into a field. You can activate a drop-down calculator in any field that displays the calculator symbol at the right end, such as the Payment field, by typing a + or clicking the icon.

The Financial Calendar

Quicken 4 for Windows' Financial Calendar gives you a tool for taking a quick look ahead to how things are going for you. You can see dates when upcoming bills must be paid as well as dates when you expect to receive a check that can be deposited. You can mark both recurring transactions and one-time payments on the calendar. You can add a note to any day and choose to display a bar chart at the bottom for an assessment of how you are doing financially. Figure 1-9 shows a month from the Financial Calendar.

Forecasting your Financial Picture

Quicken 4 for Windows adds a new Forecasting feature, which displays a graph of your future financial picture. The Forecasting feature, as shown in

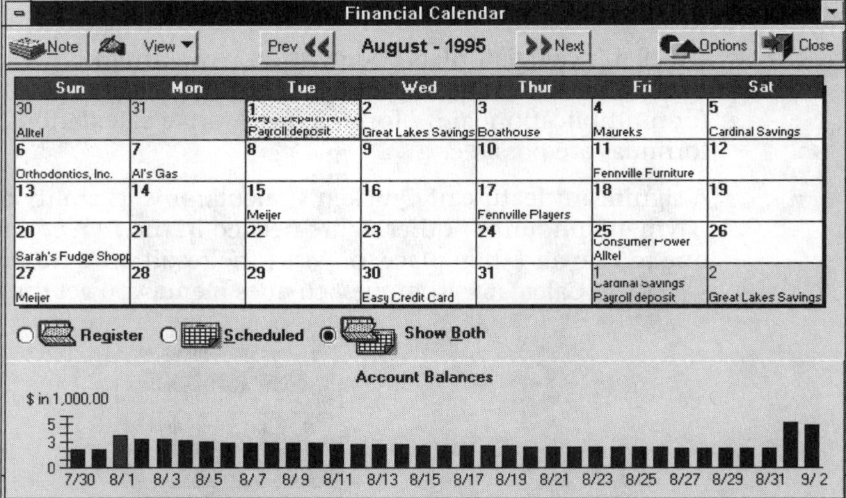

Quicken's financial planning calendar
Figure 1-9.

Figure 1-10, displays a graph of how your net worth changes over time. The Forecasting graph can pick up estimated expenses and incomes from your current register entries or budget, as well as scheduled expenses and incomes from your scheduled transactions list. You can also modify the projection by adding or removing expenses or incomes. You can create several different scenarios in the Forecasting feature, letting you compare the effect of different financial decisions on your net worth, as you can see in Figure 1-10. This feature gives you an excellent overview of what will happen to you financially, depending on your decisions.

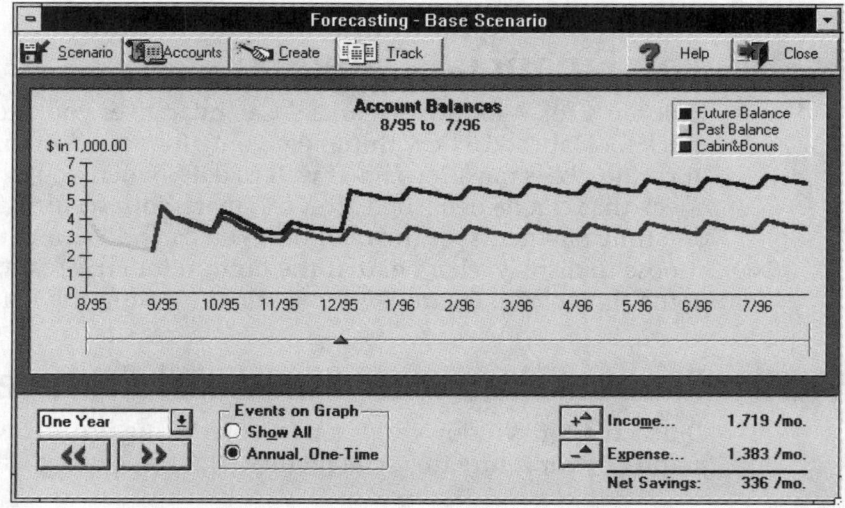

Using the Forecasting feature to compare two financial scenarios
Figure 1-10.

CHAPTER

QUICKEN 4's NEW HOMEBASE FEATURE

With version 4 of Quicken for Windows, you have a handy new way of accessing the features you will use most often. This new access method, called HomeBase, provides a comfortable operating base from which you can launch many tasks. HomeBase is ideal for new users of Quicken because it provides a graphical approach to accessing Quicken's commands.

In this chapter, you'll learn how easy HomeBase is to use, and then you'll take a mini-tour of the HomeBase options. You'll learn what HomeBase offers and preview Quicken's comprehensive financial tools. You'll also learn how you can customize HomeBase to suit your preferences.

Working with HomeBase

The HomeBase window, shown in Figure 2-1, provides access to Quicken's most frequently used features. If this window is not visible when you first start Quicken, the HomeBase feature has been turned off. You'll need to activate it again before you can make a selection.

Turning HomeBase On and Off

When you first start Quicken, HomeBase is turned on. If you close the HomeBase window, you will not be able to use it until you select HomeBase from the Activities menu or click the HomeBase icon in the icon bar.

Making HomeBase Selections

The options on the left side of the HomeBase window represent categories of tasks you can start from HomeBase. The category of tasks that is currently highlighted is the active selection. This determines which options appear at the right side of the window, since these are specific tasks you can carry out.

To select a different category of tasks, click the desired category with your mouse. Another way to select a category is to press ALT and the letter that is underlined in the category's name. No matter which method you use, when

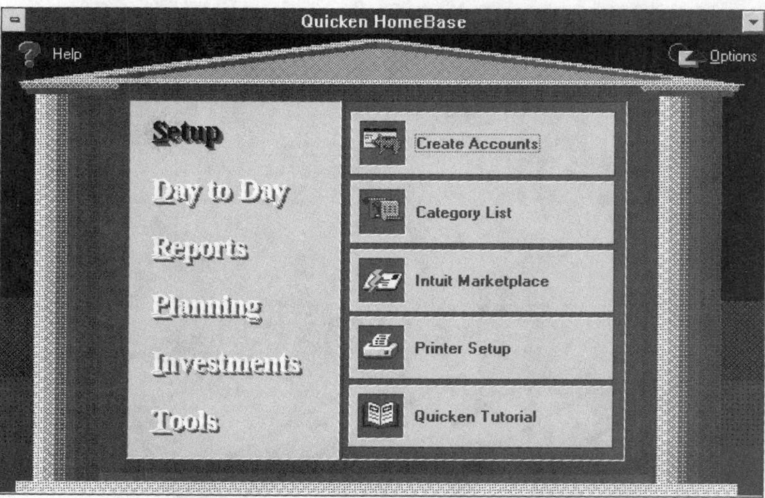

The HomeBase window
Figure 2-1.

you select a new category, a new set of tasks scrolls into view on the right side of the window. For example, to see the Day To Day options, click Day To Day or press ALT-D.

To select a specific task from the right side of the window, you can click the task with your mouse. You can also move the highlight to that button by pressing TAB to move to the next button or SHIFT-TAB to move to the last button, then press SPACEBAR to select it. What happens next depends on the task you just selected.

If you select the Setup category of tasks, then select the Create Accounts button, Quicken will display the window shown in Figure 2-2 in which you can choose the type of account you want to create. If you select the Reports category of tasks, then the More Reports button, Quicken will display the Create Report dialog box shown in Figure 2-3, from which you can choose the type of report you want to create.

HomeBase Provides Access to Many Types of Quicken Tasks

You can get a glimpse of what's to come in Quicken by quickly walking through the HomeBase options. This will familiarize you with the different task lists that HomeBase provides. Each task list represents a set of related activities that you can use for different types of Quicken tasks.

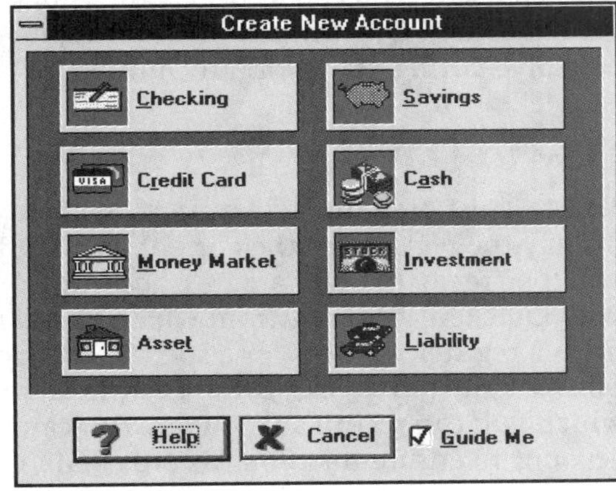

Options available after you select Create Accounts
Figure 2-2.

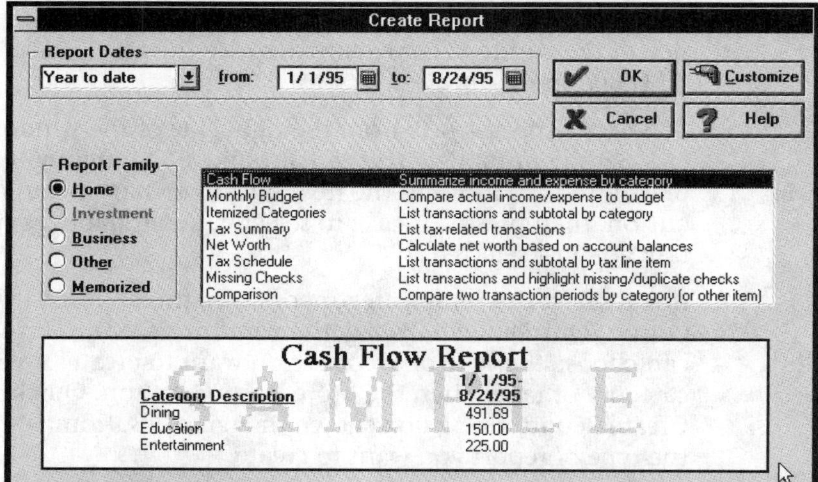

The Create Report dialog box
Figure 2-3.

Setup

HomeBase's Setup options will get you started working with Quicken. Use them to create new savings, checking, and credit card accounts. You can also review the categories that Quicken makes available for organizing your entries. Select the Intuit Marketplace if you want to order checks, other preprinted forms, or software from Intuit Corporation, the developers of Quicken. Select Printer Setup to customize your printer settings for working with Quicken. You can also start the Quicken Tutorial, which provides a guided tour of Quicken and its features, if you want more help before actually starting your work in Quicken.

Day to Day

This task list presents the transactions that you will use most often. First display the register for the current account by selecting Use Register—then you'll be ready to enter a new transaction. You can also display a list of all of your Quicken accounts, from which you can edit the accounts, or choose to open a register window for a specific account. When you are ready to pay bills or write paychecks, the Write Checks option displays a check window in which you can record a payment. You can reconcile a checking or savings account to ensure that your records match the statement sent by your bank.

Quicken's Financial Calendar lets you take a look at upcoming bills or expected deposits and schedule recurring transactions.

Reports

The Reports task list lets you create both reports and graphs as well as Quicken 4 for Windows' new Snapshots, which provide a general overview of your finances. The first four options in this task list present dialog boxes in which you can define the precise report or graph you want to create and print. Figure 2-3 shows the Create Report dialog box that appears when you select More Reports. From this dialog box, you can select any of Quicken's predefined report styles, or you can access customization options that let you create a unique report. The last Reports option, Financial Snapshot, presents a summary page with up to six simplified graphs or reports of your current financial conditions, providing a quick overview.

Planning

Use the Planning task list to access many of Quicken's features for planning your financial future. You can display a forecasting graph that uses estimated and known spending to determine how your net worth is going to be affected by your current financial habits or hypothetical financial decisions. You can also open the Budget window and create Quicken budgets to help you assess and control your spending habits. You can access any of Quicken's financial planners, which let you evaluate loans, college savings, mortgage refinancing, or retirement prospects. The Tax Planner option can draw on the transactions you've already entered in Quicken to estimate how much you're going to owe the IRS come April. This feature can help you avoid penalties due to inadequate withholdings, and make sure you've saved enough to meet the tax bill. You can use Savings Goals to set aside money that remains in an active account to pay a future expense or monitor how well you are matching your savings goal.

Investments

Whether you own just one share of stock or have a sophisticated portfolio including bonds, options, and warrants, Quicken provides tools to help you record your transactions and evaluate your current holdings. The range of investment-related tasks you can perform is shown here:

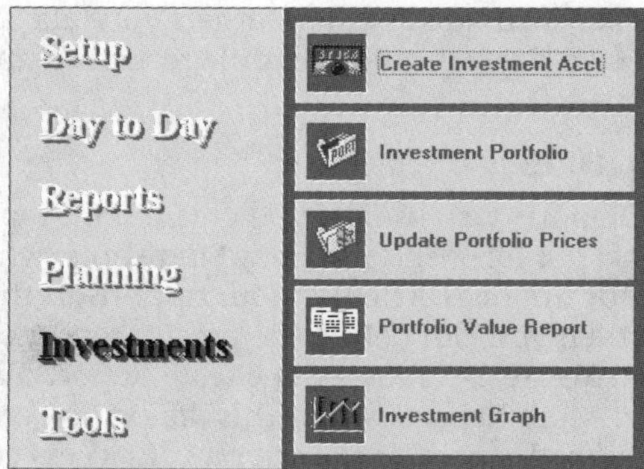

As you can see, Quicken helps you do everything from creating a new investment account to creating reports or graphs about your current investments. You can also update the market value of the securities you hold.

Tools

The Tools options are not as closely related to each other as the choices in other task lists. These are the tools you can use to work with your Quicken data or to modify Quicken itself. For example, you can find and replace text in all of your transactions, or you can re-categorize all transactions assigned to a single category. You can also amortize a loan, or set Quicken's customization options.

Customizing HomeBase

Quicken lets you customize how HomeBase works for you in several ways. To set these customization preferences, click the Options button in the HomeBase window. This displays the following dialog box:

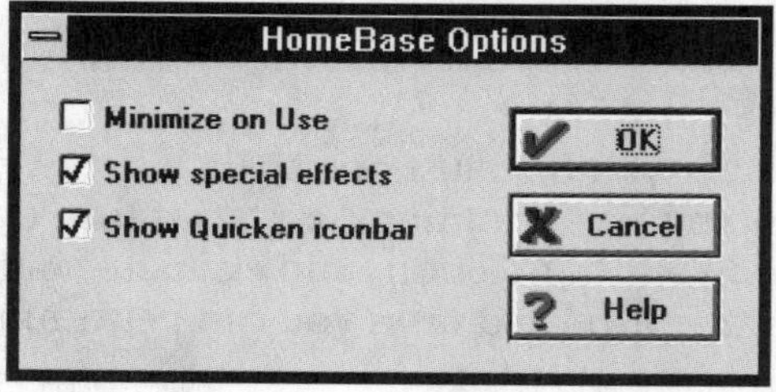

You can turn the three HomeBase options on and off by selecting their check boxes. Selecting OK finalizes the settings, and puts one or more of them into effect. You can always change the settings again in the future using the same steps.

Minimize on Use

When this option is selected, it causes Quicken to reduce HomeBase to an icon as soon as you make a selection from it. This reduces the clutter of windows and dialog boxes that can accumulate in your Quicken window as you carry out tasks. Even after you complete your task, HomeBase remains as an icon. You can open the window again by either double-clicking it or selecting it from the Windows menu.

Note: If you are running Quicken on a system with minimal memory (2MB), you may want to keep the HomeBase window minimized except when you are using it to maximize Quicken's use of your system's memory.

Show Special Effects

When this option is selected, which it is by default, HomeBase uses a special scrolling effect to change the display of individual task buttons on the right side of the HomeBase window when you select new categories of tasks on the left side. The buttons for the task list you were in scroll up to the top of the window and then disappear, while the new task list's buttons scroll up from the bottom of the window. You may prefer to turn this feature off to speed up your use of HomeBase, since you cannot select a specific task during the few seconds it takes to complete the scrolling. If this feature is turned off, then the buttons are simply replaced without the scrolling effect. This can help save memory on your system, since the scrolling effect requires the use of some memory.

Show Quicken Iconbar

When this option is selected, which it is by default, Quicken continues to display the icon bar beneath the menu bar when the HomeBase window is open. If you clear this option's check box, Quicken will hide the icon bar whenever the HomeBase window is on the screen. If you have HomeBase open, you may not need the icon bar, since all of the commands executed by the icon bar's icons can also be selected from the HomeBase window.

Deciding Whether to Use HomeBase or Other Methods

You've learned that Quicken provides you with a number of different ways to access its features. In addition to HomeBase, you can use selections from the menu bar, the icon bar, and the Quick Keys discussed in Chapter 1. While Quicken provides several different methods of accessing a specific feature, you'll get the same results no matter which method you use. For example, you can look at a list of your Quicken accounts using any one of these methods:

- Choose Account List from the HomeBase Day To Day task list.
- Choose Account from the Lists menu.
- Select the Accts button in the icon bar.
- Press CTRL-A.

If having so many options seems too confusing, you don't have to worry. In this book, we will simplify things for you. We will provide one easy-to-use option when we give you the steps for completing a specific task. Since Quicken's menus provide access to all of Quicken's features, the numbered steps in the remaining chapters of this book almost always use the menu to access the tasks you need to perform. Occasionally, a keyboard or icon bar alternative is either recommended or provided as an alternate method. When a HomeBase alternative to a menu command exists, we'll show the HomeBase option in the margin next to the numbered steps that it parallels. The HomeBase options will be marked with an icon that looks like this:

The HomeBase task list and the button you need to select will always appear beneath this icon. This will let you easily use HomeBase instead of the menus or other alternatives. As a new user, you'll find HomeBase a good tool for getting started in Quicken. However, after you've used Quicken for awhile, you will probably prefer to use the menus or other alternative.

CHAPTER

3

MAKING REGISTER ENTRIES

If you maintain a checking account or monitor a savings account, you are already familiar with the concept of the Quicken register. The register is the backbone of the Quicken system. It enables you to maintain information on checking accounts, cash accounts, and other assets and expenses.

With the register, you maintain current information for an account so you know the precise account balance. You also keep a history of all the transactions affecting the balance. The Quicken register's capabilities extend far beyond those of your normal checkbook register. With the Quicken register, you can easily categorize entries, and then use these categories to analyze your transactions and create reports.

In this chapter you will learn to create and maintain a single checking account register. The transactions are similar to those you might make in a personal account. As you work with Quicken, you will repeatedly use the techniques you learn here.

Maintaining a Register

Your register is your master record for all financial information.

Quicken's register works much like the manual checking account register shown in Figure 3-1. You start with the account balance at the beginning of the period and record each check written as a separate entry, including the date, amount, payee, and check number. You can add information to document the reason for the check. This information can be useful in preparing tax forms or verifying that invoices are paid. As you enter each check, a new balance is computed. You must enter other bank charges, such as check printing fees, overdraft charges, and service fees, that are also subtracted from the account balance. You record deposits in a similar fashion. Since interest earned on an account is often automatically credited to the account, you should enter it as it appears on your monthly bank statement.

RECORD ALL CHANGES OR CREDITS THAT AFFECT YOUR ACCOUNT

NUMBER	DATE	DESCRIPTION OF TRANSACTION	PAYMENT/DEBIT		T	FEE IF ANY (-)	DEPOSIT/CREDIT (+)		BALANCE $	
	1/1	Opening Balance 1st U.S. Bank					1,200	00	1,200	00
	1995								1,200	00
100	1/4	Small City Gas & Light	67	50					67	50
	1995	Gas & Electric							1,132	50
101	1/5	Small City Times Paper Bill	16	50					16	50
	1995								1,116	00
	1/7	Deposit - Salary monthly pay					700	00	700	00
	1995								1,816	00
102	1/7	Small City Market Food	22	32					22	32
	1995								1,793	68
103	1/7	Small City Apartments	150	00					150	00
	1995	Rent							1,643	68
104	1/19	Small City Market Food	43	00					43	00
	1995								1,600	68
105	1/25	Small City Phone Company	19	75					19	75
	1995	Phone Bill							1,580	93
	2/10	Dividend Check					25	00	25	00
	1995	Dividend from ABC Co.							1,605	93

Manual entries in a checking account register
Figure 3-1.

Note: Quicken cannot compute the interest earned on your account since it cannot know when the checks clear your bank. This information is needed to compute the interest earned.

Although it is easy to record entries in a manual check register, most people occasionally make mistakes when computing the new balance. Recording transactions in Quicken's register eliminates this problem since it handles the math for you. Quicken also provides many other advantages such as categories for classifying each entry, automatic totaling of similar transactions within a category, easily created reports, and a Find feature for quickly locating specific entries.

Before entering any transactions in Quicken's register, you need to create a file and set up an account. This means assigning a name to the account and establishing a beginning balance. You will want to learn about Quicken's built-in categories, which let you categorize all transactions. You may already categorize some transactions in your check register. For instance, you may mark transactions that you need to refer back to. Categorizing transactions is optional in Quicken, but using categories allows you to create more useful reports.

Quicken 4 for Windows lets you use both the mouse and keyboard to move around the screen and make selections. Choose the method that seems easiest to you. In this chapter, the keyboard steps are stressed because they are not as obvious as the mouse steps. In the remainder of the book, the steps simply tell you what to do, not how to do it, so you can choose the method you prefer to use.

Chapter 2 discussed the new HomeBase window, which provides an alternative method of accessing some commands. HomeBase is convenient because it groups commands by the type of work you are doing, so you don't have to remember all of the menu commands and steps. However, HomeBase does not contain all Quicken commands. You will find an icon in the margin of this book next to instructions that have a HomeBase alternative. The text beneath the icon will indicate both the section of HomeBase and the option within the section that you must select in order to carry out the command from HomeBase.

Establishing a File and an Account

Establishing a file and an account is easy once you install and start Quicken, using the instructions in Appendix A. The exact procedure you follow depends on whether you have used Quicken before.

You can have several Quicken accounts to meet your financial needs.

If this is the first time you've used the application and you don't have data from an earlier release, Quicken helps you get started with the setup, displaying the New User Setup dialog box.

If you have data from an earlier Quicken for Windows release or from Quicken 5, 6, 7, or 8 for DOS, you can use that data in Quicken 4 for Windows. Quicken locates your old files during installation and allows you to use them without change. If you have data from these earlier releases of Quicken or have already used Quicken 4 for Windows, Quicken won't display the New User Setup dialog box now. You need to set up your new file and account without Quicken's help, using the instructions later in this chapter.

Regardless of which situation matches yours, you need to create a file for storing any data you enter with Quicken. When you provide a filename, Quicken actually creates several different files with that name using different filename extensions. Your Quicken "file" consists of several files containing different parts of the data in your file. You also need to provide an account name. Quicken can store data for various account types, and one Quicken file can hold as many as 255 accounts. You will find all the steps you need to establish a file and an account in the sections that follow.

Creating a File as a New Quicken User

Most Quicken users have only one file, but you can create a second one and save it to try out new features.

The first time you start Quicken, you are presented with the Quicken New User Setup dialog box shown in Figure 3-2. Next, Quicken leads you through the process of creating accounts for your file. Quicken names this file QDATA

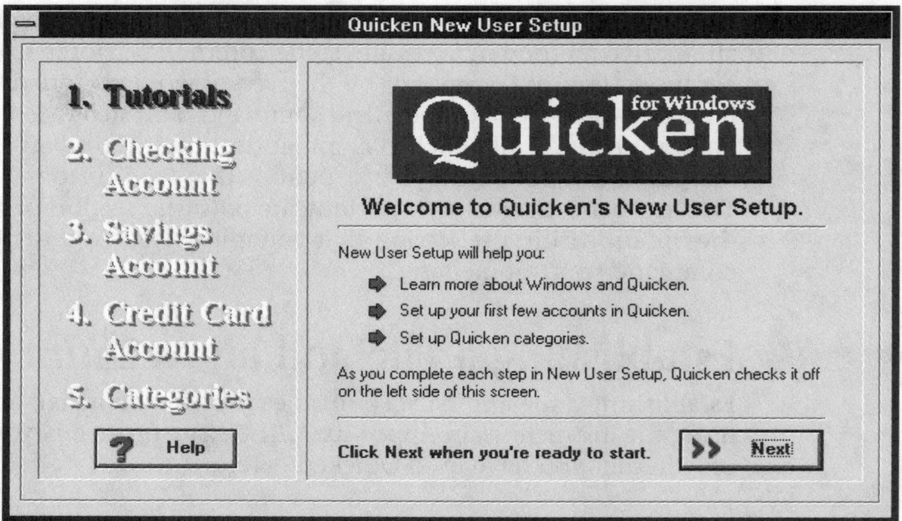

The New User Setup dialog box
Figure 3-2.

and stores information on your accounts in it. When you see the Quicken New User Setup dialog box, follow these steps:

1. Select No to skip the tutorials.
2. Select Next twice to start setting up your accounts. You won't need your checkbook, your most recent bank statement, or receipts for any uncleared transactions because you are using data provided in this book. You *will* need these items when you set up your own accounts.
3. Select Yes to set up a checking account.
4. Type **1st U.S. Bank** in the Account Name text box to give this checking account a name, and then select Next .
5. Select Yes.
6. Enter **1/1/95** in the Statement Date text box and select Next.
7. Enter **1200** in the Ending Balance text box and select Next twice.
8. Select No twice to avoid creating a savings or credit card account at this time. You will learn how to set up these accounts later.
9. Select Next twice.
10. Select Yes to use both business and personal categories.
11. Select Done.

Quicken creates the necessary files for the 1st U.S. Bank account, storing them in the Quicken directory, and opens the HomeBase window you learned about in Chapter 2. Click Use Register in the HomeBase window to display the register for the account, as shown in Figure 3-3.

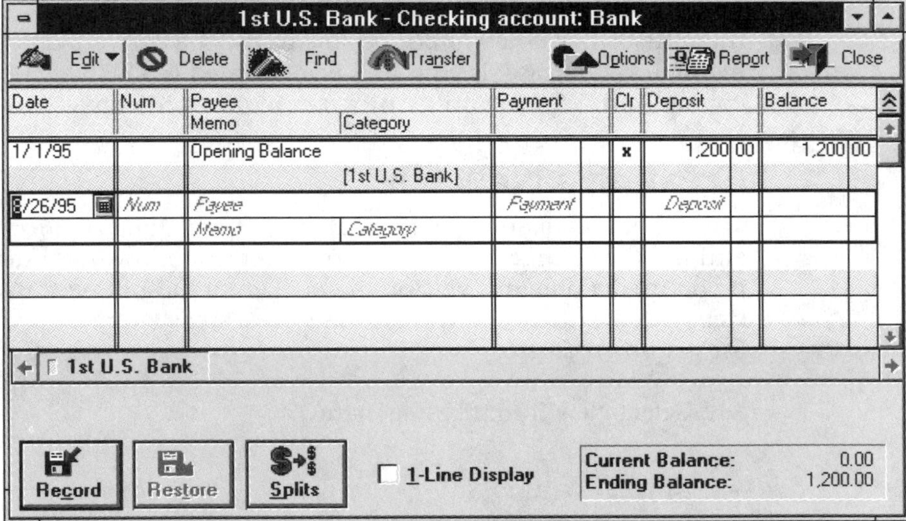

An account register window
Figure 3-3.

Note: The account used for the examples in the next few chapters is called 1st U.S. Bank. In the unlikely event that one of your own existing accounts already bears this name, you should use another name.

Quicken displays a Qcard that provides advice about what to do in the register. These Qcards can be a great deal of help when you are working with your own data, but when you use this book, you'll find they get in the way. Turn them off by selecting Show Qcards from the Help menu.

Using Data from Earlier Quicken Releases in Quicken 4 for Windows

If you followed the installation directions in Appendix A, Quicken searched your hard disk and located any files from Quicken 1, 2 or 3 for Windows or DOS Quicken 5, 6, 7 or 8. Since Quicken 4 for Windows can read these files directly, there is no need to convert them for you.

If, when you installed Quicken 4 for Windows, you changed the name of the installation directory Quicken suggested, your earlier Quicken data won't be available until you open all of the files that contain this data. To open them, select Open from the File menu, use the Directories list box to display the directory containing the file, select the file in the File Name list box, and finally select OK.

If you've been using Quicken release prior to DOS Quicken 5, your files must be converted before you can use them with Quicken 4 for Windows. DOS Quicken 3 and 4 files are converted automatically the first time you open them in Quicken 4 for Windows. You may want to create a backup copy of them first since you will not be able to use the converted version with your old Quicken release. If your files were created in Quicken 1 or 2 for DOS, contact Intuit for the utility program required to convert your data.

Creating a New File

This section explains how to create your own Quicken 4 for Windows file and how to change its location. You need to follow these steps now only if you used a previous version of Quicken or did not perform the new user steps listed earlier. You will also use these steps later when you set up a file for your own data.

1. Select New from the File menu.

2. Select the New File option button and select OK.
3. Use the Directories list box to specify the directory where you want to save the file.
4. Enter a name for the file in the File Name text box.
5. Select the check boxes for the category types that you want in your new file. Initially, both the Home and Business check boxes are selected.
6. Select OK.

Quicken displays the Create Account dialog box. You should perform the steps in the next section immediately to create the first account in this new file.

HomeBase

Setup | Create Account

Creating a New Account

The following steps explain how to create an account in your new file. If you are adding a new account to a file that contains some accounts already, you must choose New from the File menu and then select New Account and OK, or choose Create New Account from the Activities menu. You can also follow these steps if you've just created a new file as described in the preceding section:

1. Select Checking from the Create New Account dialog box.
   Quicken displays the Create Checking Account dialog box.
2. Type **1st U.S. Bank** and press TAB.

   You can use any account name you want as long as it does not exceed 15 characters. In the unlikely event that you already have a 1st U.S. Bank account, consider using 2nd U. S. Bank.
3. Type **Checking account** in the Description text box, then select Next.
4. Select Yes and Next.
5. Type **1/1/95** in the Statement Date text box and press TAB.
6. Type **1200** in the Ending Balance text box.
7. Choose Done.

Establishing a File and an Account After Using Quicken 3 for Windows

If you have used Quicken 3 for Windows, you'll already have a file with accounts set up from your earlier Quicken sessions. However, you'll still want to create a file and an account matching those in the examples in this book. You can follow the instructions in the preceding sections for creating new files and accounts.

The Quicken Register

The Quicken register looks a lot like the paper register you use with your checkbook, but it offers much more.

Figure 3-3 shows the initial register window for the 1st U.S. Bank account. Although you have not yet recorded any transactions, Quicken has already entered the account name, and the opening balance and date. Quicken has automatically entered an **X** in the Clr (cleared) field for this opening transaction, indicating that the balance has been reconciled and is correct. You will use this field in Chapter 5, "Reconciling Your Quicken Register," when you reconcile your entire account.

Currently the scroll bar at the right of the register window is inactive because there are not enough transactions to use the scroll feature. After you enter more transactions, a scroll box appears in the scroll bar, and the arrows at the top and the bottom cease being dimmed. You can use a mouse with the scroll bar to scroll through the register.

The highlighted field below the opening balance entry is where you enter the first transaction. Remember that a transaction is simply a record of a financial activity, such as a deposit or withdrawal (a credit or a debit). The same fields, which you can see in Figure 3-3, are used for all transactions. Table 3-1 provides a detailed description of each of these fields.

Another important element of the register display is the heavy blue line that appears when you enter a postdated transaction. You can see this line in Figure 3-3 above the opening balance. *Postdated transactions* are transactions with dates after the current date. To produce reports that match those shown in this book, you must use the transaction dates shown in the book for the examples, regardless of the date when you make the entries. You may or may not see the line that divides postdated transactions from current transactions. If the current date in your system is after January 1995 when you enter the examples, the line will not appear. Your results will be the same regardless of whether or not the postdated transaction line appears.

As you make the entries for the first transaction, notice that Quicken moves through the fields in a specific order. After entering data in a field, you press TAB, and the insertion point moves to the next field in which you can enter data. Some fields, such as Date, must have an entry in all transactions. Either the Payment or Deposit field requires an entry for the transaction to affect the balance. Other fields are optional, and you use them when they're needed. For example, you use the check number (Num) field only when writing checks, so it is an optional field. If you do not need an entry in an optional field, you just press TAB, and the insertion point moves to the next field. You can also click the desired field with the mouse.

You can easily change the order of the Category and Memo fields so that Quicken's register matches the order in which you note this information in your check book. All of the examples and directions in this book have the

Field	Contents
Date	Transaction date. You can accept the current date entry or type a new date.
Num (Number)	Check number for check transactions. For noncheck transactions, use other entries like DEP.
Payee	Payee's name for check transactions. For ATM transactions, deposits, service fees, and so on, enter a description in this field.
Payment	Payment or withdrawal amount. For deposit transactions, leave this field blank. Quicken supports entries as large as $9,999,999.99.
Clr (Cleared)	Skip this field when entering transactions. You will use it in Chapter 5 for reconciling accounts and noting checks that have cleared the bank.
Deposit	Deposit amounts. For a payment transaction, leave this field blank. The same rules for Payment apply.
Balance	A running total, or the sum of all prior transactions. Quicken computes it after you complete each transaction.
Memo	Optional descriptive information documenting the transaction.
Category	Optional entry used to assign a transaction to one of Quicken's categories. Categories are used to organize similar transactions and can facilitate reporting.

Fields in the Register Window
Table 3-1.

Memo field before the category. If you need to change the order of these fields to match the book, click the Options button in the register window's button bar. Then select the Memo Before Category check box so that it contains a check mark, and select OK.

Another option you may want to change to match this book is whether drop-down list boxes appear when you enter some of these fields. These boxes appeared automatically in earlier releases of Quicken, but you may find them distracting while entering the transactions in this book. To turn them off, click the Options button again, then select QuickFill. Clear the Drop Down Lists Automatically check box, and select OK. You can always open the QuickFill drop-down lists, as you will learn to do in the next section, but changing this default prevents them from opening on their own.

Special keys let you date entries quickly.

Recording Your Transactions in the Register

When you open the register window, the highlighting is already positioned for your first transaction entry. If you have used the UP ARROW key to move to the opening balance entry, you need to press CTRL-END to reposition the highlight properly. In the next sections, you enter eight sample transactions representing typical personal expenses and deposits. Don't worry if you make a mistake in recording your first transaction. Just leave the mistake in the entry and focus on the steps involved. In the second transaction, you will correct your errors. Follow these steps to complete the entries for the first transaction:

1. Type **1/4/95** and press TAB.

   Now that you have entered a date, you can see how to change dates in Quicken. Move the insertion point back to the finalized Date field by pressing SHIFT-TAB. Press + or - to increase or decrease the current date. A light touch alters the date by one day. Holding these keys down causes a rapid date change. If you use + or - to change the date, you must still use TAB to move to the next field. If you test this feature now, restore the 1/4/95 date before proceeding.

   You can also click the calendar at the right edge of the field to display a calendar that makes date selection easy. Initially, the current date is highlighted in the calendar. You can use the arrow keys to move to another date, or you can click on a different date. Also, any of the keys listed in the following table can change the highlighted date in the register:

Key	Effect
+	Increase day by 1
-	Decrease day by 1
t	Set to current date
m	First day of month
h	Last day of month
y	First day of year
r	Last day of year

2. Type **100** and press TAB to enter the check number in the Num field.
3. Type **Small City Gas & Light** and press TAB to complete the entry for Payee for this check.

Your Payee entry can be up to 40 characters long. Notice that the insertion point moves to the Payment field, where Quicken expects the next entry.

4. Type **67.50** and press TAB.

   Since this is a check transaction, the amount should be placed in the Payment field. If you click the small calculator at the right edge of the field, Quicken displays a calculator that you can use. Click numbers and arithmetic operators to compute an amount. The total is automatically placed in the field when you click =. You can also use the numeric keypad on your keyboard if the NUM LOCK key is active.

5. Type **Gas and Electric** and press TAB.

   You are limited to 31 characters on the Memo field.

6. Type **U** in the Category field.

   Initially Quicken displays "UIC" as its suggested match.

7. Type a **t** to continue selecting the category.

   Quicken displays "Utilities." Your register window should look like the one in Figure 3-4.

   If you plan to use a category, you can either select one of the standard ones and stay within Quicken's default category structure, or you can add a new one to the category list. If you click the drop-down arrow at

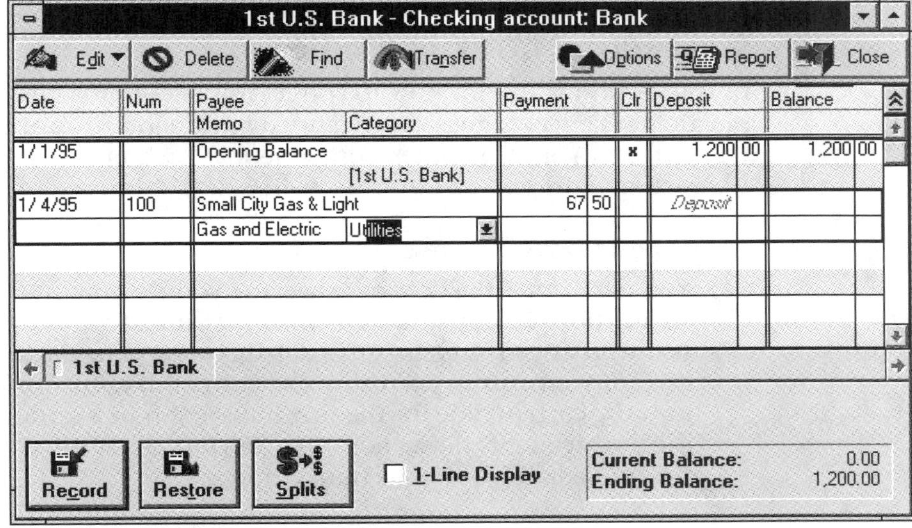

The register window before you complete the first sample transaction entry

Figure 3-4.

Categories help you organize your financial data.

the right edge of the Category field, or press ALT-DOWN ARROW, a drop-down list box appears that displays all the standard Quicken categories. You can select a category from the list box by clicking it with the mouse or by using the arrow keys to highlight it and pressing ENTER.

8. Select Record to confirm the recording of the transaction, or press ENTER.

   Your screen displays an ending balance of 1,132.50. The ending balance represents the total of all transactions entered, including any transactions that may be postdated because of the relationship between the transaction date and the current date. The current balance is the account balance as of the current date. Since all the transactions are postdated based on the date when these sample screens were captured, the current balance is zero.

You have now completed your first transaction successfully. Since everyone can make mistakes in entries, you will want to learn how to correct those errors. This is easily done with Quicken.

Making Revisions to the Current Transaction

One of the advantages Quicken has over manual register entries is that you can make changes easily and neatly. An incorrect amount or other error can be altered as soon as you notice the mistake or later. The procedure you use depends on whether you have already recorded the transaction. Quicken's QuickFill feature can save you time, whether you are correcting an existing transaction or entering a new transaction.

Correcting Your Example

In this section you learn how to correct mistakes in the current transaction, practicing the techniques covered briefly in Chapter 1, "An Overview of Quicken and Your Computer Components." First, make the following transaction entries:

1. Type **1/5/95** and press TAB.

   You must enter the date here because you are entering several days' transactions in one session. If you enter transactions daily, however, you won't need to change the date between your transactions since each of your entries will be for the current day. Quicken automatically uses the current date for the first transaction of a session, and then, for each subsequent transaction, Quicken automatically copies the date of the immediately previous transaction.

2. Type **110** and press TAB.

   Notice that the previous check number was 100. This check number should have been recorded as 101.
3. Double-click your mouse pointer at the end of the check number. Then press BACKSPACE twice to delete the 0 and the second 1 in the number entry.
4. Type **01** to change 110 to 101, then press TAB to finalize the entry.
5. Type **S**.

   The QuickFill feature makes Quicken your assistant for completing transactions quickly.

   Notice that Quicken automatically fills in the payee name from the previous transaction. This illustrates Quicken's QuickFill feature. If you accepted QuickFill's suggestion, Quicken would complete the current transaction using the entries from the previous transaction. Quicken uses QuickFill for the entries you make in the Payee and Category fields. Quicken checks the Category List for categories and looks at the payees in the Memorized Transaction List to find an entry that matches what you are typing. Quicken uses the first match it finds. You can select Memorized Transaction from the Lists menu or press CTRL-T to open the Memorized Transaction List and look through it.

   If QuickFill is not operating for you, the option has been turned off. Select Options from the register window's button bar. Select the QuickFill tab. Make sure that all of the check boxes except Drop Down Lists Automatically are selected. (If you select this check box, then the drop-down lists appear automatically when you move into the Num, Payee, and Category fields.)
6. Continue typing **malll City Times** since Quicken has not provided the match that you need.

   This entry contains an extra l. Click the mouse directly after the last l. Then press BACKSPACE to delete the character before the insertion point.
7. Press TAB to finalize the Payee entry.
8. Type **6.50** for the payment amount.
9. Move to the left of the 6 by clicking the mouse there or pressing LEFT ARROW. Type **1**, and Quicken places a 1 in front of the 6.
10. Press TAB to move to the Memo field.
11. Type **Magazine subscription** and press TAB.

    This entry is intended to be the newspaper bill, so you need to make a change. Use SHIFT-TAB to move back to the Memo field.

12. Type **Paper bill** to replace the selected entry, and press TAB.
13. Type **M** for the category.

    Quicken uses the QuickFill feature and presents the first category beginning with an M. You want to use the Misc (miscellaneous) category.
14. Click the drop-down arrow at the right edge of the field, then click Misc. Quicken enters the Misc category.

    If you had typed "Mi" in the Category field, Quicken would have presented Misc as the category. You could have stopped typing and accepted it by pressing TAB.
15. Select Record to complete your second transaction.

    Your register should look like the one in Figure 3-5.

A number of mistakes were included in this transaction, but you can see how easy it is to make corrections with Quicken.

Additional Transaction Entries

You are now somewhat familiar with recording transactions in the Quicken register. To test your knowledge and expand your transaction base for later, enter the following additional transactions in your register, using the same procedure you used to enter the previous transaction entries. For deposit entries, enter DEP in the Num field. (The QuickFill feature works for this field as well as for the Payee and Category fields.)

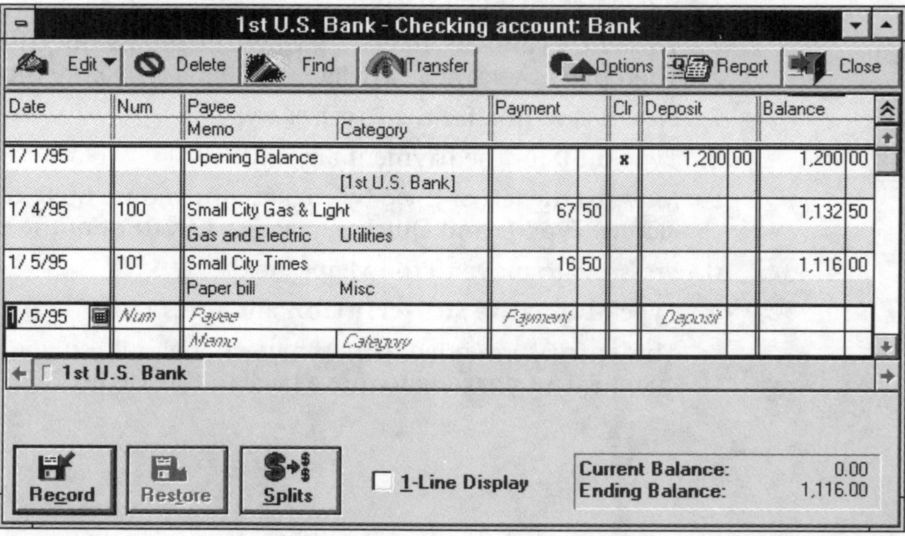

The register window after you complete the second sample transaction
Figure 3-5.

Date:	**1/7/95**
Num:	**DEP**
Payee:	**Deposit-Salary**
Deposit:	**700.00**
Memo:	**Monthly pay**
Category:	**Salary**

Date:	**1/7/95**
Num:	**102**
Payee:	**Small City Market**
Payment:	**22.32**
Memo:	**Food**
Category:	**Groceries**

Date:	**1/7/95**
Num:	**103**
Payee:	**Small City Apartments**
Payment:	**150.00**
Memo:	**Rent**
Category:	**Housing**

Date:	**1/19/95**
Num:	**104**
Payee:	**Small City Market**
Payment:	**43.00**
Memo:	**Food**
Category:	**Groceries**

When you enter the transaction for check 104, press TAB after completing the Payee field. Quicken copies the information in the Payment, Memo, and

Category fields from the transaction for check 102. Then type **43.00** in the Payment field, and select Record to save the new entries.

Date:	**1/25/95**
Num:	**105**
Payee:	**Small City Phone Company**
Payment:	**19.75**
Memo:	**Phone bill**
Category:	**Telephone**

Date:	**2/10/95**
Num:	**DEP**
Payee:	**Dividend check**
Deposit:	**25.00**
Memo:	**Dividends check from ABC Co.**
Category:	**Div Income**

After typing and recording the entries for the last transaction, your register should resemble the one in Figure 3-6.

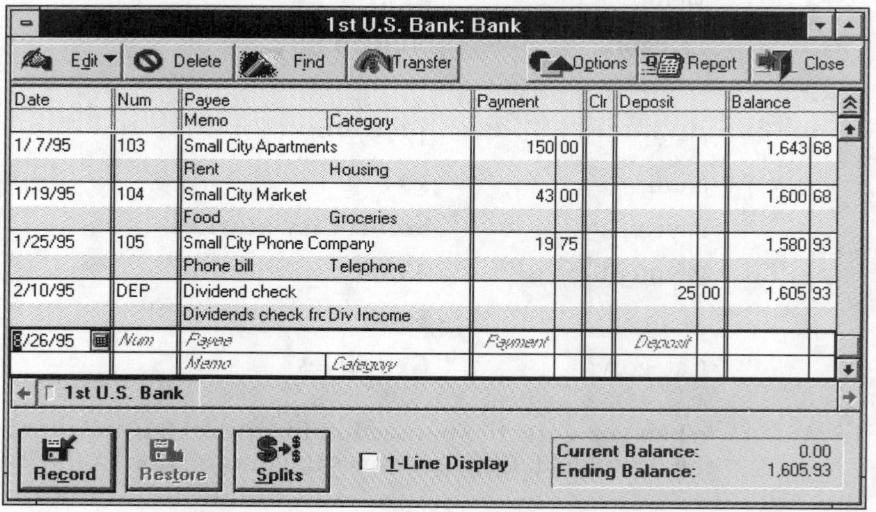

Figure 3-6. The register window after you record the entries in the last transaction

Viewing a Compressed Register

A compressed register view lets you see twice as many transactions on the screen.

You can switch back and forth between the standard register and a compressed register. A compressed register displays one line for each transaction, letting you see twice as many transactions at a time. To switch to the compressed register view, as in Figure 3-7, select the 1-Line Display check box. Clearing this check box displays the register in the original format.

Ending a Quicken Session

You do not need to finish all your work with Quicken in one session. You can end a Quicken session after entering one transaction or you can continue to enter transactions representing several months of financial activity. When you end a Quicken session, you should always use the orderly approach provided here. Never turn your system off without first exiting from Quicken.

To end a Quicken session, select Exit from the File menu. All the data you entered will be saved for use in subsequent sessions. Quicken even backs up the data, making copies of the files in the \QUICKENW\BACKUP directory.

3

Sometimes, when you exit Quicken, it prompts you to make backups onto floppy disks. If you want to backup your data onto a floppy disk, select Backup. If you don't feel it's necessary, select Exit. Backups on a floppy disk provide security in case your hard disk should break or your computer should be destroyed. The next section describes how to create floppy disk backups without Quicken's prompt.

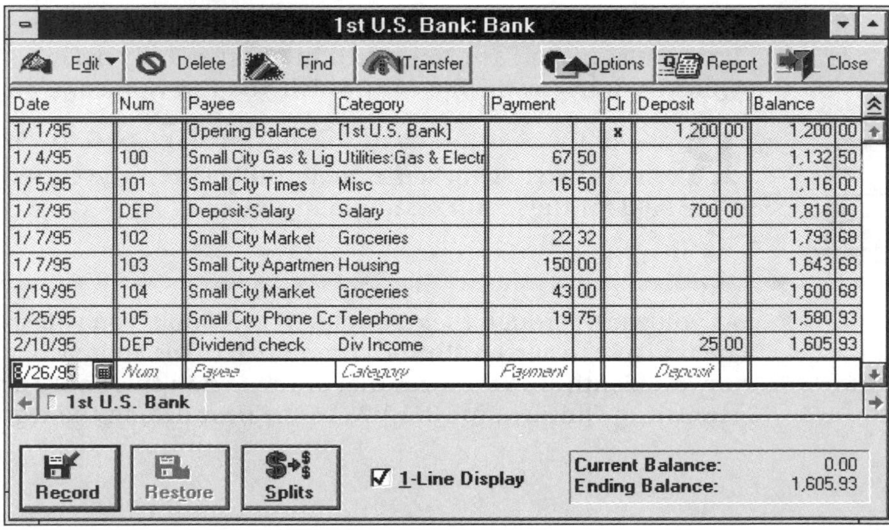

Compressed register view, showing one line for each transaction

Figure 3-7.

Creating Backups

While having a backup file on your hard disk is useful if your main file becomes corrupt, it's not going to help much if something goes wrong with your entire hard drive. You should do regular backups onto a floppy disk that you can then store in a safe place.

Quicken makes backup creation easy. Just select Backup from the File menu. Quicken displays the Select Backup Drive dialog box, shown here:

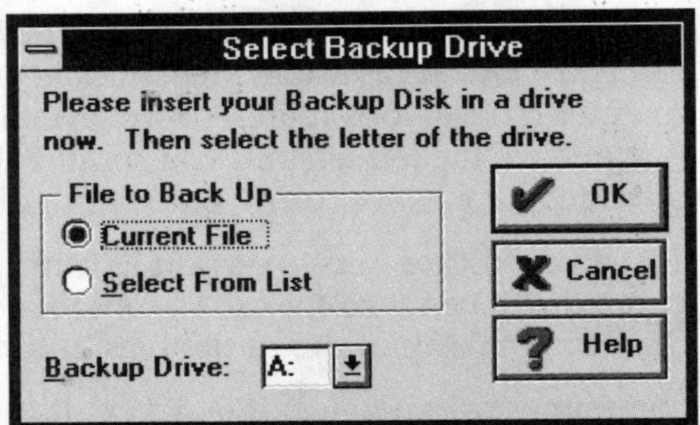

Make sure the Current File option button is selected and the correct drive is listed in the Backup Drive text box. If the incorrect drive is listed, click the drop-down arrow and select the correct one. Select OK.

Beginning a New Quicken Session

To restart Quicken after exiting, start the program from the Windows Program Manager, as you learned in Chapter 1. By default, when you open Quicken, it opens the file with which you last worked.

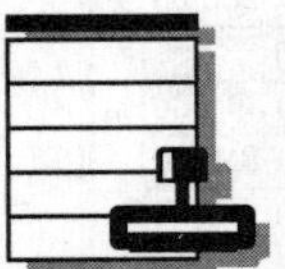

Remember: Quicken automatically enters the current date in the Date field for the first transaction in a session.

As you work through the examples in this book, you will specify dates that are unlikely to agree with the current date. This approach lets you create reports identical to the ones that are shown in this book. If you are now reentering Quicken, use 2/10/95 as the next date in the register.

Reviewing Register Entries

Reviewing transaction entries in the Quicken register is as easy as flipping through the pages of a manual register, and far more versatile. You can scroll through the register to see all the recorded transactions or you can use the Find feature to search for a specific transaction. You can also focus on transactions for a specific time period by using the Find feature from the Edit menu with the Search list box set to Date.

Scrolling Through the Register

You can use the mouse to scroll through the register quickly.

You can use the mouse to scroll through the register once you have entered enough transactions for the scroll bar to activate. The following mouse actions will help you quickly locate the place you want to be:

- Click the scroll bar arrows to scroll to the next or previous transaction.
- Point at one of the scroll bar arrows and hold down the mouse button to move quickly through the transactions.
- Click above or below the scroll box to move up or down one page of transactions.
- Drag the scroll box up or down in the scroll bar to move to a different location in the register.

If you prefer using the keyboard to move your insertion point in the register, you can put some of the keys introduced in Chapter 1 to work. You can probably guess the effects some of the keys will have from their names. The UP ARROW and DOWN ARROW keys move up or down one transaction. Once a transaction is active, you can use the LEFT ARROW and RIGHT ARROW keys to move across the current field. TAB moves to the next field, and SHIFT-TAB moves to the previous field. The PAGE UP and PAGE DOWN keys move up and down one screen at a time.

The HOME key moves to the beginning of the current field. If you press HOME twice, Quicken moves to the beginning of the transaction. When you press CTRL-HOME, Quicken moves to the top of the register.

The END key moves to the end of the current field. If you press END twice, Quicken moves to the end of the transaction. Press CTRL-END, and Quicken moves the to the last transaction in the register.

Pressing CTRL-PAGE UP moves to the beginning of the current month. Pressing it again moves to the beginning of the previous month. Pressing CTRL-PAGE DOWN moves to the last transaction in the current month; pressing it a second time will move to the end of the next month. As you enter more transactions, the value of knowing quick ways to move will be more apparent.

Using the Find Feature

The Find feature can instantly locate a transaction that you want to check.

Quicken's Find feature lets you locate a specific transaction easily. You can find a transaction by entering a minimal amount of information from the transaction in the Find dialog box. Choose Find from the Edit menu, click Find on the register's button bar, or press CTRL-F to open the Find dialog box.

Quicken can search forward or backward through the register entries for an exact match to the information you enter for a field. You can also use Quicken's wildcard feature to locate a transaction with only part of the information from a field. After looking at the examples in the next two sections, refer to the rules for finding entries in Table 3-2.

Finding Matching Entries

To find a transaction that exactly matches data, you only need to enter the data in the Find dialog box. Quicken can search all fields or restrict its search to the Payee, Category/Class, Date, Check Number, Amount, Memo, or Cleared Status field. You don't need to worry about the capitalization of your entry since Quicken is not case sensitive.

By default, Quicken searches backwards from the current transaction to the beginning of the register. Since the current transaction is usually the last one, this generally gives you a clear search of the entire register. If you prefer to search forwards through the register, towards the last entry, clear the Search Backwards check box in the Find dialog box.

Locating Transactions
Table 3-2.

Entry	Quicken Finds
electric	electric, Electric, ELECTRIC, electric power, Electric Company, Consumer Power Electric, new electric
~electric	groceries, gas—anything but electric
e..c	electric, eccentric
s?n	sun, sin, son—any single letter between an s and an n
~..	ice, fire, and anything else except blanks
..	all transactions with a blank in that field

To locate a specific check number in the 1st U.S. Bank register you developed earlier, complete the following steps:

You can search all fields or a specific field with the Find feature.

1. Select Find from the Edit menu or Find from the window's button bar to display the Find dialog box shown here:

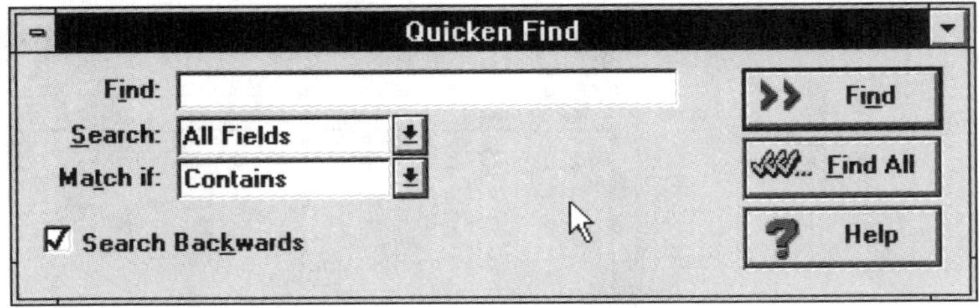

2. Type **103** in the Find text box.
3. Select Check Number in the Search drop-down list box, and press TAB.
4. Select Find to find the next matching transaction.

   When Quicken reaches the beginning of the register, it asks you about starting from the end. When Quicken can't find any matches, it displays an appropriate message.
5. Double-click the Control-menu box in the upper-left corner of the Find dialog box to close it.

3

Quicken started the search with the current transaction and proceeded toward the top of the register, attempting to find matching transactions. In this example, Quicken tried to find transactions that have 103 in the Num field. You can search for only one criterion at a time. In addition to narrowing the search by selecting a field to search in the Search drop-down list box, you can select how the criterion is matched in the Match If drop-down list box. You can specify that Quicken find a match if the transaction contains the text in the Find text box, begins with it, ends with it, exactly matches it or is greater than, greater than or equal to, less than, or less than or equal to its value.

The more transactions in the register, the more useful Quicken's Find capability becomes. For instance, you might want to find all the transactions involving a specific payee or all the transactions on a certain date. Visually scanning through hundreds of transactions could take a long time, and you could miss a matching transaction. Quicken makes no mistakes and finds the matching transactions quickly.

You can search from the current transaction toward the beginning or the end of the register.

When you select Find and there are multiple transactions that match your entry, Quicken moves to the first one that matches. You can also search for all of the records that match an entry at once. If you select Find All instead of Find, Quicken finds all of the matching transactions and displays them in a Find window like the one shown here:

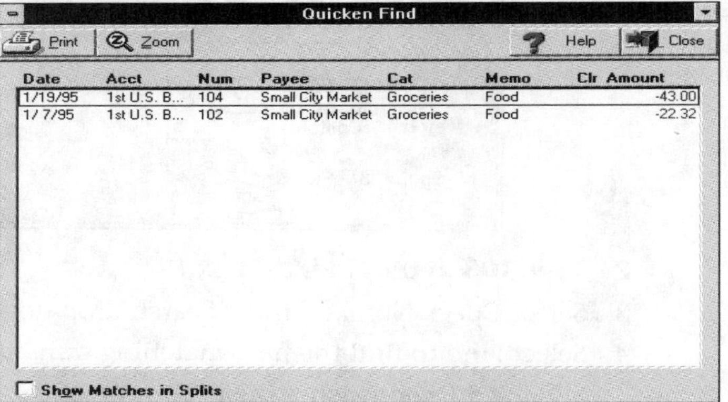

Tip: After entering transactions for months of entries, you will find it hard simply to backtrack to transactions for a specific date. One way to find those transactions is to set the Search field to Date and enter a date in the Find text box. This moves you quickly to the appropriate section of the register, making it easy to locate those old transactions.

You can use the Find All feature to locate all transactions for a specific payee or all deposits. You can print this list of transactions by selecting Print in the window's button bar. You can use this feature to reconcile accounts when your records and a bank or creditor's records don't match.

Key Word Search

You can enter a less-than-exact match and still locate the desired transactions if you search the Payee, Category, or Memo field and select a match other than Exact from the Match If drop-down list box. To look for an exact match, you must select Exact.

1. Choose Find from the Edit menu to display the Find window.
2. Type **Small** in the Find text box, and press TAB.
3. Select Payee in the Search drop-down list box.
4. Select Starts With from the Match If drop-down list box.

5. Select Find to search from the current location toward the beginning of the register. Quicken highlights the next entry for *Small City Phone Company*.

   If you continue to search with Find, Quicken moves through the transaction list, highlighting each entry starting with "Small", one at a time. Or you could select Find All to immediately locate every transaction containing "Small" at the beginning of the Payee field. Double-click the upper-left corner of the Find dialog box when you want to close it.

Revising Transactions

You have already learned how to make revisions to transactions in the check register as you are recording a transaction, but sometimes you may need to make changes to previously recorded transactions. It's important to note that although you can modify previously recorded transactions in Quicken, you can't directly change the balance unless you enter another transaction. This protects you from unauthorized changes in the register account balances. By forcing you to enter another transaction, Quicken is able to maintain a log of any changes to an account balance.

You may also find it necessary to void a previously written check, deposit, or any other adjustment to an account. Voiding removes the effect of the original transaction from the account balance, although it maintains the history of the original transaction and shows it as voided. To remove all traces of the original transaction, you must delete it.

You can use Quick Keys, the register button bar, or selections from Quicken's Edit menu to void and delete transactions. You can reinstate a voided transaction by clicking the Restore button before finalizing the transaction. However, after you've recorded a voided transaction, you must delete the entire transaction and re-create it in order to restore it to a nonvoided status.

Changing a Previous Transaction

Use the following steps to change a previously recorded transaction:

1. Move to the desired transaction.
2. Use the same techniques discussed in the "Making Revisions to the Current Transaction" section of this chapter.

Quicken does not let you change the balance amount directly. You need to enter another transaction to make an adjustment. Another option is to void or delete the original transaction and enter a new transaction.

Voiding a Transaction

Voiding a transaction is usually a better approach than deleting it, because the Void option maintains an audit trail for you.

When you void a transaction, you undo the financial effect of the transaction. Voiding creates an automatic audit trail, or record, of all transactions against an account, including those that have already been voided. Let's try the Void option with check number 100. Follow these steps:

1. Move to check number 100.
2. Choose Void Transaction from the Edit menu, or press CTRL-V. The word "VOID" is entered in front of the payee name, as shown in Figure 3-8.
3. Press ENTER to record the modification to the transaction.

If you change your mind and do not want to void the transaction, you can select Restore instead of recording the changes.

Deleting a Transaction

You can delete a transaction by pressing CTRL-D, selecting Delete Transaction from the Edit menu, or clicking the Delete button. Try this now by deleting the voided transaction for check number 100.

1. Move to the voided transaction for check number 100.
2. Choose Delete Transaction from the Edit menu, click the Delete button, or press CTRL-D. Quicken displays The Delete The Current Transaction? dialog box.
3. Select Yes to confirm the deletion.

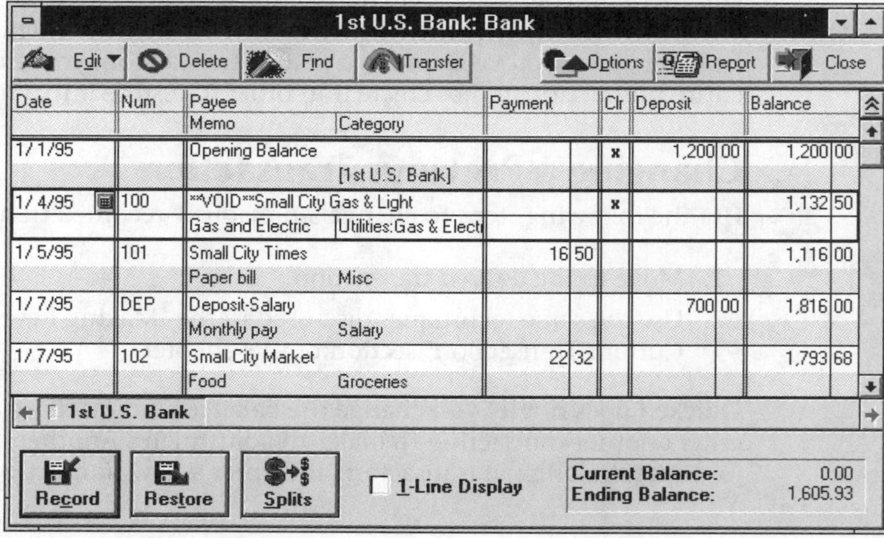

A voided transaction

Figure 3-8.

Reinstating a Transaction

To reinstate a transaction deleted in error, you must retype it.

There is no "undo" feature to eliminate the effect of deleting a transaction. You must reenter the transaction. For practice, reinstate the transaction for check number 100 with these steps:

1. Press CTRL-END to move to the end of the register.
2. Type **1/4/95**, and press TAB to set the date to 1/4/95.
3. Type **100** and press TAB to supply the check number in the Num field.
4. Type **Small City Gas & Light**, and press TAB to complete the entry for the payee for this check.

Note: If the QuickFill feature is turned on, Quicken fills out the rest of the check for you, using the original entry. However, you can't just select Record after pressing TAB to exit the Payee field since you'll be changing an entry.

5. Type **67.50** and press TAB.
6. Type **Gas and Electric** and press TAB.
7. Type **Utilities:Gas & Electric**, or use QuickFill to select it, then select Record to complete the transaction. The transaction is reentered into the register.

   Note that this category is not the same as the one you previously entered for this transaction. This subcategory of Utilities is used so that you can later create reports with greater detail. As a rule, you should use meaningful subcategories to help you better analyze your expenses later.

Obviously, in this example you have expended a considerable amount of effort to reenter this transaction. Avoid unnecessary work by confirming a void or deletion before you complete it.

CHAPTER

4

QUICKEN REPORTS

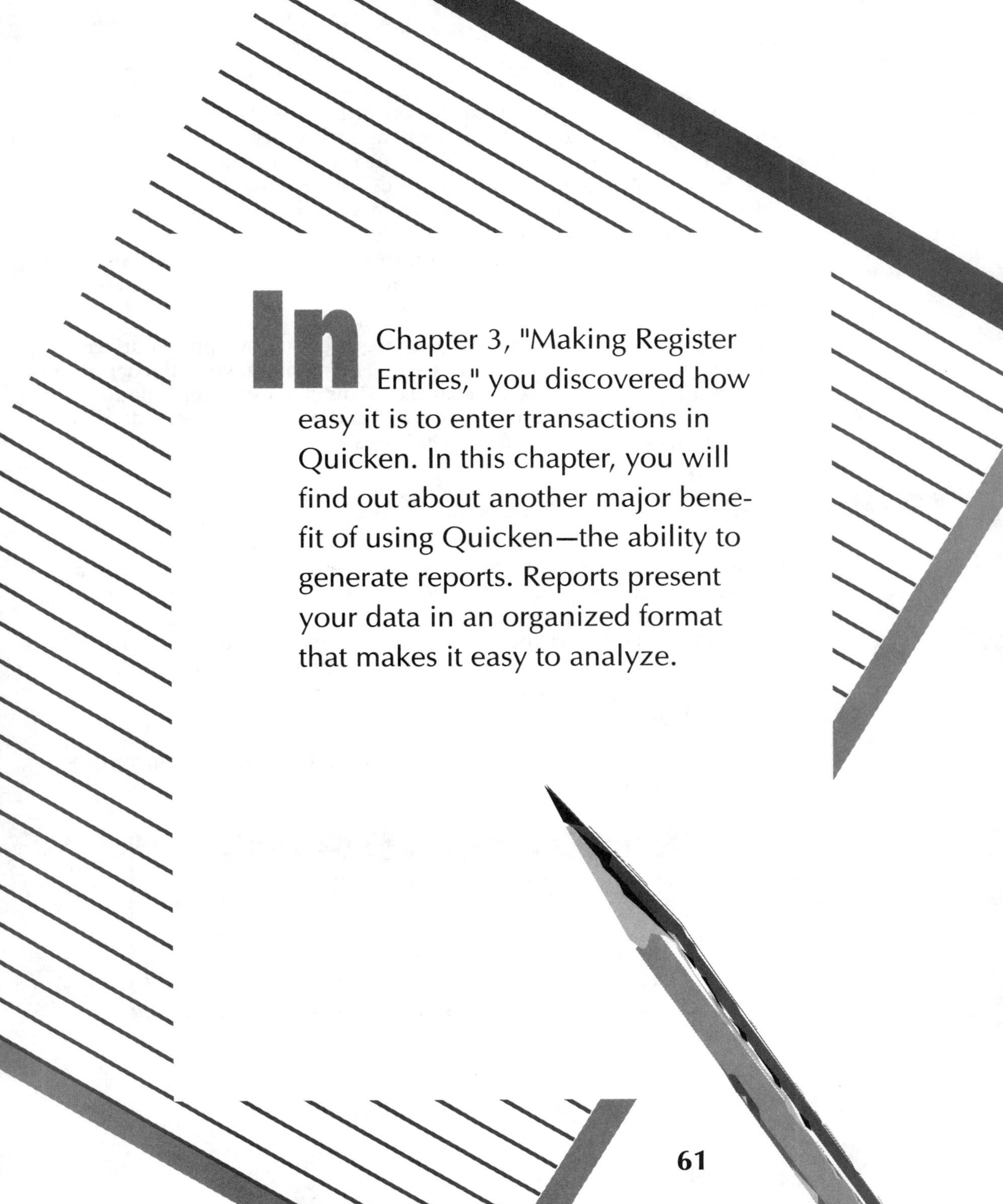

In Chapter 3, "Making Register Entries," you discovered how easy it is to enter transactions in Quicken. In this chapter, you will find out about another major benefit of using Quicken—the ability to generate reports. Reports present your data in an organized format that makes it easy to analyze.

With Quicken 4 for Windows, the Reports menu lets you customize a report while viewing it and zoom in for a close-up look at details. You can use Quicken to produce a quick printout of the register, or more complex reports that analyze and summarize data. Some of these reports, such as the Cash Flow report and the Itemized Categories report, would require a significant amount of work if compiled manually. This chapter focuses on the basic reports and some customizing options. Later chapters of this book will cover Snapshots, which provide an overview of your financial picture, as well as more complex reports.

Quicken, like other Windows products, uses the Windows printer drivers to print. While Windows handles most aspects of printing, you can change the settings for printing from within Quicken. This chapter teaches you to change the basic print settings. You can alter these if your reports do not print acceptably with the default Windows settings.

Printing the Check Register

Although it's convenient to enter transactions on the screen, a printed copy of your entries is often easier to review and is much more portable than a computer screen. Try printing the register first without changing the print settings. If your output is very different from the sample shown in this chapter, try customizing your print settings, then print the register again. You'll find instructions for customizing the settings at the end of this chapter. To print your register, follow these steps starting from the register you want to print:

1. Select Print Register from the File menu. Quicken displays the Print Register dialog box, shown here:

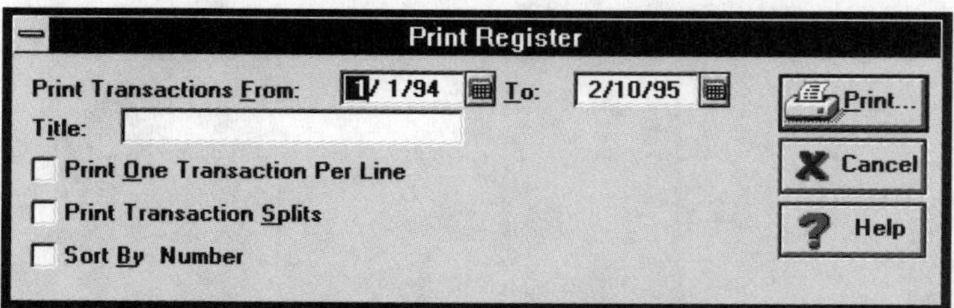

Tip: Pressing CTRL-P opens the Print Register dialog box directly, without accessing the File menu.

2. Type **1/1/95** in the Print Transactions From text box.

   This entry selects the first transaction to be printed, by date. Another way to select the date is to click the small calendar or press ALT-DOWN ARROW, which displays a calendar like this:

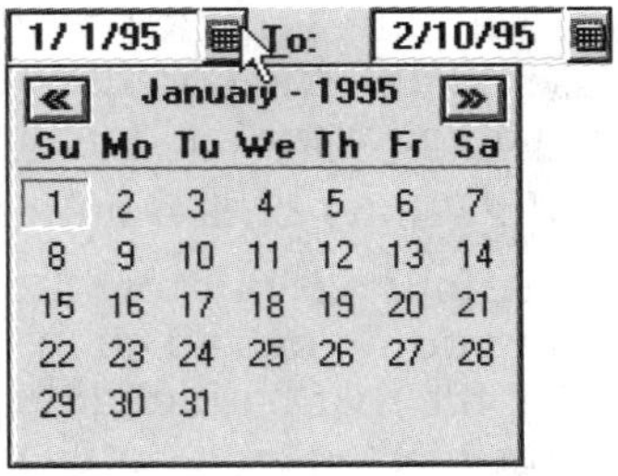

   1/1/95 To: 2/10/95

   « January - 1995 »

Su	Mo	Tu	We	Th	Fr	Sa
1	2	3	4	5	6	7
8	9	10	11	12	13	14
15	16	17	18	19	20	21
22	23	24	25	26	27	28
29	30	31				

   You can click the arrows at the top of the calendar, or press UP ARROW or DOWN ARROW to move to a new month. To enter the correct date, you can click on the date, or you can use LEFT ARROW or RIGHT ARROW to move to the date and then press ENTER. Since you already know the precise dates used in the examples in this book, however, it's probably easier just to type them. The calendar is available for all date fields in Quicken 4 for Windows.

Printing your check register at regular intervals provides a paper backup of your Quicken accounts.

3. Type **1/31/95** in the To field.

   This entry establishes the last transaction to be printed. The dates supplied in steps 2 and 3 are inclusive; that is, Quicken will print all register transactions with dates from 1/1/95 through 1/31/95.

4. Type **January Transactions** in the Title text box.

   This customizes the title of the check register. If you do not make an entry in this field, Quicken uses the default title "Check Register" for the report heading. Your heading can be up to 26 characters long.

5. Clear the Print One Transaction Per Line check box, if necessary.

   The Print One Transaction Per Line check box is blank by default; this causes Quicken to use three lines to print each transaction. To print more transactions on each page, select this check box. Then Quicken prints the register using only one line per transaction by abbreviating the information printed.

6. Clear the Print Transaction Splits check box, if necessary.

   You can ignore transaction splits for the time being. This type of transaction is introduced in Chapter 7, "Expanding the Scope of Financial Entries." For now, leave the check box cleared to print your reports properly.

7. Clear the Sort By Number check box, if necessary.

   The Sort By Number check box is also clear by default, so that Quicken sorts transactions by date and then by check number. If you wanted to print the register sorted by check number and then by date, you would select this check box.

8. Select Print. The Print Report dialog box opens, as shown in Figure 4-1. You use the Print Report dialog box to select where you are printing to and what you want included in your printed document.

9. Select the Printer option button, if necessary.

   There are four options for where to print your report. Printer is the default option. You can choose to print to a printer, to an ASCII file, to an ASCII file that has delimiters to separate your data, or to a .PRN file like those created with Lotus 1-2-3. Choose the destination by selecting the appropriate option button under Print To. As a rule, you'll want to print to your printer. However, you may want to print to a file so that you can use the copy of your register in another program.

   If you select Preview, Quicken prints your report to the screen so you can preview it. Another window appears, showing your report as it will appear when printed, as shown in Figure 4-2. From this window, you can print the report by selecting Print.

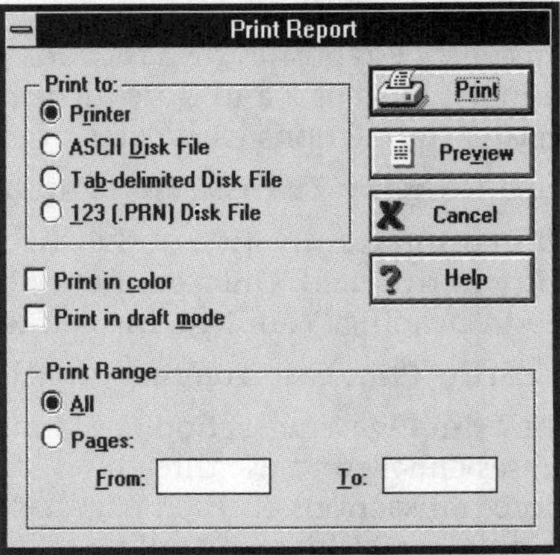

The Print Report dialog box
Figure 4-1.

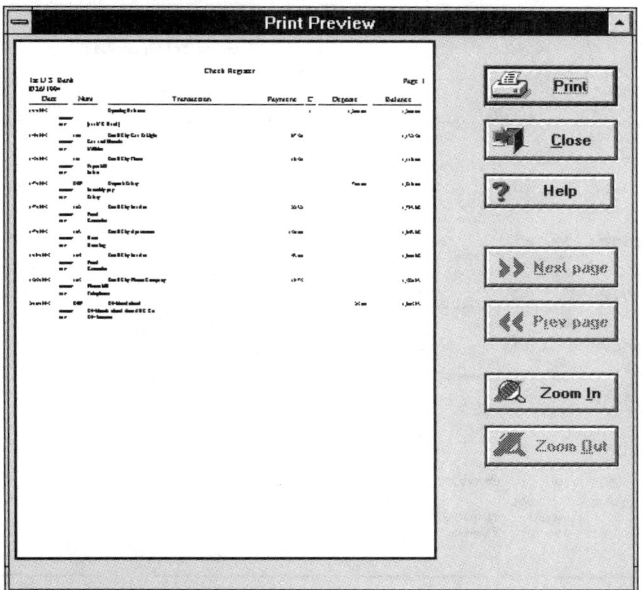

Previewing a report before printing
Figure 4-2.

10. Clear the Print In Color check box if necessary.

    If you have a color printer, you can select this check box to have Quicken print your register using colors. If you don't have a color printer, selecting this check box has no real effect.

11. Clear the Print In Draft Mode check box, if necessary.

    Printing in draft mode is faster than printing with final quality. However, your printed register won't look as good because it is printed in a lower resolution.

12. If you know the register is more than one page long and you know the pages you want to print, select the Pages button, and enter the first and last page to print in the From and To boxes.

13. Select Print.

    Once you have completed the Print Report dialog box, Quicken is ready to print the check register for the period you defined. Make sure your printer is turned on and ready to print before you select Print.

Your printed register should look like Figure 4-3. Notice that the date at the top-left corner of your report is the current date, regardless of the month for which you are printing transactions.

January Transactions

1st U.S. Bank
8/23/1995

Page 1

Date	Num	Transaction	Payment	C	Deposit	Balance
1/1/1995		Opening Balance		x	1,200.00	1,200.00
	memo:					
	cat:	[1st U.S. Bank]				
1/4/1995	100	Small City Gas & Light	67.50			1,132.50
	memo:	Gas and Electric				
	cat:	Utilities:Gas & Electric				
1/5/1995	101	Small City Times	16.50			1,116.00
	memo:	Paper bill				
	cat:	Misc				
1/7/1995	DEP	Deposit-Salary			700.00	1,816.00
	memo:	Monthly pay				
	cat:	Salary				
1/7/1995	102	Small City Market	22.32			1,793.68
	memo:	Food				
	cat:	Groceries				
1/7/1995	103	Small City Apartments	150.00			1,643.68
	memo:	Rent				
	cat:	Housing				
1/19/1995	104	Small City Market	43.00			1,600.68
	memo:	Food				
	cat:	Groceries				
1/25/1995	105	Small City Phone Company	19.75			1,580.93
	memo:	Phone bill				
	cat:	Telephone				

Printing the January transactions in the 1st U.S. Bank checking account register
Figure 4-3.

Printing the Cash Flow Report

Quicken's Cash Flow report compares the money you received during a specified time period with the money you spent. Quicken provides this information for each category you've used in the register. The Cash Flow report combines transactions from your checking, cash, and credit card accounts. (Cash and credit card accounts are discussed in Chapter 7.) To prepare a Cash Flow report for the transactions you recorded in the 1st U.S. Bank account in Chapter 3 follow these steps:

1. Select Home from the Reports menu, and then Cash Flow. You can also click the Reports icon in the icon bar.
2. Make sure the Home option button is selected, and that Cash Flow is selected in the list box. (These options are selected by default if you use the menu, but you may have to select them manually if you use the Reports icon.)
3. Type **1/1/95** in the From text box.

   Quicken automatically enters January 1 of the current year in this text box. It may be easier to change this date by pressing + or - rather than typing, depending on the current date in your system.
4. Type **1/31/95** in the To text box.

You can enter dates in the from and to text boxes as you've just done, or you can select options from the drop-down list box in the first text box. The Create Report dialog box now looks like Figure 4-4.

5. Select Customize.
6. Type **Cash Flow Report** - and your name in the Title text box under Report Layout.

   If you don't enter a report title, Quicken uses the default title, "Cash Flow Report." Your report title can be up to 39 characters long. If you don't see the Title text box, make sure the Report Layout option button is selected under Customize. Each option button under Customize displays a different set of customization options for your report.
7. Select OK, and the Cash Flow report appears on your screen.

   Notice that the Cash Flow report has inflows and outflows listed by category.

Tip: If your report window is very small, you can only see a part of the report. Use your mouse to drag the window border out, displaying more of the report. In some types of reports, the fields Category, Memo, and Payee appear. If your report window is narrow, these fields will be truncated; only the first few letters of the entry appear. Making the report window wider displays the entire contents of these fields.

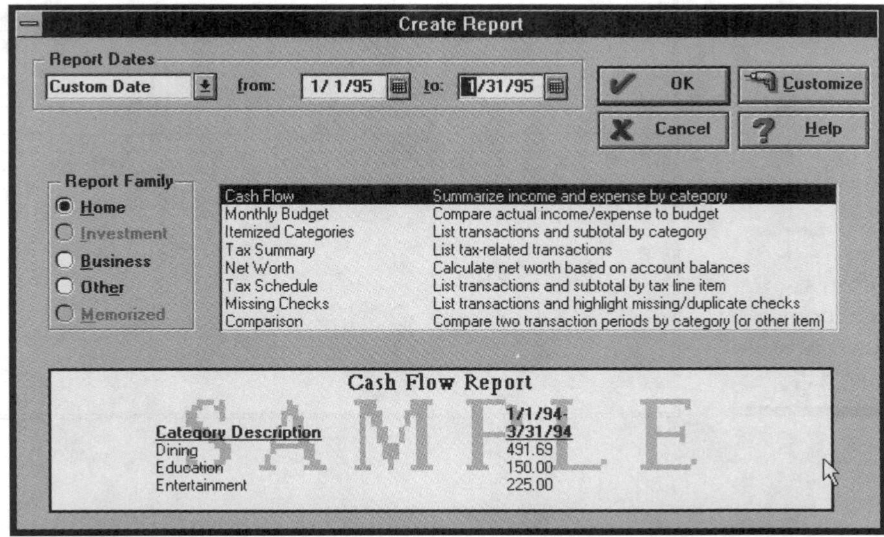

The Create Report dialog box
Figure 4-4.

8. Click the groceries outflow, or move to it using the arrow keys.
9. Double-click the groceries outflow, or press CTRL-Z or ENTER to use Quicken's QuickZoom. This feature shows you all of the transactions that make up the 65.32 total for groceries, as you can see in Figure 4-5.
10. Click Close in the QuickZoom report's button bar, or press ESC to return to the Cash Flow report.

    You can continue to examine the details for any of the entries using QuickZoom. When you're done, print the report.
11. Select the Print button, shown here, on the button bar in the Cash Flow Report window.

Quicken displays the Print Report dialog box. You need to select where you are printing the report. The default is to print to the default Windows printer.

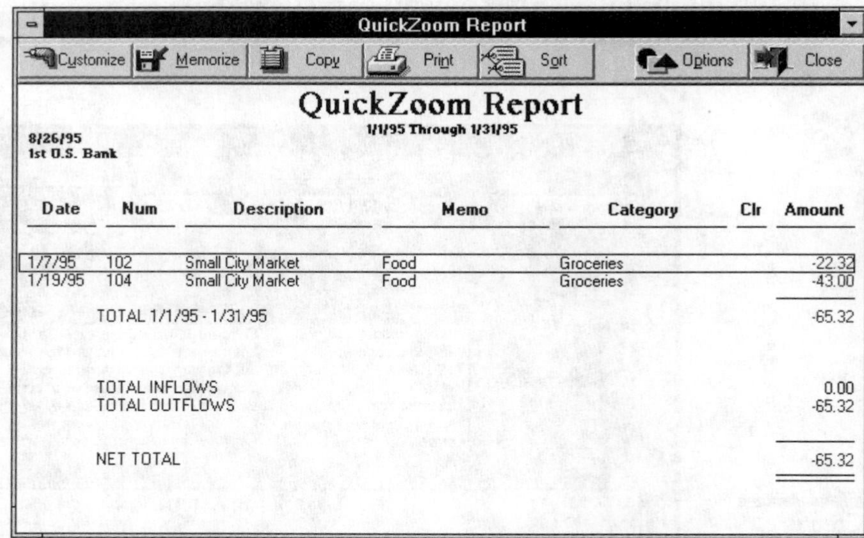

QuickZoom Report

1/1/95 Through 1/31/95

8/26/95
1st U.S. Bank

Date	Num	Description	Memo	Category	Clr	Amount
1/7/95	102	Small City Market	Food	Groceries		-22.32
1/19/95	104	Small City Market	Food	Groceries		-43.00
	TOTAL 1/1/95 - 1/31/95					-65.32
	TOTAL INFLOWS					0.00
	TOTAL OUTFLOWS					-65.32
	NET TOTAL					-65.32

Using Quicken's QuickZoom feature
Figure 4-5.

Note: CTRL-P is the Quick Key for printing.

12. Select Print to have Quicken print the report shown in Figure 4-6.

    You can have Quicken send the Cash Flow report to the default printer, to a disk as an ASCII file, or to a disk as a 1-2-3 file. You can also preview the report by selecting Preview. If you need to customize any of the printer settings, select Cancel and use the Printer Setup command from the File menu to change the printer settings.
13. To close the report, press ESC or select Close.

Memorizing a Report

If you find that you frequently create a specific type of report, you'll want to be able to re-create it quickly. To do this, you need to memorize the report when you create it.

Cash Flow Report-Mary Campbell
1/1/95 Through 1/31/95

Category Description		1/1/95-1/31/95
INFLOWS		
Salary		700.00
TOTAL INFLOWS		700.00
OUTFLOWS		
Groceries		65.32
Housing		150.00
Misc		16.50
Telephone		19.75
Utilities:		
Gas & Electric	67.50	
Total Utilities		67.50
TOTAL OUTFLOWS		319.07
OVERALL TOTAL		380.93

A standard Cash Flow report

Figure 4-6.

1. Select the Memorize button, shown here, from the report window's button bar.

The Memorize Report dialog box appears:

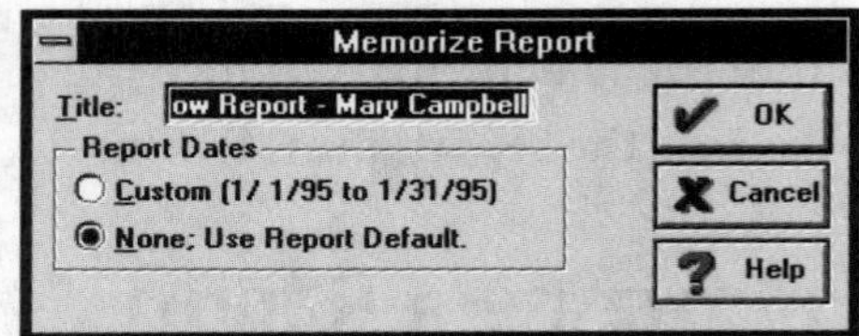

2. Enter the title you want in the Title text box.
3. Select the Custom option button to repeatedly create the report with the same range of dates. If you prefer creating the report using the then-current default dates, select None.
4. Select OK to memorize the report.

You can save time by memorizing your frequently used reports.

Later, when you want to quickly re-create the report, select Memorized Reports from the Reports menu, highlight the report title in the dialog box, select Use, and select OK to recall the report. You can also select the Reports icon to open the Create Report dialog box. Then select the Memorized option button, highlight the report name, and select OK.

Because the report you just created was quite simple, memorizing it does not save you many steps. However, your reports will become more complicated and customized as you gain experience with Quicken, and re-creating them will become equally complicated. Memorized reports save you a lot of time when the reports you're working with are more advanced.

Printing the Itemized Categories Report

The Itemized Categories report gathers together all of the transactions affecting each category for your review.

The Itemized Categories report lists and summarizes all the transactions for each category used in the register during a specific time period. Although in this example you will use this report to work with only the information in the 1st U.S. Bank checking account, the report is much more sophisticated than it might appear. It can summarize information from your Bank, Cash, and Credit Card accounts and, unlike the Cash Flow report, it incorporates category information from Asset and Liability accounts, which you will establish in Chapter 7.

You can print an Itemized Categories report by following these steps:

HomeBase

Reports | Itemized Category Report

1. Select Home from the Reports menu and then Itemized Categories. You can also select the Reports icon from the icon bar to open the Create Report dialog box, and then select Home and Itemized Categories from the list box.
2. Type **1/1/95** in the from text box.

   Quicken automatically enters January 1 of the current year in this text box. You can change the date by using + and -, instead of typing in a new date.
3. Type **1/31/95** in the To text box.

   This tells Quicken to create a report of itemized categories through the end of January.
4. Select OK.

   The Itemized Categories report appears on the screen. You can scroll down the report by using the scroll bar or PAGE DOWN.
5. Select the Print button or press CTRL-P, opening the Print Report dialog box.
6. Select Print to print the Itemized Categories report.

   You have the same print options here that you have with the Cash Flow report. You can choose to print to a printer, create an ASCII file with or without delimiters, or create a 1-2-3 file. You can look at the report on the screen if you select the Preview button. Use the Printer option button, which is the default. Note that the report is two pages long. The top of page 1 of the Itemized Categories report is shown in Figure 4-7.
7. To close the report, press ESC or select Close.

Itemized Category Report
1/1/95 Through 1/31/95

Page 1

Date	Num	Description	Memo	Category	Clr	Amount
		INCOME/EXPENSE				
		INCOME				
		Salary				
1/7/95	DEP	Deposit-Salary	Monthly pay	Salary		700.00
		Total Salary				700.00
		TOTAL INCOME				700.00
		EXPENSES				
		Groceries				
1/7/95	102	Small City Market	Food	Groceries		-22.32
1/19/95	104	Small City Market	Food	Groceries		-43.00
		Total Groceries				-65.32
		Housing				
1/7/95	103	Small City Apartments	Rent	Housing		-150.00
		Total Housing				-150.00
		Misc				
1/5/95	101	Small City Times	Paper bill	Misc		-16.50
		Total Misc				-16.50
		Telephone				
1/25/95	105	Small City Phone Company	Phone bill	Telephone		-19.75
		Total Telephone				-19.75
		Utilities:				
		Gas & Electric				
1/4/95	100	Small City Gas & Light	Gas and Electric	Utilities:Gas & Electric		-67.50
		Total Gas & Electric				-67.50
		Total Utilities				-67.50
		TOTAL EXPENSES				-319.07
		TOTAL INCOME/EXPENSE				380.93
		Balance Forward				
		1st U.S. Bank				
1/1/95		Opening Balance		[1st U.S. Bank]	x	1,200.00

A standard Itemized Categories report
Figure 4-7.

Customizing Reports

When you create the Cash Flow and Itemized Categories reports, there are many customization options available. These customization options are the same ones used to create custom reports, which are discussed in later chapters.

There are many customizing options you can select to create reports that meet your specific needs.

You can access the customization options from the Create Report window by selecting Customize, as you did to add a custom title to the Cash Flow report. You can also access this dialog box from the report window by selecting the Customize button from the button bar. Remember that once you open the customization dialog box, you can get help on each of the options by pressing F1.

There are six major categories of customization changes you can make. You can select a set of customization options by clicking an option button under Customize on the left side of the Customize Report dialog box. Depending on which button you select, different options appear on the right side of the dialog box. The options that these option buttons make available are shown and explained in Tables 4-1 through 4-6.

There are many options you can change for each type of report. For the most part, these options are the same for all types of reports. However, some of them vary depending on the type of report, simply because some options make no sense for a particular report type.

Option	Effect on Report
Title	Sets the title to appear at the top of the report.
Row	Sets whether rows display information by category, class, payee, or account name. (Summary and Comparison reports only.)
Column	Sets whether columns display totals for periods of time, categories, classes, payees, or accounts. (Summary, Comparison Budget, and Account Balance reports only.)
Subtotal by	Sets whether transactions are grouped by time period, category, class, payee, account, or tax schedule, with totals displayed for each group. (Transaction reports only.)
Interval	Displays a column for total account balances for a time period. (Account Balance reports only.)
Sort By	Sets how transactions are sorted in the report. (Transaction reports only.)

Report Layout Options
Table 4-1.

Option	Effect on Report
Cents in Amounts	Sets whether cents or only dollar amounts are shown in reports.
Totals Only	Sets whether individual transactions or only totals for sets of transactions are shown.
Memo	Sets whether transaction memos are shown in the report. (Transaction reports only.)
Category	Sets whether categories are shown in the report. (Transaction reports only.)
Split Transaction Detail	Sets whether the details of split transactions or only the totals of the transactions are shown. (Transaction reports only.)
Amount as %	Sets whether summary amounts display as percentages. (Summary reports only.)
Differences as %	Sets whether difference amounts display as percentages. (Comparison reports only.)
Differences as $	Sets whether difference amounts display as dollar values. (Comparison reports only.)
Account Detail	Sets whether the report contains subtotals by class or by security. (Balance Sheet, Net Worth and Account Balances reports only.)
Organization	Sets how the report data is organized.

Report Layout Options *(continued)*
Table 4-1.

To Include	Select
Specific accounts	Individual accounts in the list by clicking or highlighting and pressing SPACEBAR
Types of accounts	Account type button (Bank, Cash, Credit Card, Investment, Asset, or Liability)
All or no accounts	Mark All or Clear All to toggle between all or none

Accounts Options
Table 4-2.

Option	Effect on Report
Amounts	Includes all transactions or only those that are equal to, greater than, or less than the amount you specify.
Include Unrealized Gains *(Transaction reports)*	Generates transactions for changes in the prices of securities (unrealized gains/ losses).
Include Unrealized Gains *(Summary reports)*	Includes income or inflows for unrealized gains.
Tax-related Transactions Only	Includes only transactions assigned to tax-related categories.
Transaction Types	Includes all transactions or only one type (deposits, unprinted checks, or payments).
Status	Sets whether transactions are included that have not cleared, are marked by you as cleared, or have been cleared during reconciliation.

Transactions Options
Table 4-3.

Option	Effect on Report
Transfers	Includes all transfers, excludes all transfers, or excludes transfers between accounts included in the report.
Subcategories	Displays subcategories and subclasses beneath their parent categories or classes, hides all subcategories and subclasses, or displays subcategories or subclasses with parent categories or classes beneath them.
Categories	Includes all categories, regardless of use, includes only categories used or with assigned budget amounts, or includes only categories with assigned budget amounts. (Budget reports only.)

Show Rows Options
Table 4-4.

Report Customization Categories/Classes Options
Table 4-5.

To Include	Select
A specific category	Categories, then the category in the list
A specific class	Classes, then the class in the list
All or no categories	Categories, then Mark All or Clear All to toggle between all and none
All or no classes	Classes, then Mark All or Clear All to toggle between all and none

Matching Options
Table 4-6.

Field	Includes
Payee Contains	Transactions that have the entered text in the Payee field
Category Contains	Transactions that have the entered text in the Category field
Class Contains	Transactions that have the entered text in the Class field
Memo Contains	Transactions that have the entered text in the Memo field

There is no reason for you to be concerned with most of these report customization options at first. For most of Quicken's predefined reports, you'll want to change only one or two options appropriate to that report type. It's only later when you create custom reports that you really need to know about all these selections.

Although the customization options for the reports require a little time to learn, the result can be a dramatic difference in the appearance and content of your reports. Since the Cash Flow and Itemized Categories reports share several layout features, you may find some of the same options useful in both reports. Don't change these options unless the changed report will be more useful to you than the unchanged one. You can change the labeling information on a report as well as the basic organization of the entries.

Changing Column Headings

Quicken lets you change the column headings on reports. You can print a report for the standard monthly time period, or you can change it to one week, two weeks, half a month, a quarter, half a year, or one year. Make this change by selecting Customize from the report's button bar, and then selecting Report Layout. Simply choose the time period you want to use from the Column drop-down list box:

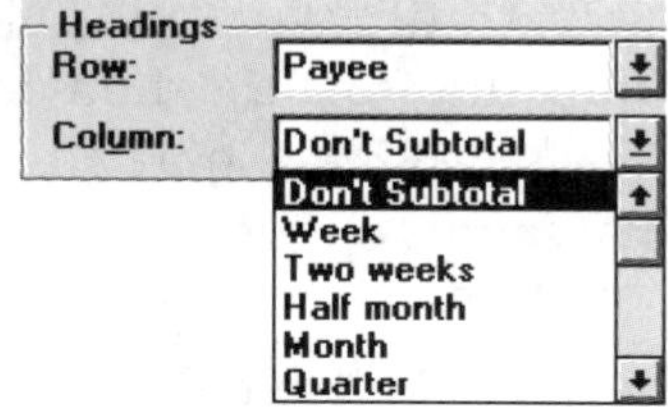

Figure 4-8 shows a report created with half-month time periods used as the column headings.

Follow these steps to create the report in Figure 4-8.

HomeBase

Reports | More Reports

1. Select Home from the Reports menu, and then select Cash Flow. You can also click the Reports icon and choose Home, and then Cash Flow, from the Create Reports dialog box.

Cash Flow Report by Half Month
1/1/95 Through 1/31/95

Category Description	1/1/95-1/15/95	1/16/95-1/31/95	OVERALL TOTAL
INFLOWS			
Salary	700.00	0.00	700.00
TOTAL INFLOWS	700.00	0.00	700.00
OUTFLOWS			
Groceries	22.32	43.00	65.32
Housing	150.00	0.00	150.00
Misc	16.50	0.00	16.50
Telephone	0.00	19.75	19.75
Utilities:			
Gas & Electric	67.50	0.00	67.50
Total Utilities	67.50	0.00	67.50
TOTAL OUTFLOWS	256.32	62.75	319.07
OVERALL TOTAL	443.68	-62.75	380.93

A half-month report for cash flow

Figure 4-8.

2. Type **1/1/95** in the From text box.
3. Type **1/31/95** in the To text box. (If you were to select OK at this point, Quicken would create the report without customization.)
4. Select Customize.
5. Move to the Column text box. Open the drop-down list box by clicking the drop-down arrow or pressing ALT-DOWN ARROW.
6. Select Half month from the drop-down list box.
7. If you've created any accounts other than the 1st U.S. Bank account, select the Accounts option button underneath Customize, and make sure that only this account is selected.
8. Select OK to create the report.
9. Quicken displays the completed report on the screen. Figure 4-8 shows the result of the preceding steps.

Changing Row Headings

The Customize Report dialog box also lets you change the row headings shown in a report. Instead of using categories as row headings, as in Figure 4-8, you can use payees. Figure 4-9 shows the same report as Figure 4-8 after Payee has been selected in the Row drop-down list box, and Don't Subtotal in the Column drop-down list box.

You can make these customization changes by using the button bar at the top of the report window. To change the row headings, select Customize. Then click the Report Layout button under Customize, if necessary. Select Payee from the Row drop-down list box. To change the column headings, select Don't Subtotal from the Column drop-down list box.

Cash Flow Report
1/1/95 Through 1/31/95

Payee	1/1/95- 1/31/95
Deposit-Salary	700.00
Small City Apartments	-150.00
Small City Gas & Light	-67.50
Small City Market	-65.32
Small City Phone Company	-19.75
Small City Times	-16.50
OVERALL TOTAL	380.93

Using payee names as row headings
Figure 4-9.

Changing Other Report Layout Options

There are many other customization options you can set. Some of these options let you select the organization of your report or determine how transfers are handled. The Report Layout options under Show at the right side of the dialog box include a few more items for the Itemized Categories report than for the Cash Flow report. More items appear because there are more things you may want to show or not show in this report: the Itemized Categories report shows complete transactions, whereas the Cash Flow report shows a summary of transactions. The Report Layout options for the Itemized Categories report are shown here:

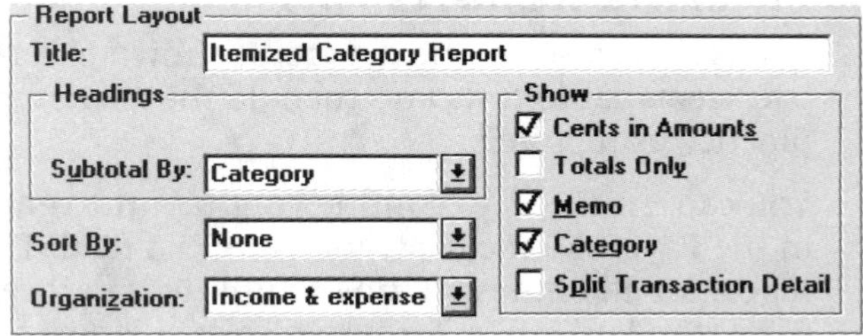

The Organization drop-down list box lets you change from the default organization, which shows separate totals for income and expenses, to an organization that shows information on a cash flow basis.

The check boxes under Show at the right side of the dialog box let you specify the combination of totals, memos, and categories to be shown on the report. You can also elect to show the details of split transactions. Split transactions are discussed in Chapter 7, "Expanding the Scope of Financial Entries." Notice that you have the option of showing cents in the report form. The default setting for this option is to display cents.

Setting Row Contents

When you select Show Rows under Customize in the Customize Report dialog box, you find options that let you determine which row contents are shown in your report. The Show Rows options look like this:

Show Rows
Transfers: Include All
Subcategories: Show All

The Transfers drop-down list box allows you to define how you want your reports to handle transfers between accounts. For example, when Quicken transfers cash from your checking account to your savings account, do you want these transfers included or excluded from the individual reports? Transfers are covered in detail in Chapter 11, "Creating Custom Reports."

The Subcategories drop-down list box lets you define how you want your reports to display the contents of subcategories. You can choose to show all subcategories, to hide all of them, to only show totals for the parent categories, or to reverse the display of categories and subcategories so that the report is divided by subcategories rather than by categories.

Filtering Reports

Filters let you select the data to be shown in a report. You should read the overview that follows and then do the exercise at the end of this section to practice using filters.

You can use filters to confine your report to entries that have specified text in the Payee, Memo, Category, or Class field. This allows you to create a report for all entries relating to utilities or groceries, for example. You can use a standard report form to display a report for a specific payee, such as Small City Times, or you can display a report for all records that contain "Small". To establish filters based on Payee, Memo, Category, or Class field matches, select Matching under Customize in the Customize Report dialog box. This displays the following options:

Include Transactions if
Payee Contains:
Category Contains:
Class Contains:
Memo Contains:

You can filter reports to search for specific payees, categories, classes, or memo contents.

If the dialog box contains the word "Small" in the Payee Contains text box, then processing this request would create a report of all the records with a Payee entry containing "Small." You can modify the printed report further by limiting the report to transactions that have specified text in any combination of the Payee, Memo, Category, and Class fields.

If you want to further narrow searches, you can use special characters. You can enter **=** to specify an exact match, **..** to specify any text, **~** to specify anything but the following text, or **?** to substitute for any one character. For example, you could search for all transactions without "Small" by entering **~Small** in the Payee field.

Another way to filter a report is to determine which transactions to include based on their amount, type, or status. To set this type of filter, select Transactions under Customize. You can designate whether to include transactions below, below and equal to, equal to, above, or above and equal to a designated amount by selecting an option from the Amounts drop-down list box and then, in the following field, entering a value to compare with the transaction amounts. You can limit which transactions are included based on their type by selecting Payments, Deposits, Unprinted Checks, or All Transactions from the Transaction Types drop-down list box.

Use these options to create a Cash Flow report for all the transactions that begin with "Small" in the Payee field. Complete the following steps:

HomeBase

Reports | More Reports

1. Select Home from the Reports menu, and then select Cash Flow. You can also click the Reports icon in the icon bar and select Home, then Cash Flow from the Create Reports dialog box.
2. Enter **1/1/95** in the From text box and **1/31/95** in the To text box.
3. Select Customize.
4. Type a new title in the Title text box. If this text box is not displayed, select Report Layout under Customize to display it.
5. Select Matching under Customize.
6. Type **Small** in the Payee Contains text box.
   If QuickFill is turned on, it attempts to complete the entry for you just as if you were entering "Small" in the Payee field of a register. Press DEL to remove "City Apartments" so that the Payee Contains text box contains "Small" only.
7. Select OK to create the report.

Since the report shows categories for the row headings, you cannot tell if the correct information is displayed. To correct this problem, you can customize the report so that Quicken lists the payee names as the row headings. You can use the button bar at the top of the report to make your changes.

1. Select Customize from the report window's button bar.
2. Select Report Layout under Customize, if necessary.
3. Select Customize Payee from the Row drop-down list box, and then select OK to return to the report.
4. Press ESC to close the report window.

Working with Category Totals

You can create an Itemized Categories report that shows only the totals for each category. To create a totals report for the January transactions, follow these steps:

HomeBase

Reports | Itemized Categories Report

1. Select Home from the Reports menu, and then select Itemized Categories. You can also select the Reports icon from the icon bar , and then select Home and Itemized Categories from the Create Reports dialog box.
2. Type **1/1/95** in the From text box and **1/31/95** in the To text box.
3. Select Report Layout beneath Customize, if necessary.
4. Select the Totals Only check box under Show at the right side of the dialog box.
5. Select OK to create the report.

Changing Printer Settings

As mentioned previously, Quicken 4 for Windows, like other Windows products, uses the Windows printer drivers when printing. A printer driver is a file containing all the information specific to your printer needed to print a document on that printer. When you print a document from Quicken, it is read into a special temporary file. Then the Windows Print Manager program sends the information to the printer while you continue working with Quicken, so you don't lose much time to the printing process.

Within Quicken, you can select which printer to use, how the paper is fed to the printer, and which of the available fonts to use for the body and the headings of your report. You can also use Quicken to activate the Windows dialog box that sets the defaults for some of your printer's features. When you make these changes, the defaults change not only for Quicken but for all Windows applications.

The following examples illustrate making setting changes to an HP LaserJet III printer. If you use another type of printer, some of your options will be quite different. Therefore, you won't be able to make identical choices. However, you may be able to make parallel choices, depending on the features that your printer supports.

HomeBase

Setup | Printer Setup

You can follow these steps to change the print settings:

1. Select Printer Setup from the File menu.
2. Select Report/Graph Printing Setup. The Report Printer Setup dialog box appears, as shown in Figure 4-10.

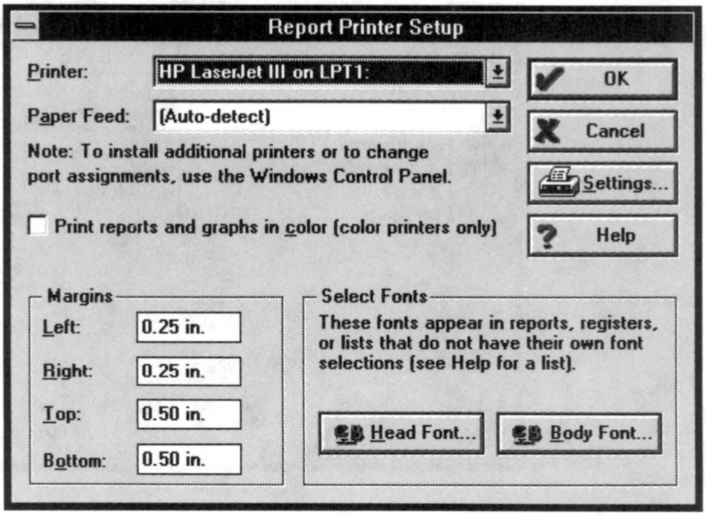

The Report Printer Setup dialog box
Figure 4-10.

3. Select the printer you want to use from the Printer drop-down list box. This list includes all the printers currently installed in Windows. If you want to use an uninstalled printer, you need to use the Windows Control Panel to install that printer. For more details, consult your Windows manual.
4. Enter the margins you want to use for your report in the Left, Right, Top, and Bottom text boxes under Margins. Margins are the spaces between the edges of the paper and the printed text. By default, the top and bottom margins are set to .5 inch and the side margins to .25.
5. From the Paper Feed drop-down list box, select how the paper will be fed into the printer. You should leave this set to the default, Auto-detect, unless Quicken is not printing properly on your paper.
6. Select Head Font to change the font you wish to use for the headings of your report. The Report Default Headline Font dialog box opens, as shown in Figure 4-11.
7. Select a font in the Font list box, a style in the Font Style list box, and a size in the Size list box. Then select OK to return to the Report Printer Setup dialog box.
8. Select Body Font to change the font used to print the body of your report. A dialog box opens that looks just like the Report Default Headline Font dialog box shown previously and is used in the same fashion.

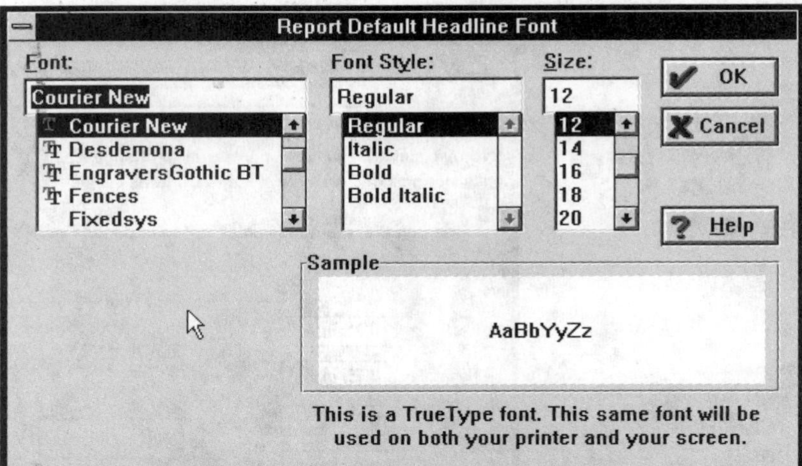

The Report Default Heading Font dialog box

Figure 4-11.

9. To make changes to the printer's default settings, select Settings. A Setup dialog box opens, similar to the one shown in Figure 4-12.

The options available in this dialog box depend on the features that your printer supports, so your printer probably won't have the options shown here. When you are finished setting these options, select OK. Remember that the settings you make in this dialog box are now the default for all Windows applications, not just for Quicken.

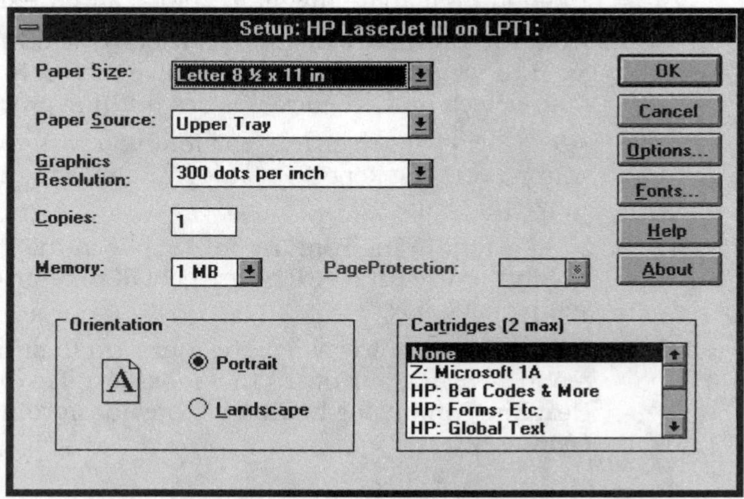

The Setup dialog box for printing

Figure 4-12.

CHAPTER

5

RECONCILING YOUR QUICKEN REGISTER

The process of comparing your entries with those of the bank is known as *reconciling* your account. The reconciliation procedure lets you determine whether discrepancies between the bank's record of your balance and your record are due to errors or timing differences.

Timing differences occur because your own Quicken balance includes transactions up to the present date, whereas your bank statement was compiled before all your transactions had cleared the bank. These timing differences must be reconciled to ensure that neither you nor the bank has made an error. If you are serious about monitoring your financial activities, you should consider a monthly reconciliation of your checking accounts, both personal and business, a necessary step in your financial record-keeping.

Monthly bank statement reconciliations should be part of your personal financial planning program.

In addition to timing differences, there may be errors in the amounts entered. With manual check registers, you might also make addition and subtraction errors when you record checks and deposits. This is one type of error you do not need to worry about with Quicken since its calculations are always correct, as long you record the amounts correctly.

Also, sometimes your bank statement may reflect transactions that you haven't entered in your register. For example, you may have automatic monthly withdrawals for house or car payments, or savings transfers to another bank account or mutual fund. In addition, there may be a bank service charge for maintaining your checking account or for printing checks, or you may have earned interest. This chapter will closely examine these kinds of discrepancies.

In this chapter you will look at how reconciliation works, and you will walk through a reconciliation exercise. The last part of this chapter deals with problems that can occur and with methods for getting your account to agree with your bank's records.

Quicken's Reconciliation Process

Quicken reduces the frustration of the monthly reconciliation process by providing a systematic approach to reconciling your checking accounts. Since this process includes more steps than any of the exercises you have completed so far, a brief overview may help you to understand each step in relation to the overall objective of the procedure.

A Few Key Points

There are three points to remember when using the Quicken reconciliation system. First, Quicken reconciles only one checking account at a time, so you have to reconcile each of your personal and business accounts separately.

Second, you should make a habit of reconciling your checking accounts on a monthly basis. You can easily monitor your checking balances once you begin a monthly routine of reconciling your accounts, but attempting to reconcile six months of statements at one sitting is a frustrating experience, even with Quicken.

Third, before beginning the formal Quicken reconciliation process, examine your bank statement for any unusual entries, such as check numbers that are out of the range of numbers you expected to find on the statement. For example, if you find checks 501 and 502 listed as cleared, and all the other cleared checks are numbered in the 900s, the bank might have charged another customer's checks against your account. This examination indicates what you should look for during the reconciliation process.

An Overview of the Process

Quicken leads you through the reconciliation process.

When you begin reconciliation, Quicken asks for information from your current bank statement, such as the opening and ending balances, service charges, and any interest earned on your account. Quicken will record these transactions in the check register and mark them as cleared since the bank has already processed these items.

Once you enter this preparatory information, Quicken presents a summary window for marking cleared items. All the transactions you recorded in the account, as well as the service charge and interest-earned transactions, are shown on this window.

Your next step is to check the amounts of your Quicken entries against the amounts listed on the bank statement. Where there are discrepancies, you can switch to your Quicken register and check the entries. You may find incorrect amounts recorded in the Quicken register or incorrect amounts recorded by your bank. You may also find that you forgot to record a check or a deposit. You can create or change register entries from the register window. Once you have finished with an entry, you mark the transaction as cleared. A check mark appears in the Cleared column until you complete the reconciliation. If you look at the register again after reconciliation you will see that Quicken has placed an X in the register's Cleared column for each transaction cleared.

Quicken maintains a running total of your balance as you proceed through the reconciliation process. Each debit or credit is applied to the opening balance total as you mark it cleared. You can determine the difference between your cleared balance amount and the bank statement balance at any time. Your objective is to achieve a difference of zero at the end of the reconciliation process.

After resolving any differences between your balance and the bank's, you can print the reconciliation reports.

Preparing the Printer for Reconciliation

Before you begin reconciliation, you should check your printer settings. This is important because at the end of the reconciliation process, you are given an opportunity to print reconciliation reports. You can't change printer settings after Quicken presents you with the Print Reconciliation Report window; it's too late. If you attempt to make a change by pressing ESC, the dialog box is closed, and you have to start over. However, you don't need to complete the detailed reconciliation procedure again, as the reconciliation has already been completed.

Select Printer Setup from the File menu to check your printer settings now. Then you are ready to start the reconciliation example.

A Sample Reconciliation

HomeBase

Day To Day | Use Register

From reading about the objectives of the reconciliation process, you should understand its concept. Actually doing a reconciliation will fit the pieces together. The following exercise uses a sample bank statement and the entries you made to the 1st U.S. Bank register in Chapter 3, "Making Register Entries."

1. Open your 1st U.S. Bank register, if necessary, by selecting Use Register from the Activities menu or clicking the Register icon in the icon bar. (This step is necessary only if your register does not appear in the Quicken window.)

Tip: You can also press CTRL-R to open the account register.

HomeBase

Day To Day | Reconcile Account

2. Select Reconcile from the Activities menu or click the Recon icon in the icon bar to start Quicken's reconciliation system.

   You see the Reconcile Bank Statement dialog box:

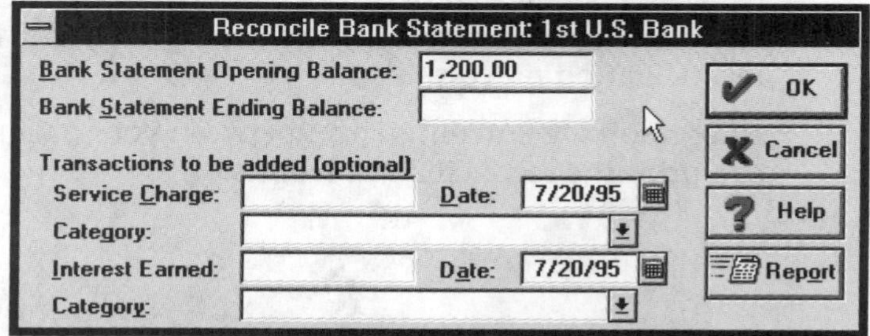

Figure 5-1 is a copy of your first bank statement from 1st U.S. Bank; you will use it to respond to Quicken's prompts for information.

The first time you reconcile an account, the Reconcile Bank Statement dialog box displays the same opening balance as the one in your Quicken register. This amount should also match the balance shown on your first monthly bank statement.

3. Enter **1398.21** in the Bank Statement Ending Balance text box.
4. Enter **11.50** in the Service Charge text box.

   You must enter all the service charges and similar charges in a lump sum. In this case, the bank has charged you a monthly service charge and a check printing charge that total 11.50 (3.50 + 8.00).
5. Enter **2/1/95** in the Date text box as the date for the bank charge.

   Remember that the dates in the examples are used so that your reports and data will exactly match what is in this book. You can use the calendar to select this date.
6. Enter **Bank Chrg** in the Category text box.

   Entering a category is optional; however, to take full advantage of Quicken's reporting features, you should use a category for all transactions. You can ensure that the category is entered correctly by starting to type it and then letting QuickFill complete the entry, or by selecting the entry from the drop-down list.
7. Enter **1.03** in the Interest Earned text box.
8. Enter **2/1/95** in the Date text box.
9. Enter **Int Inc** in the Category text box.
10. Select OK.

    The Reconcile Bank Account window shown in Figure 5-2 appears. Here you mark cleared items. The payments and checks are on the left side of the window and the credits or deposits are on the right because many bank statements divide transactions by whether they add money to your account or remove it. The new service charge and interest transactions appear in these list boxes, which also list the transactions you entered in Chapter 3.

    The Reconcile Bank Account window also shows totals in the bottom right corner. The cleared balance shown at the bottom of the window is your opening balance of 1200.00 modified by the two new transactions. Quicken also monitors the difference between this cleared total and the bank statement balance.

1st U.S. Bank
P.O. Box 123
Small City, USA

DATE 2/10/95
PAGE 1 OF 1

Mary Campbell
P.O. Box ABC
Small City, USA

DATE	DESCRIPTION	AMOUNT	BALANCE
1-1	Deposit	1,200.00	1,200.00
1-6	100 check	77.50-	1,122.50
1-7	Deposit	700.00	1,822.50
1-11	101 check	16.50-	1,806.00
1-12	103 check	150.00-	1,656.00
1-20	102 check	22.32-	1,633.68
2-1	Loan payment deduction	225.00-	1,408.68
2-1	Service charge	11.50-	1,397.18
2-1	Interest	1.03	1,398.21

Date	Check No.	Amount
1-6	# 100	77.50-
1-11	# 101	16.50-
1-20	# 102	22.32-
1-12	# 103	150.00-

STATEMENT

Bank statement for the 1st U.S. Bank account

Figure 5-1.

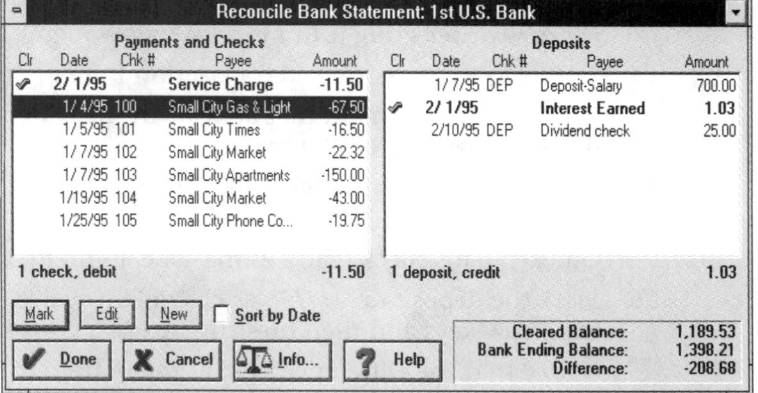

The Reconcile Bank Account window

Figure 5-2.

11. Make sure that the entry for check number 100 is highlighted in the Payments and Checks list box. Since the bank statement entry and this entry do not agree, select Edit to move to the register.

    The register window looks like Figure 5-3. Make sure that check number 100 is highlighted. If you looked at your canceled check for this transaction, you would see that it was for 77.50 and that it cleared the bank for that amount. Since the register entry is wrong, you must make a correction.

12. Move to the Payment field, type **77.50**, and then select Record or press ENTER.

5

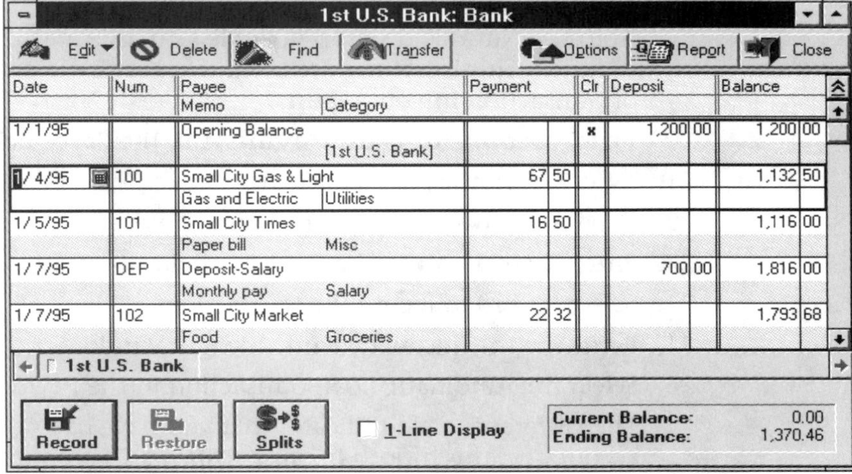

The Check Register window

Figure 5-3.

13. Return to the Reconcile Bank Account window by clicking on that window or selecting it from the Window menu.
14. Select the newly corrected transaction to mark it as cleared.

    Notice the check mark that appears in the Clr column, indicating that this item has cleared the bank.
15. Select checks 101 through 103 by clicking 101, then pressing SHIFT while clicking 103.

    Quicken adds check marks to the Clr column for checks 101 through 103.
16. Mark the deposit on 1/7/95 as cleared by clicking it or moving to it with the arrow keys and then pressing SPACEBAR.

    Notice that the Difference field at the bottom of the window displays 225.00. When you check the bank statement, you see that this difference is the amount of the automatic deduction for an automobile loan you have with 1st U.S. Bank. Since this amount is not shown on your list of uncleared items, the transaction is not yet recorded in your register.

When the Difference field shows no amount remaining, your reconciliation is complete.

17. Move to the register window by clicking on it or by selecting it from the Window menu.
18. Move to the end of the register by using the scroll bar or by pressing CTRL-END.
19. Enter **2/1/95** in the Date field.

    For this exercise, enter 2/1/95 as the date so that the recorded transaction shows the date that the bank deducted the amount from your account. (When using Quicken to reconcile your own accounts, you can use the current date if you prefer.) Since this is an automatic deduction, you don't use a check number. You can enter EFT (which stands for Electronic Funds Transfer) in the Num field, or select EFT from the Num field's drop-down list, to indicate an automatic transfer of funds. This is not required, but it makes it easier to identify this type of transaction in your reports.
20. Type **Automatic Loan Payment** in the Payee field.
21. Type **225** in the Payment field.
22. Type **Auto payment** in the Memo field.
23. Enter **Auto:Loan** in the Category field.
24. Select Record to record the transaction.
25. Return to the Reconcile Bank Account window.
26. Select the Automatic Loan transaction in the Payments and Checks list.

    The Difference field indicates that you have balanced your checking account for this month because it shows an amount of 0.00. Figure 5-4

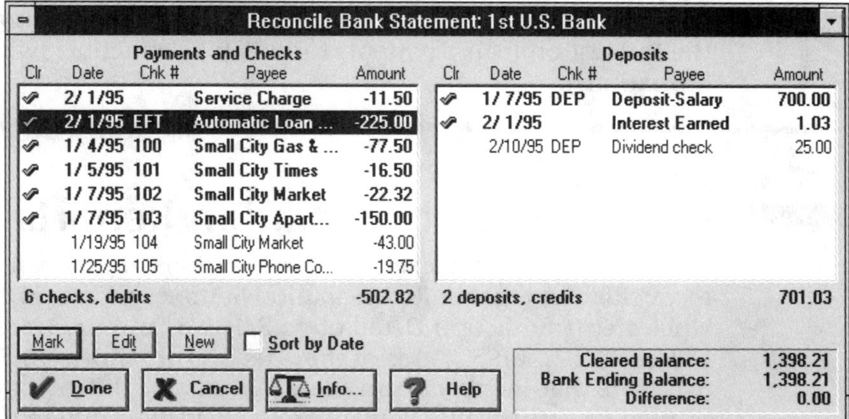

The new entry reconciles the account.
Figure 5-4.

shows the Reconcile Bank Account window with the account balanced. You can refer to this figure to complete the reconciliation.

27. Select Done, and the Reconciliation Complete dialog box appears.
28. Select Yes from this dialog box. The Reconciliation Report Setup window appears:

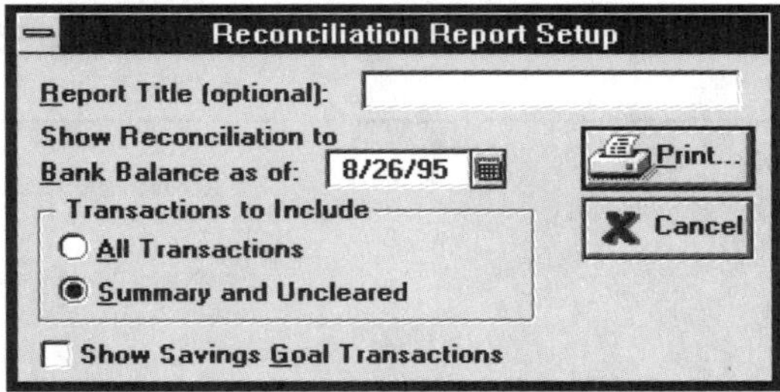

You must complete this window to print the reconciliation reports.

29. Type **2/10/95** in the Show Reconciliation to Bank Balance As Of text box.
    This changes the reconciliation date to conform to the example date.
30. Select All Transactions.
31. Select Print.
32. Select Printer in the Print Report dialog box, if necessary, and then select Print.

You have now completed the reconciliation process, and Quicken is printing your reconciliation reports.

Note: If the automobile referred to in the reports is used for business, the interest on loan payments for it is tax deductible (with certain limitations).

Quicken's Reconciliation Reports

Since you selected Quicken's All Transactions option, you have received four reconciliation reports: Reconciliation Summary, Cleared Transaction Detail, Uncleared Transaction Detail up to 2/10/95, and Uncleared Transaction Detail after 2/10/95. Three of these reports are shown in Figures 5-5 through 5-7. Note that the spacing in these figures may differ from that in your printed reports because you are probably using a different printer.

Note: Remember that the dates on these reconciliation reports will vary depending on when they are created. The dates in the upper-left corner of your document will not match those shown here. However, if you enter the dates of the transactions and the reports as given in this book, your reports should match those shown in all other particulars.

Reconciliation Report

1st U.S. Bank
2/10/95

Page 1

Reconciliation Summary

BANK STATEMENT -- CLEARED TRANSACTIONS:			
Previous Balance:			0.00
Checks and Payments	6	Items	-502.82
Deposits and Other Credits	2	Items	701.03
Ending Balance of Bank Statement:			198.21
YOUR RECORDS -- UNCLEARED TRANSACTIONS:			
Cleared Balance:			1,398.21
Checks and Payments	2	Items	-62.75
Deposits and Other Credits	1	Item	25.00
Register Balance as of 2/10/95:			1,360.46
Checks and Payments	0	Items	0.00
Deposits and Other Credits	0	Items	0.00
Register Ending Balance:			1,360.46

Figure 5-5. The Reconciliation Summary report

Reconciliation Report

1st U.S. Bank
2/10/95

Page 2

Cleared Transaction Detail

Date	Num	Payee	Memo	Category	Clr	Amount
Clr Checks and Payments						
1/ 4/95	100	Small City Gas & Light	Gas and Electric	Utilities	x	-77.50
1/ 5/95	101	Small City Times	Paper bill	Misc	x	-16.50
1/ 7/95	102	Small City Market	Food	Groceries	x	-22.32
1/ 7/95	103	Small City Apartments	Rent	Housing	x	-150.00
2/ 1/95	EFT	Automatic Loan Payment	Auto payment	Auto:Loan	x	-225.00
2/ 1/95		Service Charge		Bank Chrg	x	-11.50
Total Clr Checks and Payments				6 Items		-502.82
Clr Deposits and Other Credits						
1/ 7/95	DEP	Deposit-Salary	Monthly pay	Salary	x	700.00
2/ 1/95		Interest Earned		Int Inc	x	1.03
Total Clr Deposits and Other Credits				2 Items		701.03
Total Clr Transactions				8 Items		198.21

The Cleared Transaction Detail report
Figure 5-6.

In the Reconciliation Summary report, shown in Figure 5-5, the section labeled "BANK STATEMENT — CLEARED TRANSACTIONS" lists the beginning balance of 1,200.00 and summarizes the activity the bank reported for your account during the reconciliation period. The first part of the section headed "YOUR RECORDS — UNCLEARED TRANSACTIONS" summarizes the difference between your register balance at the date of the reconciliation—2/10/95—and the bank's balance. In this case, there are two checks written and one deposit made to your account that were not shown on the bank statement. The report shows any checks and deposits recorded since the reconciliation date. In your sample reconciliation, no transactions were entered after 2/10/95, so the register balance at that date is also the register ending balance.

The Cleared Transaction Detail report, shown in Figure 5-6, contains two sections: "Clr Checks and Payments" and "Clr Deposits and Other Credits." The items they contain were part of the reconciliation process. Notice that this report provides detail for the "CLEARED TRANSACTIONS" section of the Reconciliation Summary report.

The Uncleared Transaction Detail up to 2/10/95 report, shown in Figure 5-7, contains the sections "Uncleared Checks and Payments" and "Uncleared Deposits and Other Credits," which provide the details of uncleared transactions included in your register up to the date of the reconciliation. This report provides detail for the "UNCLEARED TRANSACTIONS" section of the Reconciliation Summary report.

Reconciliation Report

1st U.S. Bank
2/10/95

Page 3

Uncleared Transaction Detail up to 2/10/95

Date	Num	Payee	Memo	Category	Clr	Amount
Uncleared Checks and Payments						
1/19/95	104	Small City Market	Food	Groceries		-43.00
1/25/95	105	Small City Phone Company	Phone bill	Telephone		-19.75
Total Uncleared Checks and Payments				2 Items		-62.75
Uncleared Deposits and Other Credits						
2/10/95	DEP	Dividend check	Dividends check from ABC Co.	Div Income		25.00
Total Uncleared Deposits and Other Credits				1 Item		25.00
Total Uncleared Transactions				3 Items		-37.75

The Uncleared Transaction Detail report
Figure 5-7.

The Uncleared Transaction Detail after 2/10/95 report (not shown) provides detail for those transactions recorded in the check register that have a later date than the reconciliation report. In this example no transactions dated after the reconciliation date were recorded, as you can see in the final section of the Reconciliation Summary report.

These four reports are all printed automatically when you select Quicken's All Transactions option. If you had selected Quicken's Summary and Uncleared option, which is the default option, you would have received only the Reconciliation Summary report and the Uncleared Transaction Detail up to 2/10/95 report.

Additional Reconciliation Issues and Features

The reconciliation procedures discussed so far provide a foundation for using Quicken to reconcile your accounts. This section covers some additional issues that may prove useful in balancing your accounts in the future.

Updating Your Opening Balance

The importance of maintaining a regular reconciliation schedule has already been noted. You should balance your checking account before you begin to

Although you can wait to begin reconciling your bank accounts, you should begin as soon as you start using Quicken.

use Quicken to record your transactions. However, there may be times when the opening balance Quicken enters in the Reconcile Bank Statement window differs from the opening balance shown in the check register.

This can happen in three situations. First, when you reconcile a Quicken register for the first time, there may be a discrepancy due to timing differences. Second, there may be a difference if you start Quicken at a point other than the beginning of the year and then try to add transactions from earlier in the year. Third, balances may differ if you use the reconciliation feature *after* recording Quicken transactions for several periods.

First-Time Reconciliations

If you open a new account and begin to use Quicken immediately, there won't be a discrepancy, but a discrepancy will occur if you do not enter the first transaction or two in Quicken. For example, suppose you open an account on 12/31/94 for 1300.00 and immediately write a check for a 1994 expenditure of 100.00. Then you decide to start your Quicken register on 1/1/95, when the balance in your manual register is 1200.00. The bank statement would show the opening balance as 1300.00. To reconcile the difference between the bank statement and the Quicken register balance on 1/1/95, you can do one of two things.

The first alternative is to switch to the check register while performing the reconciliation procedures, enter the 100.00 check, correct the opening balance to reflect the beginning bank balance of 1300.00, and proceed with the reconciliation process, without any opening balance difference.

The second option is to simply make your change to the bank balance in the initial reconciliation screen and proceed. After you have marked all of the cleared transactions and accounted for all other differences in the ending balances, Quicken can enter an adjustment in the reconciliation to correct for the difference between the check register's and the bank statement's beginning balances.

When Quicken enters the opening balance as 1200.00 and you change it to agree with the bank statement's 1300.00, Quicken adds an Opening Bal Difference field to the bottom of the Reconcile Bank Account window and places a -100.00 balance in it. Then, because a difference remains, Quicken displays a Create Opening Balance Adjustment dialog box when you select

Done. This dialog box provides a written description of the nature of the problem and offers to make an adjustment:

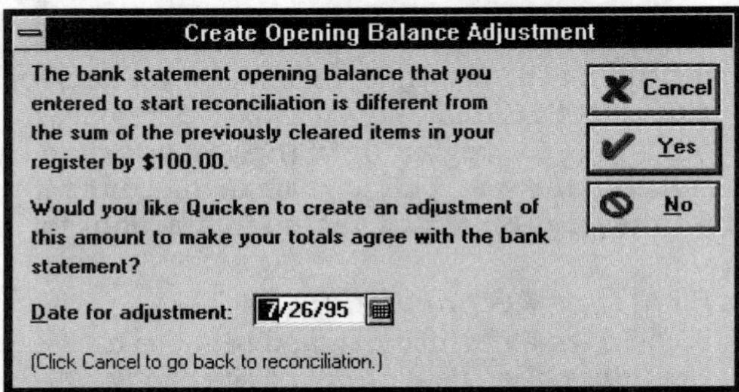

If you want to search for the problem on your own, select Cancel to return to the Reconcile Bank Account window. If you prefer to have Quicken make the necessary correction, follow these steps:

1. Enter a date in the Date for adjustment text box.
2. Select Yes.

   Quicken reconciles the opening balances by making an adjustment to the check register for the 100.00 transaction. The Adjust Balance dialog box appears.
3. If you want Quicken to make an adjustment for you, select Adjust Balance.

   The Reconciliation Complete:Balance Adjusted dialog box appears after Quicken makes an adjustment for the difference.
4. Select Yes to have Quicken display the Reconciliation Report Setup dialog box.

   You can now complete the reconciliation report printing process. Note that if you select Cancel in any of these dialog boxes, you will be returned to the reconciliation process.

Adding Previous Transactions to Quicken

You probably purchased Quicken at a point other than the beginning of your personal or business financial reporting year. In this case, you probably started recording your transactions when you purchased Quicken and entered your then-current checking account balance as your opening balance. This discussion assumes that you have been preparing reconciliations with Quicken and you now want to go back and record all your previous transactions for the current year in Quicken. Obviously, your bank balance and the Quicken balance won't agree after the transactions have been added.

Follow these steps:

1. Since you are going to add transactions in your account register, be sure you have an up-to-date printout. If you don't, print it now before you enter any additional transactions. This gives you a record of your transactions to date, which is important should you later need to reconstruct them. You may also want to back up your Quicken file.
2. Go to your Quicken register window and change the Date and Deposit fields of the Opening Balance transaction to match the bank statement from the beginning of the year.

Note: The importance of saving your bank statements is obvious. Old statements are important not only for the reconstruction of your Quicken system but also in the event you are audited by the Internal Revenue Service. It takes only one IRS audit for you to realize the importance of maintaining a complete and accurate history of your financial transactions.

3. Using your manual records and past bank statements, enter the previous transactions in your Quicken register. Remember to enter bank service charges and automatic payment deductions in case you have not previously entered them in your register, but only used them during reconciliation.
4. When you have completed the updating process, compare your ending check register balance with the one on the printed copy you made in step 1. This is important because if these balances do not match, you have made an error in entering your transactions. If this is the case, determine whether the discrepancy is due to an opening account balance difference or some other error. (Your options for fixing discrepancies between opening balances are described earlier in this chapter in the section "First-Time Reconciliations.")
5. Before starting the new reconciliation, go to the check register and type **X** in the Clr column for all transactions that have cleared in previous months.
6. Reconcile the current month's transaction. (Go to the section "A Sample Reconciliation" if you need help.)

Remember to type the opening balance on the latest bank statement over the one provided by Quicken in the Reconcile Bank Statement window.

First-Time Reconciliation for Existing Users

Although you may have been using Quicken for some time, you may not have used the Reconciliation feature before. If you are in this situation, the process we'd recommend for reconciling your account is:

1. Begin with the first bank statement that applies to your Quicken account. Reconcile your account for the time period covered by that statement, as if you had just received it.
2. Repeat this process for each of the later statements until you have caught up with the current bank statement.

Correcting Errors

Hopefully there won't be many times when you need Quicken to correct errors during the reconciliation process. However, there may be times when you can't find the amount displayed in the Difference field on your reconciliation screen, and rather than searching further for your error, you want to have Quicken make an adjustment to balance your register with your bank statement.

This situation could have occurred in the 1st U.S. Bank reconciliation process described in the section "Quicken's Reconciliation Process." In that section you made an adjustment of 10.00 to check number 100 in order to correct your recording error. If you had been careless you might have missed the error when comparing your bank statement with your check register. In this case, the Difference field in your Reconcile Bank Account window would show a 10.00 difference after clearing all items. If you can't find an error, you can perform the following steps to have Quicken make an adjustment.

Caution: The adjustment process could have a serious impact on your future reports and check register; don't take this approach to the reconciliation difference lightly.

1. In the Reconcile Bank Account window, select Done. The Adjust Balance dialog box appears, as shown here:

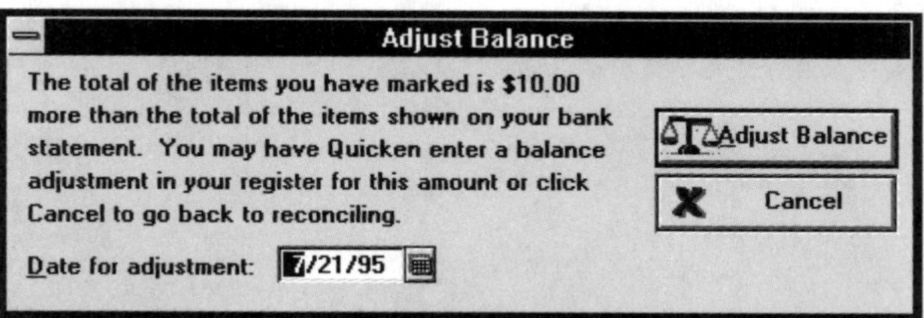

At this point, by selecting Cancel, you can still return to the register and search for the cause of the difference.

2. Select Adjust Balance.

   This tells Quicken that you don't want to search for the cause of the difference any longer, and that you simply want Quicken to make an adjustment. The adjustment uses the current date and has "Balance Adjustment" entered in the Payee field.

3. Select Yes. The Reconciliation Report Setup window appears. Now you can complete the window as described in the "A Sample Reconciliation" section of this chapter.

CHAPTER

WRITING and PRINTING CHECKS

Not only can you record your checks in Quicken's register, you can also enter check writing information and have Quicken print the checks for you. Although this requires you to order preprinted checks from Intuit or another check printer that conform to Quicken's check layout, it means that you can enter a transaction once—in the Write Checks window—and Quicken will both print your check and record the register entry.

You can order Quicken checks in five different styles. Checks for both tractor-feed printers and laser printers are available. Regardless of the check style, you won't have any problem with acceptance by banks, credit unions, or savings and loans since the required account numbers and check numbers are preprinted on the checks.

The available check styles include standard 8 1/2 by 3 1/2-inch checks, voucher-style checks that have a 3 1/2-inch tear-off stub, and 2 5/6 by 6-inch wallet-style checks with a tear-off stub. You can order all these check types for traditional printers, and you can order the regular or voucher checks for laser printers, directly from Intuit.

To print out a check order form, you choose from the menu.

As you can see on the order form, Quicken also sells window envelopes to fit the checks as well as matching deposit slips, stamps, and stationery. Intuit can also add a company logo to your checks.

HomeBase

Setup | Intuit Marketplace

Even if you don't know whether you want to order preprinted checks, you should still try the exercises in this chapter. You may be so pleased with the ease of entry and the professional appearance of the checks that you will decide to order checks for your own transactions. However, you definitely don't want to print your own checks without the preprinted check stock, since banks will not cancel (or stop) payments on checks that don't have a preprinted account number.

Using CheckFree with Quicken allows you to pay bills electronically.

You can also enter transactions in Quicken for transmission to the CheckFree payment processing service via a modem. Your Quicken register entries are updated after transmission, and the CheckFree processing center handles the payment for you. This chapter provides some information on this service, since you might want to consider it as a next step in the total automation of your financial transactions.

Writing Checks

Writing a check in Quicken is as easy as writing a check in your checkbook. Although a Quicken check has a few more fields to fill in, most of these are optional and are designed to provide better records of your expense transactions. All you really need to do is fill in the blanks on a Quicken check form.

Entering the Basic Information

There are several ways to activate the check writing features. You can select Write Checks from the Activities menu, select the Check icon on the icon bar, or press CTRL-W. The exercise presented here is designed to be entered after the reconciliation example in Chapter 5, "Reconciling Your Quicken Register," but it can actually be entered at any time.

Day To Day | Write Checks

Figure 6-1 shows a blank Quicken check form. The only field that has been completed is the Date field; by default, the current date is placed on the first check. On later checks, the date matches the one on the last check written. For this exercise, you will change the dates on all the checks written to match the dates on the sample transactions. When an electronic payment check box appears, you need to clear it if you plan to mail out checks yourself. You should already be familiar with most of the other fields on the Write Checks window, since they are similar to fields you've seen in Quicken's register. However, the Address field was not part of the register entries. It is added to the check for use with window envelopes. When the check is printed, all you have to do is insert it in a window envelope and mail it; the recipient's address shows through the window.

As many as three monetary amounts may appear in the bottom-right corner of the window. The Checks to Print field shows the total dollar amount of any checks written but not yet printed. This field is not displayed until you fill in the first check and record the transaction.

The Current Balance field appears if you write checks with dates after the current date, called *postdated checks*. Postdated checks do not affect the current balance, but they alter the ending balance. They are written to record future payments. All of the checks shown in this book are postdated because the dates they are assigned are after the dates this book is being written. They may or may not be postdated for you as you enter them,

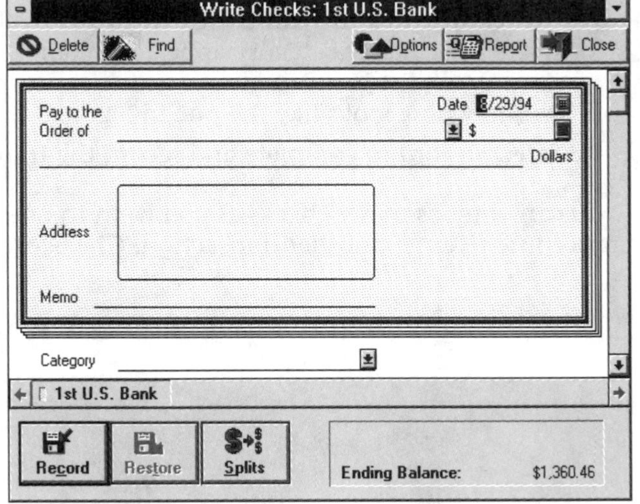

A blank check form in the Write Checks window
Figure 6-1.

6

depending on when you are reading this book. The Ending Balance field shows the balance in the account after all the checks written have been deducted.

If you are using the keyboard to enter checks, you can use TAB and SHIFT-TAB to move from field to field on the check form. When you are finished entering the check information, select Record to record the transaction.

Follow these instructions to enter the information for your first check:

1. Type **2/13/95** in the Date field. You can use + or - to change the date, or you can use the drop-down calendar to select a date.
2. Type **South Haven Print Supply** in the Pay To The Order Of field.
3. Type **58.75** in the amounts field under the date. Quicken supports amounts as large as $9,999,999.99. Notice that when you complete the amount entry, Quicken spells out the amount on the next line and positions you in the Address field. Although this entire field is optional, entering the address here allows you to mail the check in a window envelope.
4. Move to the Address Field, type ' to copy the payee name, and press ENTER.
5. Type **919 Superior Avenue**, and press ENTER.
6. Type **South Haven, MI 49090**, and move to the Memo field.
7. Type **Printing Brochure - PTA Dinner** in the Memo field.
8. Enter **Charity** in the Category field since you are donating the cost of this printing job by paying the bill on behalf of the Parent-Teacher Association.

   Remember that you can use Quicken's QuickFill feature by typing **Ch** to make the Charity category appear on your screen, or you can use the drop-down list box. No matter which approach you choose, the window now looks like the one in Figure 6-2.
9. Select Record to complete and record the transaction.

Writing a check with Quicken is easier than using your checkbook.

You can enter as many checks as you want in one session. Use the preceding procedure to enter another transaction. Check each field before you move to

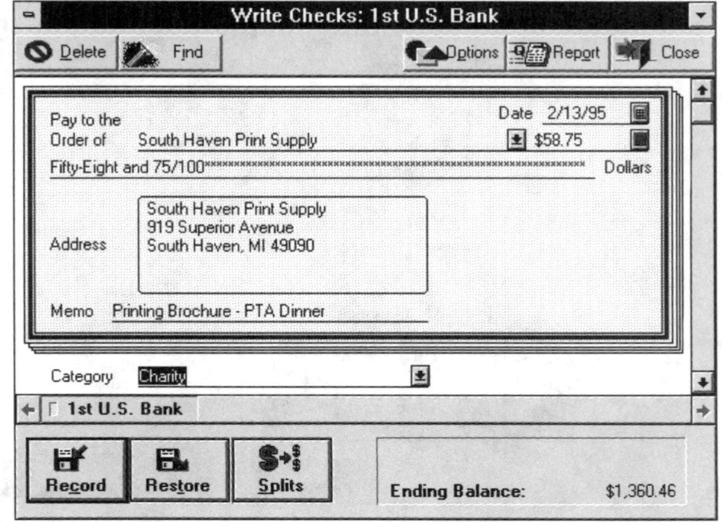

Entering the first check transaction
Figure 6-2.

the next, but don't worry if you make a mistake or two; you'll learn how to make corrections in the next section. Enter this check now:

Date:	**2/13/95**
Payee:	**Holland Lumber**
Payment:	**120.00**
Address:	**Holland Lumber**
	2314 E. 8th Street
	Holland, MI 49094
Memo:	**Deck repair**
Category:	**Home Rpair**

Remember that you can select Home Rpair from the drop-down category list, or you can use QuickFill.

When you have finished, select Record to record the transaction. Although Quicken moves you to the next check, you can use the scroll bar or press PAGE UP to see the check you've just completed, which is shown in Figure 6-3.

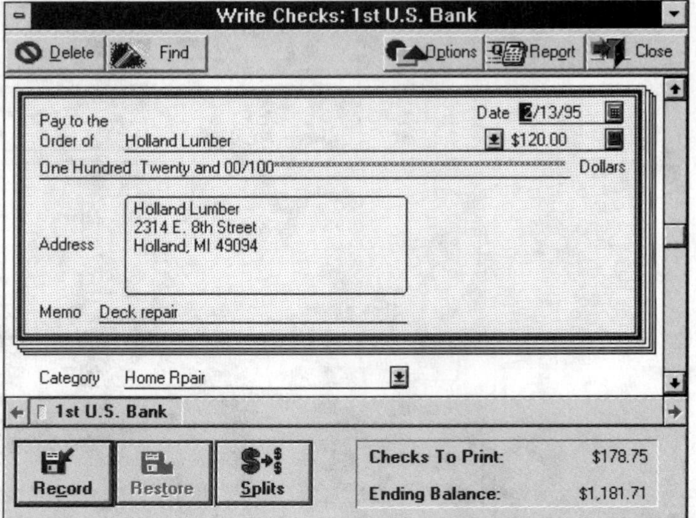

Entering a check for Holland Lumber
Figure 6-3.

Reviewing Checks and Making Corrections

You can make corrections to a check before or after completing the transaction. Although it is easiest to make them before completion, the most important thing is catching the error before printing the check. To prevent problems, you always want to review your transactions before printing.

Enter one more transaction exactly as shown in Figure 6-4, including the spelling error ("func") in the Memo field. Then you'll take a look at making the required corrections.

Press PAGE DOWN to move to a new check form if you are still looking at the check for Holland Lumber, and make the following entries without recording the transaction. (Do not correct the misspelling.)

Date:	**2/13/95**
Payee:	**Fennville Library**
Payment:	**10.00**
Address:	**Fennville Library**
	110 Main Street
	Fennville, MI 49459
Memo:	**Building func contribution**
Category:	**Charity**

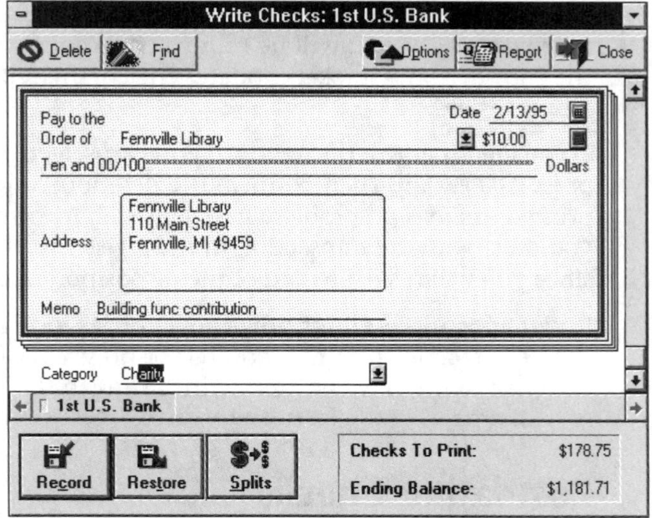

Entering a check with errors
Figure 6-4.

One mistake in the entries in Figure 6-4 is obvious. The word "fund" in the Memo field is spelled wrong. Suppose you were planning to be a little more generous with the contribution; the amount you intended to enter was 100.00. Quicken has already generated the words for the amount entry, but it changes the words if you change the amount. Since the transaction has not been recorded yet, all you need to do is move back to the fields and make corrections. Follow these instructions:

1. Move to the amount field by clicking it with the mouse or pressing SHIFT-TAB.
2. Position the insertion point immediately after the 1 in the amount field.
3. Type another **0**.

   The amount now reads "100.00."
4. Move to the Memo field.
5. Delete the *c* in "func," and then type **d**. The corrected check is for $100.00 and has "Building fund contribution" in the Memo field.
6. Select Record to record the transaction.

You can browse through the other transactions by using the scroll bar or by pressing PAGE UP and PAGE DOWN to move from check to check. Pressing HOME three times takes you to the first check, and pressing END three times takes you to the last check, which is a blank check form for the next transaction. You can make any changes you want to a check, but you should record your changes by selecting Record before you use PAGE UP or PAGE DOWN to move to a new check, or you will be prompted to confirm that you want to update the transaction. Quicken updates the balances if you change the entry in an amount field.

To delete an entire transaction, you can select Delete from the button bar or press CTRL-D, and then confirm the deletion. Since the checks have not been printed, there is no problem in deleting an incorrect transaction. After printing, you must void the transaction in the register instead of deleting the check, since you will need a record of the disposition of each check number.

If you are curious about how these entries look in the register, you can select the Registr icon from the icon bar or press CTRL-R. In the register, you will see the checks you have written with "Print" in the Num field. Figure 6-5 shows several entries made from the Write Checks window.

Postdating Checks

Postdated checks are written for future payments. The date on a postdated check is after the current date; if you enter a check on September 10 for a December 24 payment, the check is postdated. Postdated entries permit you to schedule future expenses and write the check entry while you are thinking

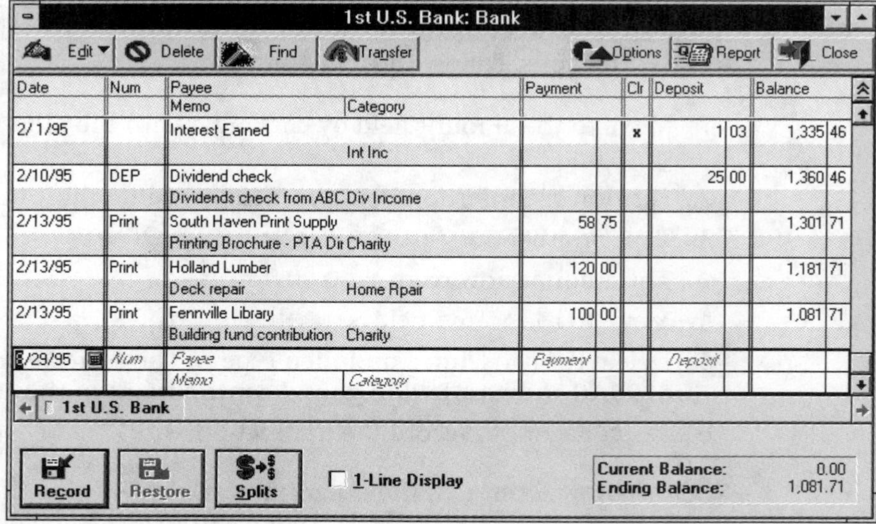

Check transactions in the register with "Print" for check numbers

Figure 6-5.

of it. It is not necessary to print postdated checks when you print checks. Quicken displays both a current and an ending balance for your account.

Depending on when you are entering the February 1995 checks in these examples, Quicken may be classifying the entries as postdated. When you print checks, you have the option of printing those checks that are dated before a particular date. This is another convenience that postdating enables you to take advantage of.

Return to the Write Checks window by selecting Write Checks from the Activities menu or using any of the previously discussed methods. Complete these entries to write a check for an upcoming birthday:

Date:	**3/8/95**
Payee:	**Keith Campbell**
Payment:	**25.00**
Memo:	**Birthday gift**
Category:	**Gifts**

Note that the Address field was deliberately left blank since this is a personal check that won't be mailed. What makes this check different from the others you have entered is that although the current date is supposedly 2/13/95, the check is written for 3/8/95 (later than the current date). Select Record to finalize the transaction.

Now that you have written a few checks, you should try printing a few. You should use plain paper even if you have check stock since these are just practice examples.

Putting Earlier Tactics to Work

Even though you are working with the Write Checks window, many of the special features you learned to use in earlier chapters still work. You can use the drop-down calculator in the amounts field if you need to total a few invoices or perform another computation. All you have to do is move to the amount field, and then select the drop-down arrow or press ALT-DOWN ARROW.

The Find feature also works. You can select Find from the Edit menu or you can press CTRL-F to open the Find dialog box. (See Chapter 3, "Making Register Entries," for more information about the Find option.)

Printing Checks

Quicken lets you print checks when you record the transaction, or you can wait until another session.

Printing checks is easy. The only difficult part of the process is lining up the paper in your printer, but after the first few times even this will seem easy, especially since Quicken has built some helps into the system for you.

You can print some or all of your checks immediately after writing them, or you can defer the printing process to a later session. Some people wait until a check is due to print it, and others elect to print all their checks immediately after they are written.

Check Stock Options

Quicken checks come in three sizes: regular checks, wallet checks, and voucher checks. Figure 6-6 shows a sample wallet check. The voucher design is shown in Figure 6-7. All styles are personalized and can be printed with a logo. The account number, financial institution number, and check number are printed on each check. Special numbers are added to the edges of checks for tractor-feed printers to assist in the alignment process.

Setting Up a Check Printer

The first step in printing checks is to set up the check printer. When you set up the check printer, you select the printer to use, how the paper is fed to the printer, and the orientation of partial pages of checks. You can also select the font used to print the checks. Finally, you can select other printer settings that depend on what printer you are using.

HomeBase

Setup | Printer Setup

1. Select Printer Setup from the File menu.

SAMUEL G. HARRISON
767 W. FOURTH STREET
PEORIA, ILLINOIS 60565
FIRST STATE BANK
1928
PAY TO THE ORDER OF
Date
$
DOLLARS
SAMPLE-VOID
Memo

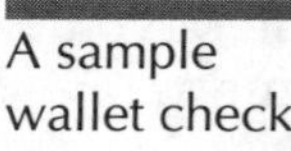

A sample wallet check
Figure 6-6.

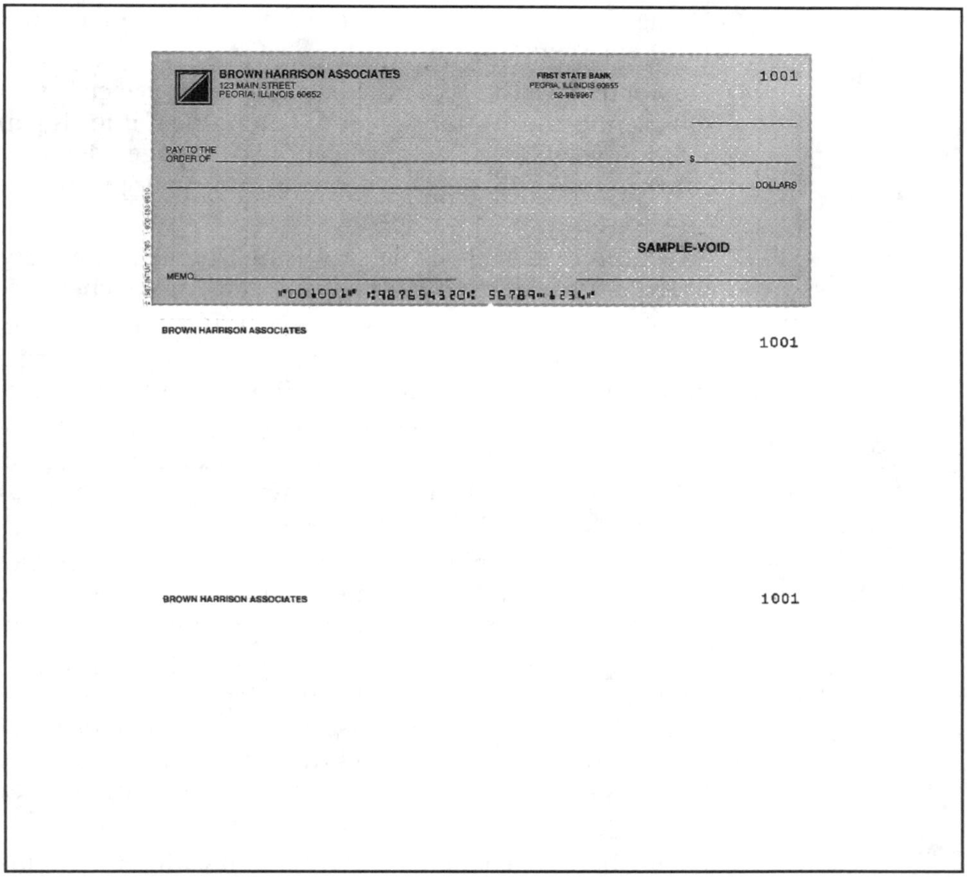

A sample voucher check
Figure 6-7.

2. Select Check Printer Setup from the cascading menu. The Check Printer Setup dialog box opens, as shown here:

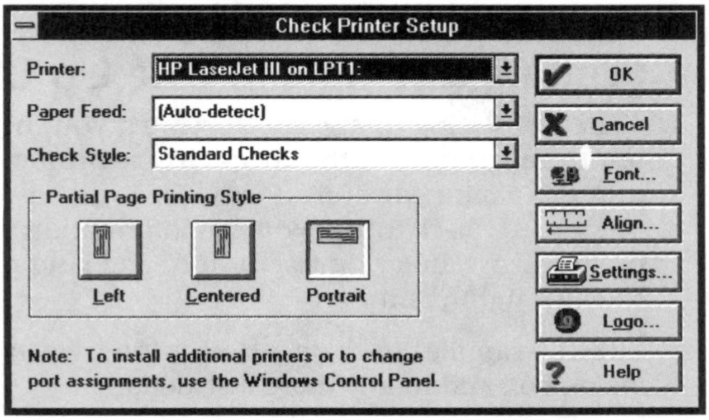

6

3. In the Printer drop-down list box, select the printer you want to use to print your checks.
4. Do not change the Paper Feed default, Auto-detect. This option causes Quicken to check your printer to determine if it feeds paper continuously like a tractor feeder or if it is page oriented like a laser printer. You can force Quicken to assume your printer uses a specific type of paper feed by selecting one of the other options.
5. Select the style of check you are using from the Check Style drop-down list box. You can choose wallet, standard, or voucher checks.
6. Select one of the options under Partial Page Printing Style to tell Quicken how the page is oriented when you print on a partially used page. If you are using a tractor-feed printer, the only option is Portrait.
7. To change the font used to print your checks, select the Font button and make your selections from the Check Printing Font dialog box. When you are finished making your selections, choose OK to return to the Check Printer Setup dialog box.
8. To add a logo to your checks, select Logo; then select File, and enter the name of the graphic image file that contains the logo. Quicken can use .BMP files, such as those created by Windows' Paintbrush program.
9. To change other settings specific to your printer, select Settings. The contents of the resulting dialog box depend on the printer you have selected. One of the options is always the height, or size, of the paper you are using. You must select the size of the checks you are printing. When you have finished making your selections, select OK to return to the Check Printer Setup dialog box.

   Remember that changing printer settings affects the Windows default settings for that printer. Make sure that you reinstate your original settings after you print your checks.
10. Select OK to save your Check Printer settings.

Printing a Sample to Line Up Checks

Before printing your first check, print a sample to test the alignment.

As part of setting up the check printer, you should print a sample check to test the alignment of the checks in the printer. You can then adjust the printer's alignment, if necessary. This will ensure perfect alignment of the preprinted check forms with the information you plan to print. This procedure is similar for tractor-feed and laser printers, but the steps are somewhat different.

To test a sample check on a laser printer, open the Check Printer Setup dialog box and follow these instructions:

1. Insert the sample checks as you would any printer paper.

Tip: If you are using a tractor-feed printer, you can purchase form leaders from Intuit that assure proper alignment of the checks in the printer. This way you won't waste a check at the beginning of each check writing session.

2. Turn on your printer, and make sure that it is on line and ready to begin printing.
3. Select Align, and then select Test.
   Quicken prints your sample check. Check the vertical alignment by observing whether the date and amount, the words "Jane Doe" (for the Pay To The Order Of field), and the phrase "We appreciate your business." (for the Memo field) are printed just above the lines on the sample check.
4. If your sample check is properly aligned, select OK. If it did not align properly, continue with the following steps, or look at Table 6-1 and make the appropriate corrections.

Print Problem	Suggestion Correction
Print lines are too close	The printer is probably set for eight lines to the inch. Change to six.
Print lines wrap, and the date and amount are too far to the right	The font selected is too large. Change to 12-point type.
Print does not extend across the check, and the date and amount print too far to the left	The font selected is too small (perhaps compressed print). Change to 12-point type, and turn off compressed print if necessary.
Print does not align with the lines on the check	The checks are not aligned properly in the printer. Reposition them by following the instructions in this chapter.
Print seems to be the correct size but is too far to the right or left	Reposition the checks from right to left.
Printer is spewing paper or producing illegible print	The wrong printer has probably been selected. Check the selection in the printer list.
Printer does not print	The printer is probably not turned on, not on line, or not chosen in the printer list; or the cable may be loose.

Correcting Printer Errors
Table 6-1.

Note: If you are using a tractor-feed or continuous-feed printer, you have a choice of how to adjust your check stock. If the sample check is only slightly off, you can choose Fine and use the same dialog box you use for adjusting laser-printed checks. If the check is off vertically by more than one line, select Coarse. Quicken then helps you adjust the check stock, using the line numbers on the edges of your stock. These numbers make positioning tractor-feed check stock much easier.

5. Make the check shown in the Check Printer Alignment dialog box shown in Figure 6-8, look like the misaligned check you have printed by selecting and dragging text within the check, using the mouse.

   If you are not using a mouse or if you want to make very small alignment changes, you can enter measurements in the Horiz and Vert text boxes to tell Quicken how much to move the text in that direction. Changes you enter in these text boxes are not shown on the check in the dialog box.
6. Select Test again to print another sample check.
7. If your check is still misaligned, try steps 5 and 6 again, repeating them until the check is correctly aligned.
8. Select OK when your sample check is properly aligned.

   You are now ready to print your checks.

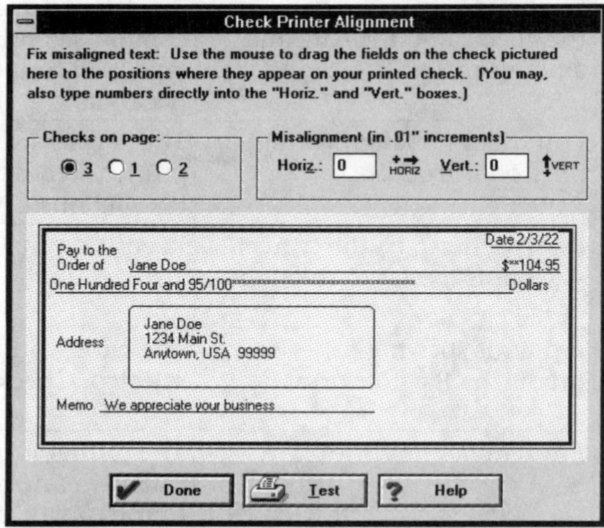

The Check Printer Alignment dialog box
Figure 6-8.

Note: If you are using a tractor-feed printer, you will want to align a specific object on the check stock with some part of the printer, like the top of the tractor feeds, and note that alignment somewhere. This prevents you from having to test your check alignment and adjust it each time you print checks because you will be able to vertically align the check stock on these markers.

Selecting Checks to Print

When you are ready to print checks, you need to tell Quicken the printer you want to use, the check style you have selected, the checks to print, and the first check number. The instructions that follow assume that you have already checked the alignment for your check stock when setting up your check printer and are now in the Write Checks window.

1. Select File, and then select Print Checks.

   Another option is to press CTRL-P instead of opening the File menu. The Select Checks To Print dialog box appears.
2. Type **1001** in the First Check Number text box and press TAB.

   Always make sure that this check number agrees with the number of the first check in the printer. Double-check this entry since Quicken uses it to complete the register entry for the check transaction. When Quicken prints the check, it replaces "Print" in the Num field with the actual check number.
3. Select the Selected Checks option button to print only certain checks.
4. Select Choose to select the checks to be printed. The Select Checks to Print dialog box opens, as shown here:

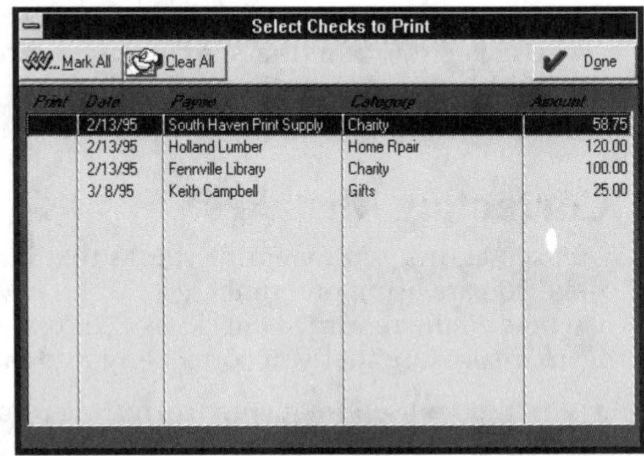

5. Select Mark All so all checks have a check mark in the Print column.

6

Checks that will be printed have check marks in the Print field. To add or remove the check marks, double-click the check, or highlight it and press the SPACEBAR. Select Done when you have finished marking the checks to print.

6. Select Print to open the Print Checks dialog box shown here:

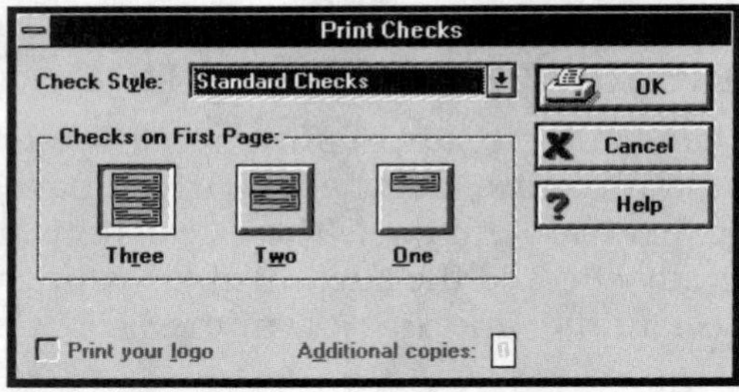

7. Select the style of check you are using from the Check Style drop-down list box.
8. If you are using a page-oriented printer, such as a laser printer, and some of the checks on the first page you are using have already been used, select the option under Checks On First Page to tell Quicken how many checks on that page are usable.
9. Select OK to print your checks.

   Quicken responds with a Did Checks Print OK? dialog box.
10. Review the checks printed, and check for errors in printing. If you used preprinted check forms, your checks might look something like the ones in Figure 6-9 which uses Quicken's sample checks.
11. If there are no errors, select OK to close the check printing dialog box and return to the Write Checks window. Select the Registr icon or select Use Register from the Activities menu to look at the register entries with the check numbers inserted. If there are problems with the checks, follow the directions in the next section.

Correcting Mistakes

Quicken allows you to reprint checks that have been printed incorrectly. Since you are using prenumbered checks, new numbers will have to be assigned to the reprinted checks as Quicken prints them. Before starting again, make sure that you correct any feed problems with the printer.

If you find yourself frequently correcting printer jams and having to reprint checks, you may want to print checks in smaller batches or set your printer to wait after each page.

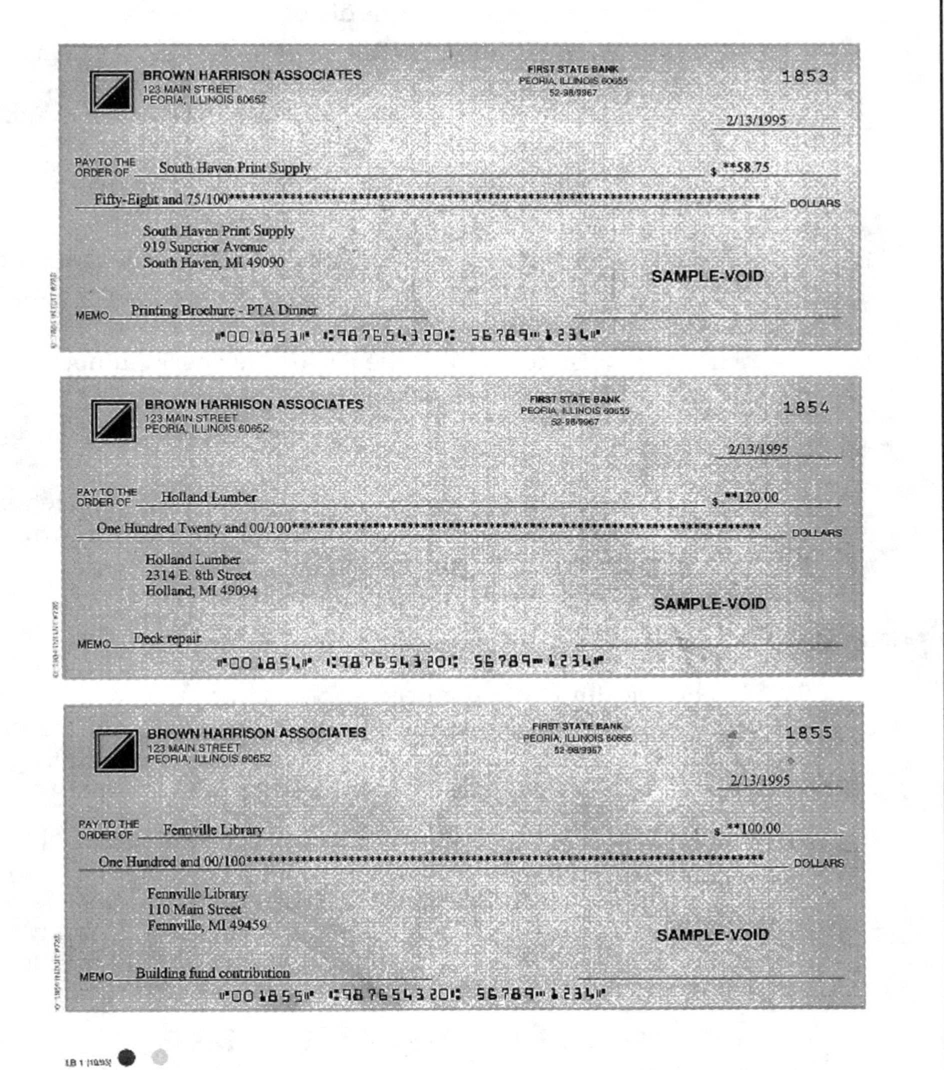

BROWN HARRISON ASSOCIATES
123 MAIN STREET
PEORIA, ILLINOIS 60652

FIRST STATE BANK
PEORIA, ILLINOIS 60655
52-98/9967

1853

2/13/1995

PAY TO THE ORDER OF South Haven Print Supply $ **58.75

Fifty-Eight and 75/100** DOLLARS

South Haven Print Supply
919 Superior Avenue
South Haven, MI 49090

SAMPLE-VOID

MEMO Printing Brochure - PTA Dinner

BROWN HARRISON ASSOCIATES
123 MAIN STREET
PEORIA, ILLINOIS 60652

FIRST STATE BANK
PEORIA, ILLINOIS 60655
52-98/9967

1854

2/13/1995

PAY TO THE ORDER OF Holland Lumber $ **120.00

One Hundred Twenty and 00/100** DOLLARS

Holland Lumber
2314 E. 8th Street
Holland, MI 49094

SAMPLE-VOID

MEMO Deck repair

BROWN HARRISON ASSOCIATES
123 MAIN STREET
PEORIA, ILLINOIS 60652

FIRST STATE BANK
PEORIA, ILLINOIS 60655
52-98/9967

1855

2/13/1995

PAY TO THE ORDER OF Fennville Library $ **100.00

One Hundred and 00/100** DOLLARS

Fennville Library
110 Main Street
Fennville, MI 49459

SAMPLE-VOID

MEMO Building fund contribution

Standard check sample printout using Quicken's sample check stock

Figure 6-9.

Complete the following steps to restart and finish your printing batch:

1. Since you did not select OK when you finished printing checks, Quicken is still waiting for you to identify the first incorrectly printed check so that it can reprint any checks that didn't print or that printed incorrectly. Type the check number of the first check you want to reprint, and select OK.

The Select Checks To Print dialog box appears.

2. The Check Number text box now shows the next available check number. Check the first Check Number text box against the number of the next check in your printer. Type a new check number in the Check Number text box, if appropriate.
3. Select the Selected Checks option button and then select Choose to open the Select Checks To Print window.
4. Select the checks to be reprinted by double-clicking on them or highlighting them and then pressing the SPACEBAR. After selecting these checks, select Done.
5. Select Print to confirm the beginning check number for this batch. The Print Checks dialog box opens.
6. Check that the settings for the checks to be printed are correct, and then select OK.
7. When the checks stop printing, select OK to indicate that all the checks have printed correctly. If they haven't all printed correctly, repeat the steps described in this section.

Using CheckFree

CheckFree eliminates the need for you to print checks. After you enter data into Quicken, you can electronically transmit it to CheckFree. The CheckFree service handles the payments for you by printing and mailing a paper check or by initiating a direct electronic transfer.

Although the ability to interface with CheckFree is part of Quicken, you must subscribe to the service before you can use it. To subscribe, complete the CheckFree Service Form included in the Quicken package or contact CheckFree at (614) 899-7500. Currently, CheckFree's monthly charge is $9.95, which entitles you to 20 transactions without an additional charge.

Setting Up Quicken to Interface with CheckFree

To use CheckFree with Quicken, you must set up your modem so that you can use Quicken's electronic payment ability. Next, on the CheckFree Service Form, you must specify which of your bank accounts your electronic payments will proceed from. You are then ready to compile an electronic payee list and write electronic checks.

Modem Settings

To set up your modem so that you can establish a link between your computer and the CheckFree service via the telephone line, select Check Free from the Activities menu, then select Set Up Modem. The dialog box shown here is displayed:

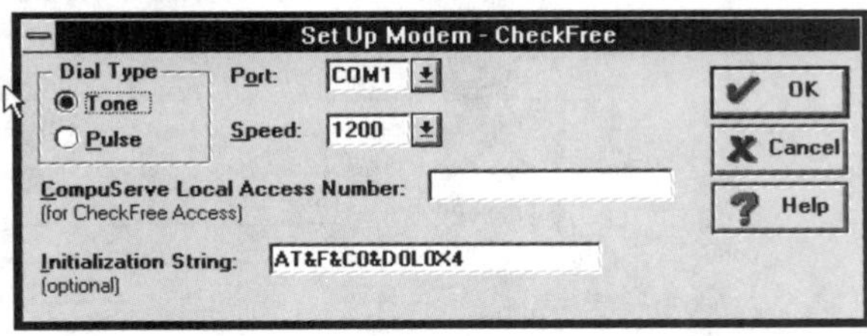

You can accept the defaults for the modem speed and the computer port to which the modem is attached, or you can change them to match your modem and computer setup.

You must enter the phone number supplied by CheckFree when you sign up with the service for transmission. When you enter the phone number, type a comma if your phone system requires a pause. For example, if you must dial an 8 or a 9 to get an outside line, type a comma after the 8 or 9 to allow a pause so that the connection with the outside line can be established. Check your modem's documentation for the appropriate initialization string to enter in the Initialization String text box. An initialization string may not be required with your modem, but you will have to check its documentation to be sure. Now you can edit the settings for the current account to use it with CheckFree, as discussed next.

Account Settings

You can set up electronic payments for any bank account, provided that you specify the account on the CheckFree Service Form. To set up an account for use with CheckFree, choose CheckFree from the Activities menu, and then select Set Up Account. Quicken presents an Account List dialog box listing your bank accounts, like the one shown here:

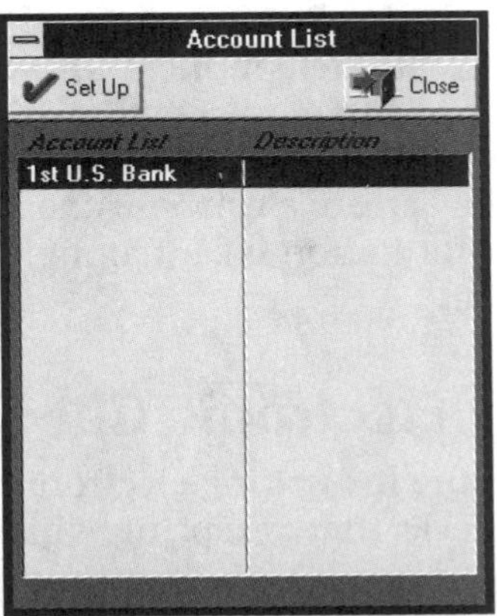

Highlight the account you want to enable for electronic transmissions, and select Set Up. Make sure the Enable Electronic Payments for Account check box is selected, and complete the dialog box as shown here:

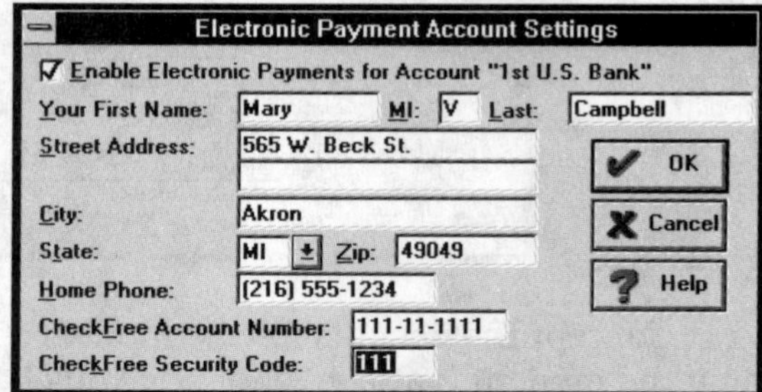

After you subscribe, CheckFree supplies you with the number for the CheckFree Security Code text box. After you select OK, you are ready to enter electronic payees and transmit electronic transactions from either the Write Checks window or the Quicken register.

Compiling an Electronic Payee List

You cannot write electronic checks for regular payees. Instead, you must compile an electronic payee list which includes information that the CheckFree service needs. To do this, follow these steps:

1. Select CheckFree from the Activities menu, and then select Electronic Payee List to open the Electronic Payee List window.
2. Select New to add a new payee to this list, opening the Choose Type of Electronic Payee dialog box.
3. Select either the Normal Payee or the Fixed, Recurring Payee option button, depending on whether or not you plan to send many checks to this payee. Then select OK.
4. In the Set Up Electronic Payee dialog box, enter the payee's name, address, and telephone number, and your account number with that payee, and then select OK.

You can now create electronic checks for the payee you have added to the list. This information is sent along with the check to the CheckFree service for their use.

Writing Electronic Checks

The procedure for writing electronic checks is almost identical to that for creating checks that you print, which is covered earlier in this chapter. To identify the check you are writing as an electronic payment, your check displays two lightening bolts where the address field normally appears. You can toggle between electronic payments and paper checks at any time by clearing or selecting the Electronic Payment check box that now appears in the Write Checks window.

You can write both electronic payments and regular checks during the same Quicken session.

Quicken automatically postdates the payment date by five working days to allow for transmission of the payment to the payee. The Pay To The Order Of field must contain the name of an electronic payee. If your entry does not match an existing payee, Quicken allows you to add it. Once you are finished with your entries, select OK.

Quicken lists your electronic checks in the register. The Num field contains "XMIT" before transmission and "EPMT" after transmission. You can enter these electronic payments directly in the register rather than using the Write Checks window, if you prefer.

Transmitting Electronic Payments

You can transmit electronic payments from the Write Checks window or the register. Select CheckFree from the Activities menu, and then select Transmit to display the Transmit Payments window. You can preview your transmission by selecting Preview, or you can select Transmit to start the transmission process.

TIPS

PC and WINDOWS TIPS

Whether

Quicken is the first program you have used on your system or is one of many, you will want to look through the PC and Windows tips in this section. Even if your primary interest is in Quicken, you may be able to learn a little bit more about your computer and Windows if you read a few of these tips each day.

1. Think about using a fax board in your computer rather than a separate fax machine. It can save money and take up less space. A fax board allows you to fax a document directly from your computer, without printing it out.
2. Always create labels for your floppy disks before you store data on them.
3. Write-protect disks that contain backup copies of data, and don't rely on just one backup copy.
4. Wrist pads may help you avoid carpal tunnel syndrome.
5. If you insist on eating while working at the computer, consider buying a keyboard membrane to protect your keyboard from food and beverages.
6. Always keep disks in boxes to protect them from dust and spills.
7. If you spill something into your keyboard, save your file immediately, then turn your keyboard upside down and shake it gently. Contact your computer store for additional options, which will depend on the type of keyboard and the liquid spilled.
8. Use static spray on carpets or install an anti-static carpet near the computer, especially in cold, low-humidity climates.
9. Avoid placing disks near magnetic fields, including the not-so-obvious ones such as television sets, vacuum cleaners, and conveyor belts at airports.
10. Consider propping your monitor up on a monitor stand or even a small box if the height is better for reading screen information.
11. If your printer tells you that your toner cartridge is low, pull it out and shake the cartridge gently from side to side before reinserting it. You may get several hundred pages more. We usually do this once or twice before recycling the cartridge.

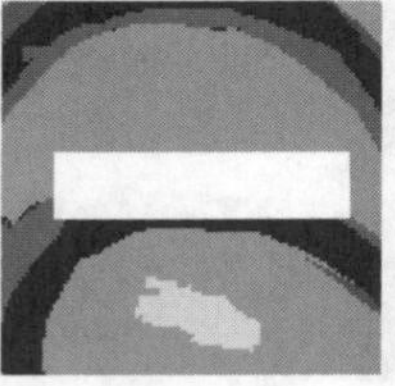
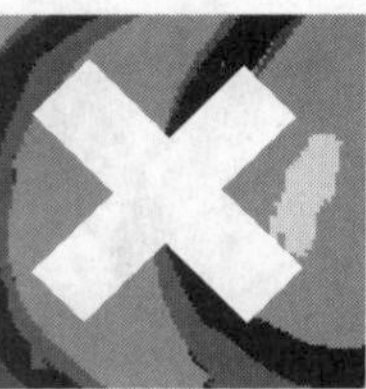

12. Look for a reliable supplier who can refill toner cartridges or re-ink ribbons.

13. Don't leave disks in a hot car or car trunk. Your data is likely to become unreadable.

14. Establish a directory structure for your PC that is modeled after your manual filing system.

15. Keep the area around your PC dust free. If it is not, you should consider having your PC cleaned at your computer store periodically. Simply cleaning a PC can fix apparent malfunctions.

16. Keep your PC away from windows. Heat, sunlight, and moisture can damage it. Also, a system in the window is more likely to attract the attention of a burglar.

17. Before setting up the entire system, position the PC monitor and check the glare on the screen. Hallway lights or light reflected from outside can make it difficult to read the display.

18. If you cannot avoid glare, buy an anti-glare screen or screen cover. The best way to reduce glare is to use indirect lighting, which you can produce by using a strong overhead light source.

19. Make sure you are using a comfortable chair if you sit at the computer for hours. Some users prefer backless computer chairs.

20. Secure your system with wire cables to the floor or wall if you cannot restrict access to the system after hours.

21. Arrange cables so they are out of the way—tripping over them causes as much harm to the cables as it does to your ego.

22. Use surge protectors to keep your PC from being damaged by sudden surges in your power line. Universal power sources can be used to give you time to save data if your power goes out.

23. During a storm, turn your PC off or, better yet, unplug it.

24. Create a schedule for regular backups of your computer files, and assign responsibility for meeting it.
25. Back up important files that are updated regularly after each major update, even if this is twice or more each day.
26. Consider joining a computer users' group or participating in online forums to learn more about PCs.
27. Write-protect disks that contain important data so they cannot be formatted accidentally. To do this, cover the notch on a 5 1/4-inch disk with a small gummed tab, or slide the tab on a 3 1/2-inch disk toward the outside edge to expose the hole beneath it.
28. If you are frequently short of hard-disk space, try the following solutions: Delete old files regularly. You can start saving data files on floppy disks instead of your hard drive. Consider getting a disk compression utility that squeezes files into smaller spaces on your disk, or zipping old files with a file compression program and expanding them only when they are needed. Keep all of your Windows temporary files in one directory and delete them regularly.
29. If you find that you simply need more disk space or memory, see if you can add it to your existing unit instead of upgrading to a new computer. You can greatly enhance your computer by adding memory, a second or a larger hard disk, or features such as internal modems, usually at less cost than buying a new system. On the other hand, if you have a model that is more than a couple of years old, its CPU's clock speed may be so slow that upgrading it would not be a good idea.
30. If you are just starting to use the computer, you may want to use the mouse. A mouse lets you select items by pointing at them and pressing a mouse button.

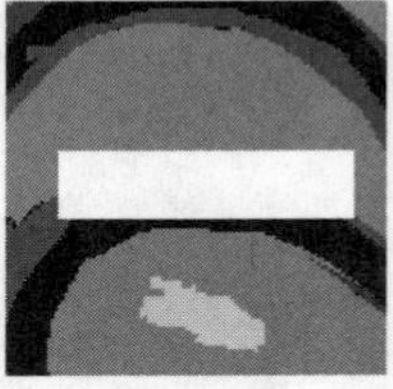

31. If your desk tends to be cluttered, use a trackball instead of a mouse. Unlike a mouse, a trackball is not actually moved around on the desk; instead, you move the ball itself.

32. Use a screen-saver program to provide security for your work. A screen-saver takes control of your screen and hides it by displaying an image whenever you haven't touched the keyboard or mouse for awhile. Some screen-savers let you assign a password that must be entered before the screen will clear.

33. Consider buying a power strip and plugging all of your computer's elements into it. You can then use the power switch to turn your entire system on at once. Many power strips are also surge suppressors.

34. If you have more than one computer, but only one printer, use a printer switch box that lets you control which computer has access to the printer at any one time. This makes it easier to share one printer. Small office networking systems are another option. They offer other advantages such as E-mail between staff members but do have a higher price tag.

35. You can create very professional-looking documents by using special paper. Paper that is preprinted with a design can make even the simplest document look professionally prepared and thus enhance your image when you present business or financial papers.

36. Another quick way to create more professional looking documents is to buy a font package. Several font packages are available for Windows, and you can use these new fonts in most Windows applications.

37. Avoid storing vital files on your computer only. Maintain backup hard copies, possibly stored off-site, and keep them appropriately organized. Circumstances that can destroy your computer files may not destroy your printouts. It is a good idea to keep a printout

of financial data, or other crucial documents, in a fireproof safe box.

38. Invest in a high-resolution monitor. Even programs that use lower resolutions will look better on high-resolution systems. More recent programs that require higher resolutions may be unreadable on a low-resolution monitor.

39. Make sure your computer is 100 percent DOS-, Windows-, and IBM-compatible. Some aren't. Programs written to run under DOS may not run correctly if the system is not completely compatible. This problem is not as common today as it used to be, but can still be a nasty surprise.

40. Make sure cables are securely attached to their connectors. If you simply attach them, but don't secure them by screwing them in place, they may fall out, or you may experience errors because information can get lost when the connections are loose.

41. Make sure you know your disk drive capacities, and buy disks that match. If your disks are of higher capacity than your disk drive, the drive will not be able to read the disks. If you attempt to format a disk to a higher capacity than your disk drive is designed for, then any information you try to save on that disk will be gibberish.

42. Remember to clean your mouse ball and keyboard occasionally, using compressed air or a special PC vacuum. Most mouse units can be opened so that you can remove the internal roller ball and clean it separately.

43. Never spray cleaners directly on your computer or computer screen; the moisture may damage your equipment. You can spray cleaner on a cloth and then wipe the monitor screen or keyboard.

44. Tackle one new computer program at a time. Trying to learn several new programs at the same time will lead to frustration.

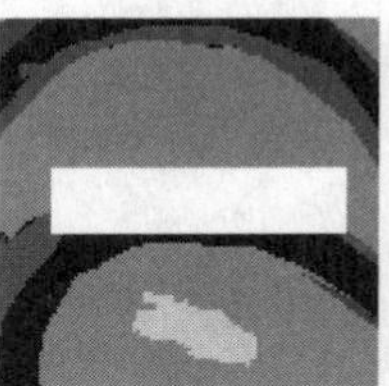

45. Learn applications at your own pace. You probably will not use every Windows accessory or program you have on your computer. Remember that it is important that you use the computer to make other tasks easier for you. You do not have to learn a lot to make a computer useful; you only have to learn what you need to complete the tasks you want to finish.

46. Create your own documentation, outlining which computer reports you find useful and how you produce them.

47. Use the DOS ATTRIB command to assign the read-only attribute to important files that you will not need to update. For example, you would enter **ATTRIB MYFILE +R** at the DOS prompt to make MYFILE read-only.

48. Establish a naming standard for all of your files. Although you will probably not be creating new Quicken files, you may create data for other programs. These naming standards are essential to keeping your data organized and to using the features of DOS that allow you to select more than one file at a time. For example, if you write a monthly budget report with your word processing program, you might want to use a name such as BGT94JAN or 94JANBUDG, and follow the pattern you create consistently throughout the year rather than entering the next months as FEB94BGT, and BUDG0394.

49. Create a batch file to simplify the task of backing up your data.

50. Don't assume that there will be room for your data on a specific disk because it seems to have the correct number of bytes of free space. You may not be able to use every byte on your disks for data storage, since space is allocated by allocation units. These vary in size by disk, but the smallest allocation units in common use today are 512 or 1,024 bytes. A file that contains only one character will still require this minimum space on the disk.

51. When naming files, avoid the use of special characters other than the underscore (_) since they are not accepted by all programs. Also, do not use spaces in filenames.

52. If a file is larger than the capacity of your floppy disk, use BACKUP (or MSBACKUP in DOS 6) to copy the file onto several disks.

53. Knowing some commonly used filename extensions will make it easier to determine what your files contain. Check this list:

.ASC	ASCII file
.BAK	Backup file
.BAT	Batch file
.COM	Program file
.EXE	Program file
.SYS	System file
.TXT	Text file

54. Remember that you cannot restore backup data with COPY. Only the RESTORE command can read data written with BACKUP.

55. Run a defragmentation program if you begin to get sluggish performance from your hard disk. Norton Utilities Speed Disk is one option.

56. You can delete commands like FDISK and FORMAT from computers that are accessed by many people; this will prevent anyone from using these programs, accidentally or purposely, to eliminate the data on a hard disk. If you're worried about needing the programs yourself, try renaming them instead of deleting them.

57. In Windows, remove the highlight from selected text by clicking somewhere else on your screen.

58. Reduce a window to an icon by clicking the Minimize button or by selecting Minimize from the control box menu that appears when you click the upper-left box in the window.

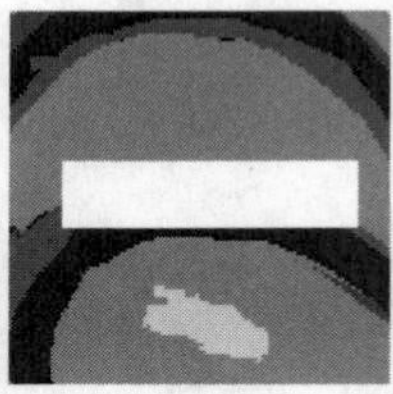

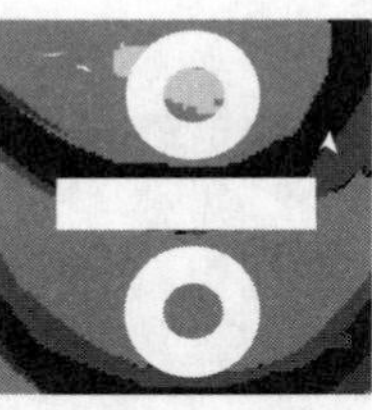

59. You can double-click the Program Manager control menu box to display the Exit Windows dialog box.

60. You can cascade open windows to display an edge of each in order to move between them with a quick click. To cascade document windows, select Cascade from the application's Windows menu. To cascade application windows, select Cascade from the Active Task List.

61. If you want to see more of each open window than cascading allows, tile the windows to make a floor tile pattern by selecting Tile from the Active Task Manager for application windows, or Tile from the Windows menu from an application. You can also individually size each window for the exact look you want.

62. To open the control menu for a document window, click on the control menu button at the left edge of the title bar, or press ALT--(hyphen).

63. To open a control menu for an application window, press ALT-SPACEBAR.

64. Windows provides several game and accessory programs. When you have time you will want to explore these extra programs, which include everything from a drawing application to a word processing application.

65. Reset the date and time on your computer from within Windows by opening the Control Panel, usually found in the Main program group, then selecting the Date/Time icon.

66. Get a close-up look at the Windows print queue by double-clicking the Print Manager icon. When you are finished, minimize the Print Manager again using the Minimize button or Minimize from the control menu. Don't exit the Print Manager until all of your printing is done.

67. Windows performs best under more recent versions of DOS.

68. If Windows' performance is sluggish, close applications you are not using.

69. If you have problems running an application, you may need to change your PATH command. This is a command in your AUTOEXEC.BAT file that DOS, Windows, and other applications use when you tell the computer to run a program that is not in the current directory. Most applications that require their directory be included in the PATH command will modify the file for you when you install the application. If that is not the case, you may need to add the directory yourself.

70. You can avoid the DOS prompt by setting up Windows so that it starts automatically when you turn your computer on. Simply include WIN as the last line in your AUTOEXEC.BAT file.

71. Program items included in the Start Up program group are loaded automatically when you start Windows. You can include program items in this group that you want loaded all the time, and thus make getting started easier.

72. You can associate various file extensions with their related programs. For example, you could associate the extension .QDT with Quicken 3 for Windows. You can open associated programs either by selecting a program item or double-clicking on them in the File Manager.

73. Program items can be either programs or documents. For example, if you keep track of your work hours in a spreadsheet, create a program item for that document. Windows will automatically load the program with that spreadsheet, if you have associated the spreadsheet extension with the spreadsheet.

74. Organize your program groups so that your most frequently used program items are grouped together.

75. You can change the colors of your display by starting the Windows Control Panel, then selecting the Colors icon. If you use dark

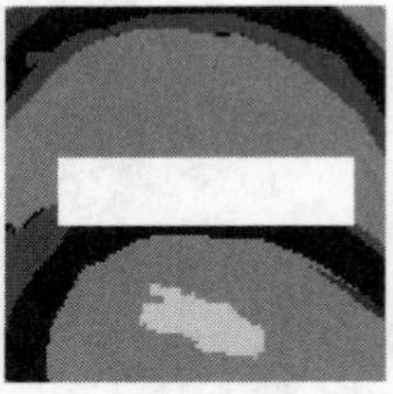

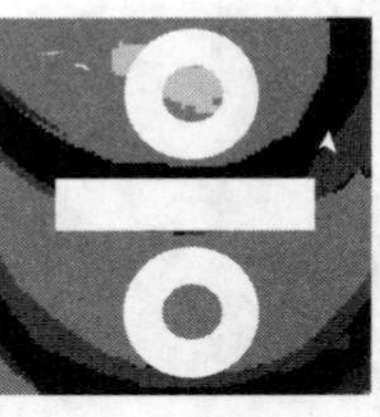

background colors, you will reduce the radiation emitted by your monitor and help reduce eyestrain.

76. You can program Windows so that when it first starts, the File Manager comes up instead of the Program Manager. In Windows 3.1, simply open the file SYSTEM.INI using Notepad, and change the line that reads **shell=progman.exe** to read **shell=winfile.exe**. (You can start a program from the File Manager by double-clicking on the program's name.)

77. Use the File Manager instead of the DOS prompt to arrange, copy, and delete files. The File Manager will prompt you for the information it needs, and you can use the mouse to highlight items from a list instead of having to remember the exact names of files to type in.

78. Add your favorite DOS programs as program items to the Program Manager. You can use Windows Setup in the Main application group and then select Setup Applications in the Options menu to have Windows find installed applications on your hard drive, including DOS programs that are not Windows applications.

79. You can maximize a program window so it takes up the whole screen, or a document window so it fills the space in the application window by clicking on the Maximize button at the upper-right end of the title bar, or by opening the window's control menu and selecting Maximize.

80. There are two ways to do virtually everything in Windows: the keyboard way and the mouse way. Use the method you are most comfortable with. The mouse is usually the easier method for new users, but it can also be slower. Try memorizing keyboard commands for tasks you perform often.

81. If you use the mouse with your left hand, you can switch the mouse buttons. Simply open the Control Panel, select the Mouse icon, and select the Swap Left/Right Button check box, then OK.

82. You can use the Mouse dialog box in the Windows Control Panel to change the double-click speed setting for your mouse. The faster the setting, the closer together the clicks have to be for Windows to recognize a double-click.

83. You can control how quickly the mouse pointer reacts when you move the mouse. Again, use the Mouse dialog box in the Windows Control Panel.

84. The Windows Print Manager controls the printing of documents in all Windows programs. The Print Manager lets you continue working in Windows applications while your documents print. When you are printing, however, do not move to a window in which you are running a DOS-based program, or else your printing will stop. (DOS-based programs are not set up to let the Print Manager continue printing in the background.)

85. All Windows programs use the same printer drivers, which are files containing the information that lets your computer communicate with your printer. Make sure that you install your printer in Windows with default settings so that you can alter settings as needed in each program (to print in landscape mode, for example) without changing the basic printer driver file.

86. Windows allocates memory among all open applications. You can change settings to allocate memory differently by using the Control Panel's 386 Enhanced dialog box. (You cannot do this, however, if you are running Windows on a 286-based computer.)

87. Windows running on a 386 or higher computer uses virtual memory, in which it treats part of your hard disk as a part of memory by storing some information on the disk. The file it stores this information in is called a swap file. You can change the type and size of the swap file from the 386 Enhanced dialog box in the Control Panel.

88. Swap files can be temporary or permanent. A temporary swap file is one that is added when necessary and deleted when you exit

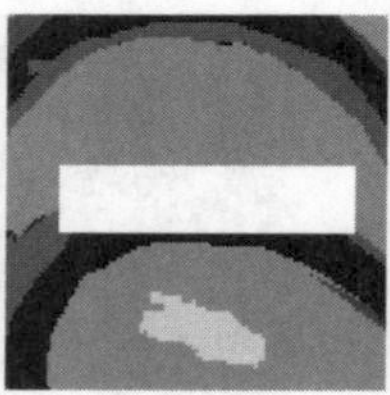

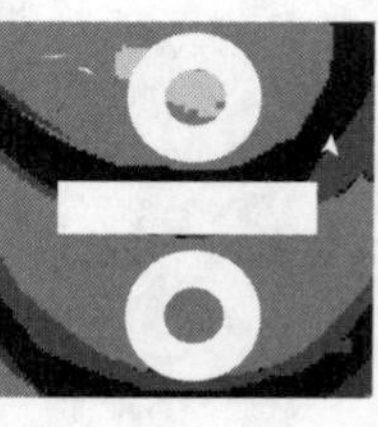

Windows. You can set a maximum size for your temporary swap file. A temporary file is slower and less efficient than a permanent file. A permanent swap files always take the same amount of space on your hard disk, and is never deleted. However, it will read and write data much faster.

89. Unless you are short on disk space, make the Windows' swap file a permanent file that is as large as possible.

90. Windows comes with a number of icons you can use for program items that do not have their own. Some icons are part of the PROGMAN.EXE file. Others are included in the MORICONS.DLL file. MORICONS.DLL includes many icons for popular DOS-based applications.

91. Use different icons for different applications. For example, if you add several non-Windows applications as program items to run from Windows, make sure that they have different icons. The different icons help you select the right application you want.

92. The mouse pointer changes shapes to let you know when you can perform certain actions. For example, you will know that the mouse pointer is in the correct position to size a window when it becomes a two-headed arrow.

93. In all Windows applications, you press ALT and the underlined or boldfaced letter in menu or dialog box elements to activate that feature. These letters are called *mnemonics*.

94. Different symbols in menus of Windows applications tell you different things. A menu item without anything after it activates a command. A menu item followed by an arrow opens a submenu that offers further options. A menu item followed by an ellipsis opens a dialog box.

95. Different dialog box elements do different things. You can type entries in text boxes and select items from list boxes. Click an

arrow button after what looks like a normal text box, and a list box will appear. You can also press ALT-DOWN ARROW.

96. If you think your system has locked up, leave it alone for a few minutes. Your computer may be unresponsive simply because it requires so much memory to carry out another task, such as loading a program, that it has none left to respond to you.

97. If you get a general format error, don't panic. Windows will stop an application if it is trying to do something that is not allowed. Depending on the error message you see, you can start the application again, or you may want to first leave Windows, then restart it, or leave Windows and reboot your computer.

98. Don't quit applications just by turning your system off. When you leave an application or Windows, Windows performs several housekeeping tasks. Also, exiting the application as designed by the program will alert you if you need to save your data. If you turn the computer off to close the application, the housekeeping is not done. Also, when you turn it on again you may see a message saying that Windows' swap file is corrupted.

99. Use the automatic save features in applications that have them to ensure that you don't lose the changes you are making.

100. Remember that there are several Windows key combinations that work the same in most applications. These include F1 for help, ALT for the menu, and ALT-F4 to close the Windows application.

101. When you have a problem with your computer, take a deep breath, calm down, and try to work through the problem step by step. When you are rushed, you can forget the most obvious things—that you can't start your favorite Windows packages without starting Windows first, for example, or that in order to print, you must first remember to turn the printer on.

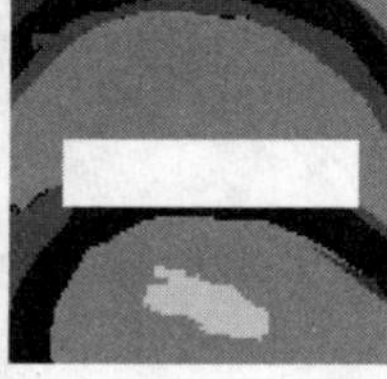

PART

HOME APPLICATIONS

CHAPTER

7

EXPANDING the SCOPE of FINANCIAL ENTRIES

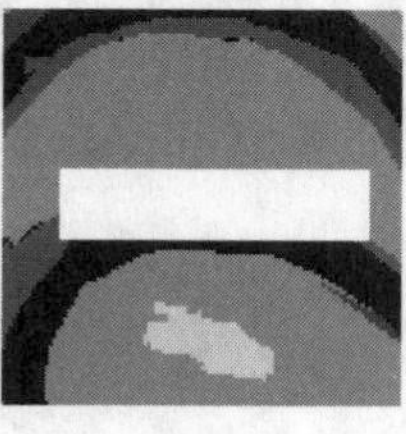

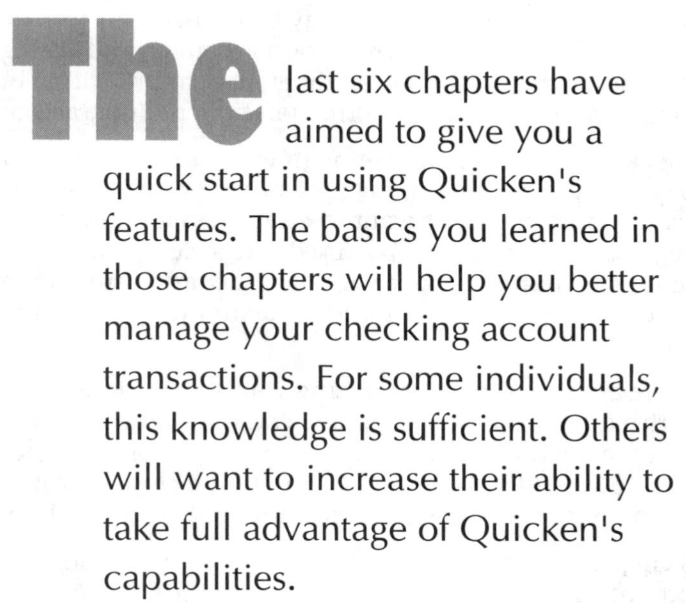

The last six chapters have aimed to give you a quick start in using Quicken's features. The basics you learned in those chapters will help you better manage your checking account transactions. For some individuals, this knowledge is sufficient. Others will want to increase their ability to take full advantage of Quicken's capabilities.

Even though you may want to start entering your own transactions right away, read the first two sections in this chapter. These sections will teach you about Quicken files and setting up an account separate from the one you used for the practice exercises. Then, if you feel you know enough to meet your needs, stop reading at the end of the section titled "Quicken Files" and enter some of your own transactions.

Even personal finances can be too complex to be handled with a single account. In one household, there may be transactions for both individual and joint checking accounts, credit card accounts, and savings accounts. Quicken allows you to set up these different accounts within one Quicken file, which enables you to include information from multiple accounts in reports.

Accounts alone are not always enough to organize transactions logically. You may find you need to change the categories you assign to your transactions; you may even want to establish main categories with subcategories beneath them. You used categories earlier to identify transactions as utilities expense or salary income. Using subcategories, you might create several groupings under the utilities expense for electricity, water, and gas.

Classes are another way of organizing your transactions to provide a perspective different from categories. You might think of classes as answering the "who," "what," "when," or "where" of a transaction. For example, you could assign a transaction to the clothing category and then set up and assign it to a class for the family member purchasing the clothing.

In this chapter, you will also learn how to assign transactions to more than one account—for example, how to transfer funds between accounts.

All of these features in this "Home Applications" section are presented assuming that you are recording transactions for your personal finances. If you are interested in using Quicken to record both personal and business transactions, first read the chapters in this section (Chapters 7 through 11). When you get to Chapter 12, you learn how to set up Quicken for your business. You can then select a category structure and create accounts that will allow you to manage both business and personal transactions.

The material in these chapters builds on the procedures you have already mastered. Feel free to adapt the entries provided to match your actual financial transactions. For example, you may want to change the dollar amount of transactions, the categories to which they are assigned, and the transaction dates shown.

Again, be aware of the dates for the transaction entries in these chapters. As you know, the date of the transaction entry, relative to the current date, determines whether a transaction is postdated. As you will see, Quicken can "remind" you to process groups of transactions at some specified date in the future. When you designate the date on which you want a particular group of transactions to go into effect (which will also be the date after which Quicken will prompt you to enter these transactions), be careful you don't use the *current* date by mistake. If you do this, the reminder will probably not occur.

Also, creating reports that match the examples in this book will be difficult unless you use the same dates as those presented in the examples. The varied dates used permit the creation of more illustrative reports.

Quicken Files

One Quicken file can contain many accounts. Once you start recording your own data, you will probably keep all of your accounts in one file.

When you first started working in Chapter 3, Quicken created several files on your disk to manage your accounts and the information within them. Since all the files have the same filename, QDATA, but different filename extensions, this book refers to them collectively, as if they were a single file. When you copy a Quicken data file, all of these files must be copied.

You worked with only one account in QDATA, but you can use multiple accounts within a file. You might use one account for a savings account and a different one for checking. You can also have accounts for credit cards, cash, assets, and liabilities, although most individuals do not have financial situations that warrant more than a few accounts.

You could continue to enter the transactions from this chapter in the 1st U.S. Bank account in the QDATA file, or you could set up a new account in the QDATA file. However, if you do this and you also adapt the chapter entries to reflect your own actual transactions, your new data will be intermingled with the practice transactions from the last few chapters. To avoid this, you need to establish a separate file for the practice transactions. In this section, you will learn how to set up new transactions that are stored separately from the already-existing entries. You will also learn how to create a backup copy of a file to safeguard the data you enter.

Adding a New File

You already have the QDATA file that contains all the transactions you entered in the first section of this book. Now you will set up a new file and create new accounts within it. Later, if you wish, you can delete the QDATA file to free the space it occupies on your disk.

The new file will be called PERSONAL. Initially, it will contain a checking account called Cardinal Bank. This account is similar to the 1st U.S. Bank checking account you created in QDATA. Since it is in a new file, a different name is used. Other appropriate names might be Business Check or Joint Checking, depending on the type of account. Naturally, if you have more than one account at Cardinal Bank, they cannot all be named Cardinal Bank. Later in this chapter, you will create both a savings and a credit card account.

Follow these steps to set up the new file and to add the first account to it:

1. Select New from the File menu.

   Quicken displays the dialog box shown here:

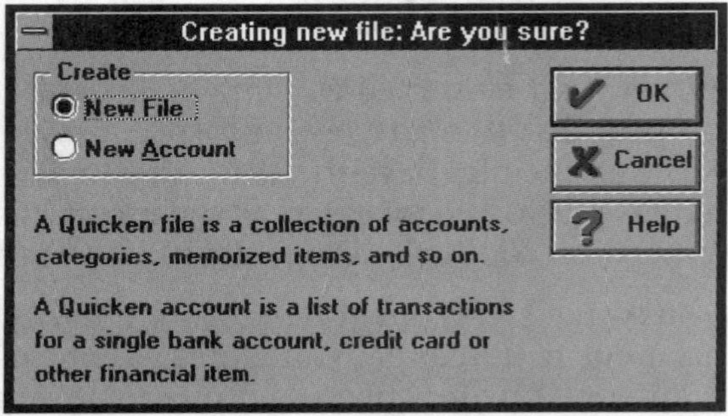

2. Select the New File option button and then select OK.
3. Type **PERSONAL** as the name for the file in the File Name text box.
4. Check the directory shown in the Directories list box and make changes if a change is required.
5. Clear the Business check box under Predefined Categories. This restricts your available categories to the Home categories. (You can always create different categories in your accounts later, of course. This step simply limits the number of predefined categories in the drop-down list in the Quicken register.)
6. Select OK to complete the creation of the new file.

   Quicken creates several files for each filename by adding different filename extensions to the name you provide. You must provide a valid filename of no more than eight characters. Do not include spaces or special symbols in your entries for filenames.

   Quicken displays the Create New Account dialog box, shown here:

7. Select Checking for the account type.

Tip: If you leave the Guide Me check box selected, Quicken guides you through creating a new account, as described here. If you clear this check box, Quicken displays a single dialog box in which to make all of the entries.

8. Type **Cardinal Bank** in the Account Name text box.
9. Type **Personal Checking** in the Description text box and then select Next.
10. Select the Yes option button and then select Next.
11. Type **7/13/95** in the Statement Date text box or select it using the drop-down calendar.
12. Type **2500** in the Ending Balance text box.
13. Select Done.

    Quicken displays the register for the Cardinal Bank account in the Personal file.

Note: Before you start with the examples in this chapter, select Options from the register window's button bar and then select QuickFill. Select the Automatic Memorization Of New Transactions check box and clear the Drop Down Lists Automatically check box. Select Display, and then the Memo Before Category check box. Click OK. You will want this feature turned on for the entries you are going to make in the new Quicken file so that you can carry out the examples in this chapter.

Changing the Active File

The result of the last exercise was the creation of a second Quicken file. You can work in either this file or the QDATA file, and you can select any account in either file at any time. To switch from the current file, PERSONAL, to QDATA, follow these steps:

1. Select Open from the File menu.
2. Select QDATA in the File Name list box and then select OK.

   The QDATA file is now active. When you open the register and check writing windows, they display the 1st U.S. Bank account. Switch back to the PERSONAL file following the same steps. The register and check-writing windows now display the Cardinal Bank account.

Tip: As a shortcut, you can press CTRL-O to open the Open Quicken File dialog box rather than making selections from the menu.

Backing Up a File

You will want to create backup copies of the data managed by Quicken on a regular basis. Backups let you recover most of your entries in the event of a disk failure, since you can just use your copy to restore the file. To record the backup information the first time, you need a blank formatted disk. You can also use this disk for later backups without reformatting it. You can format a blank or previously used disk with the Windows File Manager by choosing Format Disk from the Disk menu.

Creating Backup Files

Quicken's backup command lets you safeguard the investment you have made in entering your data. You can back up all your account files. Follow these steps to back up the current file:

1. Select Backup from the File menu.
2. Select Current File.
3. Place your blank, formatted disk in drive A, and then select A in the Backup Drive drop-down list box.
4. Select OK.
5. Select OK to acknowledge the completion of the backup when Quicken displays the successful backup message.

With backups, if you ever lose your hard disk, you can recreate your data directory, and then select Restore from the File menu to copy your backup files from the disk to this directory.

Customizing Categories

When you set up the new PERSONAL file, you selected Home categories as the standard categories option. This selection provides access to the more than 40 category choices displayed in Table 7-1. You can see that some categories are listed as expenses and others as income; some of them even have subcategories. The last column in the table shows which categories are tax related.

Category	Type	Tax Related
Bonus	Income	Yes
CPP (Canadian Pension Plan)	Income	Yes
Div Income	Income	Yes
Gift Received	Income	Yes
Int Inc	Income	Yes
Invest Inc	Income	Yes
Old Age Pension	Income	Yes
Other Inc	Income	Yes
Salary	Income	Yes
Salary Spouse	Income	Yes
Auto	Expense	No
Fuel	Subcategory	No
Loan	Subcategory	No
Service	Subcategory	No
Bank Chrg	Expense	No
Charity	Expense	Yes
Cash Contrib	Subcategory	Yes
Non-Cash	Subcategory	Yes
Childcare	Expense	Depends on income bracket
Christmas	Expense	No
Clothing	Expense	No

Standard Home Categories
Table 7-1.

Category	Type	Tax Related
Dining	Expense	No
Dues	Expense	No
Education	Expense	No
Entertain	Expense	No
Gifts	Expense	Yes
Groceries	Expense	No
GST (Goods and Services Tax)	Expense	Yes
Home Rpair	Expense	No
Household	Expense	No
Housing	Expense	No
Insurance	Expense	No
Int Exp	Expense	Yes
Invest Exp	Expense	Yes
Medical	Expense	Yes
Doctor	Subcategory	Yes
Medicine	Subcategory	Yes
Misc	Expense	No
Mort Int	Expense	Yes
Other Exp	Expense	Yes
PST (Provincial Sales Tax)	Expense	Yes
Recreation	Expense	No
RRSP (Registered Retirement Savings Plan)	Expense	No
Subscriptions	Expense	No
Supplies	Expense	No
Tax	Expense	Yes
Fed	Subcategory	Yes
Medicare	Subcategory	Yes
Other	Subcategory	Yes
Prop	Subcategory	Yes
Soc Sec	Subcategory	Yes
State	Subcategory	Yes

Standard Home Categories (*continued*)
Table 7-1.

Standard Home Categories (*continued*)
Table 7-1.

Category	Type	Tax Related
Tax Spouse	Expense	Yes
Fed	Subcategory	Yes
Medicate	Subcategory	Yes
State	Subcategory	Yes
Telephone	Expense	No
UIC (Unemployment Insurance Commission)	Expense	Yes
Utilities	Expense	No
Gas & Electric	Subcategory	No
Water	Subcategory	No

Editing the Existing Category List

You can change the name of any existing category, change its classification as income, expense, or subcategory, or change its tax-related status. To modify a category:

HomeBase

Setup | Category List

1. Display the category list by selecting Category & Transfer from the Lists menu or pressing CTRL-C.
2. Highlight the category you want to change.
3. Select Edit to edit the information for the category.
4. Change the entries you wish to alter using the Edit Category dialog box, shown here:

Edit Category
Name: Salary
Description: Salary Income
Type
Income
Expense
Subcategory of:
Tax-related
OK
Cancel
Help

5. Select OK to complete the changes.

If you change the name of the category, Quicken automatically changes it in any transactions that have already been assigned to that category.

Adding Categories

You can also add your own categories to provide additional options specific to your needs. For example, if you have just set up housekeeping, buying furniture might be a major budget category. Since you would otherwise have to lump these purchases with others in the Household category, you might want to add a Furniture category as well. Typing **Furniture** in the category field when you enter your first furniture transaction automatically makes it a category. When Quicken does not find the category in the existing list, it displays a window in which you can create the category.

However, if you have a number of categories to add, it is simpler to add them before starting to enter data. To use this approach for adding the Furniture category, follow these steps:

HomeBase

Setup | Category List

1. Open the Category & Transfer List by selecting Category & Transfer from the Lists menu or pressing CTRL-C.
2. Select New.

   You enter the new category using the Set Up Category dialog box. As shown here, it contains the entries for a new Furniture category to add to your Category list:

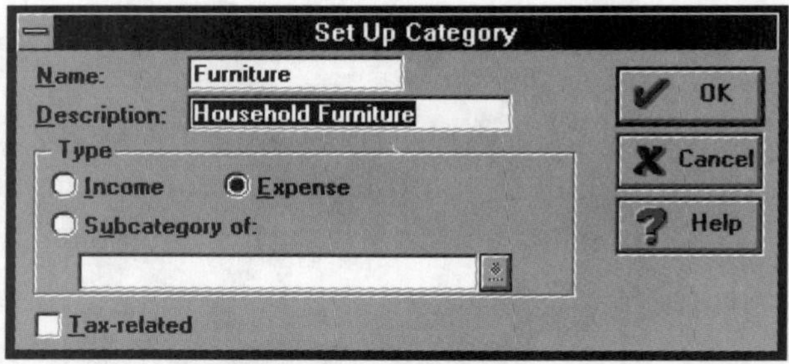

3. Type **Furniture** in the Name text box.
4. Type **Household Furniture** in the Description text box.
5. Select the Expense option button.
6. Clear the Tax-related check box, and then select OK to complete the entry.

You'll add more categories later in this chapter, but you'll add them as you enter transactions. Feel free to customize the categories as you enter them.

Requiring Categories in All Transactions

Categories help you classify and analyze your transactions. You can have Quicken remind you to enter a category whenever you attempt to record a transaction without one. While you can confirm that you want to enter the transaction without a category, this will help you avoid accidentally not entering a category.

To turn this option on:

1. Open a register window.
2. Select Options, and then select Miscellaneous.
3. Select the Warn Before Recording Uncategorized Transactions check box and then select OK to finalize the settings change.

The next time you try to record a transaction without a category entry, Quicken prompts you to confirm your choice before saving.

Using Subcategories

Now that you've set up your new file and account and have customized your categories, you are ready to enter some transactions. Since you are already proficient at basic transaction entry from earlier chapters, you will want to look at some additional ways of modifying accounts as you make entries.

One option is to create categories that are under existing categories. For instance, rather than allocating all of your utility bills to the Utilities category, you could create more specific subcategories under Utilities that let you allocate expenses to electricity, water, or gas. You could add the subcategories just as you added the new category for furniture. You can also create them when you are entering transactions and you realize that the existing categories do not provide the level of breakdown you would like.

Note: Remember that in Chapter 3, you entered a subcategory when recreating a deleted transaction. Now, you'll learn more about how to use and work with subcategories.

Entering a New Subcategory

When you enter both a category and a subcategory for a transaction, you type the category name, followed by a colon (:) and the subcategory name. It is important that the category be specified first and the subcategory second.

You will enter utility bills as the first entries in the new account. Follow these steps to complete the entries for the gas and electric bills, creating a subcategory under Utilities for each:

1. With the next blank transaction in the register highlighted, enter **7/25/95** as the date for the first transaction. Type **101** as the check number.
2. Type **Consumer Power** in the payee field. Enter **35.45** as the payment amount. Type **Electric Bill** in the Memo field. Type **Utilities:Electric** in the Category field.
3. Select Record to record the transaction.

   Quicken prompts you to create the category by displaying the Set Up Category dialog box.
4. Type **Electric Utilities** in the Description text box. Although this description is optional, it is a good idea to enter one so your reports will be informative. Your dialog box now looks like this:

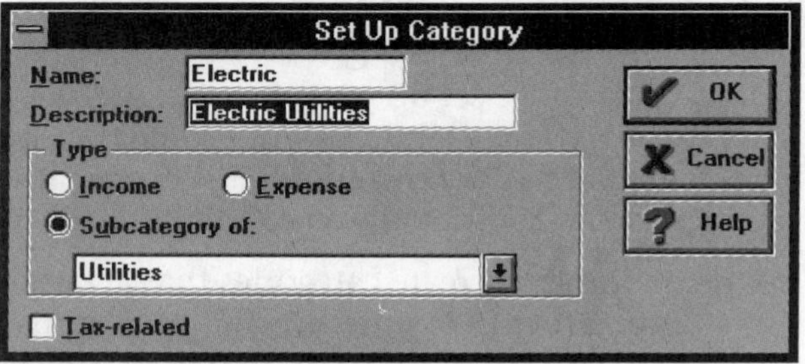

   Please note that the Name text box was already filled in, and that the new category is already marked as a subcategory of Utilities, based on the entry you made in the Category field.
5. Select OK to complete the settings and record the transaction.

Completing the Utility Subcategories

To create a subcategory for the gas bill, enter the following information in the fields shown.

Date: **7/25/95**
Num: **102**
Payee: **West Michigan Gas**
Payment: **17.85**
Memo: **Gas Bill**

Do not record the transaction. With the insertion point in the Category field:

1. Select Category & Transfer from the Lists menu or press CTRL-C to display the Category & Transfer List window.
2. Move to Utilities: Gas & Electric.
3. Select Edit to edit the current category.
4. Change the Name text box in the Edit Category dialog box to **Gas**.
5. Change the Description text box to **Gas Utilities**.
6. Select OK.
7. Double-click the Utilities:Gas entry to enter it in your transaction.
8. Select Record to finalize the transaction entry.

You still need to enter the telephone bill, but since Quicken already defines Telephone as a Home category, you cannot consider Telephone as a subcategory of Utilities. However, you could edit the Telephone category and change it to a subcategory. For now, leave it as a separate category and put the following entries in the transaction fields.

Date:	**7/30/95**
Num:	**103**
Payee:	**Alltel**
Payment:	**86.00**
Memo:	**Telephone Bill**
Category:	**Telephone**

Splitting Transactions

Split transactions are transactions that affect more than one category. You can decide how the transaction affects each of the categories involved. If you split an expense transaction, you are saying that portions of the transaction should be considered as expenses in two different categories. For example, a check written at a supermarket may cover more than just groceries. You might purchase a $25.00 plant as a gift at the same time you purchase your groceries. Recording the entire amount of the check as a groceries expense would not accurately reflect the purpose of the check. Quicken lets you record the $25.00 amount as a gift purchase and the remainder for groceries. In fact, after allocating the $25.00 to gifts, it even tells you the remaining balance that needs to be allocated to other categories. You could also enter a transaction in which you cashed a check and use the split transaction capability to account for your spending. As an example of splitting transactions, enter the following transaction for check number 100.

Date: **7/20/95**
Num: **100**
Payee: **Cash**
Payment: **100.00**
Memo: **Groceries & Misc**

Do not record the transaction. With the insertion point in the Category field, follow these steps:

1. Select Splits.
2. Type **Groceries**, the name of the first category you want to use in the Category field. You can stop typing as soon as QuickFill provides a match.
3. Type **Groceries & Market** in the Memo field.
4. Type **75** in the Amount field.
5. Type **Misc** as the category for the next line.
6. Type **Drug & Hardware Store** in the Memo field.

   Quicken displays 25.00, the remainder of the total transaction amount you entered in the Payment field, in the Amount field:

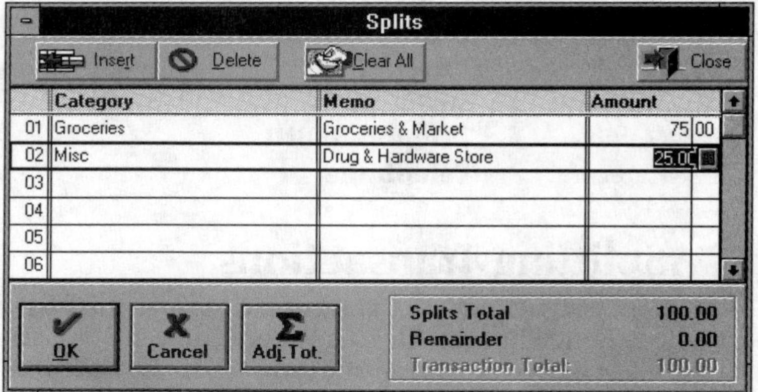

7. Select OK. In the register, the category appears as --Splits--.
8. Select Record to record the transaction.

Note: Instead of entering the amount being assigned to each category in the Amount field of the Split Transaction dialog box, you can enter a percentage. Quicken will use this percentage to calculate the exact amount, using the total amount you already entered in the Payment or Deposit field in the register.

There are many other times when you might elect to use split transactions. For example, you might want to assign part of a mortgage payment to interest and the rest to principal. Credit card purchases can also be handled in this fashion if you elect not to set up a special credit card account. Normally, using a split transaction is easier than a credit card account if you pay your bills in full each month. Notice that up to the point when you enter the category, there is no difference between a split transaction entry and any other entry in the register.

Using Multiple Accounts

Quicken makes it easy to create multiple accounts. Since all of the accounts are created in the same file, you can create separate reports for each account or a single report that shows them all. You will have an account register for each account that you create.

Types of Accounts

Setting up all of your accounts in Quicken gives you a much clearer picture of your financial conditions.

Savings, investment, cash, and credit card accounts are all possible additional accounts. Savings and investment accounts should definitely be kept separate from your checking account, since you will want to monitor both the growth and balance in each of these accounts.

The need for cash and credit card accounts varies by individual. If you pay the majority of your expenses in cash and need a detailed record of your expenditures, a cash account is a good idea. With credit cards, if your purchases are at a reasonable level and you pay the balance in full each month, the extra time required to maintain a separate account may not be warranted. There are no cash accounts in the sample files in this book. If you decide you need one, you can use the same procedures to create them that you use to create the savings account.

Creating a New Savings Account

HomeBase

Setup | Create Accounts

If you want to transfer funds from your checking account to a savings account, you must have a savings account set up. Follow these steps to create the new account:

1. Select Create New Account from the Activities menu.
2. Select Savings.

7

Note: If you clear the Guide Me check box, the options of all of the steps are compressed into a single dialog box.

3. Type **Cardinal Saving** in the Account Name text box.

   You cannot call this account Cardinal Savings with the final "s," because Quicken only allows 15 characters in an account name.
4. Type **Savings account** in the Description text box, and then select Next.
5. Select the Yes option button and then select Next.
6. Enter **7/15/95** in the Statement Date text box. Remember, you can use the drop-down calendar to select the date rather than type it.
7. Type **500** in the Ending Balance text box.
8. Select Done.

   Quicken opens the Cardinal Saving register.
9. Return to the Cardinal Bank register by clicking the window or selecting it from the Window menu.

Transferring Funds Between Different Accounts

Making a deposit from your checking account into your savings account requires a transfer between the two accounts. Transferring funds from one account to another is easy as long as both accounts are established. You might transfer a fixed amount to savings each month to cover long-range savings plans or to cover large, fixed expenses that are due annually or semi-annually. Follow these steps to make a transfer from the checking account to the savings account:

1. Complete these entries in the Cardinal Bank register for the transaction fields down to Category:

Date:	**8/5/95**
Num:	**TXFR**
Payee:	**Cardinal Savings**
Payment:	**200.00**
Memo:	**Transfer to savings**

2. In the Category field use the drop-down list box or the QuickFill feature to enter **Cardinal Saving** as the category.
3. Select Record to confirm the transaction.

Note: Depending on the year in which you are actually making these entries, Quicken may warn you if the current year is different from the one you've entered. This feature is meant to keep you from mistyping the year in your transactions. You can turn this warning off by selecting Options in the register's button bar, selecting the Miscellaneous tab, and then clearing the Warn When Recording Out Of Date Transactions box and selecting OK.

You will notice brackets around the account name in the Category field of the register, indicating that this category is also an account in its own right. Quicken has automatically created the parallel transaction in the other account, as you will see if you switch to the Cardinal Saving register. Quicken will also delete both transactions when you delete either of them.

Creating a New Credit Card Account

If you charge a large number of your purchases and do not pay your credit card bill in full each month, a separate account for each of your credit cards is the best approach. It enables you to better monitor your individual payments throughout the year. Also, your reports can then show the full detail for all credit card transactions, just as your checking account register shows the details of each check written. To set up a credit card account:

1. Select Create New Account from the Activities menu.
2. Clear the Guide Me check box, so that Quicken won't guide you through the steps of creating the account.
3. Select Credit Card. Quicken displays the Create Credit Card Account dialog box, shown here:

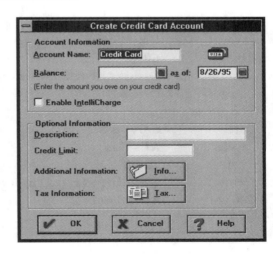

Create Credit Card Account
Account Information
Account Name: Credit Card
Balance: as of: 8/26/95
(Enter the amount you owe on your credit card)
Enable IntelliCharge
Optional Information
Description:
Credit Limit:
Additional Information: Info...
Tax Information: Tax...
OK Cancel Help

4. Enter **EasyCredit Card** in the Account Name text box.
5. Enter **0** in the Balance text box.
6. Enter **7/25/95** in the As Of text box.
7. Enter **Credit Card** in the Description text box.
8. Select OK.

After creating a credit card account, you can enter transactions throughout the month as you charge items to each of your credit cards, and you can monitor the total amount of your charges throughout the month. Or, if you prefer, you can wait until you receive your statements at the end of the month. You record credit card transaction information in the same fashion as you record checkbook entries, designating the Payee, Memo, and Category for each transaction. The Charge field is used to record transaction amounts and the Payment entry is recorded as part of the reconciliation process.

To enter all of your credit card transactions from the end-of-the-month statement:

1. Enter **8/1/95** as the date.
2. Type **Ivey's Department Store** in the Payee field.
3. Type **50** in the Charge field.
4. Type **Blue Blouse** in the Memo field.
5. In the Category field, select **Clothing**.
6. Select Record to record the transaction.
7. Now repeat this process with the following transactions:

Date:	**8/3/95**
Payee:	**Boathouse**
Charge:	**60**
Memo:	**Dinner at the Boathouse**
Category:	**Dining**

Date:	**8/7/95**
Payee:	**Al's Gas**
Charge:	**23.00**
Memo:	**Gasoline - Jeep Wagoneer**
Category:	**Auto:Fuel**

Date:	**8/11/95**
Payee:	**Fennville Furniture**
Charge:	**217.00**
Memo:	**Green Rocker**
Category:	**Furniture**

Date:	**8/17/95**
Payee:	**Fennville Players**
Charge:	**50**
Memo:	**Play Tickets**
Category:	**Entertain**

Figure 7-1 shows how your new credit card transactions appear on the screen.

Reconciling and Paying Credit Card Bills

Although it expedited your entries in this chapter to enter all of your charge transactions at one time, it is better to enter each charge as you make it, and then to reconcile your records against the credit card bill when it arrives. The reconciliation procedure is similar to the one you used for your checking account and it verifies that the charges are correct before you pay your credit card bills. To reconcile your credit card account and pay your bill:

1. With the credit card register active, select Pay Credit Card Bill from the Activities menu.

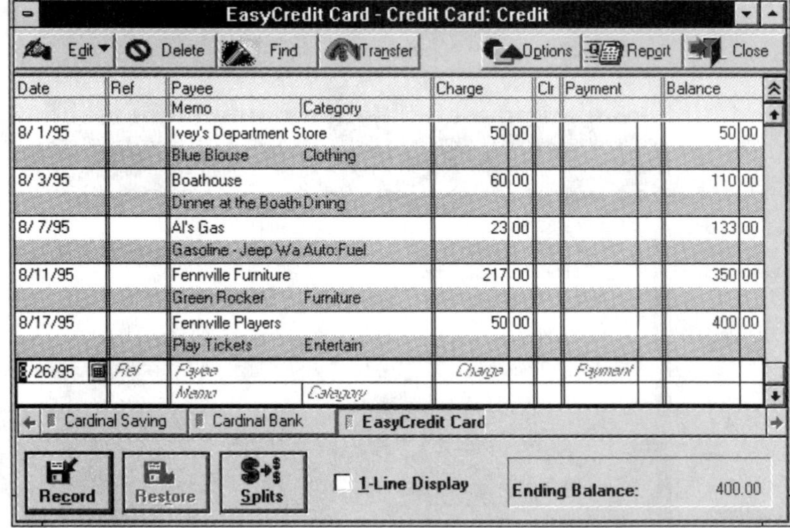

A sample credit card account
Figure 7-1.

7

2. Type **450** in the Charges, Cash Advances text box. This is the total amount you've charged since your last statement.
3. Type **0** in the Payments, Credits text box. This is the amount you've paid or had credited to your account since your last statement.
4. Type **450** in the New Balance text box. This is your current balance. If you owed anything in finance charges, you would enter this information in the text boxes below Transaction To Be Added (optional). Since you paid your bill in full last month, you don't owe any finance charges at this point.
5. Select OK. Quicken displays the Pay Credit Card Bill window, shown in Figure 7-2 This window looks a lot like the reconciliation window you used to reconcile your checking accounts.
6. Clear the five transactions in the Charges list box. You can do this by moving to each one and pressing SPACEBAR, clicking on each one, or clicking on the first one, pressing SHIFT, and then clicking on the last one. After you clear these transactions, you'll notice that there's still a $50 difference between your credit card bill's balance and your cleared balance. After checking your wallet again, you may find the receipt for your forgotten purchase at the fudge shop. Since you didn't enter this charge earlier, you need to do so now.
7. Select New. Quicken moves to the next blank transaction in the EasyCredit Card register. Enter the following transaction:

Date:	**8/20/95**
Payee:	**Sarah's Fudge Shoppe**
Charge:	**50.00**
Memo:	**Dessert, gifts, etc.**
Category:	**Misc**

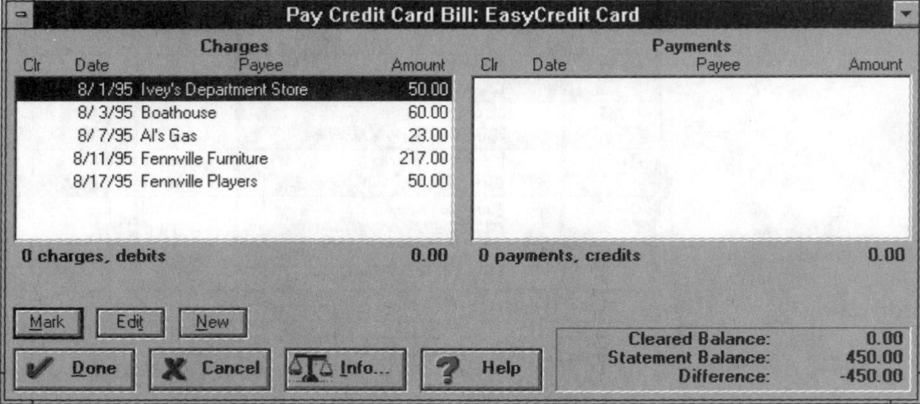

Reconcile your credit card statements before paying them

Figure 7-2.

Note: Since you gave some of the fudge away as presents, ate some yourself, and still have some saved in the freezer for future holiday parties and gifts, you're not really sure how much went to each of your usual categories. Rather than calculate it, just assign the whole purchase to the Misc category.

8. Switch back to the Pay Credit Card Bill window by clicking on it, or selecting it from the Window menu.
9. Clear this new transaction by clicking on it.

   Your difference is now 0.00. This means that you've reconciled your account. The transactions in your statement match the statements in your Quicken account.
10. Select Done. Quicken displays the Make Credit Card Payment dialog box shown here:

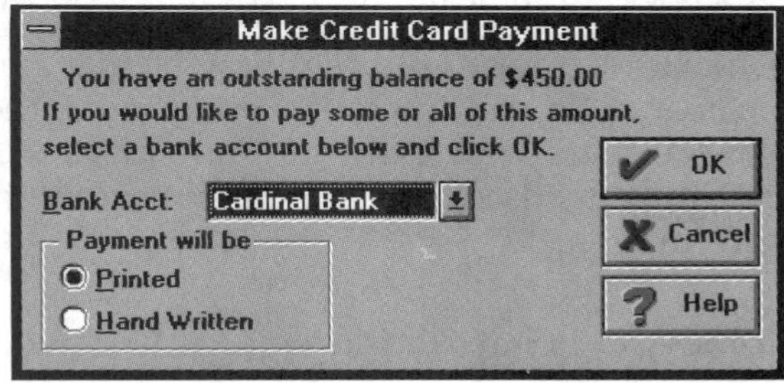

11. Select Cardinal Bank in the Bank Acct drop-down list box, if it isn't displayed there already. This is the account you are going to use to pay your credit card.
12. Select Hand Written and OK. You would select Printed if you were going to use Quicken to print the check paying your credit card bill. Quicken switches to the next blank transaction in your Cardinal Bank register.
13. Enter the following transaction:

Date:	**8/30/95**
Num:	**112**
Payee:	**Easy Credit Card**
Memo:	**August 25th Statement**

   You don't need to enter the category, because Quicken automatically enters the name of your designated credit card account (Cardinal Bank, in this case) as the category. You also don't need to enter the amount, because Quicken does that automatically for you too.
14. Select Record to record your credit card payment.

IntelliCharge

A new feature added to Quicken lets Quicken record all credit card transactions for you. IntelliCharge is your own Quicken Visa card that provides this new option. You can receive your IntelliCharge transactions on diskette or modem each month. With this feature, you select Get IntelliCharge Data from the Online menu and your data is read into your credit card account. Even the categories are completed for you as the data is recorded. You can reconcile your account and decide on the payment amount.

Memorized Transactions

Many of your financial transactions are going to repeat. You pay your rent or mortgage payments each month. Likewise, utility bills and credit card payments are paid at about the same time each month. Cash inflows in the form of paychecks are also regularly scheduled. Other payments such as groceries also repeat, but probably not on the same dates each month.

Quicken can memorize transactions that are entered from the register or check writing window. Once memorized, these transactions can be used to generate similar transactions. Amounts and dates may change, but you can edit these fields without having to reenter the payee, memo, and category information.

Memorizing a Register Entry

Memorized transactions can be recalled for later use, printed, changed, and deleted. All transactions are memorized if the Automatic Memorization of New Transactions check box in the QuickFill tab in the Register Preferences dialog box is selected, rather than cleared. To select this check box, you select Prefs in a register's button bar and then select QuickFill. The examples in this chapter assume that this check box is selected, so that all of the transactions you have entered are memorized. To try using memorized transactions, you will need to add a few more transactions to the account register to complete the entries for August. Add these transactions to your register:

Date:	**8/1/95**
Num:	**DEP**
Payee:	**Payroll deposit**
Deposit	**1585.99**
Memo:	**August 1 paycheck**
Category:	**Salary**

Date: **8/2/95**
Num: **104**
Payee: **Great Lakes Savings & Loan**
Payment: **350.00**
Memo: **August Payment**
Category: **Mort Pay**

Note: Mort Pay is a new category to add, since you do not have the information required to split the transaction between the existing interest and principal categories in the Home category list. Enter **Entire Mortgage Payment** in the Description text box when you add the category.

Date: **8/4/95**
Num: **105**
Payee: **Maureks**
Payment: **60.00**
Memo: **Groceries**
Category: **Groceries**

Date: **8/6/95**
Num: **106**
Payee: **Orthodontics, Inc.**
Payment: **100.00**
Memo: **Monthly Orthodontics Payment**
Category: **Medical**

Date: **8/15/95**
Num: **107**
Payee: **Meijer**
Payment: **65.00**
Memo: **Groceries**
Category: **Groceries**

Quicken can memorize split transactions in the same way it does any other transactions. You should carefully review the split transactions for information that changes each month. For example, the entry for the credit card payment is likely to be split across several categories if you are entering the detail in the check register rather than in a separate credit card account.

You will want to edit the categories into which the main transaction is split, and the amounts that fall into each of the categories.

You can select Memorized Transaction from the List menu or press CTRL-T to display the Memorized Transaction List; your list should match the one in Figure 7-3.

If you want to print the list once it is displayed, select Print List from the File menu, or select the Print icon from the icon bar. To remove the list from the screen, press ESC. To enter a new transaction, select New.

Memorizing Transactions Manually

Memorized transactions make it easy to enter transactions that reoccur periodically.

If your automatic memorization feature is turned off, you can still have Quicken memorize a transaction before or after it is recorded in the register or check writing window. First, fill out all the fields for the register or check transaction that you want to memorize. Then, either before or after recording the transaction, select Memorize Transaction from the Edit menu. When Quicken displays a dialog box warning you that the transaction is about to be memorized, select OK.

Changing and Deleting Memorized Transactions

Quicken lets you change a memorized transaction in the Memorized Transaction List when you activate the list, highlight the transaction, and select Edit.

Memorized Transaction List

New | Edit | Delete | Use | Report | Close

Description	Amount	Type	Memo	Cat
Al's Gas	-23.00	Pmt	Gasoline - Jeep ...	Auto:Fuel
Alltel	-86.00	Pmt	Telephone Bill	Telephone
Boathouse	-60.00	Pmt	Dinner at the Bo...	Dining
Cardinal Savings	-200.00	Pmt	Transfer to savin...	[Cardinal Saving]
Cash	-100.00	Spl	Groceries & Misc	Groceries
Consumer Power	-35.45	Pmt	Electric Bill	Utilities:Electric
Easy Credit Card	-450.00	Pmt	August 25th Stat...	[EasyCredit Card]
Fennville Furniture	-217.00	Pmt	Green Rocker	Furniture
Fennville Players	-50.00	Pmt	Play Tickets	Entertain
Great Lakes Savings ...	-350.00	Pmt	August Payment	Mort Pay
Ivey's Department Store	-50.00	Pmt	Blue Blouse	Clothing
Maureks	-60.00	Pmt	Groceries	Groceries
Meijer	-65.00	Pmt	Groceries	Groceries
Orthodontics, Inc.	-100.00	Pmt	Monthly Orthodo...	Medical
Payroll deposit	1,585.99	Dep	August 1 payche...	Salary
Sarah's Fudge Shoppe	-50.00	Pmt	Dessert, gifts, etc.	Misc

View Locked Items Only

The Memorized Transaction List
Figure 7-3.

To delete a memorized transaction, you must open the transaction list, highlight the transaction you want to delete, and select Del. A warning message appears asking you to confirm the deletion. When you select OK, the transaction is no longer memorized.

Follow these steps to delete some transactions from your Memorized Transaction List.

1. Open the Memorized Transaction List by selecting Memorized Transaction from the Lists menu or pressing CTRL-T.
2. Highlight the transaction with the description "Cash."
3. Select Del.
4. Select OK to confirm that you do want to delete the transaction from the Memorized Transaction List.
5. Repeat these steps to delete the transactions with the descriptions:

Maureks	Meijer	Al's Gas
Boathouse	Fennville Furniture	Fennville Players
Ivey's Department Store	Sarah's Fudge Shoppe	

These transactions are not regular ones. While the categories will probably remain the same whenever a check is made out to these payees, the amount will change each time. Deleting transactions you are not going to use from the Memorized Transaction List makes it easier to access the ones that you do use.

Using Memorized Transactions

To recall a memorized transaction and place it in the register, move to the next blank transaction in the register (unless you want the recalled transaction to replace a transaction already on the screen). Open the Memorized Transaction List dialog box by selecting Memorized Transaction from the Lists menu or pressing CTRL-T. Double-click the transaction you want to add to the register or highlight it and press ENTER. The selected transaction appears in the register with the date of the last transaction you entered, not the date of the transaction you memorized. You can edit the transaction in the register and select Record when you are ready to record the entry.

If you write checks with Quicken, you will want to memorize checks rather than register entries.

Memorizing a Check

Checks written in the check writing window are memorized the same way that transactions entered in the register are memorized. Memorized check and register transactions appear in the same Memorized Transaction List together and can be edited, deleted, or recalled from either the check writing or register window.

As you use Quicken more, you may find that only a few of your transactions really need to be memorized. By changing the default settings, you can keep transactions from being automatically memorized. Once you do this, you will have to memorize manually each transaction that you want memorized.

Working with Scheduled Transactions

Although you can recall memorized transactions individually as a way to reenter similar transactions, a better method can be to have Quicken automatically schedule and enter transactions for you. Quicken 4 for Windows can schedule individual transactions or groups of transactions. You can use the Financial Calendar to schedule individual transactions whether or not they are memorized, or you can schedule groups of memorized transactions using the Scheduled Transaction list.

You can use Quicken's Financial Calendar to either prompt you to enter scheduled transactions or even to enter the transactions for you at the scheduled time. You can use this automation to save you the time of entering regularly scheduled transactions. You can also use the Scheduled Transaction list to create scheduled transaction groups, which are groups of transactions scheduled to occur together.

Scheduling with the Financial Calendar

The Financial Calendar shows when each of the transactions entered in your register occurred, and you can also use the Financial Calendar to track your future obligations. In addition, the Financial Calendar provides the easiest method for quickly scheduling repeated transactions.

Scheduling Transactions

HomeBase

Day To Day | Financial Calendar

You can schedule any transaction you have entered in the Financial Calendar, whether or not it is memorized. You can schedule a transaction that will occur only a specified number of times, or you can set the transaction to recur indefinitely.

You can display the Financial Calendar by selecting Financial Calendar from the Activities menu, or selecting the Calendar icon from the icon bar. You can also press CTRL-K. Your Financial Calendar should look like Figure 7-4.

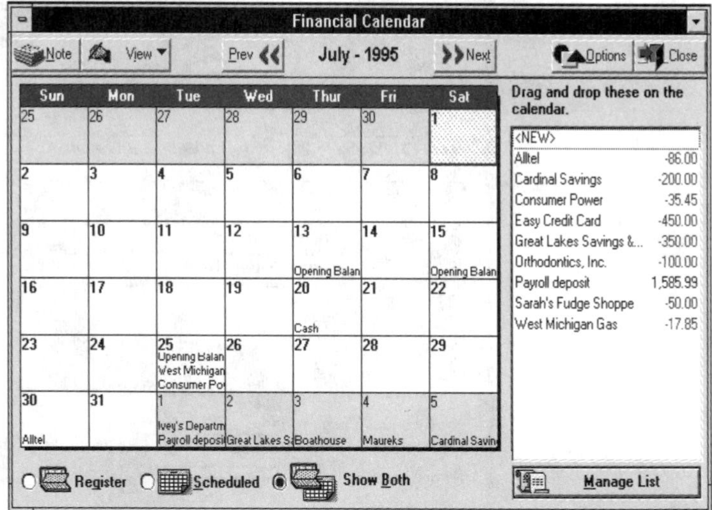

Your Financial Calendar
Figure 7-4.

Note: The Financial Calendar initially shows the calendar for the current date. Since it is unlikely that you will be using this book during the dates given for the transactions, you will probably have to change the calendar shown by selecting the Prev or Next buttons at the top of the calendar to move to July of 1995.

At the right side of the window, Quicken displays a list of the transactions you have entered. You can quickly schedule a transaction by dragging one of these transactions to a day on the Calendar with the mouse. When you release the mouse button, Quicken displays the Set Up Scheduled Transaction dialog box. For example, to schedule the regular deposit of paychecks, follow these steps:

1. Display the Financial Calendar by selecting Financial Calendar from the Activities menu or the Calendar icon from the icon bar.
2. Select Prev or Next to display the calendar for August of 1995.
3. Drag the transaction described as Payroll deposit from the list box on the right side of the window to September 1, at the bottom of the calendar.

   The Drag And Drop Transaction dialog box appears, as shown here:

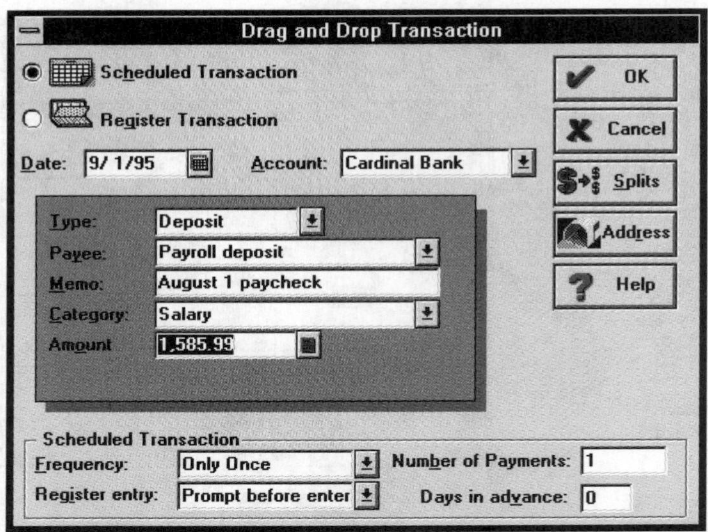

4. Enter Month in the Frequency text box.
5. Select OK.

Quicken will prompt you to enter the scheduled transaction the first time you start Quicken 4 for Windows after the scheduled date for the transaction.

Note: Notice that your scheduled transaction appears in blue, while all the other transactions in the Financial Calendar appear in black. This lets you easily distinguish between the scheduled and register transactions when both appear in the calendar.

Editing Scheduled Transactions

You can easily edit your scheduled transactions. For example, you can edit the payroll transaction you just scheduled so that Quicken will automatically enter the transaction for you on the designated date, without prompting you first. To edit a scheduled transaction, follow these steps:

1. Click on the day for which the transaction is scheduled, in this case, 9/1/95. Quicken displays the dialog box shown here:

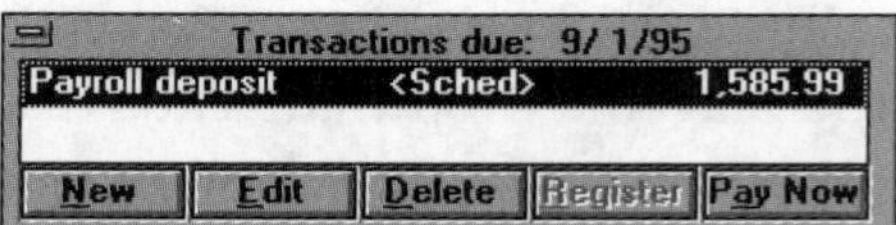

2. Select Edit, opening the Edit Scheduled Transaction dialog box shown here:

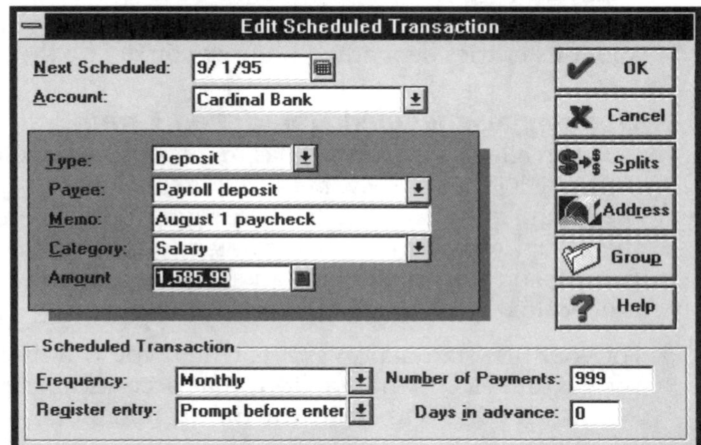

   Notice that this dialog box is nearly identical to the one you used to create the scheduled transaction originally.

3. Delete the contents of the Memo text box. You'll want to enter a new memo every month, or simply ignore it.
4. Select Automatically Enter in the Register Entry drop-down list box.

   Now Quicken will enter your payroll deposit without prompting you about it.
5. Select OK.

You may edit your transaction again when you receive a raise, or if you decide you want it entered in the register a few days before it will actually be there. This is useful as a reminder about bills you need to pay.

Paying a Scheduled Transaction Early

You may want to register a transaction as being paid early, either because you are going out of town or because you decided to pay the bill before the due date. To do this, click on the day containing the scheduled transaction, then select Pay Now.

Quicken will prompt you to review the details of the transaction. When you select Record, the transaction is entered in the register.

7

Scheduling Transaction Groups

Quicken 4 for Windows can schedule both individual transactions as described earlier or groups of transactions. If you have several memorized transactions that occur at the same time, a scheduled transaction group lets you focus on other tasks while Quicken remembers to enter the transactions you need. Quicken will record the entire group for you with or without prompting you about its entries depending on how you define the scheduled transaction.

Defining a Scheduled Transaction Group

Quicken allows you to set up as many as 12 scheduled transaction groups. Defining a group is easy, but it requires some steps. You will need to describe the group, and you will need to assign specific memorized transactions to the group. Although expense transactions are frequently used to create groups, you can also include an entry for a direct deposit payroll check that is deposited at the same time each month.

For your first transaction group, which you will title Utilities, you will group the gas and electric transactions that occur near the end of each month. Follow these steps to create the transaction group:

1. Select Scheduled Transaction from the Lists menu.
2. Select New.
3. Select Group.

   Quicken displays the Create Transaction Group dialog box, in which you define the group. The Create Transaction Group dialog box is shown here, containing the entries you will make in the steps that follow.

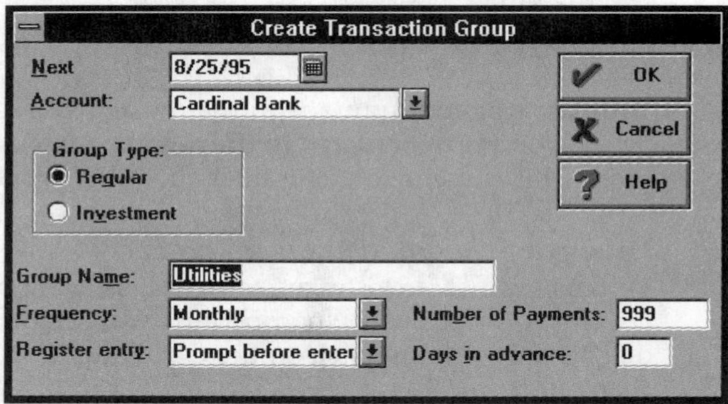

4. Enter **8/25/95** in the Next text box. Remember you can also use the drop-down calendar to select this date.

5. Enter Cardinal Bank in the Account text box as the account into which these transactions will be entered.
6. Type **Utilities** in the Group Name text box as the name for the group.
7. Select Monthly in the Frequency text box.
8. Make sure that the Number Of Payments text box is still set to 999, which causes Quicken to continue entering these transactions indefinitely.
9. Make sure that the Register Entry text box still shows "Prompt before entering" so that Quicken prompts you about the transactions before entering them in your account.
10. Select OK and Quicken displays the Assign Transactions To Group dialog box, shown here:

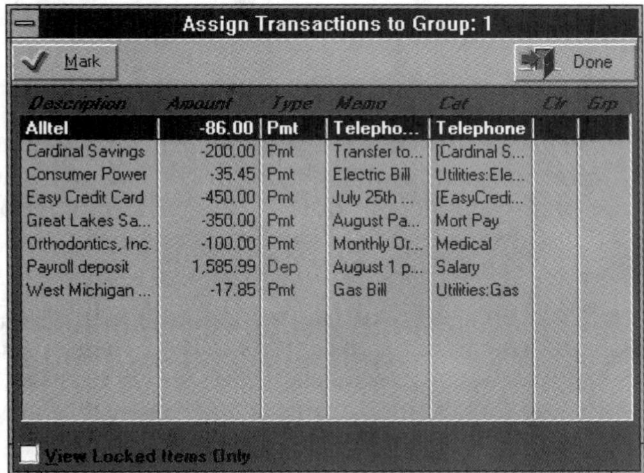

11. Double-click Consumer Power or highlight it with the arrow keys and select Mark to assign the transaction to the Utilities group.
12. The numeral 1 appears in the Grp column, which indicates that the transaction is now a part of the Utilities group.
13. Select the Western Michigan Gas and Alltel transactions by double-clicking them or highlighting them and then selecting Mark.
14. Quicken marks these transactions as part of the Utilities group, as you can see in the following illustration.
15. Select Done to indicate you are finished selecting transactions.

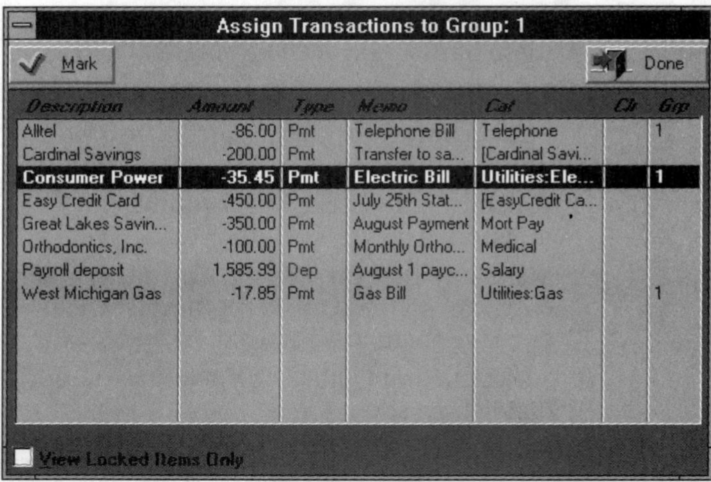

You may want to define other scheduled transaction groups to include payroll, loan payments, and anything else that you might pay at the beginning of each month. You can enter individual scheduled transactions for transactions that occur on a specific date each month, using the Financial Calendar or the Scheduled Transaction List, as described above. However, you do not need to define additional scheduled groups or transactions in order to complete the remaining exercises in this section.

You can also create transaction groups that generate checks for you. These groups contain transactions that are memorized from the check writing window. The procedure is the same as that just shown. You can identify these transactions in the Assign Transactions window because they are denoted by "Chk" in the Type field.

Changing a Scheduled Transaction Group

You can edit a transaction group at any time by selecting Scheduled Transaction from the Lists menu. Highlight the group and select Edit. As you proceed through the normal group definition procedure, you can change the description of the transaction group, how frequently it is supposed to be entered in the register, and additional transactions for inclusion in the group.

Scheduled transactions can completely automate the entry of repeated transactions such as loan payments.

To delete a scheduled transaction group, select Scheduled Transaction from the Lists menu and highlight the group you want to delete. Then select Delete. When Quicken warns you that you are about to delete the group, select OK. Quicken eliminates the group but does not delete the memorized transactions that are part of it. It also does not affect any transactions recorded in the register by earlier executions of the scheduled group.

If you want to alter a transaction that is part of the transaction group, you will need to alter the memorized transaction. This means you have to open the Memorized Transaction List, highlight the transaction and select Edit; then edit the options for the transaction.

Recording a Transaction Group

Once you have defined a scheduled transaction group, you can forget about it and let Quicken handle the entries. If you want to record the group early for some reason, you do not need to wait for Quicken. You can select it and record it yourself. Since you can memorize entries for either the register or the check writing window, make sure you have the group correctly defined for your current needs. A group type of Chk consists of transactions entered in the check writing window and can be recorded in either the account register or the check writing window. Payment (Pmt) groups consist of transactions memorized from the register and can only be used to record account register entries.

To execute a transaction group from the account register, complete the following steps:

1. Select Scheduled Transaction from the Lists menu.
2. Highlight the Utilities group.
3. Select Pay.

   Quicken displays the Record Transaction Group dialog box, which looks like this:

4. Enter **8/25/95** in the Due Date text box if needed.

   If you were actually planning to pay these bills early (as opposed to simply *recording* them early), you would enter the current date in the Due Date text box. Your register would then show the current date as the date you effected this transaction.

5. Select Record to enter the new transactions with a date of 8/25/95, as shown here:

8/25/95	Sched	Alltel		86	00		2,535	69
		Telephone Bill	Telephone					
8/25/95	Sched	West Michigan Gas		17	85		2,517	84
		Gas Bill	Utilities:Gas					
8/25/95	Sched	Consumer Power		35	45		2,482	39
		Electric Bill	Utilities:Electric					

6. Modify the Utilities transaction group entries just recorded as shown below, and add the last transaction for Meijer to complete the August transactions for your account register. Remember to record each transaction after you've made the modifications.

   Num: **108**
   Payee: **Alltel**
   Payment: **23.00**

   Num: **109**
   Payee: **Consumer Power**
   Payment: **30.75**

   Num: **110**
   Payee: **West Michigan Gas**
   Payment: **19.25**

7. Record the final transaction for the month of August as follows:

   Date: **8/27/95**
   Num: **111**
   Payee: **Meijer**
   Payment: **93.20**
   Memo: **Food**
   Category: **Groceries**

If you failed to delete the memorized transaction for Meijer earlier in this chapter, then Quicken's QuickFill feature completed the entire transaction for you when you typed **Meijer**. However, if you followed the steps given earlier, Quicken did not do this. QuickFill finds matching transactions from the Memorized Transaction list, but you deleted Meijer from this list if you carried out the exercise in the section "Changing and Deleting Memorized Transactions."

The last few transactions entered and modified should now look like this:

Date	Num	Payee / Memo	Category	Payment	Clr	Deposit	Balance
8/25/95	108	Alltel Telephone Bill	Telephone	23 00			3,048 69
8/25/95	109	Consumer Power Electric Bill	Utilities:Electric	30 75			3,017 94
8/25/95	110	West Michigan Gas Gas Bill	Utilities:Gas	19 25			2,998 69
8/27/95	111	Meijer Food	Groceries	93 20			2,905 49

Responding to Quicken Reminders to Record a Scheduled Group

You can turn BillMinder on and off by selecting Options from the Edit menu, then selecting Reminders.

If you have chosen to be prompted before a scheduled group is recorded, Quicken displays a dialog box that asks you if you want to enter the scheduled group when that day arrives. The prompt appears either in Windows when you load it or when you start Quicken. By default, when you open Windows, Quicken's BillMinder feature displays a message reminding you to pay any postdated checks or to record scheduled transaction groups. If you've turned BillMinder off, Quicken still displays the Reminder window when you start Quicken or open a file. The Reminder window also reminds you of upcoming scheduled transactions and postdated checks.

Using Classes

You have used categories as one way of distinguishing transactions entered in Quicken. Categories have to do with specified types of income and expenses, and they define transactions in these terms. They explain what kind of income or expense a given transaction represents. You can tell at a glance which costs are for utilities and which are for entertainment. Specific subcategory names and descriptions provide still more information about transactions. In summary reports, you might see totals of all the transactions contained in a category or subcategory.

Classes allow you to "slice the transaction pie" in a different way. Classes recategorize to show where, to whom, or for what time period the transactions apply. It is important not to think of classes as a replacement for categories; they do not affect category assignments. Classes provide a different view or perspective of your data.

For example, you might use classes if you have both a year-round home and a vacation cottage. One set of utility expenses is for the year-round residence, and another is for the vacation cottage. If you define and assign classes to the transactions, the categories assigned to them still mark them as utility expenses, but the classes assigned indicate which house each transaction affects.

Since the expenses for a number of family members can be maintained in one checking account, you might want to use classes for those expenses that you would like to review by family member. You can use this approach for clothing expenses and automobile expenses if your family members drive separate cars. Another method for automobile expenses is to assign classes for each of the vehicles you own. You can then look at what you have spent on a specific vehicle at the end of the year and make an informed decision regarding replacement or continued maintenance.

Quicken does not provide a standard list of classes. As with categories, you can set up what you need before you start making entries or you can add the classes you need as you enter transactions. Once you have created a class, you enter it in the Category field by placing it after your category name and any subcategories. You always type a slash (/) before entering the class name, as in Utilities: Electric/Cottage.

To create a class before entering a transaction, you can select Class from the Lists menu or press CTRL-L to open the Class List window. Select New to create a new entry. Quicken displays the Set Up Class dialog box, as shown here, where you can enter the name and description of a class:

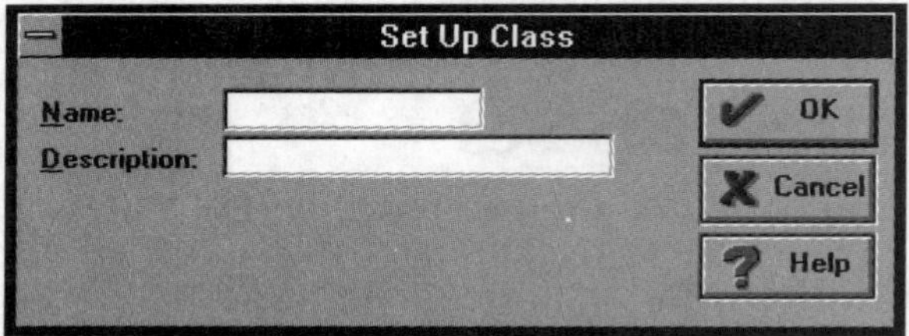

Each new class is added to the Class List dialog box. To create a class as you enter a transaction, simply type the category and any subcategories, followed by a slash and the class name you want to use. Then when you select Record, Quicken opens the Set Up Class dialog box. The following is an example of a class entry for "Jim" that could be used if you wanted to separately categorize personal expenses for each individual in the household:

8/12/95		Beach Shop		54 00			2,632 69
		New sweater	Clothing/Jim				

If Jim were not an existing class, Quicken would display the Set Up Class dialog box and you could create a class called "Jim." You will find more detailed examples of class entries in later chapters.

Adding Passwords

You can add passwords to your Quicken files to prevent other people from opening your financial records. This kind of security is especially nice if you are maintaining files on a system shared by other people, such as your kids or co-workers. To add passwords, select Passwords from the File menu. Quicken presents the following submenu:

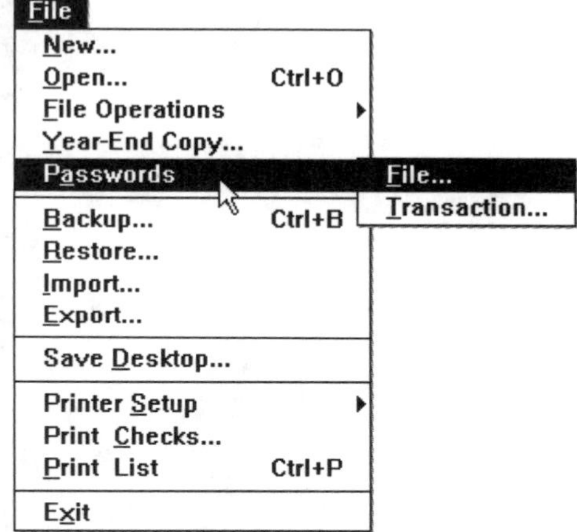

You can choose to password-protect either the file, using a file password, or existing transactions, using a transaction password. Although you can add protection with a password at both levels, you need to set each one individually.

If you select File, Quicken asks you to enter a password. Once you select OK, the password is added to the active file, and anyone wishing to work with that file must supply it. The transaction password is used to prevent changes to existing transactions prior to a specified date, without the password. If you choose Transaction, Quicken opens a window that requires you to enter both a password and a date.

If you want to change a password or remove it in a subsequent session, you must be able to provide the existing password. Quicken then provides a Change Password dialog box where you enter both the old and new passwords. After completing the entries and selecting OK, Quicken puts the new password into effect.

CHAPTER

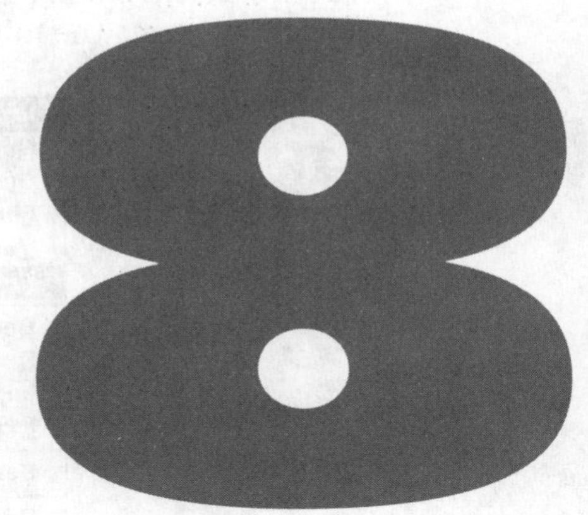

QUICKEN as a BUDGETING TOOL

You probably think of a budget as a constraint on your spending. That's not what budgets are designed to be. Instead, a budget is a financial plan that shows your projected income and expenses so you can plan your expenses within the limits of your income.

Although a budget may sometimes cause you to deny yourself a purchase, this denial will supply the funds for expenses you have given greater priority.

Given the same income, five families would prepare five different budget plans. One family might budget to save enough for a down payment on a new house. Another family might construct its budget so that they could afford a new car. A third family might enjoy eating out and traveling, and budget accordingly. Within the constraints of your income, the choice is yours.

A budget is your financial plan. It is meant to guide you as you confront financial decisions.

If a budget is meant to facilitate getting what you want, why do so many people procrastinate in putting together a budget? It may be because budgeting takes time or because it forces you to make decisions, or perhaps the reason is simply that most people are not sure where to begin. One thing is certain: budgeting is an important component of every successful financial plan. It's wise to create a budget even if you have already successfully built a financial nest egg. The budget lets you protect your investment and ensure that your spending meets both your short- and long-range goals.

Quicken is ideally suited for maintaining your budget information. The program guides you through the budget development process; you need only specify categories and make simple entries to record budgeted amounts in these categories. After a modest initial investment of time, Quicken generates reports you can use to monitor your progress toward your financial goals. You don't need to wait until the end of the budget period to record your progress. You can enter your expenses daily and check the status of your actual and budgeted amounts at any time you wish.

In this chapter, you create a budget and enter register transactions for several months. You use scheduled transaction groups from Chapter 7, "Expanding the Scope of Financial Entries," to speed up this process, providing enough transactions to give you a sense of what Quicken can do. After making your entries, you see how Quicken's standard reports can help you keep expenses in line with your budget, and you take a quick look at the insights graphs can provide.

Quicken's Budgeting Process

Quicken lets you enter projected income and expense levels for any category. You can enter the same projection for each month of the year, or you can change the amount allocated for each month. Quicken matches your planned expenses with your actual expense entries and displays the results in a Monthly Budget report. There is one entry point for budget information, but Quicken combines actual entries from all your bank, cash, and credit card accounts in the current file. Although Quicken can take much of the work out of entering and managing your budget, it cannot prepare a budget without your projections. If you have never prepared a budget before, take a look at a few budget planning considerations, shown in the "Budget Planning" box in this chapter. Once you have put together a plan, it's time to record your decisions in Quicken.

Specifying Budget Amounts

In this section, you enter budget amounts for the transaction categories you entered in the Cardinal Bank account register in Chapter 7. Later, when you create your own budget, you will need to expand the budget entries to include all the categories of income and expenses you want to monitor.

Consider a few points before you complete the budget entries:

- By default, Quicken includes categories and subcategories in budget reports if it finds budgeted amounts in the categories and subcategories. You can change this default setting so that Quicken's Monthly Budget report includes all categories found in the Category & Transfer List, or so that it includes all categories that have either budgeted or actual amounts assigned to them.
- It doesn't matter what period of time you define as the reporting period. (Although the default reporting period is monthly, you can make your reporting period quarterly or biannually, for example.)
- All the categories you have available in your Category List are shown in the Budget window. This includes Quicken's predefined personal Category List as well as any new categories you have added.
- You can assign budget amounts to subcategories as well as to categories.
- You can also assign categories to *budget supercategories*, which let you track your levels of expense or income in sets of categories. By default, Quicken assigns your income categories to either the Salary Income or Other Income supercategory, and your expense categories to the Discretionary, Non-Discretionary, or Unassigned supercategory.

HomeBase

Planning | Budgeting

To set up the budget, follow these steps from the register window:

1. Select Budgeting from the Plan menu.

   Quicken opens the Budget window, shown in Figure 8-1. Notice that the window is arranged in rows and columns, much like a spreadsheet. Notice the icons in front of the categories. If the icon displays a + (plus sign), like the one before Auto, then there are undisplayed subcategories.

You can display the subcategories by double-clicking the icon. When all subcategories are displayed, the icon displays a - (hyphen). You can hide them again by double-clicking the icon. The entries you make into subcategories are not lost when they are hidden; they are simply shown as part of the category.

Normally, you enter realistic amounts matching your budget plan in this window. In this exercise, you enter budget amounts provided for you. You also learn to use the window's button bar to help you complete your entries.

2. Move to the Salary row in the Jan column by using the mouse or DOWN ARROW.
3. Type **1586**, and move to another row or column.

   Quicken displays your entry in the Salary category, the Total Inflows row at the bottom of the window, and the Totals column at the right side of the window.
4. Move back to the Salary entry for January, and select Edit from the Budget window's button bar.
5. Select Fill Row Right, then select Yes to copy the salary across, as shown in Figure 8-2.

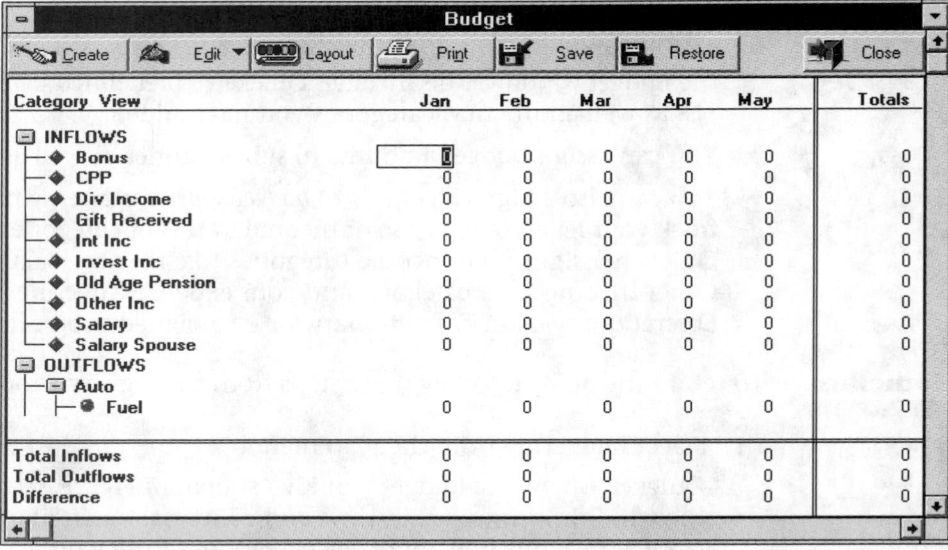

The Budget window

Figure 8-1.

Budget Planning

You must begin the budgeting process before you start making budget entries in Quicken. Start with an analysis of expected income. If your income flow is irregular, estimate on the low side. Remember to use only the *net amount* received from each income source. (The net amount is the total amount minus any taxes or other withholdings.) Also, do not include projected salary increases until they are confirmed.

The next step is analyzing projected expenses. First, budget for debt repayment and other essentials such as medical insurance premiums. In addition to monthly items such as mortgage and car loan payments, consider irregular expenses that are paid only once or twice a year. Tuition, property taxes, insurance premiums, children's and personal allowances, and church pledges are examples of irregular expenses.

Project your expenses for medical, pharmacy, and dental bills for one year. Compute the required yearly expenses, and save toward these major expenses so that the entire amount does not need to come from a single month's check.

Next, plan savings into your budget. If you wait until you cover food, entertainment, and all the other day-to-day expenses, it's easy to find that nothing is left to save. So, plan to write yourself a check for at least five percent of your net pay for savings when you pay your other bills.

The last type of expense to budget for is day-to-day expenses such as food, personal care, home repairs, gasoline, car maintenance, furniture, recreation, and gifts.

Naturally, if your totals for expenses exceed your income projections, you must reassess your budget before entering projected amounts in Quicken.

During the first few months of budgeting, err on the side of too much detail. At the end of the month, you will need to know exactly how your money was spent. You can then make realistic adjustments between expense categories to ensure that your budget stays in balance.

In step 4, you must move back to the entry because you finalized the salary entry by moving elsewhere. You can use Fill Row Right immediately after typing an entry if you haven't yet finalized the entry.

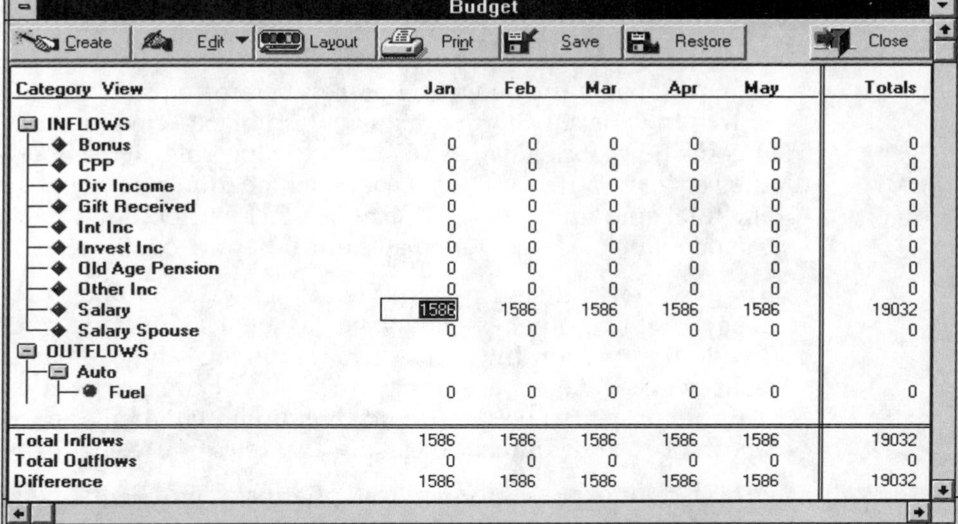

The Budget window after Fill Row Right is used for salary

Figure 8-2.

6. Highlight the January entry for the Electric subcategory under Utilities.

   If the subcategories are not currently displayed, you can double-click the icon preceding Utilities to display them.

   Notice that as you move down, the bottom part of the screen continues to show a summary of budget inflows and outflows. Quicken scrolls only the detail entries above this area.

7. Type **25**, but don't move to another field.
8. Select Edit, then select Fill Row Right and Yes to copy 25 across for all the months.

   The 25 appears as -25 because paying this bill is a cash outflow. Outflows are negative numbers. Inflows, like a salary, are positive numbers.

9. Move to the Electric entry for October, type **30**, and move to another field to replace the 25.

   Notice that Quicken changed the dollar amount for only one month. If you wanted to change the amount for November and December as well, you would need to use Fill Row Right again.

10. Move back to the October entry, select Edit, select Fill Row Right, and then select Yes.

    This time, all the values for subsequent months change to 30. You might make this type of change because new power rates are expected or because you have installed a number of new outside lights.

11. Using the following information, move to the January column and complete the budgeted amounts for the categories in that column.

Category	**Budgeted Amount**
Auto: Fuel	**30**
Clothing	**70**
Dining	**55**
Entertain	**55**
Groceries	**200**
Medical	**120**
Misc	**75**
Mort Pay	**350**
Telephone	**30**
Utilities: Gas	**20**

    Some of these expenses are assigned to categories and others to subcategories. You can do both with Quicken.

12. To enter a budgeted amount of 200 as a transfer to the Cardinal Saving account each month, start by selecting Layout from the button bar, then selecting the Show Transfers check box and OK.

    Quicken adds the transfer account categories to the list of categories. The transfers are added to both the Inflow and Outflow sections. You need to record the inflow of funds into one account separately from the related outflow of funds from another account.

13. Move to the FROM Cardinal Bank January entry at the bottom of the Inflow section, type **200**, and then select Edit, Fill Row Right, and Yes to copy 200 across for all the months.

14. Move to the TO Cardinal Saving January entry at the bottom of the Outflow section, type **200**, and then select Edit, Fill Row Right, and Yes to copy 200 across for all the months.

    In the early stages, it generally takes several months to develop sound estimates for all your expenditure categories. For example, this illustration shows a desired transfer to savings of $200.00 per month. You may anticipate that your excess cash inflows at the end of the month will be $200.00, and plan to transfer the excess to savings. If you find that your outflows actually exceed your inflows, however, you'll need to transfer money from savings. Once you establish your spending patterns and monitor your inflows and outflows, you may find that excess inflows occur during parts of the year and excess outflows during others, such as during the holiday season. You can use your Quicken budget to plan for these seasonal needs and anticipate the transfer of funds between your savings and checking accounts. As a rule, it's a good idea to transfer any excess cash to savings at the end of each month.

15. Select Layout, clear the Show Transfers check box, and then select OK to hide the transfer categories again. The amounts you entered aren't lost; they're just not displayed.
16. Select Edit, and then select Fill Columns and Yes to copy the values across from January to all the other months, as shown in Figure 8-3. This changes the figure for Utilities: Electric in Oct-Dec back to 25.

    When you use Fill Columns, you cannot copy across selectively; if you want varying amounts for different months, you need to customize the entries after using Fill Columns.
17. For the Furniture category, enter **185.00** for October and **250.00** for December.
18. Select the Save button from the Budget window's button bar to save your new budget.

Using Budget Supercategories

Budget supercategories are a new feature in Quicken 4 for Windows. They are designed to make working with your budgets even more informative. You can assign categories to any budget supercategories, creating your own supercategories if you prefer. You can then use these supercategories in

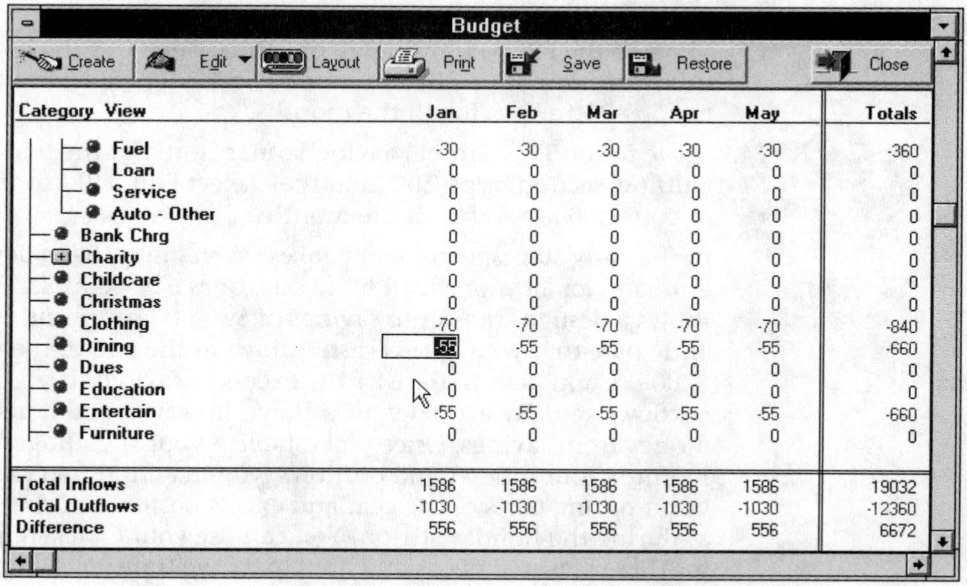

Budget

Create | Edit | Layout | Print | Save | Restore | Close

Category View	Jan	Feb	Mar	Apr	May	Totals
Fuel	-30	-30	-30	-30	-30	-360
Loan	0	0	0	0	0	0
Service	0	0	0	0	0	0
Auto - Other	0	0	0	0	0	0
Bank Chrg	0	0	0	0	0	0
Charity	0	0	0	0	0	0
Childcare	0	0	0	0	0	0
Christmas	0	0	0	0	0	0
Clothing	-70	-70	-70	-70	-70	-840
Dining	-55	-55	-55	-55	-55	-660
Dues	0	0	0	0	0	0
Education	0	0	0	0	0	0
Entertain	-55	-55	-55	-55	-55	-660
Furniture	0	0	0	0	0	0
Total Inflows	1586	1586	1586	1586	1586	19032
Total Outflows	-1030	-1030	-1030	-1030	-1030	-12360
Difference	556	556	556	556	556	6672

Figure 8-3. Some of the budget outflows after Fill Columns is used

reports and the Budget window to give you a better feel for how you are meeting your budget.

Use budget supercategories to get an overview of how you spend money.

For example, you probably have some expenses that are not negotiable, such as car payments, utility bills, or outstanding debts. This money has to be spent in full every month. However, other expenses are *discretionary*, meaning that you can change them if you wish. This might include gifts, entertainment, or dining out expenses. After all, you can choose to make your gifts or not to go out. It would help your budgeting to know, in general, whether you are overreaching your discretionary expense budget.

When you create new categories, Quicken does not assign them to any of the default supercategories. To assign them to one:

1. In the Budget window, select Edit from the button bar.
2. Select Supercategories, opening the Manage Supercategories dialog box shown in Figure 8-4.
3. Select Furniture in the Category Name list box.
4. Select Discretionary in the Supercategory Name list box.
5. Select Assign.
6. Use the same steps to assign the Mort Pay and Utilities:Electric categories to the Non-Discretionary supercategory.
7. Select OK, since you are finished reassigning categories.

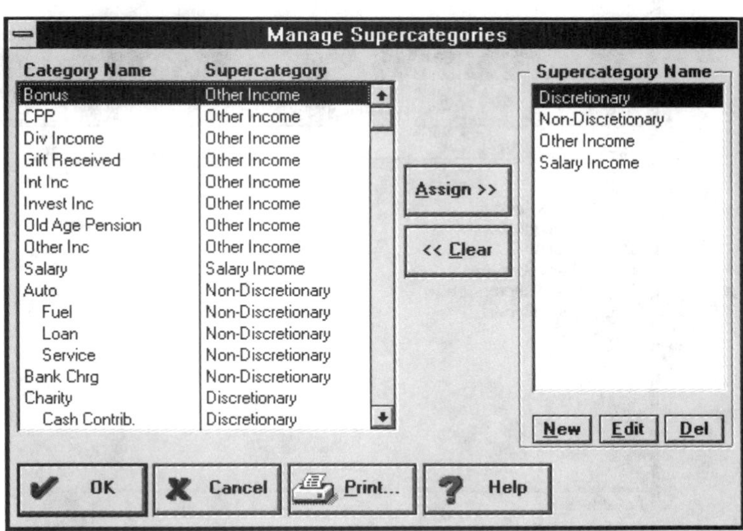

Reassigning categories to supercategories
Figure 8-4.

Note: You could create custom supercategories by selecting New in the Managing Supercategories dialog box.

You can also display your supercategories in the Budget window. Just select Layout from the window's button bar, then select the Show Supercategories check box and OK. Quicken displays the supercategories with categories beneath them. You can double-click the icons in front of the supercategories to display or hide the categories beneath them, as you can see in Figure 8-5.

Compressing your budget like this gives a better general overview of your budget. It makes it easier for you to see if there is slack in your budget, or if you are spending most of your money on necessary items.

Creating a Monthly Budget Report

HomeBase

Now that you have completed your initial budget entries, you want to prepare a monthly budget summary to compare your budgeted amounts to the actual amounts. To create a Monthly Budget report like the one shown in Figure 8-6, follow these steps:

Reports | More Reports

1. Select Home from the Reports menu, then Monthly Budget. You can also select the Reports icon from the icon bar, then choose the Home option button and Monthly Budget from the list box.

Budget

Create | Edit | Layout | Print | Save | Restore | Close

Supercategory View	Jan	Feb	Mar	Apr	May	Totals
INFLOWS						
Other Income	0	0	0	0	0	0
Salary Income	1586	1586	1586	1586	1586	19032
OUTFLOWS						
Discretionary	-255	-255	-255	-255	-255	-3495
Non-Discretionary	-775	-775	-775	-775	-775	-9300
Unassigned	0	0	0	0	0	0
Total Inflows	1586	1586	1586	1586	1586	19032
Total Outflows	-1030	-1030	-1030	-1030	-1030	-12795
Difference	556	556	556	556	556	6237

Hiding categories beneath supercategories
Figure 8-5.

2. Select Customize.
3. Enter **8/1/95** in the From text box.
4. Enter **8/31/95** in the To text box.
5. Clear the Cents In Amounts check box, and then select OK to create the report in a Monthly Budget Report window.
6. Select the Print button, and then select Print to print the report.

Note: The reports shown in this book may look different from yours because they were printed using a Hewlett-Packard LaserJet series III. You can change the appearance of your reports by changing your report printer setup.

Analyzing the Monthly Budget Report

When you print the Monthly Budget report, it's dated for the one-month period you defined. Also notice that Quicken combines transactions from all of your bank, cash, and credit card accounts to calculate the actual figures of the Monthly Budget report. This means that as you scroll down the report, you don't see the $200.00 transfer to Cardinal Saving. Quicken views all your accounts as a single unit for budget report purposes. This transfer therefore has no net effect in your file, because the money is still in one of the accounts included in the report. In the next section, you see how you can change the report to show this transfer. A transfer of $200.00 to savings can be a significant event from a budgeting perspective, and therefore, something you might want to show on a report.

The Monthly Budget report shows all your budgeted categories and the amount you were over or under budget in each. When Quicken compares your budgeted versus actual expenditures for each category, the Diff column displays *negative* numbers if your you spent more than you budgeted and *positive* numbers if you spent less. In Figure 8-6, you can see by the negative value for the overall total difference that you were over your budget for the period by $161.00. When you read the report, you can quickly see whether you met your budget objectives for each category. As already noted, your total actual outflows exceed your total budgeted outflows (1,191 - 1,030 = 161).

On closer examination, you can see that the unexpected expenditure for furniture during the month was not budgeted. This category-by-category breakdown is the heart of budget analysis and pinpoints areas for further scrutiny.

Monthly Budget Report

8/1/95 Through 8/31/95

Category Description	8/1/95 Actual	- Budget	8/31/95 Diff
INFLOWS			
Salary	1,586	1,586	-0
TOTAL INFLOWS	1,586	1,586	-0
OUTFLOWS			
Auto:			
Fuel	23	30	7
Total Auto	23	30	7
Clothing	50	70	20
Dining	60	55	-5
Entertain	50	55	5
Furniture	217	0	-217
Groceries	218	200	-18
Medical	100	120	20
Misc	50	75	25
Mort Pay	350	350	0
Telephone	23	30	7
Utilities:			
Electric	31	25	-6
Gas	19	20	1
Total Utilities	50	45	-5
TOTAL OUTFLOWS	1,191	1,030	-161
OVERALL TOTAL	395	556	-161

A Monthly Budget report for all accounts
Figure 8-6.

Since a budget is just a plan, you can make modifications as the need arises.

Modifying the Monthly Budget Report

As mentioned previously, you may want to modify the Monthly Budget report to cover only the accounts you regularly use to spend money: such as the Cardinal Bank and EasyCredit Card accounts. This change lets you see the effect of the transfer to your savings account in the report. Follow these steps to modify the Monthly Budget report:

1. Select Customize from the Monthly Budget Report window's button bar. The Customize Report Monthly Budget dialog box opens.
2. Select Accounts, and then click the Cardinal Saving account to unmark it. The Cardinal Bank and EasyCredit Card accounts should remain selected.
3. Select OK, and the modified report appears. Notice that Quicken used only the checking and credit card accounts to prepare this report and that the transfer to savings shows in the outflow section.
4. Select the Print button from the window's button bar, and then select Print to print the Monthly Budget report.

The customized report looks like Figure 8-7. Notice that the transfer to Cardinal Saving is shown in your report but that your results haven't changed. The upper-left corner of your report shows that the report is for the selected accounts only. If you look under the reports date in Figure 8-6, you'll see that that Monthly Budget report included the Bank, Cash, and CC (credit card) accounts. Unless you have chosen otherwise, Quicken lists these three account types in the budget, even if you have not created these accounts.

Tying the Monthly Budget Report to Other Quicken Reports

You have completed the basic steps involved in preparing your Monthly Budget report. Now let's see how this report relates to the reports you prepared in Chapter 4, "Quicken Reports." Figures 8-8 and 8-9 show a Cash Flow report and a portion of an Itemized Categories report for the Cardinal Bank and EasyCredit Card accounts. Since the example Monthly Budget report is based on only one month, the Cash Flow report (shown in Figure 8-8) and the Actual column in the Monthly Budget report (shown in Figure 8-7) contain the same inflows and outflows. Normally, the budget summary would cover information for a longer period of time (such as a quarter or a year) and you would prepare a Cash Flow report for each of the months included in the budget summary report. Be sure you think through your reporting requirements instead of just printing all the reports.

You might be wondering why the Cash Flow report shows a positive $194.79 net cash inflow, while the Monthly Budget report (Figure 8-7) indicates that you were over budget by $161.00. This occurs because the Cash Flow report looks only at actual cash inflows and outflows. The Monthly Budget report, on the other hand, examines what you want to spend and what you actually spent. The positive cash flow shows that you have more money at the end of the month than you did at the end of last month. The negative budget shows that you have less money than you planned. Looking at the Budget

Monthly Budget Report
8/1/95 Through 8/31/95

Category Description	8/1/95 Actual	- Budget	8/31/95 Diff
INFLOWS			
Salary	1,586	1,586	-0
FROM Cardinal Saving	0	0	0
TOTAL INFLOWS	1,586	1,586	-0
OUTFLOWS			
Auto:			
Fuel	23	30	7
Total Auto	23	30	7
Clothing	50	70	20
Dining	60	55	-5
Entertain	50	55	5
Furniture	217	0	-217
Groceries	218	200	-18
Medical	100	120	20
Misc	50	75	25
Mort Pay	350	350	0
Telephone	23	30	7
Utilities:			
Electric	31	25	-6
Gas	19	20	1
Total Utilities	50	45	-5
TO Cardinal Saving	200	200	0
TOTAL OUTFLOWS	1,391	1,230	-161
OVERALL TOTAL	195	356	-161

A Monthly Budget report for the checking and credit card accounts
Figure 8-7.

column of Figure 8-7, you can see that there should have been $356.00 to transfer to savings if you had met your budget objectives.

Figure 8-9 provides detailed information for each category. Notice that the Groceries category is printed by check number and provides details for the "Groceries" amount in the Budget and Cash Flow reports. When you're looking at Budget and Cash Flow reports that cover a longer period of time, the Itemized Categories report can provide useful insights into your spending

Cash Flow Report
8/1/95 Through 8/31/95

Category Description		8/1/95- 8/31/95
INFLOWS		
Salary		1,585.99
TOTAL INFLOWS		1,585.99
OUTFLOWS		
Auto:		
Fuel	23.00	
Total Auto		23.00
Clothing		50.00
Dining		60.00
Entertain		50.00
Furniture		217.00
Groceries		218.20
Medical		100.00
Misc		50.00
Mort Pay		350.00
Telephone		23.00
Utilities:		
Electric	30.75	
Gas	19.25	
Total Utilities		50.00
TO Cardinal Saving		200.00
TOTAL OUTFLOWS		1,391.20
OVERALL TOTAL		194.79

A Cash Flow report for the budget period
Figure 8-8.

patterns. They can show where you spent and the frequency of expenditures by category. This information can help you analyze the changes you might want to make in your spending patterns.

Creating a Quarterly Budget Report

The reports presented so far in this chapter give you an overview of the budgeting process by looking at expenditures for one month. You would need to extend your examination over a longer period of time to tell if the over-budget situation in August was unusual or if it is part of a trend that should be remedied.

Itemized Category Report by Category
8/1/95 Through 8/31/95

PERSONAL-Selected Accounts

Date	Acct	Num	Description	Memo	Category	Clr	Amount
	INCOME/EXPENSE						
	INCOME						
	Salary						
8/1/95	Cardi...	DEP	Payroll deposit	August 1 paycheck	Salary		1,586
	Total Salary						1,586
	TOTAL INCOME						1,586
	EXPENSES						
	Auto:						
	Fuel						
8/7/95	EasyC...		Al's Gas	Gasoline - Jeep Wagoneer	Auto:Fuel	x	-23
	Total Fuel						-23
	Total Auto						-23
	Clothing						
8/1/95	EasyC...		Ivey's Department Store	Blue Blouse	Clothing	x	-50
	Total Clothing						-50
	Dining						
8/3/95	EasyC...		Boathouse	Dinner at the Boathouse	Dining	x	-60
	Total Dining						-60
	Entertain						
8/17/95	EasyC...		Fennville Players	Play Tickets	Entertain	x	-50
	Total Entertain						-50
	Furniture						
8/11/95	EasyC...		Fennville Furniture	Green Rocker	Furniture	x	-217
	Total Furniture						-217
	Groceries						
8/4/95	Cardi...	105	Maureks	Groceries	Groceries		-60
8/15/95	Cardi...	107	Meijer	Groceries	Groceries		-65
8/27/95	Cardi...	111	Meijer	Food	Groceries		-93
	Total Groceries						-218
	Medical						
8/6/95	Cardi...	106	Orthodontics, Inc.	Monthly Orthodontics Payment	Medical		-100

A Partial Itemized Categories report for the budget period

Figure 8-9.

To extend the time period covered by the Monthly Budget report, you will need to add transactions for other months. Fortunately, you can use the transaction groups discussed in Chapter 7, "Expanding the Scope of Financial Entries," to make the task easy. As you add more information to the reports, you will also learn how to create wide reports with Quicken.

Additional Transactions

To create a more realistic budget, you will extend the actual budget amounts for several months by creating new register transactions. This also gives you an opportunity to practice techniques you learned in earlier chapters, such as recalling memorized transactions and making changes to split transactions. Remember that you will use the transactions recorded in Chapter 7. Figure 8-10 shows the register entries you will make in the Cardinal Bank account to expand your data for this chapter. To record the first transaction in the Cardinal Bank account register, follow these steps:

Note: You can create a register report like the one in Figure 8-10 by selecting Report in the register window. This report gives the same information as you would see if you printed the register, but prints on fewer pages and can be customized.

You can group small expenses into the Misc category. Any expense that needs to be monitored closely should be kept separate. Also, when making this decision, consider what percentage of your total budget the category represents.

1. Switch to your Cardinal Bank register window and select Memorized Transaction from the Lists menu to display the list of memorized transactions.

   In Chapter 7, you deleted some of the memorized transactions. Unless you have altered your settings again, Quicken is still set to memorize all transactions.

2. Move to the transaction you want to recall, Cardinal Saving, and select Use.
3. Make any changes necessary to reflect the transaction you want to record. In this case, change the date to 9/1/95 and the amount to 194.79, and then select Record.

   As mentioned earlier, excess cash in any month should be transferred to savings. This helps prevent impulsive buying if you are saving for larger outflows in later months of the year. But remember that when you plan your budget, you can build in varying monthly savings rather than setting a minimum amount and transferring any excess inflow or outflow at the end of each month.

4. Complete the example by entering all the information in your register as shown in Figure 8-10. This report already shows the transfer to savings that you completed in the last step. As a reminder, the report shows

Register Report
9/1/95 Through 10/31/95

PERSONAL-Cardinal Bank

Date	Num	Description	Memo	Category	Clr	Amount
9/1/95	TXFR	Cardinal Savings	Transfer to savings	[Cardinal Saving]		-194.79
9/1/95	DEP	Payroll deposit	September paycheck	Salary		1,585.99
9/2/95	113	Great Lakes Savings & Loan	September Payment	Mort Pay		-350.00
9/3/95	114	Maureks	Food	Groceries		-85.00
9/8/95	115	Orthodontics, Inc.	Monthly Orthodontics Payment	Medical		-170.00
9/8/95	TXFR	Cardinal Savings	Transfer to savings	[Cardinal Saving]		-200.00
9/25/95	116	Alltel	Telephone Bill	Telephone		-29.00
9/25/95	117	Consumer Power	Electric Bill	Utilities:Electric		-43.56
9/25/95	118	West Michigan Gas	Gas Bill	Utilities:Gas		-19.29
9/30/95	119	Maureks	Food	Groceries		-95.00
10/1/95	TXFR	Cardinal Savings	Transfer to savings	[Cardinal Saving]		-166.35
10/1/95	DEP	Payroll deposit	October Paycheck	Salary		1,585.99
10/2/95	121	Great Lakes Savings & Loan	October Payment	Mort Pay		-350.00
10/5/95	122	Maureks	Food	Groceries		-115.00
10/5/95	TXFR	Cardinal Savings	Transfer to savings	[Cardinal Saving]		-200.00
10/8/95	123	Orthodontics, Inc.	Monthly Orthodontics Payment	Medical		-100.00
10/19/95	124	Maureks	Food	Groceries		-135.00
10/25/95	125	Alltel	Telephone Bill	Telephone		-27.50
10/25/95	126	Consumer Power	Electric Bill	Utilities:Electric		-37.34
10/25/95	127	West Michigan Gas	Gas Bill	Utilities:Gas		-16.55
		TOTAL 9/1/95 - 10/31/95				837.60
		TOTAL INFLOWS				3,171.98
		TOTAL OUTFLOWS				-2,334.38
		NET TOTAL				837.60

Additional account register entries
Figure 8-10.

payments as negative numbers but when you enter them, enter them as positive numbers in the Payment column.

You will primarily be recalling memorized transactions, scheduled transactions and transaction groups, and split transactions to enter these payments and deposits. The only transactions that are not memorized or scheduled are the grocery checks. Notice that check numbers 120 and 128 are *not* entered. When you have finished, the new checking account balance is $3,293.09.

After entering these transactions in the Cardinal Bank account, you need to enter your credit card transactions, as shown in Figure 8-11.

5. First switch to the EasyCredit Card register window and enter the credit card transactions for September. The last September charge was at the Red Tomato Eatery.

   After the Red Tomato Eatery charge in September, the balance is -233.00. The shortened Memo field entries in Figure 8-1 are Gasoline - Jeep Wagoneer, Dinner at the Red Tomato Eatery, Dinner at the Boathouse, and Gasoline - Jeep Wagoneer.

Register Report
9/1/95 Through 10/31/95

PERSONAL-EasyCredit Card

Date	Num	Description	Memo	Category	Clr	Amount
		BALANCE 8/31/95				0.00
9/1/95		Fennville Players	Play Tickets	Entertain		-50.00
9/8/95		Al's Gas	Gasoline - Jeep Wag...	Auto:Fuel		-23.00
9/10/95		Sue's Stitchery	Gifts, supplies, etc.	Misc		-50.00
9/13/95		Ivey's Department Store	Red Blouse	Clothing		-50.00
9/17/95		Red Tomato Eatery	Dinner at the Red T...	Dining		-60.00
10/1/95		Fish's Furniture	Table and chairs	Furniture		-550.00
10/5/95		Boathouse	Dinner at the Boath...	Dining		-45.00
10/10/95		Al's Gas	Gasoline - Jeep Wag...	Auto:Fuel		-37.00
10/12/95		LouAnn's Clothes	White Dress	Clothing		-75.00
10/13/95		Fennville Players	Play Tickets	Entertain		-100.00
10/22/95		Ivey's Department Store	Clearance Sale	Misc		-150.00
		TOTAL 9/1/95 - 10/31/95				-1,190.00
		BALANCE 10/31/95				-1,190.00
		TOTAL INFLOWS				0.00
		TOTAL OUTFLOWS				-1,190.00
		NET TOTAL				-1,190.00

Credit card charges for September and October

Figure 8-11.

Note: Remember to enter the negative amounts you see in Figure 8-11 as positive numbers in the Charge column of the register.

6. Select Pay Credit Card Bill from the Activities menu.
7. Type **233** in the Charges, Cash Advances text box.
8. Type **0** in the Payments, Credits text box. The value you enter in this text box includes any payments and credits you made during the last month, but does not include the payment you made for last month's credit card bill.
9. Type **233** in the New Balance text box, and select OK.
10. Since you'll be paying this credit card bill in full, mark September's charges and October's payment transactions in the two list boxes.

    The payment you made from last month appears in the Payments column because it is not yet cleared. Assuming that this payment appears on the bill, you can clear it now.
11. When your difference is 0, select Done.
12. When the Make Credit Card Payment dialog box appears, make sure that Cardinal Bank is selected in the Bank Acct drop-down list box, and the Hand Written option button is selected. Since these were the settings used when you last paid your credit card bill, they should still be selected.

13. Select OK. Quicken switches to a new transaction in the Cardinal Bank register.
14. Record the transaction with the following entries:

Date	**9/30/95**
Num:	**120**
Payee:	**EasyCredit Card**
Memo:	**September 25th Statement**

15. Next, enter the remaining transactions for October that are listed in Figure 8-11.

    After all of the charges, the balance is -957.00. Remember to enter the negative amounts you see in Figure 8-11 as positive numbers in the Charge column of the register.
16. Select Pay Credit Card Bill from the Activities menu.
17. Type **957** in the Charges, Cash Advances text box.
18. Type **0** in the Payments, Credits text box.
19. Type **957** in the New Balance text box, and select OK.
20. Since you'll be paying this credit card bill in full, mark all of the transactions in the two list boxes.
21. When your difference is 0, select Done.
22. When the Make Credit Card Payment dialog box appears, make sure that Cardinal Bank is selected in the Bank Acct drop-down list box, and the Hand Written option button is selected. Since these were the settings used when you last paid your credit card bill, they should still be selected.
23. Select OK. Quicken switches to a new transaction in the Cardinal Bank register.
24. Record the transaction with the following entries:

Date:	**10/31/95**
Num:	**128**
Payee:	**EasyCredit Card**
Memo:	**October 25th Statement**

You have now entered all of the checking and credit card transactions for September and October. Using the memorized and scheduled transactions makes entering all these entries easier. While you normally don't enter two full months of transactions in one sitting, these groups can still speed up entering normal monthly transactions, especially when you have many regular payments to make. Now that you have the transactions that you need for your budget report, follow these steps to create it:

HomeBase

Reports | More Reports

1. Select Home from the Reports menu, and then select Monthly Budget. You can also click the Reports icon, and then select the Home option button and Monthly Budget from the list box.
2. Type **8/1/95** in the From text box.
3. Type **10/31/95** in the To text box.
4. Select Customize.
5. Clear the Cents In Amounts check box under Show.
6. Select the Accounts option button, and then unmark the Cardinal Saving account.
7. Select OK, and the Monthly Budget report appears.

This report lists, for each budgeted category, the amount budgeted and actually spent as well as the difference between the two. By looking over the report, you can see where you have spent more than you intended.

Wide Reports

The Monthly Budget report you just generated is wider than your window, and may be difficult to comprehend until you understand its structure. In this section, you explore the budget report and become more familiar with Quicken reports.

Use the scroll bars, the arrow keys, PAGE UP, PAGE DOWN, HOME, and END to become familiar with the appearance of the Monthly Budget report. It's easy to move around the report. Pressing HOME returns you to the top-left corner of the wide-screen report. END takes you to the bottom-right corner of the report. PAGE UP moves you up one screen, and PAGE DOWN moves you down one screen. When you are moving around in the report, you move from one actual number to another. Pressing ENTER or double-clicking an actual number creates a QuickZoom report that details the transactions that the actual number represents.

When you print wide reports, use a small font and landscape orientation, if your printer supports these options. This significantly increases the amount of information that can print on a page. When you print wide-screen reports, Quicken numbers the pages so that you can easily follow the flow of the report.

Using the Budget Report

The steps for preparing and printing a budget report will become familiar with a little practice. The real issue is how to use the information. Let's look at a budget report that combines three months, and discuss some of its findings.

Move to the lower-right side of the quarterly Monthly Budget report. The report shows that you spent $1,041.00 more than you had budgeted for the quarter. You can see that part of the explanation for the actual outflows exceeding the inflows is due to $361.00 being transferred to savings. Most of us would not view that as poor results. On the other hand, if you move up in the report, you can see that you have spent $582.00 more on furniture than you had budgeted. This may be because sale prices justified deviating from the budget, but it could also be compulsive buying that can't be afforded over the long run. If you find yourself over budget, the "Dealing with an Over-Budget Situation" box provides some suggestions for improving the situation.

Figure 8-12 shows the budget summary for the period 8/1/95 through 10/31/95. It was produced by requesting a Monthly Budget report using Half Year in the Column drop-down list box for the column heading. The report does not use quarters for the column heading because Quicken's quarterly reports use standard quarter endings. The report will combine August and September for the quarter ending September 30 and show October separately. Using a half year for the column heading and limiting the report to 8/1/95 through 10/31/95 combines these three months. The Cents In Amounts check box in the Customize Report dialog box was cleared to display only whole dollar amounts. Remember that the information in the Budget column came from the budgeted amounts you established earlier in this chapter. The information in the Actual column is summarized from the register entries recorded in your Cardinal Bank and EasyCredit Card accounts. You can also request a Cash Flow report by month for the budget period and examine the monthly outflow patterns. You might want to print out itemized category information for some categories during the period for a more detailed analysis of expenditures. This report is created by highlighting an amount and pressing ENTER or by double-clicking it.

Quicken Graphs That Show Budget Results

Quicken can create graphs that help you monitor your budget. Quicken's different graph options are under the Graphs selection on the Reports menu. Both the Income and Expense graphs and the Budget Variance graph provide tools for monitoring your budget; you can select these and other types of graphs from the Graphs submenu.

You may be interested in the composition of your expenditures in order to identify areas of major costs and see if any of them can be reduced. To display a graph showing expense composition on your screen, follow these steps:

HomeBase

Reports | Income/Expense Graph

1. Select Graphs from the Reports menu, then Income and Expense. You can also select the Graphs icon in the icon bar, then the Income and Expense Graph option button.

Budget Report by Half Year
8/1/95 Through 10/31/95

Category Description	8/1/95 Actual	- Budget	10/31/95 Diff
INFLOWS			
Salary	4,758	4,758	-0
FROM Cardinal Saving	0	0	0
TOTAL INFLOWS	4,758	4,758	-0
OUTFLOWS			
Auto:			
Fuel	83	90	7
Total Auto	83	90	7
Clothing	175	210	35
Dining	165	165	0
Entertain	200	165	-35
Furniture	767	185	-582
Groceries	648	600	-48
Medical	370	360	-10
Misc	250	225	-25
Mort Pay	1,050	1,050	0
Telephone	80	90	11
Utilities:			
Electric	112	75	-37
Gas	55	60	5
Total Utilities	167	135	-32
TO Cardinal Saving	961	600	-361
TOTAL OUTFLOWS	4,916	3,875	-1,041
OVERALL TOTAL	-158	883	-1,041

A three-month budget summary
Figure 8-12.

2. Type **8/95** in the From text box.
3. Type **10/95** in the To text box.
4. Select Create.

Quicken's graphs let you take a quick look at your budget picture.

Quicken displays the graph shown in Figure 8-13. The window actually displays two graphs. The first one, the bar graph at the top of the window, shows the comparison between inflows and outflows each month. The pie graph at the bottom of the window displays what percentage of your total income each category constituted. If you select Next 10 at the bottom of the window, you see a pie graph displaying the next ten categories. In the first pie graph, the categories that are not separately listed are combined into an "Other" category.

Dealing with an Over-Budget Situation

Expenses cannot outpace income indefinitely. The extent of the budget overage and the availability of financial reserves to cover it dictate the seriousness of the problem and how quickly and drastically cuts must be made to reverse the situation. Although the causes of an over-budget situation are numerous, the following strategies can help correct the problem:

- If existing debt is the problem, consider a consolidation loan—especially if the interest rate is lower than existing installment interest charges. Then don't use credit until the consolidated loan is paid in full.
- If day-to-day variable expenses are causing the overrun, begin keeping detailed records of all cash expenditures. Look closely at what you are spending for eating out, entertainment, and impulse purchases of clothing, gifts, and other nonessential items.
- Locate warehouse, discount, thrift, and used clothing stores in your area, and shop for items you need at these locations. Garage sales, flea markets, and the classified ads can sometimes provide what you need at a fraction of the retail cost.
- Be certain that you are allocating each family member an allowance for discretionary spending and that each is adhering to that amount.
- If you cannot find a way to lower expenses any further, consider a freelance or part-time job until your financial situation improves. Many creative people supplement their regular incomes with a small-business venture.
- Plan ahead for major expenses such as car insurance, property taxes, and so on by splitting the cost over 12 months and transferring each month's portion to savings until it is time to pay the bill. If you save for the expense, you can transfer the amount saved to your checking account the month of the anticipated expenditure.

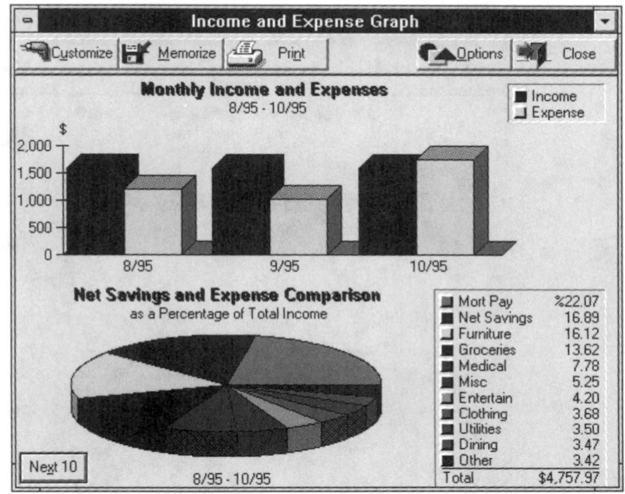

Income and Expense Graphs
Figure 8-13.

A graph can focus on the details for budget categories as well. You might want to look at categories that are either under or over budget, for example. To see a bar chart that displays the actual versus budgeted amounts for categories that are in your budget, follow these steps:

HomeBase

Reports | More Graphs

1. Select Graphs from the Reports menu, then Budget Variance. You can also select the Graphs icon in the icon bar, and then the Budget Variance Graph option button.
2. Type **8/95** in the From text box.
3. Type **10/95** in the To text box.
4. Select Create.

   The graphs shown in Figure 8-14 appear on your screen.

Feel free to experiment with the other graph types. None of your selections will affect register entries, so you don't have to worry about making mistakes.

Using the Progress Bar

Quicken 4 for Windows offers a new feature that can help you track your progress on individual budgeting goals, the Progress Bar. You can use the Progress Bar to track how well you match your budget in troublesome categories.

To set up and display the Progress Bar, follow these steps:

1. Select Progress Bar from the Plan menu. Quicken displays a blank Progress Bar at the bottom of your Quicken window.

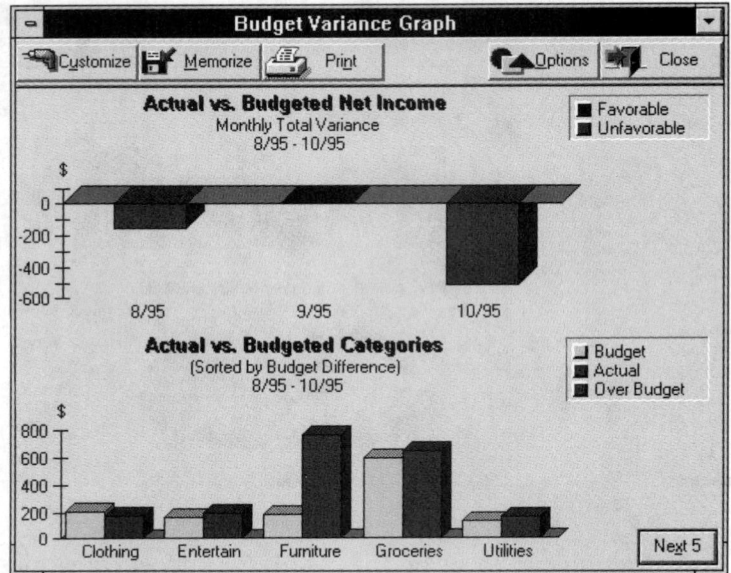

A Budget Variance Graph
Figure 8-14.

2. Select Cust at the right end of the Progress Bar to display this dialog box:

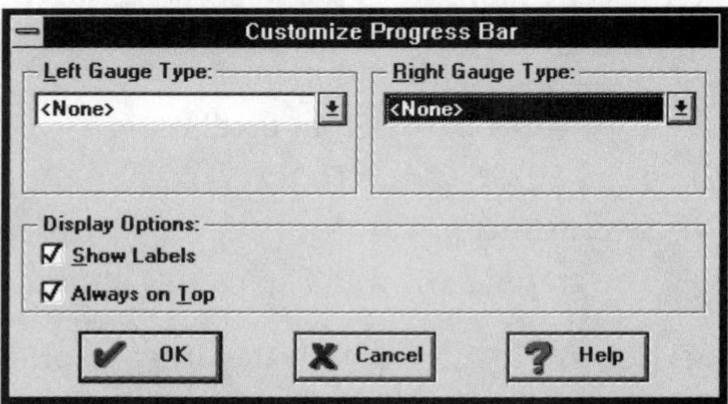

3. Select Budget Goal from the Left Gauge Type drop-down list box.
4. Select Choose Category.
5. Select Current Month from the Date Range drop-down list box.
6. Select Mort Pay from the Category list box, then OK.
7. Select Budget Goal from the Right Gauge Type drop-down list box.
8. Select Choose Category.

9. Select Current Month from the Date Range drop-down list box.
10. Select Dining from the Category list box, then OK.
11. Select OK.

You may encounter a problem, because of the dates used in this book. The Progress Bar displays your progress in this budget category for the *current* month. Since it is unlikely that you are actually entering the transactions in this book in October 1995, your Progress Bar probably shows nothing. However, if your computer system's date were 10/15/95, your Progress Bar would look like this:

Close | Mort Pay Budget 10/95 350.00 350.00 | Dining Budget 10/95 45.00 55.00 | Cust

To remove the Progress Bar, select the Close button on the left.

Creating Savings Goals

Quicken 4 for Windows has included a new budgeting tool, called *savings goals*. These are not the same as savings accounts. Savings accounts are separate accounts from your checking accounts. When you transfer money between the two accounts in Quicken, you record an actual banking transaction. Sometimes, however, you don't actually want to transfer money from your checking account to your savings account. Instead, you just want to earmark some of the money in your checking account for a future purpose. You are essentially hiding it from yourself. For example, you may save money in your checking account to buy a washing machine or to allow for a night on the town at the end of the month when you plan to celebrate your anniversary.

With savings goals, you can create an "account" that doesn't actually exist. The money is actually still in your checking account, but is marked as being unavailable. You can view the progress of your savings in a separate Quicken register or with the Progress Bar.

HomeBase

Planning | Savings Goals

Creating a Savings Goal

To create a savings goal for a new computer, follow these steps:

1. Select Savings Goals from the Plan menu.
2. Select New.

3. Type **New Computer** in the Goal Name text box.
4. Type **1500** in the Goal Amount text box.
5. Enter **8/31/96** in the Finish Date text box, and select OK. The new savings goal looks like the one in Figure 8-15.

Transferring Money to a Savings Goal

Now that you've created the savings goal, you need to indicate the money you are setting aside. To do so:

1. Select Contribute to open the following dialog box, which shows the completed entries you need to make:

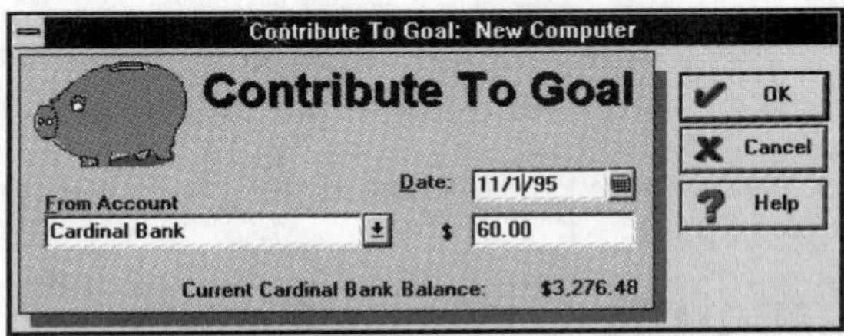

2. Select Cardinal Bank in the From Account drop-down list box.
3. Type **60** in the text box after the $, and then select OK.

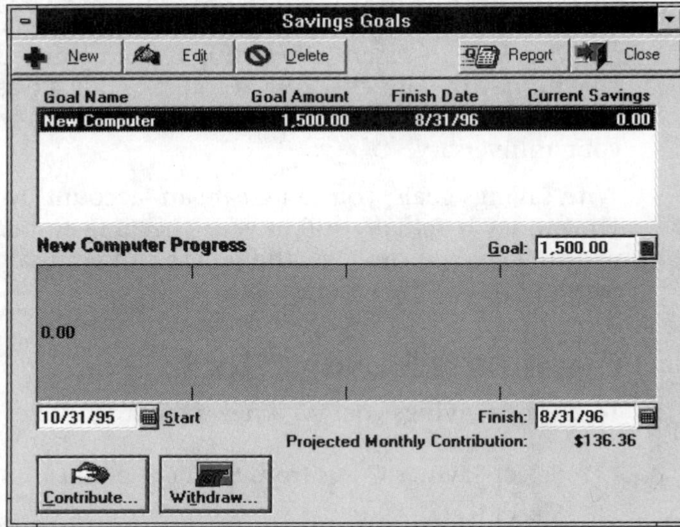

The Savings Goals feature allows you to record future savings projects.
Figure 8-15.

4. Enter **11/1/95** in the Date text box and select OK.
5. Switch to the register window for Cardinal Bank, and move to the last transaction.

   Quicken subtracts the 60 dollars you've contributed to the New Computer savings goal just as if you'd written a check to a savings account at your bank. However, you haven't actually removed any money from your checking account; you've just hidden it.
6. You'll notice the new Hide Sav. Goal check box at the bottom of the register window. Select this check box, and the transfer to the New Computer account disappears.

   Your register now shows only those transactions that the bank reports on its statement.

To see how close to achieving your savings goal you are, you can switch to the New Computer register. The easiest way to do this is select the New Computer account selector just beneath the transactions in your register window. This displays the new account register, showing the 60 dollars you've now saved for your new computer.

If you select Savings Goals from the Plan menu again, Quicken displays a "gas-gauge" of your progress to the current date. However, this gauge, like the Progress Bar, uses the current date, so this gauge remains at 0% until your computer's date is after November 1995.

Spending Savings Goal Money

Since your savings goal account isn't a real one, you can't spend money directly from it. After all, how would you write a check from an account the bank knew nothing about? To spend the money you have saved, you need to enter a transaction transferring the money back to the account in which it's really stored. Then you can write a check from that account and delete the savings goal account.

For example, suppose you won a new computer in a raffle. Rather than continuing to save the money for the computer, you want to close out this savings goal account. To do this:

HomeBase

Planning | Savings Goals

1. Select Savings Goals from the Plan menu to switch to the Savings Goals window.

2. Highlight the New Computer goal in the list box, and select Delete. Quicken displays the Delete Savings Goal dialog box shown here:

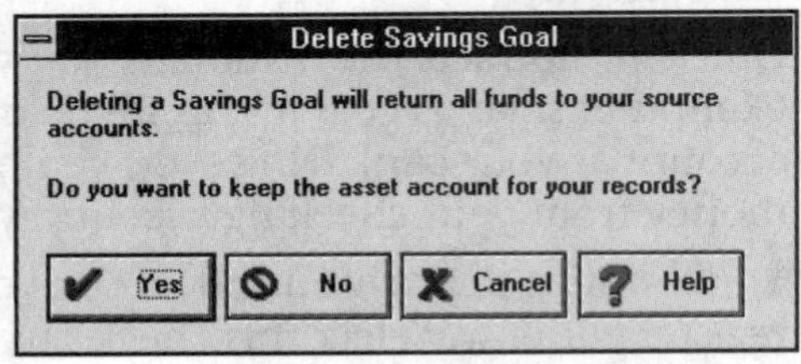

3. Select No.

   Quicken deletes the goal, the account, and all transactions between the goal's account and the Cardinal Bank account. It's as if the savings goal never existed. Now, you can write the check for the computer knowing that the account has sufficient funds.

4. Select Close to remove this Savings Goals window.

Forecasting Your Budget

Quicken 4 for Windows includes two features for forecasting your budget. You can use the Financial Calendar as a simple way to see the total effects of your current and scheduled transactions. You can use this feature to get a feel for whether your current or planned rate of expenditure is feasible. Quicken 4 for Windows also offers the more sophisticated Forecasting feature. With this feature, you can predict future budget based on estimated incomes or expenses, scheduled transactions, and historical averages. You can create several different scenarios to judge the effect of different choices.

Forecasting with the Financial Calendar

You were introduced to the Financial Calendar in Chapter 7 as a way to schedule transactions. All your transactions are noted in the calendar. The calendar can also forecast how well you comply with your budget and how your financial planning is progressing. Follow these steps to view a graph presented by the Financial Calendar that you can use to help with your financial planning.

HomeBase

Day To Day | Financial Calendar

1. Select the Calendar icon from the icon bar, or select Financial Calendar from the Activities menu to open the Financial Calendar window.
2. Select View from the Calendar's button bar.
3. Select Show Memorized Txns to remove the check mark.
4. Select View, then click Show Account Graph.

The list of transactions at the right side of the window disappears, and the calendar expands to fill the extra space. The calendar raises from the bottom of the window to have room to show account balances.

5. Click Next or Prev in the button bar to display the calendar for 8/95. The Financial Calendar should now look like Figure 8-16.

The graph shows the total account balances for all your accounts on each day of the month. The graph uses your actual transactions, scheduled transactions, and transaction groups to calculate these balances.

Predicting Your Financial Future

Quicken 4 for Windows includes a new Forecasting feature that graphs a projection of your finances based on your actual and budgeted data. This graph can help you do "what-if" planning for your budget. You can add or remove income or expenses to find out what would happen to your financial picture if a specific element changed. For example, the Forecasting graph can show you the effect of moving to a more or less expensive apartment. The Forecasting feature uses three sources of information to predict your financial picture into the future:

- Your income and expenses to date, taken from your registers or budget
- Scheduled transactions that you can see in your Financial Calendar
- Amounts you enter to affect the forecast

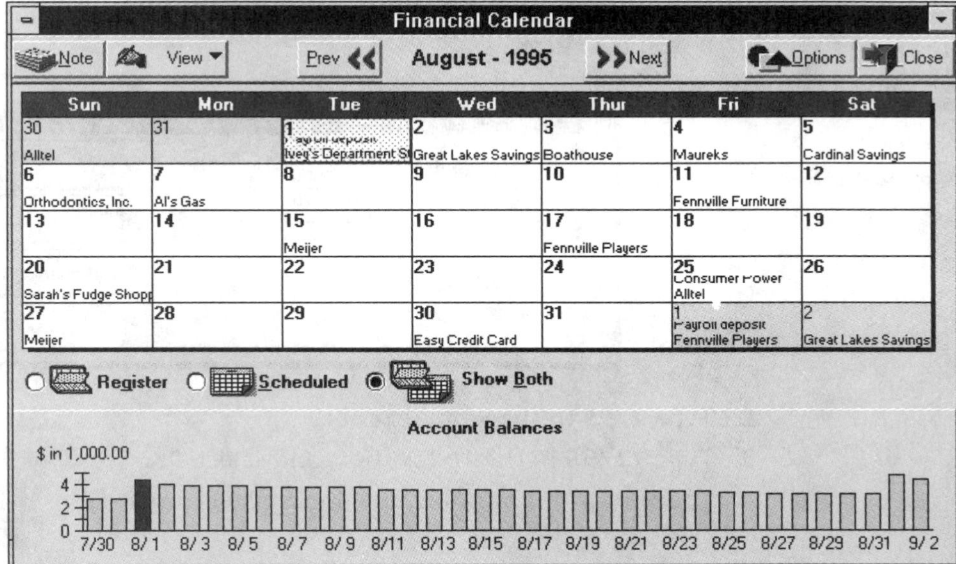

Account Balances graphs in the Financial Calendar
Figure 8-16.

Creating a Forecasting Scenario

You'll want to create your forecasting graph to see how current expenditures will affect your future financial picture. At this point, however, because of the way that the Forecasting feature works, you are going to need to change the system date on your computer. This is not something you normally do when creating forecasting graphs with your own data. However, if you want the forecasting graph you will create to match the ones shown here, you need to change the date to match the example. To change your system date:

1. Open the Windows Control Panel by double-clicking its program icon in the Program Manager. This program icon is normally found in the Main program group window.
2. Double-click the Date/Time icon in the Control Panel.
3. Change the Date to 11/1/95.
4. Select OK.

Caution: As soon as you finish with this exercise, change the date on your computer system back to the current date.

To create a forecasting scenario, follow these steps:

HomeBase

Planning | Forecasting

1. Select Forecasting from the Plan menu. Quicken opens the Forecasting window and then opens the Automatically Create Forecast dialog box, shown here:

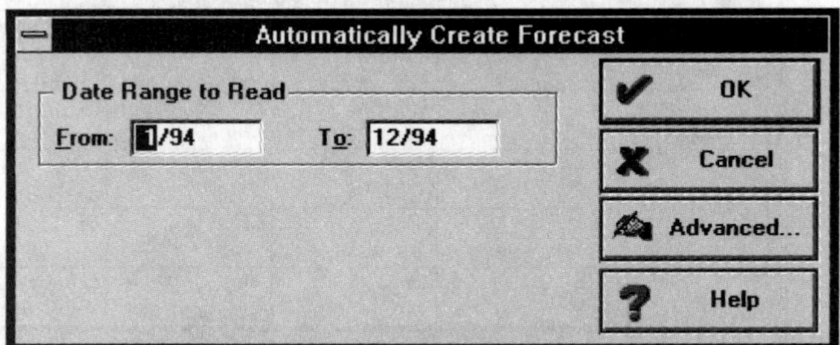

2. Type **7/95** in the From text box.
3. Type **11/95** in the To text box, and select OK.

   The Forecasting window now looks like Figure 8-17.

4. Select the Income button in the lower-right corner of the window, opening the Forecast Income Items dialog box.

   The Known Items are those that are scheduled. You've scheduled your payroll deposits so they are included there. Quicken will also estimate transactions based on those in your accounts. Since you've never recorded income from a source other than your salary, there are no estimated income items. However, you can add one. Here's how:
5. Select New.
6. Type **Yearly Bonus** in the Description text box.
7. Type **1600** in the Amount text box.
8. Select Yearly in the Frequency drop-down list box.
9. Enter **12/31/95** in the Next Scheduled Date text box, and select OK.
10. Select the Expense Items option button at the top of the dialog box.

    Now the list box displays your known and estimated expenses, like the one in Figure 8-18.
11. Select New. Since you are considering buying a cabin in the mountains, you want to enter a new projected expense, the cabin's mortgage payment, and see how that affects your budget.
12. Type **Cabin** in the Description text box.
13. Type **275** in the Amount text box.

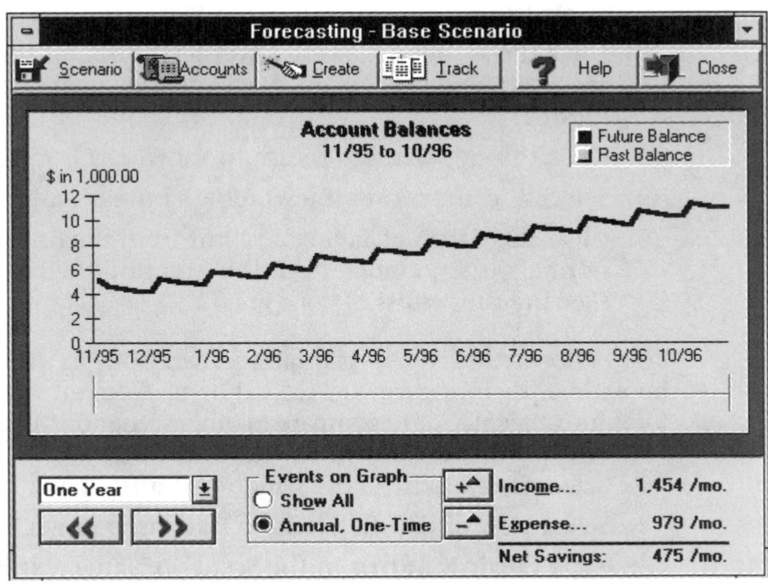

The default Forecasting graph
Figure 8-17.

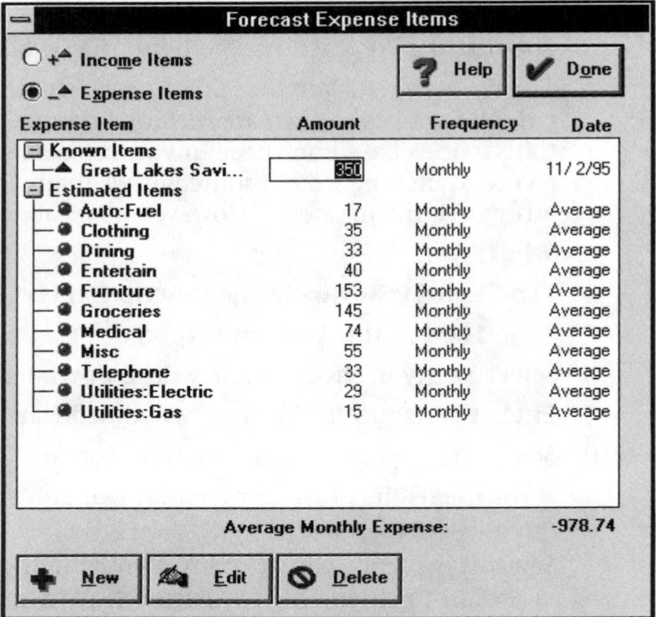

The Forecast Income/Expense Items dialog box
Figure 8-18.

14. Select Monthly in the Frequency drop-down list box.
15. Enter **11/2/95** in the Next Scheduled Date text box, then select OK.
16. Now that you've added the changed expenses you are considering, select Done.
17. Click the >> button in the lower-left corner of the Forecast window to see how these new expenses will change your budget for the next six months
18. Click the << button to return to showing 11/95 through 10/96.
19. Select Accounts from the window's button bar.
20. Clear the Cardinal Saving account from the list box. Since you don't normally spend much from this account, the large sum growing in it is skewing the results of your graph.

You've now created a new planning scenario, one in which you will earn a yearly bonus and pay mortgage on a second home. You can save this specific scenario for future reference or to compare to other scenarios. To save this scenario:

1. Select Scenario from the window's button bar.
2. Select New under the Scenario Data drop-down list box.
3. Type **Cabin&Bonus** in the Scenario Name text box, and select OK.

4. Select Done. You've now saved the scenario.

In the future, you can recall this scenario to review how the cabin and bonus would affect your budget. To compare two scenarios, open the Manage Forecast Scenarios dialog box by choosing Scenario from the button bar. Choose the Compare Current Scenario With option button and select a scenario from the adjoining drop-down list box. Quicken displays the projection line of the chosen scenario, and the selected projection line. This lets you compare the effects of two different scenarios, as shown in Figure 8-19.

Caution: You must now reset your computer's date to the current date. If you don't, you will encounter problems with some programs and in correctly identifying your files or working with your own Quicken files.

Don't hesitate to play around with the Forecasting feature. Nothing you enter in the forecasting feature will affect your scheduled transactions, budget, or register entries. By developing many alternative forecasts, you can take a variety of situations into account. For example, you can use this feature to determine the effect of changing jobs, being laid off, or buying a new car or house. These forecasts can help you plan for any number of financial windfalls and disasters and to determine the final result of your current spending practices.

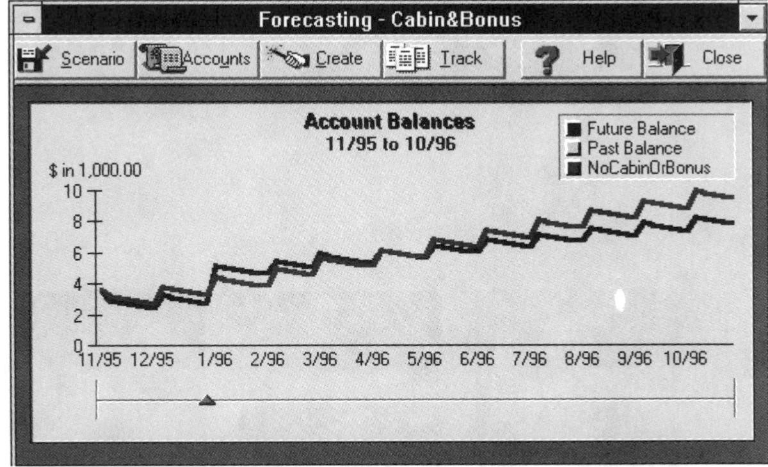

Comparing two forecasting scenarios
Figure 8-19.

CHAPTER

USING QUICKEN to ORGANIZE TAX INFORMATION

The benefits of using Quicken for your financial planning and monitoring go beyond recording transactions. In addition to handling your budget entries and reports, Quicken can also help in preparing your taxes. Although using Quicken won't necessarily make tax preparation fun, it can reduce the tax-time crunch considerably by organizing your tax information throughout the year.

If you plan your categories and classes correctly and complete all your entries faithfully, the hard part is done. You can then use Quicken's reports to provide the entries for specific lines on tax forms.

In this chapter, you'll see in more detail how Quicken can help you at tax time. After looking at a few ideas for organizing tax information, you'll learn how to:

- Modify some transactions from earlier chapters to provide additional tax information
- Prepare tax summary information as a report
- Assign Quicken categories to lines within tax schedules
- Use tax-related categories for federal income tax withholdings and state income tax withholdings
- Establish a category for local income tax withholdings
- Split entries for mortgage payments into mortgage interest and payments against the principal

In later chapters, you'll learn how to combine Quicken's personal tax-related reports with business reports. These two types of reports combine to form a powerful tax-monitoring and planning tool.

Note: Keep in mind that Quicken reports alone are not sufficient documentation for proving tax-deductible expenses. See the "Essential Tax Documentation" list in this chapter for materials that may help you substantiate expense claims in case of an IRS audit.

Quicken Tax Overview

The organization Quicken offers can make tax time much easier for you.

In Quicken, categories are defined as tax related or not tax related and can be assigned to tax schedules. You can change the tax-related status and tax schedule assignment of any of the existing categories by editing the current category in the category list. You can also define the tax-related status for any new category as you enter it.

Defining and using classes for your transactions enables you to collect useful details about your financial transactions. Assigning tax schedules and lines to categories allows Quicken to accumulate the information you need for specific line items on tax forms such as Form 1040 (U.S. individual return), Schedule A (itemized deductions), Schedule B (interest and dividends), and Schedule E (royalties and rents). Figures 9-1 and 9-2 show two of these forms.

Once you know Quicken well, you can refine information gathering even further. For example, you may decide to tag specific tax information by setting up classes for transactions that are tax related and specific to a particular tax form. At the end of the year, you can have Quicken print the transactions that you need for a particular line. In your own Quicken system, you may want to identify the specific forms associated with these items. For example, "Tax Fed/1040" indicates a class for transactions affecting Form 1040. Another approach is to create a class that represents a line item on a specific form. For example, "Mort Int/A—9A" is very specific. The class entry "A—9A" indicates Schedule A, line 9A—mortgage interest paid to financial institutions. You could then have Quicken generate the tax-related information by tax form or line item and use these totals to complete your taxes.

Essential Tax Documentation

The entries in your Quicken register are not enough to convince the IRS that you incurred expenses as indicated. If audited, you will need documentation of each expense to substantiate your deductions. Although you may be able to convince the IRS to accept estimates for some categories based on other evidence, you'll be better off if you can present optimal proof, such as the examples listed in Table 9-1.

Expense Claimed	Proof
Dependents other than minor children	Receipts for the individuals' support. Records of the individuals' income and support from others
Interest	Creditor statements of interest paid
Investments	Purchase receipts and brokerage firms' confirmation receipts
Medical and dental care	Canceled checks with receipts indicating the person treated
Medical insurance	Pay stubs showing deductions or other paid receipts
Moving expenses	Itemized receipts and proof of employment for 12 months in your previous job
Pharmacy/drugs	Itemized receipts and canceled checks
Real estate taxes	Receipts for taxes paid. Settlement papers for real estate transactions in the current year
Unreimbursed business expenses	Itemized receipts, canceled checks, and mileage logs

Items You Can Use to Prove Expenses Claimed on Your Tax Return
Table 9-1.

Form **1040** Department of the Treasury—Internal Revenue Service
U.S. Individual Income Tax Return (L) **1993**

IRS Use Only—Do not write or staple in this space.

For the year Jan. 1–Dec. 31, 1993, or other tax year beginning , 1993, ending , 19 OMB No. 1545-0074

Label (See instructions on page 12.) **Use the IRS label.** Otherwise, please print or type.

LABEL HERE

Your first name and initial | Last name | **Your social security number**

If a joint return, spouse's first name and initial | Last name | **Spouse's social security number**

Home address (number and street). If you have a P.O. box, see page 12. | Apt. no.

City, town or post office, state, and ZIP code. If you have a foreign address, see page 12.

For Privacy Act and Paperwork Reduction Act Notice, see page 4.

Presidential Election Campaign (See page 12.)

Do you want $3 to go to this fund? Yes No

If a joint return, does your spouse want $3 to go to this fund?

Note: *Checking "Yes" will not change your tax or reduce your refund.*

Filing Status (See page 12.) Check only one box.

1 Single
2 Married filing joint return (even if only one had income)
3 Married filing separate return. Enter spouse's social security no. above and full name here. ▶
4 Head of household (with qualifying person). (See page 13.) If the qualifying person is a child but not your dependent, enter this child's name here. ▶
5 Qualifying widow(er) with dependent child (year spouse died ▶ 19). (See page 13.)

Exemptions (See page 13.)

6a **Yourself.** If your parent (or someone else) can claim you as a dependent on his or her tax return, **do not** check box 6a. But be sure to check the box on line 33b on page 2

b **Spouse**

c **Dependents:**

(1) Name (first, initial, and last name)	(2) Check if under age 1	(3) If age 1 or older, dependent's social security number	(4) Dependent's relationship to you	(5) No. of months lived in your home in 1993

If more than six dependents, see page 14.

No. of boxes checked on 6a and 6b
No. of your children on 6c who:
• **lived with you**
• **didn't live with you due to divorce or separation (see page 15)**
Dependents on 6c not entered above
Add numbers entered on lines above ▶

d If your child didn't live with you but is claimed as your dependent under a pre-1985 agreement, check here ▶
e Total number of exemptions claimed

Income

Attach Copy B of your Forms W-2, W-2G, and 1099-R here.

If you did not get a W-2, see page 10.

If you are attaching a check or money order, put it on top of any Forms W-2, W-2G, or 1099-R.

7 Wages, salaries, tips, etc. Attach Form(s) W-2 — 7
8a **Taxable** interest income (see page 16). Attach Schedule B if over $400 — 8a
b **Tax-exempt** interest (see page 17). DON'T include on line 8a — 8b
9 Dividend income. Attach Schedule B if over $400 — 9
10 Taxable refunds, credits, or offsets of state and local income taxes (see page 17) — 10
11 Alimony received — 11
12 Business income or (loss). Attach Schedule C or C-EZ — 12
13 Capital gain or (loss). Attach Schedule D — 13
14 Capital gain distributions not reported on line 13 (see page 17) — 14
15 Other gains or (losses). Attach Form 4797 — 15
16a Total IRA distributions — 16a — b Taxable amount (see page 18) — 16b
17a Total pensions and annuities — 17a — b Taxable amount (see page 18) — 17b
18 Rental real estate, royalties, partnerships, S corporations, trusts, etc. Attach Schedule E — 18
19 Farm income or (loss). Attach Schedule F — 19
20 Unemployment compensation (see page 19) — 20
21a Social security benefits — 21a — b Taxable amount (see page 19) — 21b
22 Other income. List type and amount—see page 20 — 22
23 Add the amounts in the far right column for lines 7 through 22. This is your **total income** ▶ — 23

Adjustments to Income (See page 20.)

24a Your IRA deduction (see page 20) — 24a
b Spouse's IRA deduction (see page 20) — 24b
25 One-half of self-employment tax (see page 21) — 25
26 Self-employed health insurance deduction (see page 22) — 26
27 Keogh retirement plan and self-employed SEP deduction — 27
28 Penalty on early withdrawal of savings — 28
29 Alimony paid. Recipient's SSN ▶ — 29
30 Add lines 24a through 29. These are your **total adjustments** ▶ — 30

Adjusted Gross Income

31 Subtract line 30 from line 23. This is your **adjusted gross income.** *If this amount is less than $23,050 and a child lived with you, see page EIC-1 to find out if you can claim the "Earned Income Credit" on line 56* ▶ — 31

Cat. No. 12600W Form **1040** (1993)

Federal Form 1040

Figure 9-1.

9

SCHEDULES A&B (Form 1040)

Department of the Treasury Internal Revenue Service (L)

Schedule A—Itemized Deductions

(Schedule B is on back)

▶ Attach to Form 1040. ▶ See Instructions for Schedules A and B (Form 1040).

OMB No. 1545-0074

1993

Attachment Sequence No. **07**

Name(s) shown on Form 1040 | **Your social security number**

Section	Line	Description	Box	Amount	Box	Amount
Medical and Dental Expenses		**Caution:** *Do not include expenses reimbursed or paid by others.*				
	1	Medical and dental expenses (see page A-1)	1			
	2	Enter amount from Form 1040, line 32. 2				
	3	Multiply line 2 above by 7.5% (.075)	3			
	4	Subtract line 3 from line 1. If zero or less, enter -0- ▶			4	
Taxes You Paid (See page A-1.)	5	State and local income taxes	5			
	6	Real estate taxes (see page A-2)	6			
	7	Other taxes. List—include personal property taxes ▶	7			
	8	Add lines 5 through 7 ▶			8	
Interest You Paid (See page A-2.)	9a	Home mortgage interest and points reported to you on Form 1098	9a			
	b	Home mortgage interest not reported to you on Form 1098. If paid to the person from whom you bought the home, see page A-3 and show that person's name, identifying no., and address ▶	9b			
Note: Personal interest is not deductible.	10	Points not reported to you on Form 1098. See page A-3 for special rules	10			
	11	Investment interest. If required, attach Form 4952. (See page A-3.)	11			
	12	Add lines 9a through 11 ▶			12	
Gifts to Charity (See page A-3.)		**Caution:** *If you made a charitable contribution and received a benefit in return, see page A-3.*				
	13	Contributions by cash or check	13			
	14	Other than by cash or check. If over $500, you **MUST** attach Form 8283	14			
	15	Carryover from prior year	15			
	16	Add lines 13 through 15 ▶			16	
Casualty and Theft Losses	17	Casualty or theft loss(es). Attach Form 4684. (See page A-4.) ▶			17	
Moving Expenses	18	Moving expenses. Attach Form 3903 or 3903-F. (See page A-4.) ▶			18	
Job Expenses and Most Other Miscellaneous Deductions (See page A-5 for expenses to deduct here.)	19	Unreimbursed employee expenses—job travel, union dues, job education, etc. If required, you **MUST** attach Form 2106. (See page A-4.) ▶	19			
	20	Other expenses—investment, tax preparation, safe deposit box, etc. List type and amount ▶	20			
	21	Add lines 19 and 20	21			
	22	Enter amount from Form 1040, line 32. 22				
	23	Multiply line 22 above by 2% (.02)	23			
	24	Subtract line 23 from line 21. If zero or less, enter -0- ▶			24	
Other Miscellaneous Deductions	25	Other—from list on page A-5. List type and amount ▶			25	
Total Itemized Deductions	26	Is the amount on Form 1040, line 32, more than $108,450 (more than $54,225 if married filing separately)? • **NO.** Your deduction is not limited. Add lines 4, 8, 12, 16, 17, 18, 24, and 25 and enter the total here. Also enter on Form 1040, line 34, the **larger** of this amount or your standard deduction. ▶ • **YES.** Your deduction may be limited. See page A-5 for the amount to enter.			26	

For Paperwork Reduction Act Notice, see Form 1040 instructions. Cat. No. 12614K **Schedule A (Form 1040) 1993**

Schedule A for itemized deductions

Figure 9-2.

Planning to Use Quicken for Taxes

Although you can record tax information in Quicken in several ways, the best method is to tailor your transaction entries to the information that your tax forms require. This is a good approach even if you have an accountant prepare your return. If you organize your tax information, your accountant won't have to—and you'll pay less for tax preparation as a result.

Start the planning process with the forms and schedules you filed last year. Although the forms change a little from year to year and you may not need to file exactly the same forms every year, last year's set of forms makes a good starting point. Form 1040, part of which is shown in Figure 9-1, is the basic tax form used by individuals. Schedule A, shown in Figure 9-2, is used for itemized deductions.

You can choose one of three methods to have Quicken accumulate information for the various tax forms and schedules that you need to prepare. The first method is to identify tax-related information using category assignments, then produce a tax summary at the end of the year containing all tax-related category entries. Although this is the simplest method, it provides the least detail.

Use the tax schedules option if you want to make the most of Quicken's tax support features.

With the second method, you also have the option of assigning each category and subcategory to a particular line of a tax schedule. Before you can do this, you need to check an Options setting. Select Options from the Edit menu or select the Options icon from the icon bar. Then select General. Make sure the Use Tax Schedules with Categories check box is selected—select it if necessary. Select OK and Close.

To assign a category to a tax schedule, display the category list by selecting Category & Transfer from the Lists menu or by pressing CTRL-C. Then highlight the category for which you want to make a tax schedule assignment, and select Edit. When the Edit Category dialog box appears, you can select the Tax-related check box. Then select a line of a tax schedule or form from the Form drop-down list box. The lines of the forms are given names rather than numbers to make your selection easier. If you use these methods, you can produce a tax schedule report that lists all tax-related entries by line within schedules.

Classes provide another option for organizing the tax information you need.

The third option for categorizing tax data is to use a class assignment. Class assignments provide a way to further organize categories and subcategories. You can assign multiple classes to your existing categories and subcategories. You make these assignments as you enter transactions by typing / followed by the class name after a category or subcategory. Although this approach involves more work than using Quicken's tax schedule assignments, it can provide the greatest level of detail within your existing category structure.

Selecting a Method that Works for You

If you have unreimbursed business expenses that exceed a certain percentage of your income, you might want to set up a class for Form 2106, which is used exclusively for these expenses. If you have Form 2106 expenses, you won't know until the end of the year if you have enough expenses to deduct them. With the class-code approach, you use a class called 2106 for unreimbursed business expense transactions, and you check the total at year's end. Assign this class code to all travel and entertainment expenses, meals, and professional association dues and subscriptions. Another approach would be to set up new categories for unreimbursed business expenses and assign these categories to lines in tax schedule 2106 with Quicken's Tax Schedule feature.

Be sure to keep an eye out for the timing of your expenses. *Expense recognition* determines which tax year expenses at the beginning or end of the year affect. This may pose a problem for you if you charge items, since the IRS recognizes an expense as occurring the day you charge it rather than the day you pay for it. For example, unreimbursed air travel charged in December 1994 and paid by check in January 1995 is counted in 1994 totals, because you incur the liability for payment the day you charge the tickets. A separate Quicken account for credit purchases makes these necessary year-end adjustments easier than when you just keep track of credit card payments from your checkbook.

You may decide to use classes rather than tax schedule assignments to categorize tax information. You may also decide your class codes should indicate more than the number of the tax form where the information is used. If you look at the forms shown in Figures 9-1 and 9-2, you see that each line where information can be entered has a number. For example, line 7 of your 1040 is "Wages, salaries, tips, etc.," which you can probably fill in with the total from the Salary category if you have only one source of income. But when you set up Quicken categories for income from several sources, you might want to assign a class called 1040-7 to each income transaction so that you can display a total of all the entries for this class. Likewise, you can set up classes for other line items, such as A-6 for real estate tax and A-13 for cash contributions. You could also set up 1040-21a for Social Security benefits and 1040-9 for dividend income, but if you decide to use classes, establish a class for only those lines that you are likely to use.

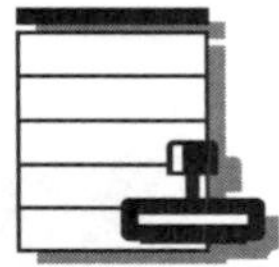

Remember: When entering a class, you must enter the category, a slash (/), and then the class.

If you own and manage rental properties, you must use Schedule E to monitor income and expenses for these properties. With Quicken, you can classify the income and expense transactions for Schedule E. Classes are almost a requirement for rental property management since the same types of expenses and incomes are repeated for each property. You might use the street address or apartment number to distinguish the transactions generated by different properties. You can use the Splits feature if one transaction covers expenses or income for more than one property.

Most of your entries will focus on the current tax year, but you might sometimes need longer-term tax-related information. When you sell assets such as a house or stock holdings, you can use information accumulated over the time you own the asset. Maintaining information on these assets in separate accounts is the best approach. Separate accounts can make it much easier to calculate the profit on the sale of the asset. For example, if you purchase a house for $100,000 and sell it five years later for $150,000, it might seem that the profit is $50,000. However, if you accurately record improvements such as a new deck and a fireplace, these amounts can be added to the cost of the asset since they are items that added value to the asset. When the $35,000 cost of these improvements is added to the price of the house, the profit is $15,000 for tax purposes. Take a look at the sample transaction in the next section and the tax reports before making your final decisions about classes and categories for your tax information. Depending on the complexity of your tax situation, simple category assignments might be sufficient.

Recording Detailed Tax Information

In Chapter 8, "Quicken as a Budgeting Tool," you recorded detailed transaction information in the account register for your Cardinal Bank checking account. Scroll through these transactions and notice the treatments of the monthly paycheck and mortgage payment transactions. For the paycheck, you entered the amount of the check after deductions for items such as FICA, federal withholdings, medical insurance, and state withholdings. For the monthly mortgage payment, you established a tax-related category called Mort Pay and used that for the entire payment. However, Quicken can provide much better tax-related information in both these areas. If you want Quicken to accumulate tax schedule information for you, you'll want to make some changes. The following sections show you how.

9

Gross Earnings and Salary Deductions

Highlight the first payroll transaction you recorded in your Cardinal Bank personal account register. The amount of the net deposit was $1,585.99—you didn't record any of the tax-related information for deductions. The entry you made there is adequate for maintaining a correct check register. It is also adequate for budgeting purposes, since you only need to match cash inflows and outflows, and the net amount of the payroll check represents the inflow for the period. However, for tax purposes, you need more information. If you complete the following entry, you will be able to monitor the amounts on your pay stub. You will also be able to verify the accuracy of your Form W-2 at the end of the year.

To expand the payroll transaction, you need some additional information. Your gross earnings for the pay period were $2,000.00. The deduction withheld for FICA taxes was $124.00, Medicare was $29.00, medical insurance was $42.01, federal taxes were $130.00, state taxes were $80.00, and local taxes were $9.00.

The following steps illustrate how you can use Quicken's Splits feature to capture all the information related to the tax aspects of your paycheck and still show the net deposit of $1,585.99 to the checking account.

1. With the August 1st payroll entry highlighted, select Splits. The Splits window appears.
2. Leave Salary as the category.
3. Type **Gross Wages Earned** in the Memo field.
4. Type **2000.00** in the Amount field.

   These modifications set your Salary category as your gross earnings for the period. When you record your paycheck this way, Quicken can accumulate your year-to-date gross earnings. After recording this portion of the transaction, you are left with -414.01 in the Amount field of the next line. This is Quicken's way of telling you there is currently a negative difference between the amount of the net deposit and the gross wages recorded. This difference equals the amount of the withholdings from your paycheck that you will record in the remaining steps.
5. Enter **Tax:Soc Sec** as the category.
6. Type **FICA Withholding** in the Memo field.
7. Type **-124.00** in the Amount field.

   Quicken records the information in the Splits window and leaves a balance of -290.01 on the next line. This category is predefined as tax related in Quicken, even though FICA withholdings are not ordinarily tax deductible on your Form 1040. Quicken works this way because you should monitor the amount of your FICA withholdings if you change jobs during the year. Since there is a limit on the amount of earnings taxed for Social Security, switching jobs can cause you to pay more than you owe. The second employer will not know the amount that the first employer withheld. You can include excess FICA payments on your Form 1040 with other withholding amounts (on line 58). If you earn less than the upper limit, you won't use this category when you prepare your taxes.

8. Enter **Tax:Medicare** as the category, **Medicare Withholding** in the Memo field, and **-29.00** in the Amount field.
9. Enter **Medical** as the category, **Health Insurance** in the Memo field, and **-42.01** in the Amount field.
10. Enter **Tax:Fed** as the category, **Federal Income Tax** in the Memo field, and **-130.00** in the Amount field.
11. Enter **Tax:State** as the category, **State Income Tax** in the Memo field, and **-80.00** in the Amount field.
12. Enter **Tax:Local** as the category.

    When you try to move to the next field, Quicken displays the Set Up Category dialog box. To set up the category, follow these steps:
13. Type **Local Tax** in the Description text box.
14. Select the Tax-related check box.
15. Select OK.
16. Type **Local Income Tax** in the Memo field.
17. Type **-9.00** in the Amount field.

    Now your Splits window looks like this:

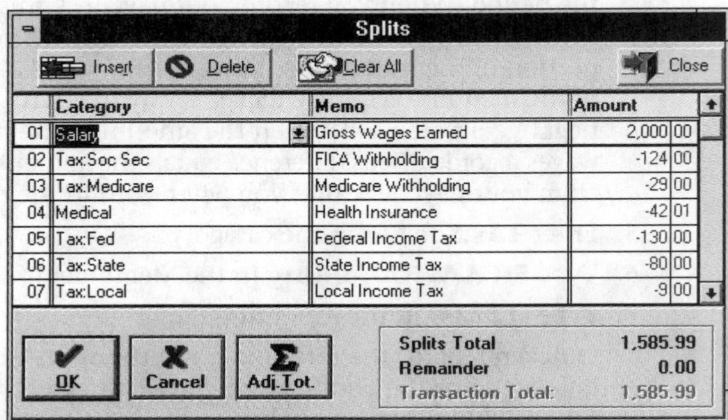

Notice that there is no balance left to explain in the Splits window.

18. Select OK, and Quicken returns you to the register window.
19. Select Record to tell Quicken to accept the changed transaction.

After you complete this process, all the information in the Splits window is recorded in your accounts. Your reports will show gross earnings for tax purposes at $2,000.00, with tax-related deductions for FICA, Medicare, medical insurance, and federal, state, and local taxes.

Mortgage Principal and Interest

The mortgage payment transaction recorded in Chapter 7, "Expanding the Scope of Financial Entries," is fine for recording changes to your checking account balance or monitoring budgeted expenses. However, it doesn't capture the tax-related aspects of the transaction. Although you identified the transaction as tax related, the mortgage principal and interest were not isolated. You would not be able to tell how much to list on your tax return as interest expense. Perhaps your bank will provide you with a statement that lists this information at the end of the year. In some cases, the bank even divides your previous month's payment among principal, interest, and escrow on the current month's bill. However, if you purchased your home from a private individual, you won't receive this information. You can have Quicken calculate it for you, since accurate records are necessary to take the mortgage interest expense as a tax deduction. Quicken will continue to assist you by organizing it in the recording process.

On your screen, highlight the first Great Lakes Savings & Loan mortgage payment of $350.00 on 8/2/95, which you recorded in Chapter 7. Using Quicken's Splits feature, you will modify the record of this transaction to distribute the payment between principal and interest. For the steps outlined here, it is assumed that you know which payment number you are making. Another assumption is that you pay your insurance and taxes directly to the insurer and local taxing unit with checks recorded separately in your register. If the financial institution has established an escrow account for these payments, you can easily add that amount to this transaction, assuming that you have defined a tax-related category called Escrow.

The following steps show you how to create a loan amortization schedule and track your mortgage principal and interest payments:

1. With the first mortgage payment entry highlighted, select Financial Planners from the Plan menu, then select Loan.
2. Type **39999** in the Loan Amount text box.
3. Type **9.519** in the Annual Interest Rate text box.

4. Type **25** in the Number of Years text box.
5. Type **12** in the Periods Per Year text box.
6. Select Schedule to view the schedule.

   The top part of the schedule is shown here:

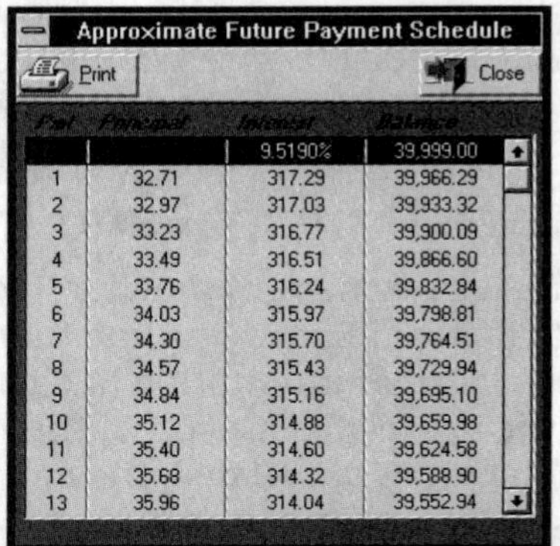

Pmt	Principal	Interest	Balance
		9.5190%	39,999.00
1	32.71	317.29	39,966.29
2	32.97	317.03	39,933.32
3	33.23	316.77	39,900.09
4	33.49	316.51	39,866.60
5	33.76	316.24	39,832.84
6	34.03	315.97	39,798.81
7	34.30	315.70	39,764.51
8	34.57	315.43	39,729.94
9	34.84	315.16	39,695.10
10	35.12	314.88	39,659.98
11	35.40	314.60	39,624.58
12	35.68	314.32	39,588.90
13	35.96	314.04	39,552.94

   You can print it out for future reference by selecting Print. Since you are about to make your fifty-third payment, look down the schedule for payment 53 to get the numbers you need.

7. Select Close, then Close to return to the register.
8. Make certain your Great Lakes Savings & Loan transaction for August is highlighted.
9. Select Splits, and the Splits dialog box appears.
10. Enter **Mort Prin** in the category field.

    Since you do not have the Mort Prin category in your Category List, Quicken prompts you to create it. Type **Mortgage Principal Exp** in the Description text box for this category. Do not select the Tax-related check box.

11. Type **Principal Part of Payment** for the memo.
12. Type **49.33** to record the portion of the transaction related to principal.
13. Enter **Mort Int** in the second category field.
14. Type **Interest Part of Payment** for the memo.

The Splits window should now look like this:

Splits

Insert | Delete | Clear All | Close

	Category	Memo	Amount	
01	Mort Prin	Principal Part of Payment	49	33
02	Mort Int	Interest Part of Payment	300	67
03				
04				
05				
06				

OK | Cancel | Adj. Tot.

Splits Total 350.00
Remainder 0.00
Transaction Total: 350.00

15. Select OK, and Quicken returns you to the highlighted mortgage payment transaction in your register.
16. Select Record to record the new split transaction information.

After you record these two transactions, you can see the benefits of having Quicken organize the information. You should now memorize this transaction again so you can easily record it each month. To do this, move to the transaction and select Memorize Transaction from the Edit menu, or press CTRL-M. Select No when prompted about memorizing percentages, then select OK and Replace. In the next section, you take a look at the tax information you have entered into your Quicken system.

Printing Quicken's Tax Reports

HomeBase

Reports | More Reports

You can use Quicken's tax reports to get the detailed information you need to prepare your taxes. In this section, you'll examine reports generated by using the information from the Cardinal Bank account register for the first month (8/1/95 through 8/31/95). Follow these steps to generate Quicken's Tax Summary report:

1. From the account register, click the Reports icon; then select the Home option button and select Tax Summary from the list box, or select Home from the Reports menu, and then select Tax Summary.
2. Enter **8/1/95** in the From text box.
3. Enter **8/31/95** in the To text box.
4. Select Customize.
5. Select the Accounts option button.

6. Clear the marks for all accounts except Cardinal Bank.
7. Select OK.

   The Tax Summary report appears on your screen. You can use the arrow keys to move through the report.
8. Select Print from the report's button bar.
9. Select Print. Quicken prints the tax summary by category, as shown in Figure 9-3.

The Tax Summary Report

By default, Quicken prints the complete details for each tax-related category. This format enables you to use the totals generated at the end of the tax year for entry on your tax returns. The following table indicates where each of the totals generated in Figure 9-3 would have been used on a 1993 1040 form.

Expense Category	Location on Tax Return
Total Salary Income	Form 1040, line 7
Total Federal Tax	Form 1040, line 54
Total Medical & Dental	Schedule A, line 1
Total Mortgage Interest Exp	Schedule A, line 9a
Total State Tax	Schedule A, line 5
Total Local Tax	Schedule A, line 5

These totals also provide an excellent summary and could prove useful in the event of an IRS tax audit inquiry.

As you will see in Chapter 11, "Creating Custom Reports," all Quicken reports can be customized for many different report formats (reports that cover months, quarters, half years, and so on). In Chapter 8, you compared a report prepared for a single account, Cardinal Bank, to a report prepared for all accounts. The report for all accounts used the Bank checking accounts, the cash accounts, and the credit card accounts from the PERSONAL file.

Here, Figure 9-3 shows a report that was prepared for a single account, Cardinal Bank. Figure 9-4 shows a Tax Summary report that includes all the accounts in the PERSONAL file. Note that in this figure, the second column from the left (Acct) shows the source of the tax-related transaction. In this report, all the sources are from the Cardinal Bank account. In a more complex situation, this type of report would be useful in tracking the source of a tax-related transaction. For year-end tax purposes, a report of all your accounts provides an overview by category that integrates the various accounts. When you prepare your taxes, you should select the report format best suited to your needs.

9

Tax Summary Report by Category
8/1/95 Through 8/31/95

8/31/95
PERSONAL-Cardinal Bank

Date	Num	Description	Memo	Category	Clr	Amount
	INCOME/EXPENSE					
	INCOME					
	Salary					
8/1/95	DEP	Payroll deposit	Gross Wages Earned	Salary		2,000.00
	Total Salary					2,000.00
	TOTAL INCOME					2,000.00
	EXPENSES					
	Medical					
8/1/95	DEP	Payroll deposit	Health Insurance	Medical		-42.01
8/6/95	106	Orthodontics, Inc.	Monthly Orthodontics Payment	Medical		-100.00
	Total Medical					-142.01
	Mort Int					
8/2/95	104	Great Lakes Savings & Loan	Interest Part of Payment	Mort Int		-300.67
	Total Mort Int					-300.67
	Tax:					
	Fed					
8/1/95	DEP	Payroll deposit	Federal Income Tax	Tax:Fed		-130.00
	Total Fed					-130.00
	Local					
8/1/95	DEP	Payroll deposit	Local Income Tax	Tax:Local		-9.00
	Total Local					-9.00
	Medicare					
8/1/95	DEP	Payroll deposit	Medicare Withholding	Tax:Medicare		-29.00
	Total Medicare					-29.00
	Soc Sec					
8/1/95	DEP	Payroll deposit	FICA Withholding	Tax:Soc Sec		-124.00
	Total Soc Sec					-124.00
	State					
8/1/95	DEP	Payroll deposit	State Income Tax	Tax:State		-80.00
	Total State					-80.00
	Total Tax					-372.00

A partial Tax Summary report for the Cardinal Bank checking account
Figure 9-3.

Tax Summary Report by Category
8/1/95 Through 8/31/95

8/31/95
PERSONAL-Bank,Cash,CC Accounts

Date	Acct	Num	Description	Memo	Category	Clr	Amount
	INCOME/EXPENSE						
	INCOME						
	Salary						
8/1/95	Cardi...	DEP	Payroll deposit	Gross Wages Earned	Salary		2,000.00
	Total Salary						2,000.00
	TOTAL INCOME						2,000.00
	EXPENSES						
	Medical						
8/1/95	Cardi...	DEP	Payroll deposit	Health Insurance	Medical		-42.01
8/6/95	Cardi...	106	Orthodontics, Inc.	Monthly Orthodontics Paym...	Medical		-100.00
	Total Medical						-142.01
	Mort Int						
8/2/95	Cardi...	104	Great Lakes Savings & Loan	Interest Part of Payment	Mort Int		-300.67
	Total Mort Int						-300.67
	Tax:						
	Fed						
8/1/95	Cardi...	DEP	Payroll deposit	Federal Income Tax	Tax:Fed		-130.00
	Total Fed						-130.00
	Local						
8/1/95	Cardi...	DEP	Payroll deposit	Local Income Tax	Tax:Local		-9.00
	Total Local						-9.00
	Medicare						
8/1/95	Cardi...	DEP	Payroll deposit	Medicare Withholding	Tax:Medicare		-29.00
	Total Medicare						-29.00
	Soc Sec						
8/1/95	Cardi...	DEP	Payroll deposit	FICA Withholding	Tax:Soc Sec		-124.00
	Total Soc Sec						-124.00
	State						
8/1/95	Cardi...	DEP	Payroll deposit	State Income Tax	Tax:State		-80.00
	Total State						-80.00
	Total Tax						-372.00

A Tax Summary report for PERSONAL file accounts
Figure 9-4.

Note: The Tax Summary and Tax Schedule reports shown in this chapter show transactions from 8/1/95 through 8/31/95 because those are the only transactions you have entered. Normally, when you create a tax-related report, you use transactions from the entire reporting period, which is usually a year.

Another report format is shown in Figure 9-5. In this case, Quicken was instructed to print only the Medical category. This information was included in the report shown in Figure 9-3, but you can see that filtered reports become useful as you increase the number of recorded transactions and want details on particular items. The procedures for generating this type of report are covered in Chapter 11.

A final point: by default, every Quicken report displays the date the report was prepared in the upper-left corner. When you use a Quicken report to make your financial decisions, always check the report date to ensure you are using the most recent report.

The Tax Schedule Report

If you choose to assign categories to tax schedules and lines, you will want to create a Tax Schedule report. This report provides useful information only if you have edited your categories and assigned them to the schedules and forms where you want the income and expenses they represent to appear. Figure 9-6 shows a section of a Tax Schedule report that displays Schedule A medical expenses. These expenses are the same as those you saw in Figure 9-5, where a filter was used to create a Tax Summary report. Keep in mind that you would have to print many filtered Tax Summary reports to get the same information contained in one Tax Schedule report.

Tax Summary Report by Category

8/1/95 Through 8/31/95

8/31/95

PERSONAL-Bank,Cash,CC Accounts

Date	Acct	Num	Description	Memo	Category	Clr	Amount
	INCOME/EXPENSE						
	EXPENSES						
	Medical						
8/1/95	Cardi...	DEP	Payroll deposit	Health Insurance	Medical		-42.01
8/6/95	Cardi...	106	Orthodontics, Inc.	Monthly Orthodontics Paym...	Medical		-100.00
	Total Medical						-142.01
	TOTAL EXPENSES						-142.01
	TOTAL INCOME/EXPENSE						-142.01

A sample Tax Summary report showing a specific category
Figure 9-5.

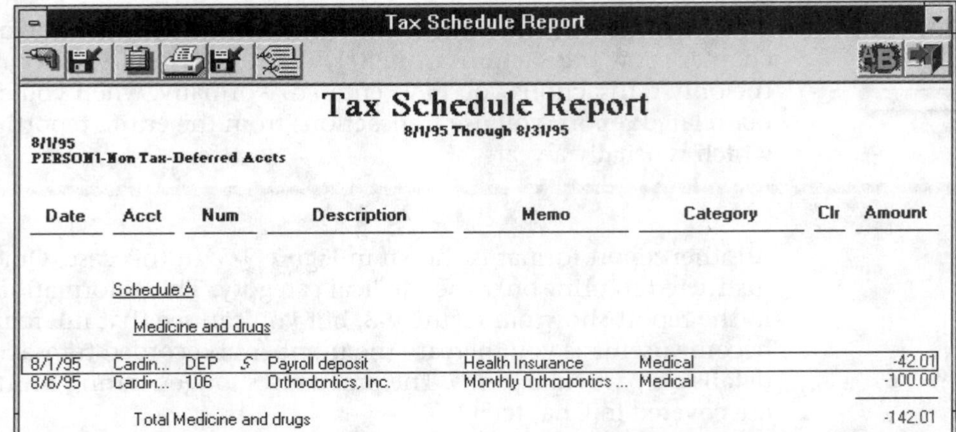

Schedule A medical expenses in a Tax Schedule report

Figure 9-6.

HomeBase

Reports | More Reports

To produce the Tax Schedule report, first make sure that medical expenses are assigned to the "Medicine and Drugs" line of Schedule A. They are selected by default, if you selected the Use Tax Schedules With Categories check box, as described earlier in this chapter. Then select Home from the Reports menu and Tax Schedule; or select the Reports icon, select the Home option button, and select Tax Schedule from the list box. Select OK to accept the default title and time period for the report, or change the title and time period and then select OK.

Quicken's Tax Planner

Use Quicken's new Tax Planner to avoid unpleasant surprises come April 15.

Quicken 4 for Windows offers a new feature, the Tax Planner. You can use the Tax Planner to estimate your taxes for the upcoming year, or to compare the effects of different financial decisions on your taxes. The Tax Planner can use the data you have entered in your Quicken register to figure out how much you are going to owe in taxes. You can also enter data to simulate changes in your financial conditions.

Note: The examples shown here use data from a different Quicken file, not the PERSONAL file you've created. This example lets you see a slightly more complex tax situation, in which there is salary income from a spouse.

To use the Tax Planner to estimate the taxes you are going to owe this year:

1. Select Tax Planner from the Plan menu.
2. Select Married-Joint from the Status drop-down list box.
3. Make sure that the current year appears in the Year text box.
4. Select Quicken Data. Quicken looks through all of the transactions entered in your accounts and extracts the data assigned to tax-related categories. Then it displays the Preview Quicken Tax Data window shown in Figure 9-7.

   This window shows the categories of data that Quicken has found in your accounts, their totals, and where Quicken is going to insert them into the Tax Planner. It also *annualizes* the information. Quicken has located the transactions from the beginning of the year to the current date. When it annualizes the amounts, it extends the data in the categories so that your data is for the entire year. However, any future changes, such as bonus income or layoffs, are not reflected.
5. Select OK to return to the Quicken Tax Planner window with the imported data. Depending on the data you have entered, the window might look something like Figure 9-8.

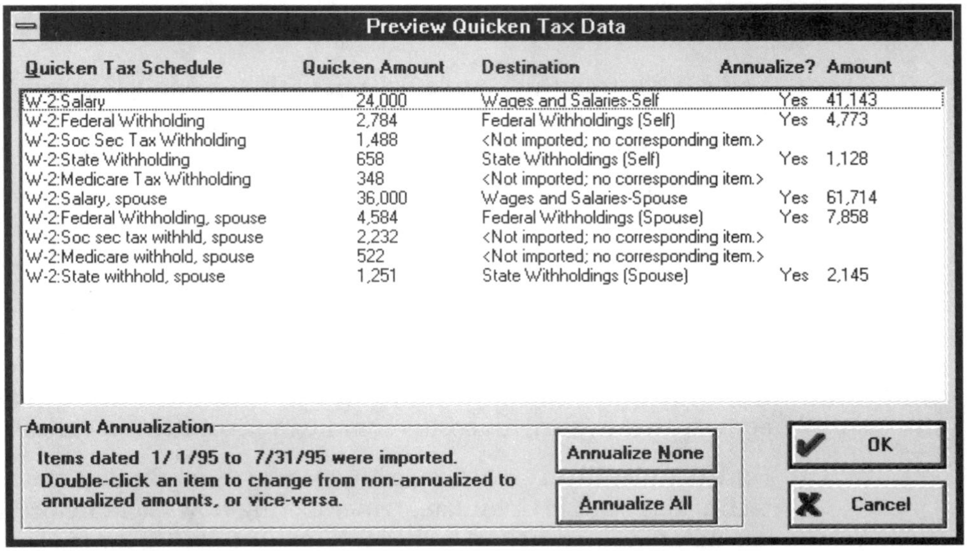

Preview Quicken Tax Data

Quicken Tax Schedule	Quicken Amount	Destination	Annualize?	Amount
W-2:Salary	24,000	Wages and Salaries-Self	Yes	41,143
W-2:Federal Withholding	2,784	Federal Withholdings (Self)	Yes	4,773
W-2:Soc Sec Tax Withholding	1,488	<Not imported; no corresponding item.>		
W-2:State Withholding	658	State Withholdings (Self)	Yes	1,128
W-2:Medicare Tax Withholding	348	<Not imported; no corresponding item.>		
W-2:Salary, spouse	36,000	Wages and Salaries-Spouse	Yes	61,714
W-2:Federal Withholding, spouse	4,584	Federal Withholdings (Spouse)	Yes	7,858
W-2:Soc sec tax withhld, spouse	2,232	<Not imported; no corresponding item.>		
W-2:Medicare withhold, spouse	522	<Not imported; no corresponding item.>		
W-2:State withhold, spouse	1,251	State Withholdings (Spouse)	Yes	2,145

Amount Annualization

Items dated 1/ 1/95 to 7/31/95 were imported.
Double-click an item to change from non-annualized to annualized amounts, or vice-versa.

Annualize None | Annualize All | OK | Cancel

The Preview Quicken Tax Data window
Figure 9-7.

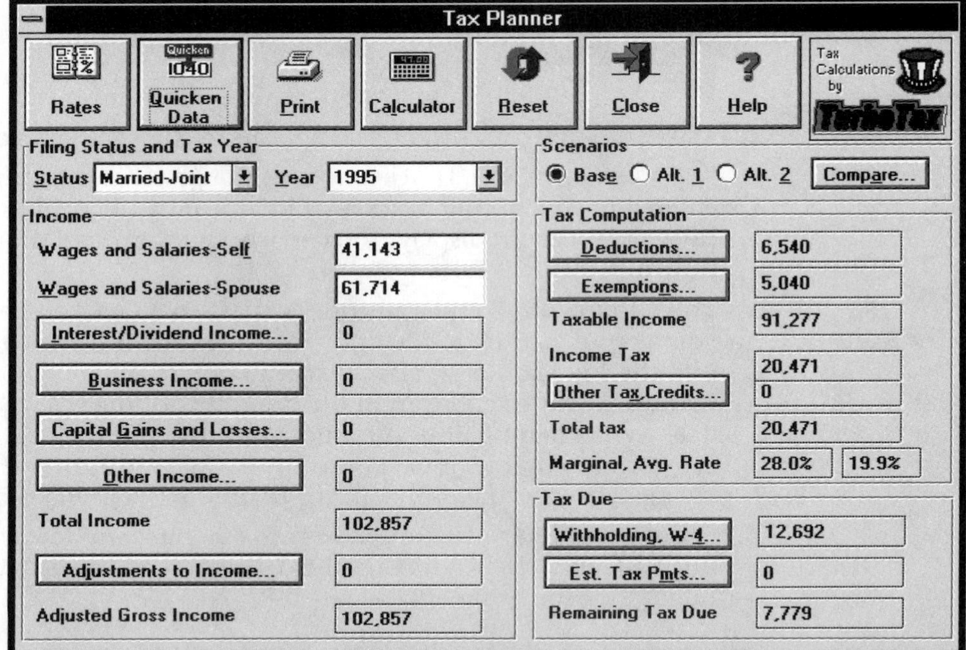

Creating a Tax Scenario using Quicken data
Figure 9-8.

You can see that this couple has not withheld enough in taxes in the last year. On April 15, they'll need to give the IRS $7,779.00 They should start thinking now about ways to reduce this tax bill or to save the money with which to pay it.

Comparing Tax Scenarios

While Quicken's new Tax Planner can warn you of unexpected tax bills coming due, it can also do a great deal more. It can help you compare the effect of different financial decisions on your tax bill. You can use this feature to help you ensure that you don't involve yourself in a financial activity that is going to cost you more in taxes than it will earn.

For example, Clara McFallon, a Quicken user, works part-time as a computer technician. An old classmate, remembering how Clara helped him learn to use his computer, has asked her to provide training for his law firm's support staff on the firm's new computers. Clara hasn't worked for herself before, but she's interested. First, though, she wants Quicken to tell her how this new business income will affect her tax bill since she will have to make a large investment in equipment and training material in order to conduct the classes.

First, Clara selects the Alt 1 option button, to create a second scenario. The base scenario is saved so that she can compare this new scenario to it later. When Quicken prompts about copying the current scenario, she selects Yes.

Then she selects Business Income, opening the Business Income/Loss - Schedule C dialog box. She enters **10000**, her projected fee, in the Revenue text box, and **8340**, her projected expenses, in the Other Allowable Expenses text box, and selects OK. Then she selects Compare, and the dialog box shown in Figure 9-9 appears.

Clara's total tax bill rises by $705.00, while her total income only rises by $1,613.00. Therefore, she'll only make $908.00 with this training contract. State and local taxes will further reduce this profit. Clara may choose either not to accept this contract, to request a larger fee, or to accept the job in the interest of establishing a reputation as a trainer.

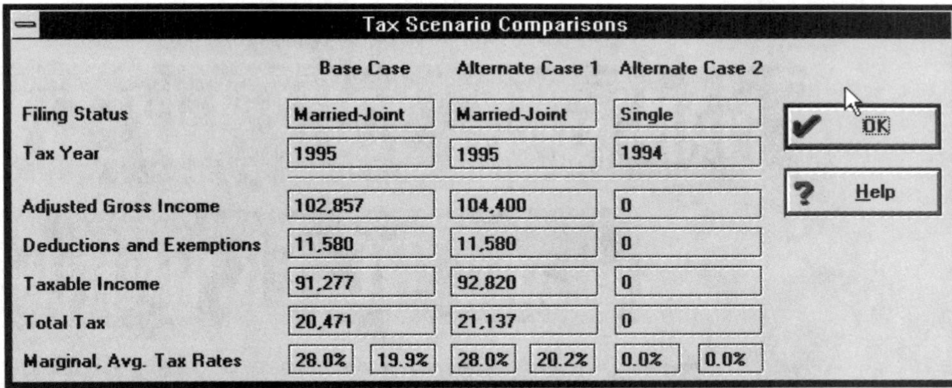

Tax Scenario Comparisons
Base Case
Alternate Case 1
Alternate Case 2
Filing Status
Married-Joint
Married-Joint
Single
Tax Year
1995
1995
1994
Adjusted Gross Income
102,857
104,400
0
Deductions and Exemptions
11,580
11,580
0
Taxable Income
91,277
92,820
0
Total Tax
20,471
21,137
0
Marginal, Avg. Tax Rates
28.0%
19.9%
28.0%
20.2%
0.0%
0.0%
OK
Help

The Tax Scenario Camparisons dialog box.
Figure 9-9.

CHAPTER

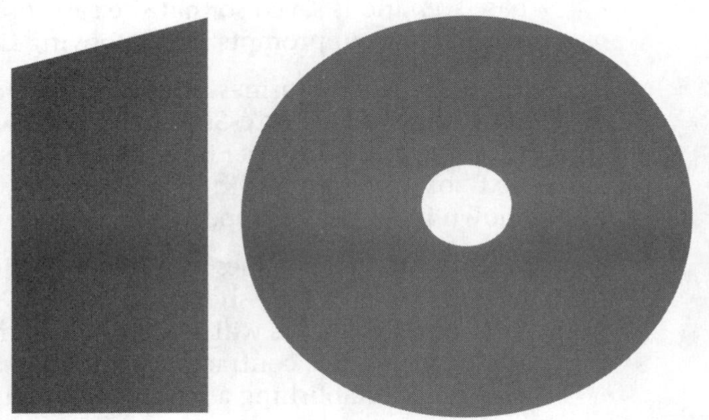

MANAGING YOUR INVESTMENTS and DETERMINING YOUR NET WORTH

In previous chapters, you used Quicken as a tool for financial planning and monitoring. Many of the activities were simply repetitive steps; you applied the same techniques repeatedly to record transactions. These activities were procedural—they did not require analysis before entry, and each transaction followed exactly the same steps.

Basic Concepts of Financial Management

You probably have financial goals you want to meet, such as buying a new car, purchasing a house, or retiring at age 60. Whatever your goals are, you need a certain level of financial resources to meet them. You can try accumulating the necessary resources by making deposits to a savings account or acquiring investments such as stocks and bonds. In this chapter, you learn to measure how successful you have been in your financial management activities.

One important measure of your financial status is your net worth. *Net worth* is a measurement of the difference between your total assets and your total liabilities at a given time. When you look at how your net worth changes over time, you can tell how well you have managed your resources and obligations. The process of preparing a statement of net worth differs from the procedural activities of earlier chapters. To estimate your net worth, you must make judgments estimating the worth of items you purchased earlier. Some investments, such as stocks, have a clearly defined market value because they are publicly traded. Other investments, such as land or real estate, require a more subjective evaluation.

Net worth is a financial measure for assessing your financial condition at a point in time.

To determine your net worth, you must look at more than just the assets you own. Although you may live in a $300,000 house, the bank probably owns more of it than you do. For calculating net worth, you must figure your remaining financial obligation on the house. If you still have a mortgage of $270,000, then you only own $30,000 of the house. The following equation is a simplified formula for determining net worth:

Financial resources - Financial obligations = Net worth

As you can see, your net worth describes your financial position after you consider all your financial holdings and deduct all your financial obligations. In accounting terms, your financial resources are items of value that you hold (*assets*). Your assets may include checking, savings, and money market accounts. These are examples of *liquid assets*—you can convert them readily into cash. Stocks, bonds, real estate holdings, and retirement funds (Individual Retirement Accounts [IRAs], SEP-IRAs, and Keogh plans) are other examples of investments you might hold. These assets are not as liquid as those in the previous group because they are harder to convert to cash. Also, since their cash value depends on the market at the time you try to sell them, you may not be able to get their full value at any one point in time. Your residence, vacation property, antiques, and other items of this nature are classified as *personal assets*. These assets are the least liquid because you may need considerable time to convert these assets to cash.

To plan strategies effectively, assess your financial condition at least once a year.

The other part of the net worth equation is your financial obligations. These include credit card balances and other short-term loans such as those for automobiles. In addition, you must consider long-term loans for the purchase of a residence, vacation property, or other real estate.

Net worth is the measure most people focus on when monitoring the success of their financial planning activities. The key point to remember is that net worth increases when your financial resources increase—through savings, compounding interest on an investment, appreciation, and reducing the amount of your financial obligations. Take a look at Table 1, which shows the effects of compounding interest on $100.00 invested monthly for 20 years. Here you can see the effects of compounding interest on an investment and the rapid rate at which even a small investment can grow.

Financial obligations are not necessarily a sign of poor financial management. If you borrow money and invest it so that it returns more than you are paying to use it, you have *leveraged* your resources. Of course, there is more risk in this avenue of financial planning. Don't take on more risk than you can handle—either financially or emotionally.

After completing this chapter, you will be able to begin monitoring your financial condition. In accounting terms, you can look at the bottom line. The *bottom line* in personal financial management is your net worth if you value your assets realistically. How you manage your financial assets and related obligations determines your net worth.

If you set an annual goal of increasing your net worth by a certain percentage, you can use Quicken to help you record your financial activities and monitor your success. For example, let's say you start using Quicken in January, and you record your assets and obligations throughout the year. You can then contrast your financial condition at the beginning and end of the year and compare the results with your goals. As a result of this comparison, you might decide to change your strategy in some areas of your financial plan. For instance, you might decide to switch from directly

Cash Value after	4% per year	6% per year	8% per year
1 year	$1,222	$1,234	1,245
2 years	$2,494	$2,543	$2,593
3 years	$3,818	$3,934	$4,054
4 years	$5,196	$5,410	$5,635
5 years	$6,630	$6,977	$7,348
10 years	$14,725	$16,388	$18,295
15 years	$24,609	$29,082	$34,604
20 years	$36,677	$46,204	$58,902

Effects of Compounding Interest on $100.00 Invested Monthly for 20 Years
Table 10-1.

managing your portfolio of stocks to using a mutual fund with its professional managers. Perhaps you want to shift some assets from real estate to liquid assets that can be converted to cash more quickly.

Establishing Accounts for This Chapter

In earlier chapters, you used bank accounts in a file called PERSONAL to record all your transactions. In this chapter, you learn about Quicken's other account types. These accounts are ideally suited for recording information about assets you own, debts you have incurred, and investments. You establish a file called INVEST for the examples in this chapter. This makes it easy to obtain the report results shown in this chapter even if you did not complete the examples in earlier chapters. This new file will be established for illustration purposes only. For your own financial planning, you will probably record all your activities in a single file. That way, Quicken will have access to all your personal information when preparing your reports and assessing your net worth.

Adding a New File

You have already used the following process in the "Adding a New File" section of Chapter 7, "Expanding the Scope of Financial Entries." In the new file, INVEST, you establish six new accounts to use throughout this chapter. Follow these steps to set up the new file:

1. Select New from the File menu.
2. Select New File, and select OK.
3. Type **INVEST** as the name of the file.

   Quicken creates several files using this filename and differing filename extensions. You must provide a valid filename of no more than eight characters. Do not include spaces or special symbols.
4. Make sure the selected directory is the one in which you normally store your data files.
5. Clear the Business check box to restrict this file to home categories, and select OK.

   Quicken displays the Create New Account dialog box, shown in Figure 10-1.
6. Select Investment to start creating your investment account.

HomeBase

Investments | Create Investment Acct

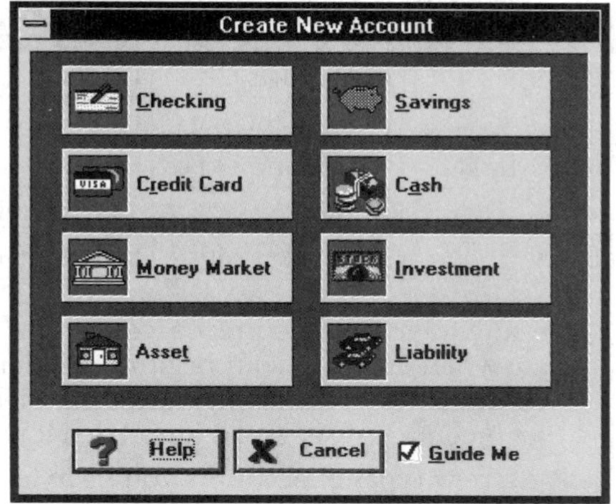

The Create New Account dialog box
Figure 10-1.

10

Note: These steps assume that you have left the Guide Me check box selected.

7. Type **Investments** in the Account Name text box.
8. Type **Personal Investments** in the Description text box, and select Next.
9. Select No, and then Next.

   If you were establishing a tax-deferred account, you would select Yes instead of No.
10. Select Schedule D:LT Gain/Loss-Security from both the Transfers In and Transfers Out drop-down list boxes, then select Next.
11. Select No, and then Done. (You would select Yes to establish an account containing only a single mutual fund.)
12. Quicken asks whether you want to add an icon that opens the investment account in Portfolio View to your icon bar. Select No.
13. Quicken may display a warning message to inform you of the advanced nature of investment accounts. Press ENTER to exit this warning. Because investment accounts are always established with a zero balance, you will not be asked to supply a beginning balance or date, as you are when you create other types of accounts.
14. Establish the five remaining accounts as follows:

Account Type	Account Name	Account Description	Balance
Checking	Great Lakes Chk	Personal Checking	4,000
Savings	Great Lakes Svg	Personal Savings	2,500
Money Market	Price Money Mkt	Money Market Account	15,000
Asset	Residence	444 Tardell	100,000
Liability	Great Lakes Mtg	Mortgage on Tardell	85,000

Be sure to enter the correct account type and balance. Use 8/1/95 as the date when entering your beginning balance for each account. When you establish your Liability account, select No when prompted to avoid having Quicken set up an amortized loan.

The three new types of accounts you have just established are used to separately maintain records for different assets and liabilities. A little background on when to use each account type will help you make selections when you start recording your own information.

Investment Accounts

Investment accounts are tailored to investments that have fluctuating prices, such as stocks, mutual funds, bonds, Individual Retirement Accounts (IRAs), and 401(K) plans. You can establish an investment account for each of your investment holdings or you can establish one investment account to parallel your transactions with a brokerage firm. In addition to recording information in special fields such as Shares and Amounts, you can use these accounts to track a cash balance in an account.

Asset Accounts

Asset accounts are appropriate for investments that have a stable price, such as CDs or Treasury bills. This type of account is also the most appropriate selection for assets that don't have a share price, such as real estate holdings.

Liability Accounts

You use liability accounts to record debts. A mortgage on a property and a car loan are examples of obligations that decrease your net worth and should be recorded in a liability account.

Establishing the Initial Balance in Your Investment Account

Investment accounts are always established with an initial balance of zero. To transfer existing holdings to an investment account, you transfer the shares in at cost. You can establish a complete list of securities before you begin or add the information for each security as you enter the information establishing its cost. To activate the investments account and record the securities, follow these steps:

1. Open the Account List, if necessary, by selecting the Accts icon from the icon bar.
2. Highlight the Investments account in the Account List window, and select Open.

   Quicken presents the Investments register. Notice that the fields differ from the bank account registers you have used previously. The Investments register is tailored to investments that have a share price.

   You can enter one of the actions listed in Table 10-2 by typing it or selecting it from the Action field's drop-down list box. You can also select one of the buttons in the window's button bar to display the appropriate action dialog box. Only the More button displays a list of the actions themselves. The other buttons open dialog boxes in which you enter data. Quicken interprets the data you enter, and enters the appropriate action into your register.
3. Select More from the button bar.

   ShrsIn is highlighted, as shown here:

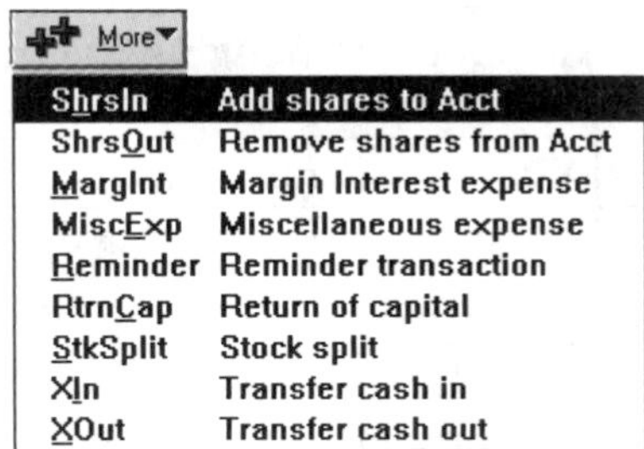

4. Select ShrsIn. The Add Shares To Account dialog box appears.
5. Enter **10/10/88** in the Date text box.
6. Type **Haven Publishing** in the Security text box, and press TAB to leave the text box.

Button	Action	Associated Transaction
Buy	Buy	Buying a security with cash from an investment account
	BuyX	Buying a security with cash from another account
Income	Div	Recording cash dividends in an investment account
	DivX	Transferring cash dividends to another account
	IntInc	Recording interest income in an investment account
	CGLong	Recording cash received from a long-term capital gains distribution
	CGLongX	Transferring cash received from a long-term capital gains distribution to another account
	CGShort	Recording cash received from a short-term capital gains distribution
	CGShortX	Transferring cash received from a short-term capital gains distribution to another account
	MiscInc	Recording cash received from miscellaneous income sources
More	ShrsIn	Transferring shares into an investment account
	ShrsOut	Transferring shares out of an account
	MargInt	Paying a margin loan from a cash account
	MiscExp	Paying miscellaneous expenses from a cash account
	Reminder	Used with the BillMinder feature to notify you of a pending event
	RtrnCap	Recognizing cash from the return of capital
	StkSplit	Changing the number of shares resulting from a stock split
	XIn	Transferring cash into an investment account
	XOut	Transferring cash out of an investment account
Reinvest	ReinvDiv	Reinvesting dividends in additional shares
	ReinvInt	Reinvesting interest in additional shares
	ReinvLg	Reinvesting long-term capital gains distribution
	ReinvSh	Reinvesting short-term capital gains distribution
Sell	Sell	Selling a security and leaving the proceeds in an investment account
	SellX	Transferring the proceeds of a sale to another account

Investment Actions
Table 10-2.

Quicken displays a Set Up Security dialog box. When the dialog box is completed for this example, it looks like this:

Note: You can use CTRL-Y at any time from the Investments register to open and update the entire Security list at once.

7. Type **HPB** in the Symbol text box.
8. Select Stock from the Type drop-down list box.
9. Select Growth from the Goal drop-down list box.
10. Clear the Tax-Free Security check box.
11. Enter **1.60** in the Est. Annual Income($) text box, and select OK.
12. Type **500** in the Number of Shares text box.
13. Type **20** in the Price Per Share text box and press TAB to leave this text box. Quicken calculates the contents of the Total Cost Basis text box.
14. Type **Initial Cost** in the Memo text box.
15. Select OK to record the transaction.

HomeBase

Investments | Investment Portfolio

Repeat the process for Ganges Mutual Fund and Glenn Packing, using the entries shown in Figure 10-2. Figure 10-3 shows a view of the same transactions in the Portfolio View window. You can get to this view by selecting the Port View button from the Investments register. You can record all your investment transactions in this view if you like. When the Set Up Securities dialog box appears for the new securities, use the following information.

	Ganges Mutual Fund	Glenn Packing
Symbol:	GMF	GPK
Type:	Mutual Fund	Stock
Goal:	Growth	Income
Est. Annual Income:	.40	1.00
Tax-free Security:	No	No

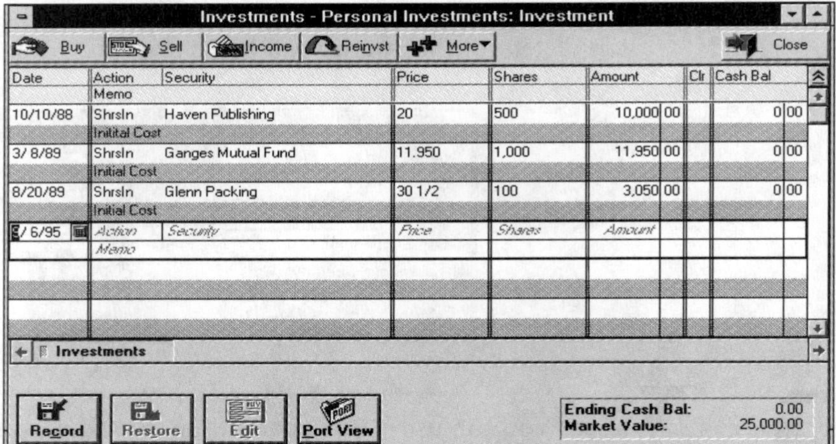

Initial transactions in the Investments register
Figure 10-2.

Although you now have your stock holdings entered at cost, you must perform an additional step to establish a current market value for your holdings.

Note: You can use the mouse in the Portfolio View window to display a list of special security actions. If you move the mouse pointer to either of the first two fields, it turns into a magnifying glass with a Z inside it. When you click the field with the right mouse button, you will be able to choose New Security, Edit Security, Delete Security, or Price History or Quick Report from the pop-up list box.

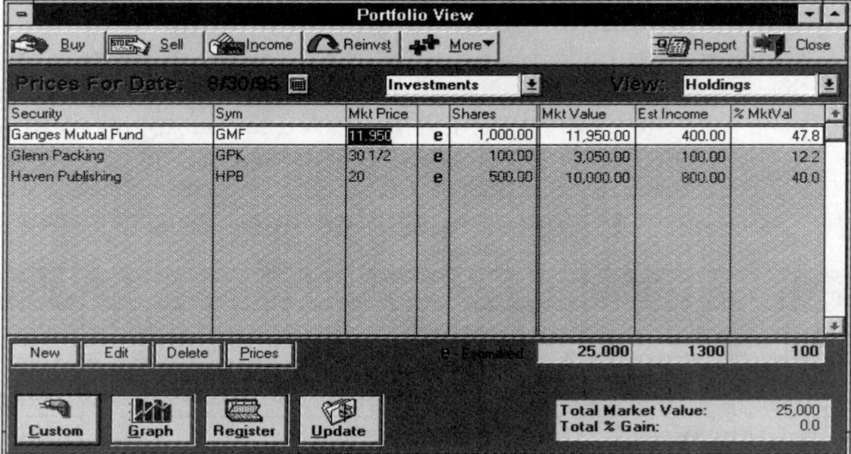

Initial investment transactions in the Portfolio View window
Figure 10-3.

Revaluing Your Assets to Market Value

When using Quicken to determine your net worth, you must assign values to your investments, liabilities, and assets. This means that you need to exercise some judgment in evaluating an asset's worth. Don't be intimidated; the task is not as complex as you might think. The easiest assets to evaluate are your checking, savings, and money market accounts. You know what your cash balance is in each of these accounts, so you can easily determine their value at any time. After you complete your monthly reconciliation, you have the current value of your accounts. If you own stocks and bonds, you can generally determine their current value by looking in the financial section of your local newspaper. If you own stock in a closely held corporation, you will have to use other sources for valuation—for example, recent sales of similar companies in that industry or in your area. If your assets are land holdings, you can ask a realtor familiar with the local area about the approximate value of your lot or other property holdings. You might also be able to use recent sale prices of similar properties in your area.

Valuing your residence presents similar problems. You know what you paid for the property, and with Quicken you can accumulate the additional cost incurred in improving it. It's more difficult to know what value to place on the property when you prepare your Net Worth report. Once again, try to determine the sale prices of properties in your area, and consider how your house compared in price with neighboring properties when you bought it. This provides a basis for comparison in the future. However, remember that improvements you made to your house may increase the value of your home relative to others in the area. For example, adding a new bath and renovating the kitchen may significantly enhance the value of your home over time.

When revaluing your assets, use prudent judgment so that your net worth determination produces a realistic assessment of your financial condition.

The amount you owe, or the associated liability, on your home should be easy to track. You receive annual statements from the financial institutions from which you have borrowed money for your residence and any home improvements. These statements indicate your remaining financial obligation.

Use prudent judgment when determining values for your assets. A conservative but not very useful approach would be to say that any assets whose values you cannot determine from external sources should be valued at what you paid for them. Accountants call this *historical cost.* For your own planning and monitoring, this is not a realistic approach to determining your net worth. Try to determine fair value, or what you think your home could be sold for today, by taking into consideration current national and local economic conditions, and use reasonable values. Those familiar with the local market will certainly have some knowledge of the value of homes in your area. Inflating the value of your properties does not help you accurately assess your net worth.

Follow these steps to enter the current value of your stocks:

1. From the Investments register, select Port View, and then select Price Update from the View drop-down list.

   Your next step is to establish the date for which you want to enter the market values: 7/31/95.
2. Press CTRL-G, enter **7/31/95**, and then select OK.

   You can also select 7/31/95 from the drop-down calendar in the Prices For Date field.
3. With Ganges Mutual Fund highlighted, type **13.210** in the Mkt Price field, and press DOWN ARROW.
   You can enter new market prices for any of the investments, or you can use the + and - keys to change them by 1/8 point in either direction.
4. With Glenn Packing highlighted, press - four times to change the market price to 30, and then press DOWN ARROW.
5. With Haven Publishing highlighted, type **22**, and press UP ARROW.

   Figure 10-4 shows the Portfolio View window after you have entered the new prices. Notice that Quicken shows arrows that indicate whether the new price is higher or lower than the previous price.
6. Select Register to return to the Investments register.

Viewing Portfolio Information at a Glance

Later you will see how to use Quicken to prepare reports from the Investment Report menu. However, if you're like most investors, you'll want

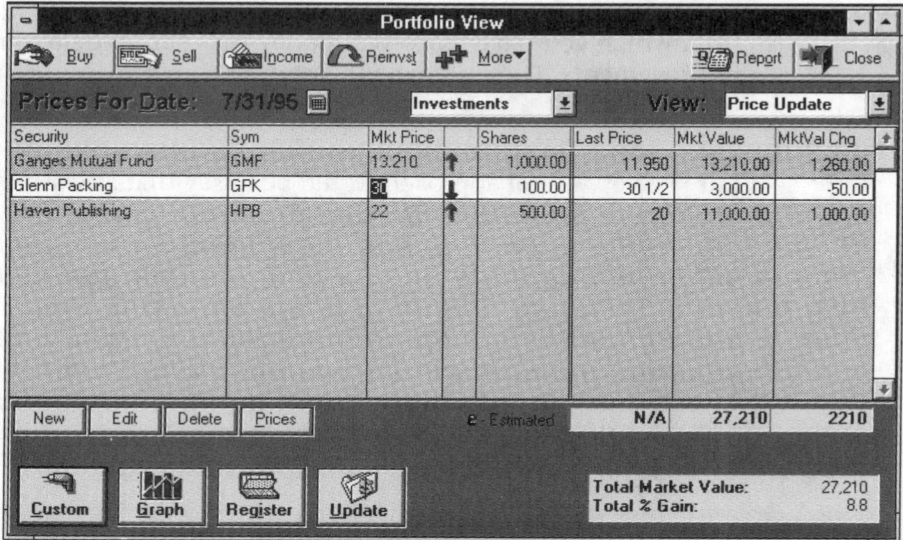

Updated prices in the Portfolio View window
Figure 10-4.

to take a quick look at your investments without preparing the formal reports. You can get a quick glance at your investment account from the Portfolio View window by using the View drop-down list. This list gives you several options for viewing your investment account data: Holdings (the default setting for the Portfolio View window), Performance, Valuation, Price Update, Custom 1, and Custom 2.

The Holdings view shows the percentage of your total account balance that each element in your portfolio represents. You also see the estimated income expected for each security based on past payouts for the security, and the latest market price for each security.

The Performance view shows the return on investment for each of your account holdings, both in dollar values and as a percentage. This view also displays the amount invested in each security.

The Valuation view compares the current market value of each of your holdings with the amount you have invested in each security. The total shows the market value of your holdings at the most recent date at which you updated your valuations.

The Price Update view compares the current and previous price of each of your holdings. It also shows the current market value of each holding and how much the price update changed the total market value.

The preset Custom 1 view illustrated in Figure 10-5 shows the percentage gain or loss on each security in your portfolio. It also shows the average cost, the number of shares held, and the latest market price entered for each security.

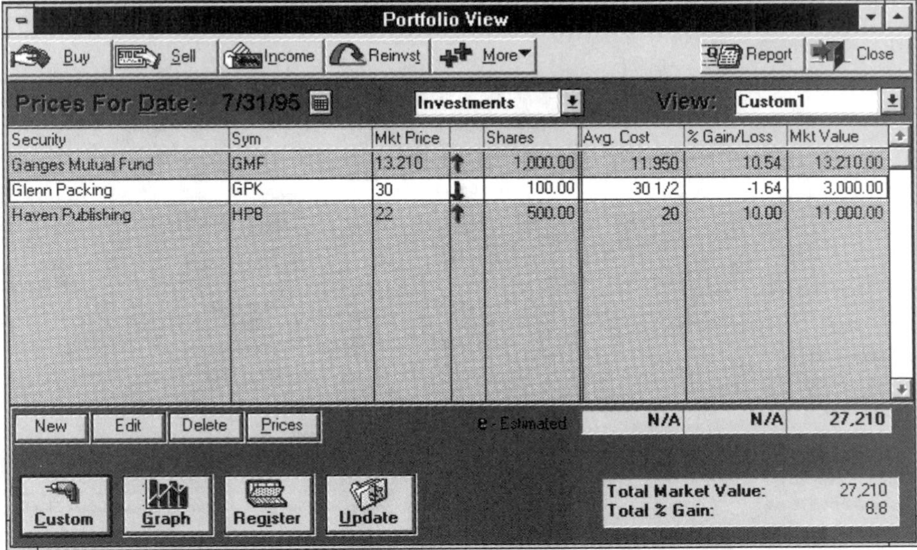

Preset Portfolio View column headings for the Custom 1 view

Figure 10-5.

In addition to using these preset views of your portfolio, you can create customized views. Select the Custom button in the Portfolio View window to open the Portfolio View Settings dialog box shown in Figure 10-6. You can select different customization options on each of the four tabs: Accounts, Securities, Miscellaneous, and Custom Views.

The Accounts tab lets you select which of your investment accounts you want to include in the Portfolio View window. You might only want to view your holdings with a single broker. The Securities tab lets you select which securities you have set up that you want to appear in the Portfolio View window. For example, you may choose to look at only your technology or utilities securities.

The Miscellaneous tab provides access to a number of customization features. You can select the period for which you want Quicken to compute your portfolio's returns under Return Calculations. The default setting is Entire History, which shows information recorded throughout the entire history of your Investment account. You can also select This Year; Last 365 Days; or From..., to specify a day from which you want your return computed. Finally, you can choose a layout for presenting basic information about each security: the default Name/Symbol, Name Only, Name/Type, or Name/Type/Symbol.

Select the Custom Views tab to set up the Custom 1 and Custom 2 view options. You can select from 18 column heading options for the last three columns of your Portfolio View window. The preset views for both custom settings are Avg. Cost in Column 1, % Gain/Loss in Column 2, and Mkt Value in Column 3. You can assign a custom name to your reports in the View Name text boxes.

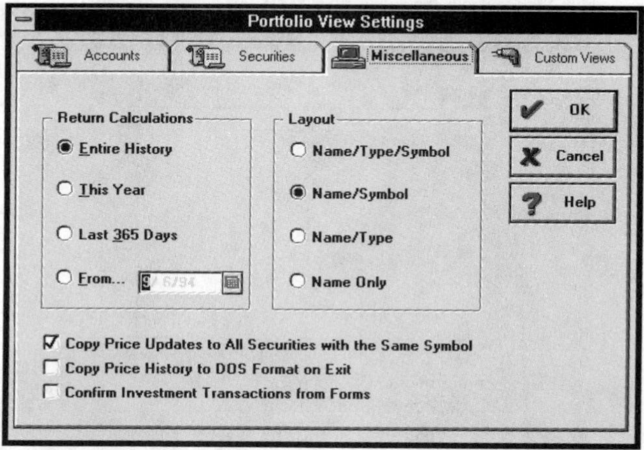

Portfolio View Settings dialog box
Figure 10-6.

Using Quicken's Portfolio Price Update

You can use Portfolio Price Update to update your investment reports in a timely and efficient manner.

The manual method of updating security prices works fine when you have only a few stocks. If your portfolio is large, keeping your stock values up to date takes a lot of time. Quicken offers a new trick to make updating your stock prices in a timely fashion much easier. The fee for this service is quite reasonable. A charge of $2.95 a month lets you update your portfolio prices six times a month. You can update as many as 250 stocks at a time. Simply include the standard ticker code for the stock as its symbol when you set up the stock. Then, using a modem, you can obtain the latest stock prices from Quicken's Portfolio Price Update service. This service automatically updates your stock prices. To try it out, follow these steps:

1. Check your Quicken investment list to make sure that you've assigned the correct ticker symbol for each of your securities. You can open the list by pressing CTRL-Y. If you aren't sure what the correct ticker symbol is, call a broker, visit your local library, or read newspaper financial sections. The Portfolio View of your investments might look similar to the one in Figure 10-7.
2. Make sure your modem is turned on and connected to the phone line.
3. Select Update Portfolio Prices from the Online menu.
4. Select OK after Quicken displays a dialog box confirming that this is one of your three free calls to the Portfolio Price Update service. If you've already used your three free calls, a dialog box appears requesting information so you can set up an account with the service.

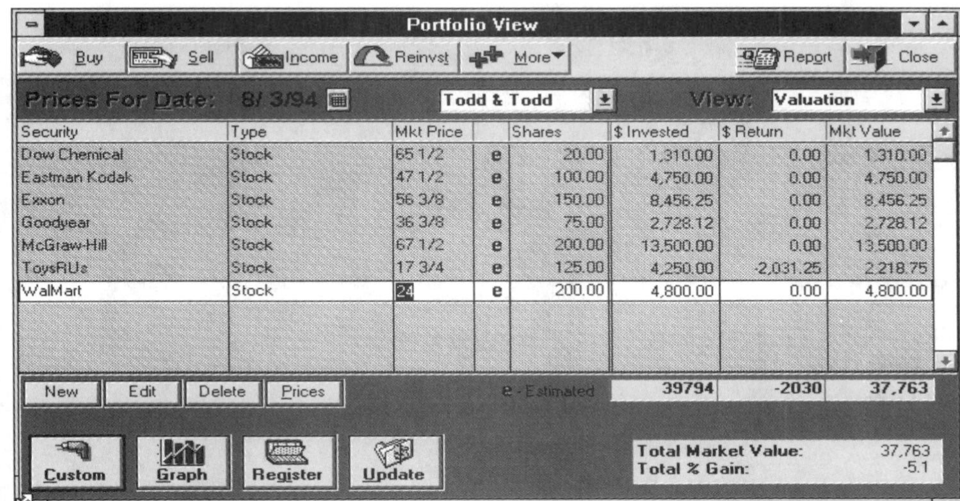

A sample set of investments
Figure 10-7.

5. Quicken prompts you for any dialing prefix you need to dial out. Select OK after making any required entry.

After this, your computer can handle the remaining steps alone. Quicken automatically sets up your modem, calls the service, updates the stocks in your investment account, and then disconnects from the service. Unless some trouble arises with setting up your modem, you don't have to do anything else. After updating your securities, your Portfolio View window will look similar to the one in Figure 10-8.

Your First Net Worth Report

When you set up securities earlier in the chapter, you recorded balances in all the accounts in your INVEST file. At this point, you can determine your net worth. Remember that your net worth is determined by the following formula:

Financial resources - Financial obligations = Net worth

Follow these steps to print your first Net Worth report:

1. Return to the Investments account register and select Home from the Reports menu. Then select Net Worth.

   The Create Report dialog box appears.
2. Type **8/1/95** in the Report Balance As Of text box, and select OK.

   The Net Worth report appears on your screen.
3. Select Print. The Print Report dialog box appears.

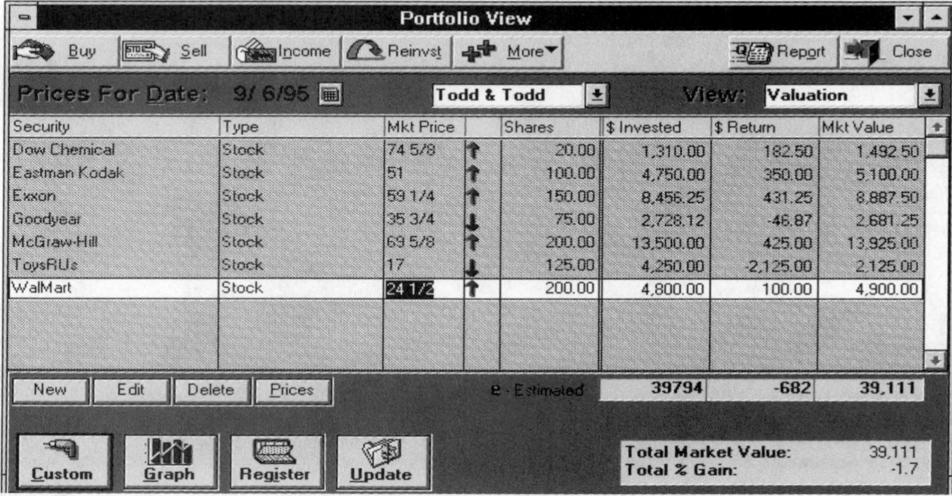

Securities after being updated with the Update Portfolio Prices service

Figure 10-8.

4. Select Printer, and then select Print. Your resulting printout will resemble the report shown in Figure 10-9.

Note: Again, the spacing in your report may differ from that shown in the figure because of adjustments made to fit the material onto these pages.

Notice that the Net Worth report is presented for a specific date—in this example, 8/1/95. The report presents your assets and liabilities at this date and gives you a base point against which to make future comparisons. As you can see, your net worth on 8/1/95 is $63,710. At the end of this chapter, you prepare another Net Worth report and compare how your net worth has changed.

Net Worth Report
(Includes unrealized gains)
As of 8/1/95

Acct	8/1/95 Balance
ASSETS	
Cash and Bank Accounts	
Great Lakes Chk	4,000.00
Great Lakes Svg	2,500.00
Price Money Mkt	15,000.00
Total Cash and Bank Accounts	21,500.00
Other Assets	
Residence	100,000.00
Total Other Assets	100,000.00
Investments	
Investments	27,210.00
Total Investments	27,210.00
TOTAL ASSETS	148,710.00
LIABILITIES	
Other Liabilities	
Great Lakes Mtg	85,000.00
Total Other Liabilities	85,000.00
TOTAL LIABILITIES	85,000.00
OVERALL TOTAL	63,710.00

A Net Worth report for 8/1/95
Figure 10-9.

The Impact of Investments and Mortgage Payments on Net Worth

In this section, you record various transactions in the INVEST file to demonstrate the effects of certain types of transactions on your net worth. You will see how Quicken can monitor your mortgage balance as part of your monthly record-keeping in your checking account. You will also see how you can record a transaction only once and trace the financial impact on both your checking and your investment account registers.

Additional Stock Transactions

You will now record the acquisition of some additional stock, dividends, dividends reinvested, and the sale of stock. The following steps demonstrate how easy it is to record transactions in a Quicken for Windows' investment account:

1. Go to the Investments account register, if you are not already there.
2. Move to the last entry.
3. Select Buy from the button bar.
4. Type **8/2/95** in the Date text box.
5. Type **Douglas Marine** in the Security text box, and press TAB.

   Because this security is not in the Security list, it must be added.
6. Type **DGM** in the Symbol text box.
7. Select Stock in the Type text box.
8. Select Growth in the Goal text box.
9. Make sure the Tax-Free Security check box is clear.
10. Type **.30** in the Est. Annual Income($) text box.
11. Select OK to finalize the Security list entry.
12. Type **100** in the Number Of Shares text box, and press TAB.
13. Type **25** in the Price text box, and press TAB to have Quicken calculate the content of the Total Of Sale text box.
14. Type **50** in the Commission/Fee text box, and press TAB to have Quicken adjust the content of the Total Of Sale text box.
15. Select [Price Money Mkt] from the Transfer Acct drop-down list box.

    The transfer amount is automatically computed as the price of the stock plus the commission.
16. Type **Buy 100 Douglas Marine** in the Memo text box.
17. Select OK to finalize the transaction.

The next transactions record dividends and transfer them to another account or reinvest them in shares of the stock. Rather than transferring funds in and out for each transaction, you can choose to leave a cash balance in your brokerage account. Quicken allows you to mirror almost any investment situation. To record the dividend transaction, follow these steps:

1. Select Income. The completed Record Income dialog box for this example is shown in Figure 10-10.
2. Type **8/10/95** in the Date text box.
3. Select Haven Publishing from the drop-down list in the Security text box.
4. Type **200** in the Dividend text box, and press TAB to have Quicken fill the Total text box.
5. Select [Great Lakes Svg] from the Transfer Account drop-down list box.
6. Type **Div @ .40 per share** in the Memo text box.
7. Click OK to finalize the transaction.

The next transaction also recognizes a dividend distribution. These dividends are reinvested in shares purchased at the current market price. Follow these steps to record the transaction:

1. Select Reinvst from the button bar.
2. Type **8/15/95** in the Date text box.
3. Select Ganges Mutual Fund from the Security drop-down list box. Another option is to type **G**, and Quicken then completes the name for you using the QuickFill feature. You have seen QuickFill at work in entries

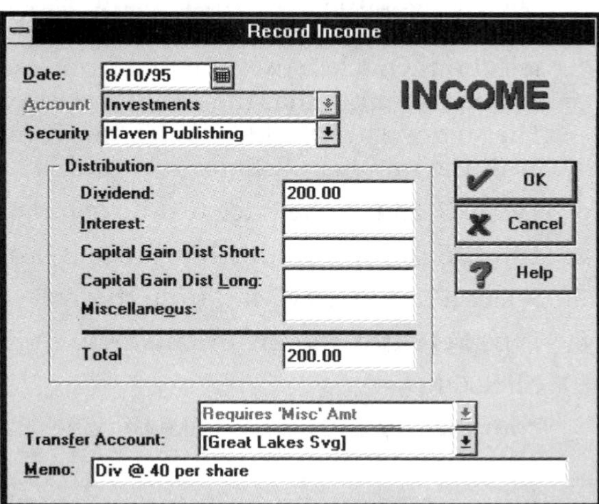

The Record Income dialog box
Figure 10-10.

you made in earlier chapters. Quicken tries to match the characters that you type for the Payee, Category, Security, and Action fields to entries in existing lists. If you want to use the Glenn Packing security, you must select it from the drop-down list box.

4. Type **100** in the Dividend text box in the Dollar Amount column, and press TAB.

   Quicken supplies the new price per share, if you enter the number of shares and the amount of the dividend that you are reinvesting.
5. Type **7.531** in the Dividend text box in the Number Shares column, and press TAB.
6. Type **Dividend Reinvestment** in the Memo text box.
7. Select OK.

To record the sale of stock with the transfer of proceeds to another account, follow these steps:

1. Select Sell from the button bar.
2. Type **8/25/95** in the Date text box.
3. Select Haven Publishing from the drop-down list in the Security text box.
4. Type **100** in the Number Of Shares text box, and press TAB.

   If you select Lots, Quicken presents a Specific Identification of Shares dialog box that allows you to select specific shares from various acquisition dates for the security being sold. You designate the specific shares that are being sold in this situation. This allows you to assign the cost of the shares that are being sold when gain or loss is being determined on this sale for tax purposes. In this example, all the shares were purchased at one time, so you let Quicken do the work for you. Unless you make a selection, Quicken uses the first-in-first-out selection method. That method assumes that the oldest shares of this stock are being sold first. The shares will be sold in order, beginning with the oldest shares held, until the number of shares sold in this sale transaction is reached.
5. Type **23 1/4** in the Price text box, and press TAB.
6. Type **25** in the Commission/Fee text box, and press TAB.
7. Select [Price Money Mkt] from the Transfer Acct drop-down list box.
8. Type **Sell 100 Haven Publishing** in the Memo text box.
9. Click OK.

   Your register entries look like the ones in Figure 10-11.

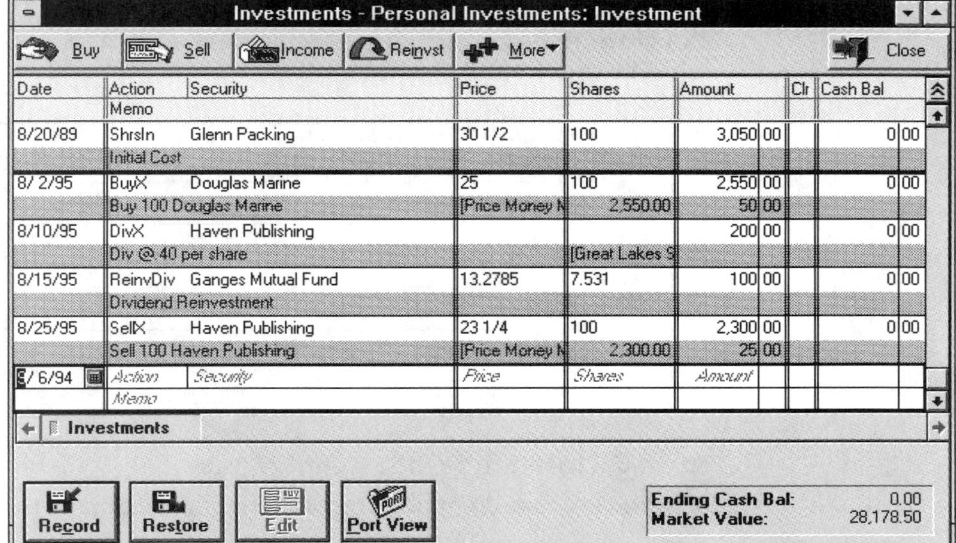

The Investments register after the August 1995 transactions have been made
Figure 10-11.

A Mortgage Payment Transaction

You recorded mortgage payments in earlier chapters, but here you will see how you can monitor your principal balance when you make your payment. In this example, you make your monthly payment from your checking account and monitor the impact of the payment on your principal balance in the Great Lakes Mtg liability account. Follow these steps to record this transaction:

1. Enter the Great Lakes Chk register, move to the Date field of the next transaction, and type **8/5/95**.
2. Type **100** in the Num field.
3. Type **Great Lakes Bank** in the Payee field.
4. Type **875.00** in the Payment field.
5. Select Splits to open the Splits window.
6. Enter **[Great Lakes Mtg]** in the Category field. Type **Principal Payment** in the Memo field, type **25.00** in the Amount field, and press TAB.

   You have recorded the first part of the transaction.

7. Select Mort Int from the Category drop-down list box. Type **Interest Portion of Payment** in the Memo field, and press TAB. Your Splits window should look like this:

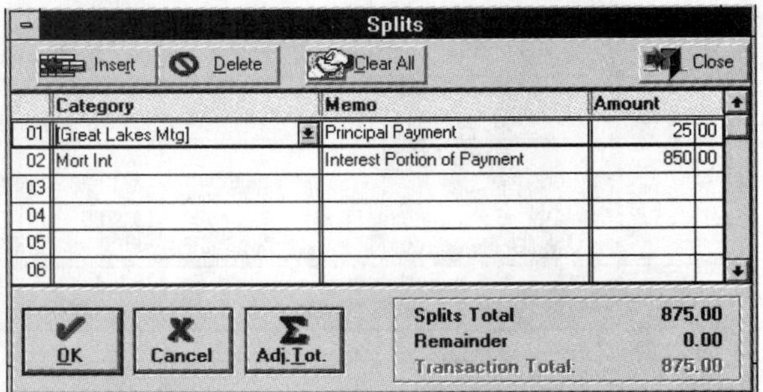

8. Select OK to return to the account register.
9. Select Record, and Quicken records the transaction in the register.

As you can see, the balance in the account has been reduced by the amount of the payment. At the same time, Quicken has recorded the transaction in your Great Lakes Mtg account and reduced the obligation by the $25.00 principal portion of the payment.

How Transactions Affect Your Net Worth

Let's take a look at the effect of the previous transactions on your net worth. If you compare the report in Figure 10-12 to the previous Net Worth report, you'll see that your net worth has increased by $68.50 compared to the net worth shown in Figure 10-9. This difference is the net effect of the transactions you recorded during the month of August in your investment, cash, and bank accounts.

Your net worth can grow if you either increase the value of your financial resources or decrease the amount of your obligations. In the following section, you will see how increases in the value of your investments are recorded and the effect they have on your net worth.

Recording Appreciation in Your Investment Holdings

In this section, you record the increased appreciation in your investments and residence occurring since the Net Worth report prepared on 8/1/95. Although the amounts may seem high, remember that this is an example.

Net Worth Report
(Includes unrealized gains)
As of 8/31/95

Acct	8/31/95 Balance
ASSETS	
Cash and Bank Accounts	
Great Lakes Chk	3,125.00
Great Lakes Svg	2,700.00
Price Money Mkt	14,750.00
Total Cash and Bank Accounts	20,575.00
Other Assets	
Residence	100,000.00
Total Other Assets	100,000.00
Investments	
Investments	28,178.50
Total Investments	28,178.50
TOTAL ASSETS	148,753.50
LIABILITIES	
Other Liabilities	
Great Lakes Mtg	84,975.00
Total Other Liabilities	84,975.00
TOTAL LIABILITIES	84,975.00
OVERALL TOTAL	63,778.50

The Net Worth report after stock is acquired and a mortgage payment is made
Figure 10-12.

Also, remember that what you make in the stock market and housing market this year could be lost next year.

Appreciation of Your Investments

Quicken permits you to record increases and decreases in the value of your holdings. As noted in the net worth formula, changes in the value of your holdings have the potential to significantly affect your net worth over a period of years. Remember the effect of compounding interest on your investments. Follow these steps to enter the changes to your investments for the month of August:

1. Move to the Investments account register by opening the Account list window, highlighting the Investments account, and selecting Open.
2. Select Port View.

3. Select Price Update from the View drop-down list.
4. Press CTRL-G, enter **8/31/95**, and select OK. You can also select the date from the Prices For Date drop-down calendar.

   Notice the letter *e* next to the prices. An *e* tells you that Quicken is using an estimated value for the investment. For example, Quicken valued the Glenn Packing shares at $30.00 per share. Because you didn't buy or sell any shares of this stock during August, Quicken uses the 7/31/95 price shown in Figure 10-11 until you revalue the stock. The Ganges Mutual Fund stock is shown at its actual value on 8/15/95 because you recorded the dividend reinvestment transaction in your account on that date. Quicken automatically updates your market valuation each time you provide new price information in recording account transactions throughout the year.
5. Enter the new market prices for the stocks, as shown in Figure 10-13. Press UP ARROW or DOWN ARROW after you record each new price.
6. Select Register to return to the account register.

Appreciation of Your Residence

As your home increases in value, you will want to record this change in Quicken in order to see how it affects your net worth. In this example, as a result of recent sales in your neighborhood, you believe that $105,000 would be a conservative estimate of the market value of your home. Follow these steps to value your home at $105,000:

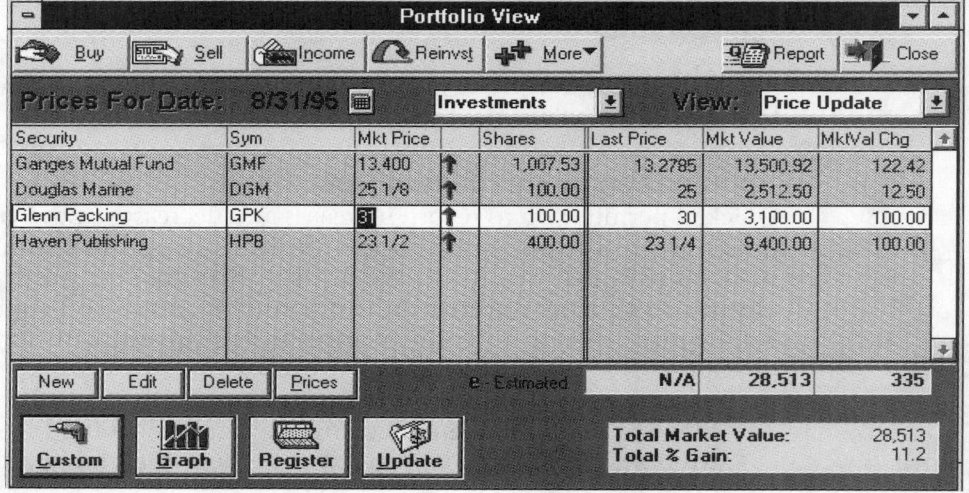

Figure 10-13. The Portfolio View window after revaluations are recorded

1. From the Account List window, highlight the Residence account, and select Open.

   Quicken opens the register for this account and highlights the next blank transaction.
2. Select Update Balances from the Activities menu.
3. Select Update Cash Balance.
4. Type **105000**, and press TAB twice to avoid specifying a category.
5. Type **8/31/95**, and select OK.

Your register should look like Figure 10-14.

Your Ending Net Worth Determination

Having prepared the adjustments to the various accounts in the INVEST file, you are now prepared to print your Net Worth report for the end of the period.

1. Select Home from the Reports menu, and then select Net Worth. The Create Report dialog box appears.
2. Type **8/31/95** in the Report Balance As Of text box, and select OK.

   The Net Worth report appears on your screen.
3. Press CTRL-P. The Print Report dialog box appears.

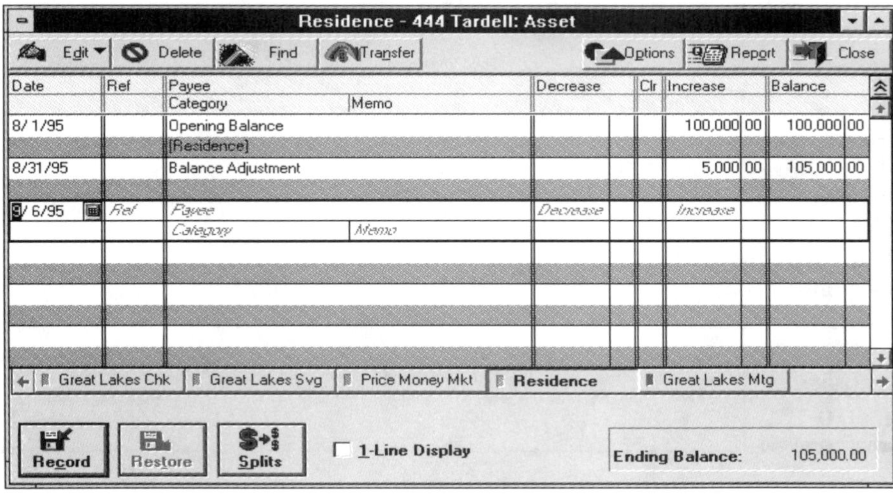

The Residence register after a value increase is recorded

Figure 10-14.

4. Complete the appropriate selections in the dialog box. When you select OK to leave the dialog box, your printer prints the report shown in Figure 10-15.

An examination of Figures 10-9 and 10-15 reveals that your net worth increased by almost $6,000 during the time period. What were the reasons for these changes? For the most part, the increased values of your investments and residence explain the greater net worth.

Net Worth Report
(Includes unrealized gains)
As of 8/31/95

Acct	8/31/95 Balance
ASSETS	
Cash and Bank Accounts	
Great Lakes Chk	3,125.00
Great Lakes Svg	2,700.00
Price Money Mkt	14,750.00
Total Cash and Bank Accounts	20,575.00
Other Assets	
Residence	105,000.00
Total Other Assets	105,000.00
Investments	
Investments	28,513.42
Total Investments	28,513.42
TOTAL ASSETS	154,088.42
LIABILITIES	
Other Liabilities	
Great Lakes Mtg	84,975.00
Total Other Liabilities	84,975.00
TOTAL LIABILITIES	84,975.00
OVERALL TOTAL	69,113.42

Figure 10-15. The Net Worth report for 8/31/95 after all transactions affecting the INVEST file are recorded

The importance of monitoring your net worth has been stressed throughout this chapter. This book's focus is teaching you how to use Quicken to assist in your financial planning and monitoring activities. Once you have a good picture of your net worth from the Quicken reports, you can focus on additional planning. You might want to set your net worth goal for a future point or make plans to protect your existing holdings.

If you have not taken any actions regarding estate planning, this is another area to address. Making a will is a very important part of the estate planning process and should not be delayed. The complexities of planning for the transfer of your estate are significant. However, you may be surprised to learn that a lawyer's fee for a simple will can be relatively low. You can also write a will with one of the new software programs specifically designed for that purpose.

The Need for a Will

A will is important to ensure that your heirs benefit from the net worth that you have accumulated and to make sure that your wishes control the distribution of your assets at your death. Without a will, the laws of your state and the rulings of a probate court decide what happens to your assets and award the custody of your minor children. The following may also occur:

- A probate court may appoint an administrator for your estate.
- State laws may distribute your assets differently than you would wish.
- Fees for probate lawyers may consume from 5 to 25 percent of your estate. The smaller your estate, the higher the percentage will be for the probate lawyer.
- If your estate is large enough to be affected by federal estate taxes ($600,000 or more), absence of a will and lack of other estate planning can increase the tax obligations on your estate.

Quicken's Investment Reports

Quicken offers five investment reports that provide information on your investments from different perspectives. You can use these reports to look at detailed investment transactions or to assess gains or losses in investment value over a period of time. The many options available provide variations on each basic report.

Portfolio Value Report

A Portfolio Value report gives you the values of all the investments in your portfolio at a given date based on price information stored in Quicken. The Portfolio Value report displays the number of shares, the current price, the cost basis of the shares, the gain or loss, and the current value of the shares. Follow these steps from the Investments account to create a Portfolio Value report:

HomeBase

Investments | Portfolio Value Report

1. Select Investment from the Reports menu.
2. Select Portfolio Value.
3. Enter **8/31/95** in the Report Value As Of text box, and select Customize.
4. Clear the Cents in Amounts check box, and select OK.

   The report is displayed on your screen. A printed copy of the report is shown in Figure 10-16.
5. Select Close to close the report window.

Investment Performance Report

The Investment Performance report lets you look at your investments' gains or losses over time. The Investment Performance report indicates your return for the period and projects an average annual return based on the results of the period selected. Follow these steps to create an Investment Performance report:

1. Select Investment from the Reports menu, and then select Investment Performance.

Portfolio Value Report
As of 8/31/95

Security	Shares	Curr Price	Cost Basis	Gain/Loss	Balance
Douglas Marine	100.00	25 1/8	2,550	-38	2,513
Ganges Mutual Fund	1,007.53	13.400	12,050	1,451	13,501
Glenn Packing	100.00	31.000	3,050	50	3,100
Haven Publishing	400.00	23 1/2	8,000	1,400	9,400
Total Investments			25,650	2,863	28,513

A Portfolio Value report
Figure 10-16.

2. Enter **8/1/95** in the From text box.
3. Enter **8/31/95** in the To text box.
4. Select Customize.
5. Clear the Cents In Amounts check box, and select OK.

   A printed version of the report, showing an annualized return of 64.5 percent, is shown in Figure 10-17.
6. Select Close.

Capital Gains Report

The Capital Gains report is useful for tax purposes because it shows the gain or loss on sales of investments. One Capital Gains report you can create allows you to look at the difference between short- and long-term capital gains. Follow these steps to create the report:

1. Select Investment from the Reports menu.
2. Select Capital Gains.
3. Enter **8/1/95** in the From text box.
4. Enter **8/31/95** in the To text box.
5. Select Customize.
6. Clear the Cents In Amounts check box, and select OK.

   Figure 10-18 shows a printout of this report.
7. Select Close to close the report window.

Investment Performance Report
8/1/95 Through 8/31/95

Date	Action	Description	Investments	Returns	Avg. Annual Tot. Return
	8/1/95 - 8/31/95				
7/31/95		Beg Mkt Value	27,210		
8/2/95	BuyX	100 Douglas Marine	2,550		
8/10/95	DivX	Haven Publishing		200	
8/25/95	SellX	100 Haven Publishing		2,300	
8/31/95		End Mkt Value		28,513	
	TOTAL 8/1/95 - 8/31/95		29,760	31,013	64.5%

Figure 10-17. An Investment Performance report

Capital Gains Report
8/1/95 Through 8/31/95

Security	Shares	Bought	Sold	Sales Price	Cost Basis	Gain/Loss
LONG TERM						
Haven Publishing	100	10/10/88	8/25/95	2,300	2,000	300
TOTAL LONG TERM				2,300	2,000	300

A Capital Gains report
Figure 10-18.

Investment Income Report

The Investment Income report shows the total income or expense from your investments. Dividends as well as realized and unrealized gains and losses can be shown on this report. Follow these steps to create the report:

1. Select Investment from the Reports menu.
2. Select Investment Income.
3. Enter **8/1/95** in the From text box.
4. Enter **8/31/95** in the To text box.
5. Select Customize.
6. Clear the Cents In Amounts check box.
7. Select Show Rows.
8. Select Exclude All from the Transfers drop-down list box.
9. Click OK to display the report on your screen.
   Your report will resemble the printout shown in Figure 10-19.
10. Select Close to close the report window.

Investment Transactions Report

The Investment Transactions report is the most detailed of the five investment reports Quicken offers. It reports on all investment transactions during the selected period.

Follow these steps to create an Investment Transactions report:

1. Select Investment from the Reports menu.
2. Select Investment Transactions.

Investment Income Report
8/1/95 Through 8/31/95

Category Description	8/1/95-8/31/95
INCOME/EXPENSE	
INCOME	
_DivInc	300
_RlzdGain	300
TOTAL INCOME	600
TOTAL INCOME/EXPENSE	600

Figure 10-19. An Investment Income report

3. Enter **8/1/95** in the From text box.
4. Enter **8/31/95** in the To text box.
5. Select Customize.
6. Clear the Cents In Amounts check box.
7. Select Transactions, and mark the Include Unrealized Gains check box.
8. Select OK to display the report on your screen.
   Your report will resemble the printout shown in Figure 10-20.
9. Select Close to close the report window.

Graphing Your Investments

Quicken gives you an opportunity to visually review your investment activities at specified points in time or over a period of time. Graphing options include an Investment Performance graph that shows your portfolio's value and average annual return over a selected time period. You can also use Quicken's QuickZoom feature to view your portfolio's composition, graph the price history for individual securities, and prepare a Price and Value History report for securities. From the Price and Value History report, you can use QuickZoom to select individual security transactions from their origination transactions. Graphing activities begin from the Investments register.

1. Select Graphs from the Reports menu, and then select Investments. Quicken presents a Create Graphs dialog box with the Investment Graph option button already selected. You can also open this dialog box by

Investment Transactions Report
(Includes unrealized gains)
8/1/95 Through 8/31/95

Date	Action	Secur	Categ	Price	Shares	Commssn	Cash	Invest. Value	Cash + Invest.
BALANCE 7/31/95							0	27,210	27,210
8/2/95		Douglas M...	_UnrlzdGain	25.000				-50	-50
8/2/95	BuyX	Douglas M...		25.000	100	50	-2,550	2,550	
			[Price ...				2,550		2,550
8/10/95	DivX	Haven Publ...	_DivInc				200		200
			[Great...				-200		-200
8/15/95		Ganges Mu...	_UnrlzdGain	13.2785				69	69
8/15/95	ReinvDiv	Ganges Mu...		13.2785	7.531		-100	100	
			_DivInc				100		100
8/25/95		Haven Publ...	_UnrlzdGain	23 1/4				300	300
8/25/95	SellX	Haven Publ...		23 1/4	100	25	2,000	-2,000	
			[Price ...				-2,300		-2,300
			_RlzdGain				300		300
8/31/95		Haven Publ...	_UnrlzdGain	23 1/2				100	100
8/31/95		Ganges Mu...	_UnrlzdGain	13.400				122	122
8/31/95		Glenn Packi...	_UnrlzdGain	31.000				100	100
8/31/95		Douglas M...	_UnrlzdGain	25 1/8				13	13
TOTAL 8/1/95 - 8/31/95							0	1,303	1,303
BALANCE 8/31/95							0	28,513	28,513

An investment Transactions report including unrealized gains and losses

Figure 10-20.

HomeBase

Investments | Investment Graph

clicking the Graphs icon on your icon bar, and then selecting Investment Graph. From this dialog box, you can select the investment accounts you want to include in the graph and also whether you want to limit your selection of securities.

2. Type **7/95** in the From text box.
3. Type **8/95** in the To text box, and select Create.

   Quicken presents a graph similar to the one in Figure 10-21, showing the monthly portfolio value by security. As you specified in the previous steps, a two-month period is shown in this illustration. Quicken also presents a graph of your average annual total return for the portfolio, as well as the return for your individual securities.
4. Move the mouse pointer to the 8/95 bar on the Monthly Portfolio Value graph. The pointer changes to a magnifying glass with a Z inside. Double-click the left mouse button. You will see this graph:

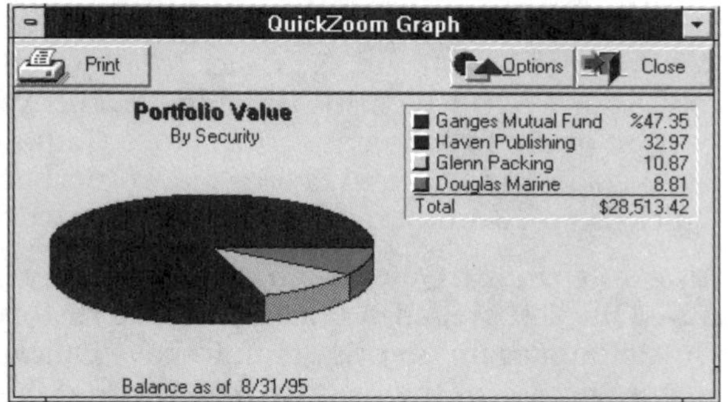

QuickZoom prepares a pie chart that shows the composition of your portfolio by individual security. From the graph, you can see that Ganges Mutual Fund comprises about 47 percent of your portfolio's total value, Haven Publishing 33 percent, Glenn Packing 11 percent, and Douglas Marine 9 percent.

5. If you want to print either of these graphs, click the Print button on the button bar.

The default is for Quicken to use all of your investment accounts to create your Investment graphs. Only the Investments account is used to create the graph in Figure 10-21 because it is your only investment-type account. If you have several investment accounts, you can select the Accounts button in the Create Graph dialog box and choose the accounts you want included in the graph. If you have an IRA, a 401(K), and a personal investment account, you can choose to graph each account separately. If you do not make a selection, Quicken merges all three accounts into one graph.

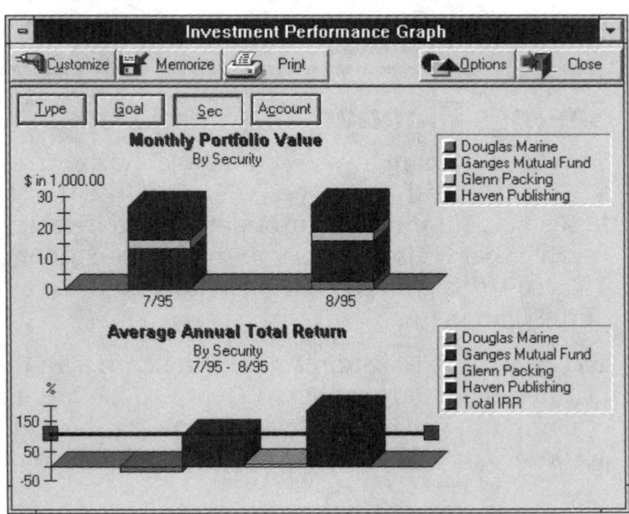

An Investment Performance graph
Figure 10-21.

Several additional graphing features enable you to view the Investment Performance Graph and the QuickZoom pie chart. You can use QuickZoom to view any of the securities included in the Average Annual Total Return portion of the Investment Performance Graph. Then Quicken can prepare an Average Annual Total Return report for that security. You can then use QuickZoom again to trace individual transactions to their original entry.

Also, you can use QuickZoom on any security in the QuickZoom pie chart to have Quicken prepare a Price and Value History graph for that security. Use QuickZoom again on this graph to have Quicken prepare a Price and Value History report for the security. You can also use QuickZoom on an individual report transaction to view its original entry in the Sell, Buy, or other investment entry dialog box in which you placed it.

Using Quicken's Financial Planning Tools

Quicken for Windows has several financial planning tools that perform calculations to help you plan and make decisions about your financial goals. You have already used one financial tool, the Loan Planner, to calculate the split between mortgage principal reductions and interest in Chapter 9. In this section, you learn about the Savings, Retirement, College, and Refinance Planners. These are similar to the Loan Planner and each other because they provide information you need to make an informed decision, and they enable you to compare different scenarios. To open a financial planning tool, select Financial Planners from the Plan menu.

Note: All the financial planning tools require you to make assumptions about interest rates, yields, and so on. Continue to monitor your assumptions over time and make corrections as the economy or other factors change.

Savings Planner

Early in this chapter, you saw a table illustrating the effects of investing $100.00 a month for 20 years. You can use the Savings Planner in Quicken to see how future value information is generated. The Savings Planner is so flexible that it also allows you to calculate other things such as current value. To access this planner, select Savings from the Financial Planners submenu of the Plan menu.

To complete this example, make the entries in the Investment Savings Planner dialog box shown in Figure 10-22. You must tell Quicken that the opening balance is zero, because you are starting with no money in the account. The other entries are the annual yield of 8 percent, a period of 240

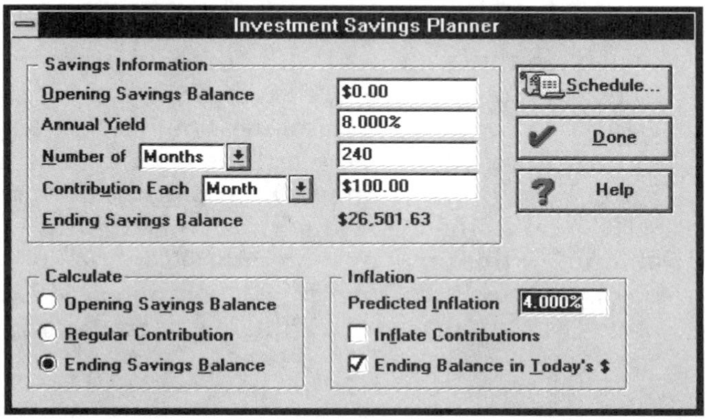

The Investment Savings Planner dialog box showing the return for the investment example

Figure 10-22.

months, and a $100.00 monthly payment. You'll have to make an educated guess about the expected yield.

Quicken calculates an ending savings balance of $26,501.63. If you check the table shown earlier in this chapter called "Effects of Compounding Interest on $100.00 Invested Monthly for 20 Years," you'll notice that this future balance does not match the one calculated there. This is because Quicken has adjusted the ending savings balance so that it appears in today's dollars, taking inflation into account. This example assumes an inflation rate of 4 percent over the 20-year period.

If you clear the Ending Balance In Today's $ check box, Quicken displays the ending savings balance as the actual dollar amount, which will be $58,902.04. This is a good example of the effect inflation can have on money saved over a period of time. If you select Schedule, Quicken presents a schedule of your payments and the accumulated savings during the 240 periods assumed in this illustration.

You can also have Quicken adjust your payments for inflation, although it was not done in this example. To illustrate, you might want to contribute the equivalent of $100.00 in today's dollars, taking into account inflation, every month for the next 20 years. You should select the Inflate Contributions check box then select Schedule. Quicken provides a payment schedule that is adjusted for the 4-percent annual inflation rate. Your first payment would still be $100.00, but your last payment would be $221.52. Your final account balance would be $81,126.62 if you maintain your 8-percent yield and adjust for inflation.

You can see how easy it is to enter a few numbers and get help from Quicken on your investment decisions. There are many changes that you can make as you select weekly, monthly, quarterly, or annual payment periods from the drop-down list boxes. You can adjust annual yield and inflation expectations.

You can also select whether to calculate the regular contribution required to match a future value and whether to calculate the opening value necessary to reach a future value. For example, if you expect an 8-percent return and want to know how much money you need to deposit today to have $58,902 in the future, you would select the Opening Savings Balance option button. Select Years in the Number Of drop-down list, press TAB, and enter **20**. Then select Year in the Contribution Each box, press TAB and DEL to clear the amount in this text box, enter **58902** in the Ending Savings Balance text box, and press TAB. Quicken will compute a $12,637.32 deposit that you might want to make with a finance or insurance company.

Retirement Planning

You can also use Quicken to help project your expected income flows from your various retirement investments (for example, your SEP-IRA, Keogh plan, Individual IRA, 401(K), or retirement savings account). Figure 10-23 shows the Retirement Planner dialog box, which appears when you select Financial Planners from the Plan menu, and then select Retirement.

To complete the dialog box, you must provide your best estimates for some of the information. You should review this information at least once a year to see if modifications are needed and what effect the changes have on your expected retirement income. The following sections describe the type of information you must provide.

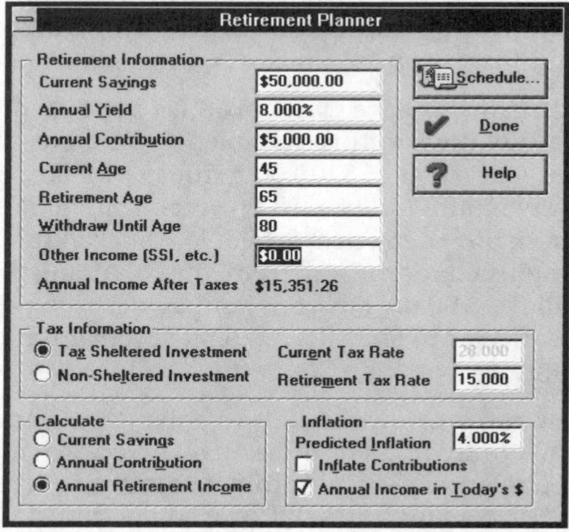

The Retirement Planner dialog box with sample entries
Figure 10-23.

Current Savings Enter the current balance in your investment account. For example, if your IRA has a $50,000 balance at the beginning of the year, you would enter that balance here. Enter your current tax rate and your expected retirement tax rate, or accept the defaults.

Annual Yield Enter your estimate of the expected annual return on this investment. You could use past returns on this investment as a guide; however, you cannot rely solely on this source. Use a conservative but realistic estimate of your expected annual yield.

Annual Contribution Enter your best guess of the future annual contributions that will be made to this investment. Remember to include matching contributions from your employer in addition to your own contributions to the account.

Age Information Change Quicken's default ages to match your situation. If you are 45, wish to retire at 65, and wish to have income provided from this investment until you are 80, enter that information.

Tax Information Indicate whether or not the current account is tax sheltered. Enter your current tax rate and your expected retirement tax rate, or accept the defaults. Most retirement investments are tax sheltered; however, personal savings (CDs, mutual fund accounts, and so on) that you may plan to use to supplement your retirement plans are taxable.

Predicted Inflation Accept Quicken's default annual rate of 4 percent, or modify it to see what the potential impact of various rates would be. Select the Inflate Contributions check box if you would like Quicken to adjust your yearly payment schedule to reflect the increasing amount you will need to contribute to protect your investment against inflation. The default setting is for no inflation adjustment to your yearly payments.

When you enter this information, Quicken provides you with retirement planning information, as shown in Figure 10-23. The Annual Income After Taxes amount shows what your expected future income in today's dollars will be. If Quicken shows that this investment will provide $10,000, that is the spending value of your investment in today's dollars. That is, Quicken has taken your future payments and adjusted them for inflation.

Quicken also allows you to enter expected payments from Social Security or other sources to give you a better picture of your total future retirement income. When you select Schedule, you can ask Quicken to print out your payment schedule for the retirement investment account. This process provides valuable information for retirement planning. As a result of this type of exercise, you might decide that you need to increase your retirement investment contributions or that you are on track for future financial security. This type of review should be an annual planning assessment. It is very important to protect your retirement quality of living, and this easy-to-use Quicken feature can be a valuable tool toward that goal.

College Planning

The College Planner is shown in Figure 10-24. The assumptions for this college-planning scenario are that:

- Your child will attend a nationally known private university with a current tuition of $15,000 a year.
- It will be 18 years before your child enrolls in this university.
- Your child will pursue a major that requires five years of study to complete the degree requirements.
- Your annual yield will be 8 percent over the period.
- Predicted inflation for tuition is 6 percent.

Figure 10-24 shows that you would need to make annual payments of $4,977.74 from 1995 to 2017. Note that the calculations are based on your continuing payments during the five years that your child is in school. When you select Schedule, you can see that tuition will rise to $42,815 for your child's freshman year if you assume a 6-percent annual increase. If you change the assumptions to have your child complete a major in an area requiring only four years of study, your annual payments would decrease to $4,086.16.

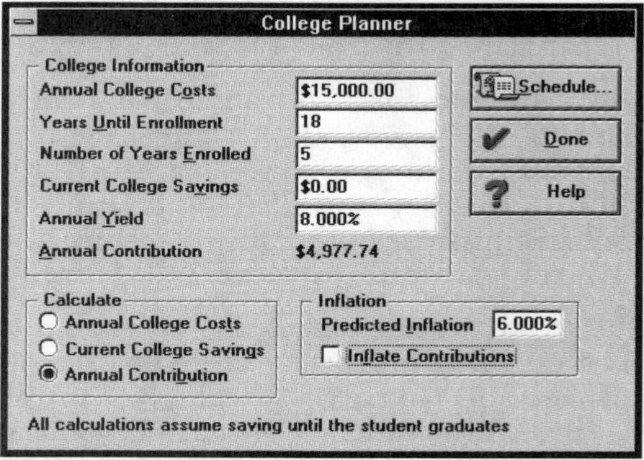

The College Planner dialog box

Figure 10-24.

Refinance Planner

As interest rates fall, you can use the Refinance Planner to assess whether to approach your financial institution about refinancing your loan. You can use the information from the Loan Planner example in Chapter 10 for an example of an actual loan. In the example in Chapter 10, you had a $40,000 loan at 9.519 percent interest for 25 years with payments of $350 a month. If you were considering refinancing after 36 months, you could print out the payment schedule to see that you still had a balance of $38,642.29. The Refinance Planner will show you how much a lower interest rate will reduce your payments and how long it will take to recover the cost of refinancing. Follow these steps to provide the information you need:

1. Select Financial Planners from the Plan menu, and then select Refinance.
2. Type **350.00** in the Current Payment text box, and then press TAB.

   In Chapter 10, the illustration did not provide for an escrow account (insurance, property taxes, and so on) held by the mortgage company. If escrow had been included, you would have entered the monthly escrow account as well. You can obtain your escrow information from the monthly statement that your mortgage company provides.
3. Type **38642.29** in the Principal Amount text box, and then press TAB.

   This is the principal for the remaining mortgage after 36 $350 payments are applied.
4. Type **22** in the Years text box, and then press TAB.

   This number assumes that you want the house paid off within the 25-year goal for the original mortgage. You can negotiate a 15-year or a 30-year loan if you prefer, in which case you would change the Years information accordingly.
5. Type **8.375** in the Interest Rate text box, and then press TAB.

   This is the interest rate quoted by your financial institution.
6. Type **900** in the Mortgage Closing Costs text box, and then press TAB.

   Even when you refinance with your existing loan holder, you can expect to pay closing costs for the new loan. In this example, your lender has provided an estimate of $900.
7. Type **.25** in the Mortgage Points text box, and then press TAB. Your screen displays the Refinance Planner shown in Figure 9-25.

   The .25 represents the 1/4 point that your lender will charge to give you the 8.375 percent interest rate on the 22-year loan.

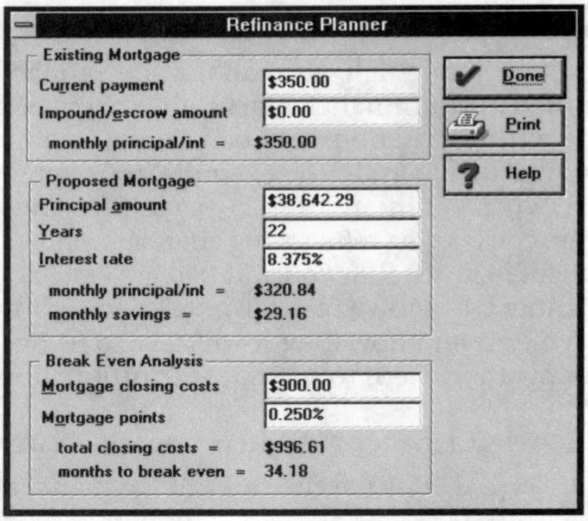

Refinance Planner

Existing Mortgage
Current payment $350.00
Impound/escrow amount $0.00
monthly principal/int = $350.00

Proposed Mortgage
Principal amount $38,642.29
Years 22
Interest rate 8.375%
monthly principal/int = $320.84
monthly savings = $29.16

Break Even Analysis
Mortgage closing costs $900.00
Mortgage points 0.250%
total closing costs = $996.61
months to break even = 34.18

Done
Print
Help

The Refinance Planner dialog box
Figure 10-25.

Notice that if you refinance your home under these conditions, your monthly payments will be reduced to $320.84 (principal and interest), saving you $29.16 a month. Since you must pay out $900.00 in closing costs plus 1/4 point, the last line on the screen tells you that you must stay in the home another 34.18 months before your monthly savings will offset the closing costs and points. You can shop around for better terms with other institutions and use the Refinance Planner to pick the best deal.

CHAPTER

CREATING CUSTOM REPORTS

As you grow accustomed to managing your finances with Quicken, you'll periodically want to step back from the detail in the register and look at the reports and graphs Quicken can create. You can view the reports onscreen, or you can print them to share with others. Graphs allow you to analyze your data in just a few minutes.

Quicken can prepare both standard and custom reports. Standard reports have a predefined format most Quicken users will find acceptable for their personal, business, and investment reporting needs.

However, as you become more familiar with Quicken, you may want to customize your reports to make them even more useful to you. Custom reports allow you to alter the report format to meet your specific requirements.

Quicken can create eight different standard reports for personal use: Cash Flow, Monthly Budget, Itemized Categories, Tax Summary, Net Worth, Tax Schedule, Missing Checks, and Comparison. You can create any of these reports by selecting Home from the Reports menu, as shown here:

With Quicken, you can prepare 13 preset standard and custom reports.

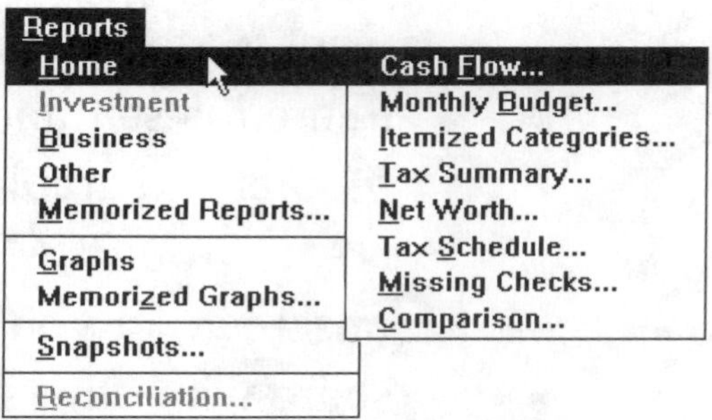

You have seen several examples of standard reports in earlier chapters. Quicken allows you to customize any of the standard reports while you are creating them or after they are displayed on your screen. You can see from the Memorized Reports command in the preceding menu that Quicken can access reports that you have memorized. (More information about memorized reports appears at the end of this chapter.)

Quicken also provides five custom report types that you access by selecting Other from the Reports menu: Transaction, Summary, Comparison, Budget, and Account Balances. Notice that you can access the Comparison report through either the Home or the Other selection in the Reports menu. Selecting any of the custom report types from the Reports menu opens the Create Report dialog box, from which you can choose many different report frameworks. From this dialog box, you can select Customize, opening the Customize Report dialog box. Although the exact contents of the Customize Report dialog box depend on the type of report you are creating, you can always enter information such as the accounts you want to use, directions for totaling and subtotaling the report, the type of cleared status you want to use for included transactions, and specific transactions you wish to include.

You used a custom option in Chapter 8, "Quicken as a Budgeting Tool," when you selected the current account item to customize the Monthly Budget report for Cardinal Bank. (This report is shown in Chapter 8.) In this chapter, you will look at additional custom report options and report filtering features as you build additional custom reports. After completing the exercises in this chapter, you will be able to create your own custom reports and memorize them for later use. Be sure to review the boxed information below to learn how you can safeguard your time investment.

Documenting Your Decisions

As you work with Quicken's custom report features, you will probably try a number of custom report options before you decide on the exact set of reports that meets your needs. If you had an accountant prepare these reports for you, there might also be some trial and error before the exact format to use was determined. Once the decisions were made, the accountant would document them to ensure you received the exact reports you requested on a regular basis. You will benefit by following the same procedure with Quicken: Document the custom reports and options you select. Follow these steps when putting together your documentation:

- Place all your report documentation in one folder.
- Include a copy of each report you want to produce on a regular basis.
- If you are using a Quicken report to obtain information for another form, such as an income tax form, include a copy of this form in your folder and note on it which line or lines in the Quicken report have been used to obtain the necessary information for this form.
- Include the selections you used in the Customize Report dialog boxes. If you have a screen-capture utility, you can capture and print these screens when you create the report the first time. If not, make a note of the selections you used.
- If you are creating multiple copies of some reports, write down the information for creating the report on the extra copies and write down what must be done with the copies.
- Memorize each custom report to make it instantly available when you need it again.

In Chapter 8 you created graphs of your budget performance. Graphs are designed to give you a quick picture of your account information, without all the detail of reports, to help you spot trends and make analyses.

Customizing Report Options

By selecting Quicken's customizing option, you can modify any of the preset formats to meet your specific reporting needs.

You can create reports in many different formats. As noted earlier, the standard settings are sufficient for most reporting needs. However, as you become familiar with Quicken's customization options, you may want to modify some of the formats to meet your special needs. Once you customize a report the way you want, memorize it so that you can always access an updated report with just a few commands. Figure 11-1 shows the Customize Comparison Report dialog box. To open this dialog box, select Other from the Reports menu, and then select Comparison. Select Customize from the Create Report dialog box. The Customize Report dialog box varies slightly depending on the type of report you are preparing, but the vast majority of the selections are available when preparing all standard and custom reports.

In Figure 11-1, the customization features you can access when preparing your report appear in the left side of the dialog box. You can explore the options selecting various customization option buttons and then reviewing the default setting for each report. (Some of these options vary between reports.) Each time you select a customization option, Quicken presents a view that shows the current settings for each feature controlled by that option.

The first customization option shown for the Comparison report—Report Dates—allows you to modify your specified reporting dates. If you had a

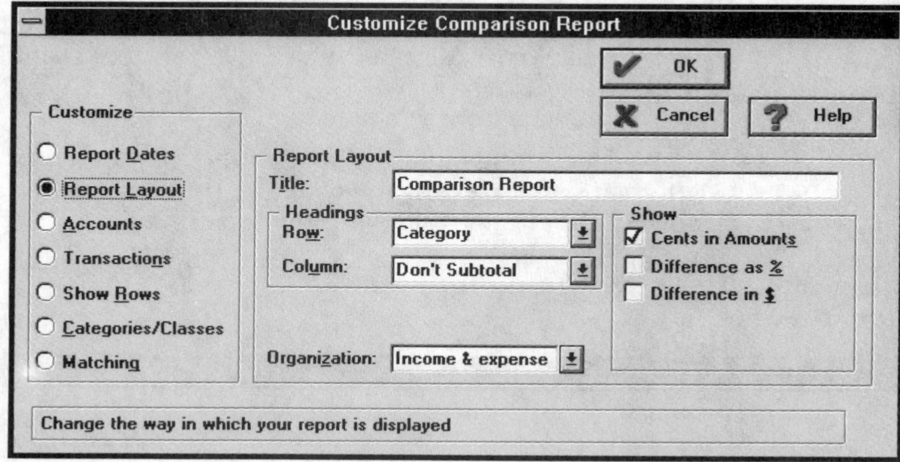

The Customize Comparison Report dialog box
Figure 11-1.

Comparison report on your screen and wanted to modify the reporting dates, you could just select this option and change the compared period. For all other reports, you make a change in the reporting dates by using the Report Layout option.

The Report Layout option allows you to customize your report title and modify the settings for row and column heads. You can change the setting in the Column drop-down list box from Don't Subtotal to various time periods ranging from a week to a year.

If you don't specify an interval, the default selection is the date identified in the Report Dates option. In this case, you may have defined your comparison dates as the years 1994 and 1995. In this example, if you request the report interval of Month, Quicken will prepare a Comparison report that shows monthly comparisons of inflows and outflows during 1994 and 1995. You can also use the Report Layout option to change the report organization to the cash flow or income & expense format. Finally, you can use the Report Layout option to have Quicken show cents in your report and to show the differences between the comparative periods in percentages or in dollar amounts. You can change these settings by clearing or selecting the check boxes in the Show selection box. The check marks shown in Figure 11-1 are the default settings for the Comparison report.

The Accounts option lets you select the accounts to include in the current report. Depending on the type of report being prepared, Quicken may select just one account, some accounts, or all your accounts by default. With this option, you can modify these preset selections to meet your needs.

You can filter your report to include only transactions that contain a specific payee, category, class, or memo.

Selecting Transactions lets you modify several features. You can designate specific amounts to be included in your report. The default is all amounts, but you may want a report to include only amounts that are less than, equal to, or greater than a specified amount. You can also use this option to designate transaction types, specify whether to include unrealized gains and tax-related transactions, and designate the status of the transactions to include in your report. By toggling a check box, you can indicate whether you want blank, newly cleared, and reconciled transactions included in the report.

The Show Rows option allows you to designate if you want to show or hide all subcategories, or display them reversed with their parent categories. You can also choose to include all transfers, exclude all transfers, or exclude only those to other accounts in the report. The Categories/Classes option allows you to select specific categories and classes to include in your report. The final customization option, Matching, lets you filter your report to include only transactions that contain a specific payee, category, class, or memo.

Adjusting Your Transactions

In Chapter 9, you updated the paycheck and mortgage payment transactions in August to show more detail. However, you would never really enter some paychecks with the tax details and other paychecks without. Doing so would create inaccurate reports. To ensure that the reports you create in this chapter will be accurate, you're going to modify all of your previous transactions to include the detail entered in the Splits window for the August transactions. To do this:

1. Select Open from the File menu.
2. Select the PERSONAL file from the File Name list box, and select OK.
3. If necessary, press CTRL-A or select the Accts icon from the icon bar to open the Account list. Highlight the Cardinal Bank account, and select Open. Quicken opens the Cardinal Bank account register.
4. Move to the 8/1/95 payroll deposit transaction and press CTRL-M to memorize it.
5. Select No to avoid saving the splits at percentages.
6. Select OK in response to the prompt that it is memorizing the transaction.
7. When Quicken asks if you want to replace the previous Payroll Deposit memorized transaction, select Replace.
8. Move to the 9/1/95 payroll deposit transaction and delete it by pressing CTRL-D or selecting Delete from the button bar, then selecting Yes.
9. Move to the blank transaction at the bottom of the register. Enter **9/1/95** in the Date field and **DEP** in the Num field. In the Payee field, start typing **Payroll deposit**. When QuickFill recognizes this entry, press TAB. Enter **September paycheck** in the Memo field and select Record.
10. Move to the 10/1/95 payroll deposit transaction and delete it by pressing CTRL-D or by selecting Delete from the button bar, and then selecting Yes.
11. Move to the blank transaction again. Enter **10/1/95** in the Date field and **DEP** in the Num field. In the Payee field, starting typing **Payroll deposit**. When QuickFill recognizes this entry, press TAB to have it fill in the remainder of the transaction. Enter **October paycheck** in the Memo field and select Record.
12. Now move to the 8/2/95 payment to the Great Lakes Savings & Loan. Memorize this transaction as described earlier. Remember not to save as percentages.
13. Move to the 9/2/95 payment to the Great Lakes Savings & Loan, and then delete it.

14. Move to the blank transaction, and enter **9/2/95** in the Date field, and **113** in the Num field. Enter **Great Lakes Savings & Loan** in the Payee field. When QuickFill finishes this entry, press TAB. Enter **September payment** in the Memo field. Select Record.
15. Move to the 10/2/95 payment to the Great Lakes Savings & Loan, and then delete it.
16. Move to the blank transaction, and enter **10/2/95** in the Date field, and **121** in the Num field. Enter **Great Lakes Savings & Loan** in the Payee field. When QuickFill finishes this entry, press TAB. Enter **October payment** in the Memo field. Select Record.

You've now used the memorized transaction feature to reenter these transactions with the split transaction details. This will make the reports you create in this chapter much more meaningful, because you are now using the same level of detail in these transactions for each month.

Creating a Comparison Report

A comparison report lets you review your financial activities during two time periods for comparative purposes.

To create a Comparison report, select Home or Other from the Reports menu and then select Comparison. If you accept the default settings for this report, Quicken provides a comparison of any two time periods you specify. For example, you might want to compare your checking account inflows and outflows for 1994 and 1995 to give you a feeling for how your spending habits have changed during the past year. You could also see whether you have been able to decrease expenditures or increase revenues to increase your savings during the past year.

Follow these steps to produce a Comparison report.

HomeBase

Reports | More Reports

1. Select Home from the Reports menu.
   Quicken displays the menu shown at the beginning of this chapter.
2. Select Comparison, and a Create Report dialog box appears.

   If you wanted to accept the standard settings, you would enter your comparative dates and press OK. Then the standard report would appear.
3. Select Customize.

   Quicken displays the Customize Comparison Report dialog box with the Report Dates customization option selected. You now designate the time periods you want to use as your comparative periods. Remember that you can select reporting subperiods, such as weekly or monthly, by using the Report Layout option discussed earlier.
4. Enter **8/1/95** in the Compare From text box.
5. Enter **8/31/95** in the Compare To text box.

6. Enter **9/1/95** in the To From date text box.
7. Enter **9/30/95** in the To To date text box.
8. Select Report Layout.
9. Clear the Cents in Amounts check box.

   As discussed in the previous section, there are many additional customization options you can select while deciding on the final format that meets your reporting needs.
10. Select OK, and a Comparison report resembling the one shown in Figure 11-2 appears on your screen.

Comparison Report

8/1/95 Through 9/30/95

Category Description	9/1/95-9/30/95	8/1/95-8/31/95	$ Difference
INFLOWS			
Salary	2,000	2,000	0
TOTAL INFLOWS	2,000	2,000	0
OUTFLOWS			
Auto:			
Fuel	23	23	0
Total Auto	23	23	0
Clothing	50	50	0
Dining	60	60	0
Entertain	50	50	0
Furniture	0	217	-217
Groceries	180	218	-38
Medical	212	142	70
Misc	50	50	0
Mort Int	301	301	0
Mort Prin	49	49	0
Tax:			
Fed	130	130	0
Local	9	9	0
Medicare	29	29	0
Soc Sec	124	124	0
State	80	80	0
Total Tax	372	372	0
Telephone	29	23	6
Utilities:			
Electric	44	31	13
Gas	19	19	0
Total Utilities	63	50	13
TOTAL OUTFLOWS	1,439	1,605	-166
OVERALL TOTAL	561	395	-166

A Comparison report
Figure 11-2.

If you have not updated your payroll deposits and mortgage payments as described at the beginning of this chapter, the numbers in your report will look different, but the format will be exactly the same.

Creating a Custom Transaction Report

A custom transaction report lets you group transactions in many different ways for making decisions.

You can print all the transactions in any Quicken account register by selecting Print Register from the File menu. Quicken prints a list of all the transactions in a given time frame. You can use this approach for printing a complete listing of register activity for backup purposes. However, that sort of listing doesn't provide much information for decision making. The custom Transaction report provides an alternative. When creating this report, you can subtotal transaction activity in many different ways, use all or only selected accounts, or show split transaction details to include the specific transaction details you need for better decision making. Let's take a look at some examples.

Showing Split Transaction Details

If a transaction is split among several categories, the word "SPLIT" appears in the Category field when the account register is printed. Suppose you want to prepare a custom report that captures all the details recorded in each split transaction within a selected time frame. Follow these steps:

HomeBase

Reports | More Reports

1. Select Other from the Reports menu, and then select Transaction. Quicken displays the Create Report dialog box.
2. Select Customize.
3. Enter **8/1/95** in the From text box.
4. Enter **8/31/95** in the To text box.
5. Select the Split Transaction Detail check box so it contains a check mark. Your dialog box looks like Figure 11-3.
6. Select OK, and the Transaction report appears on the screen.
7. Select the Print button.
8. Select the Printer option button, and then select Print to create the report. Figure 11-4 shows the first few transactions in this report. Notice that the report shows the details of the split transactions on 8/1 and 8/2.
9. Press ESC to clear the report from the screen.

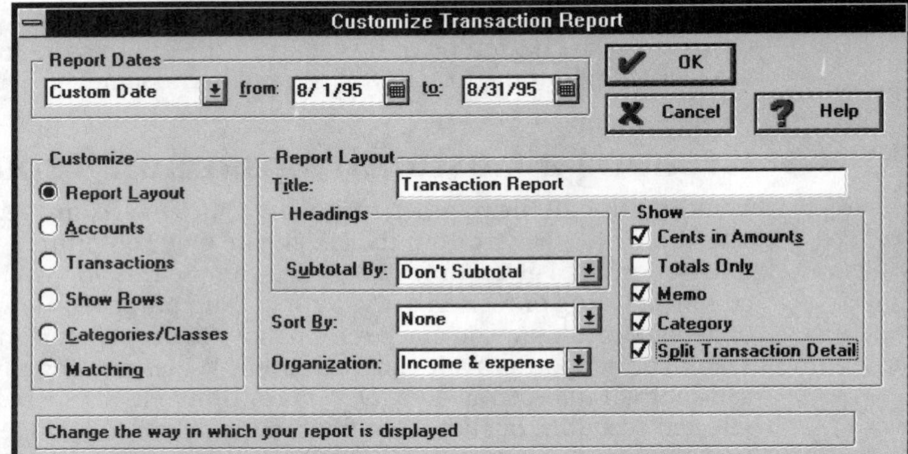

The Customize Transaction Report dialog box
Figure 11-3.

Adding Subtotals to the Transaction Report

When you produce a Transaction report without subtotals, the transactions are simply listed in order by date, as shown in Figure 11-4. You can also change the Subtotal By drop-down list box setting in the Customize Transaction report dialog box to Week, Two Weeks, Half Month, Month, Quarter, Half Year, or Year. The report still lists the transactions by date, but

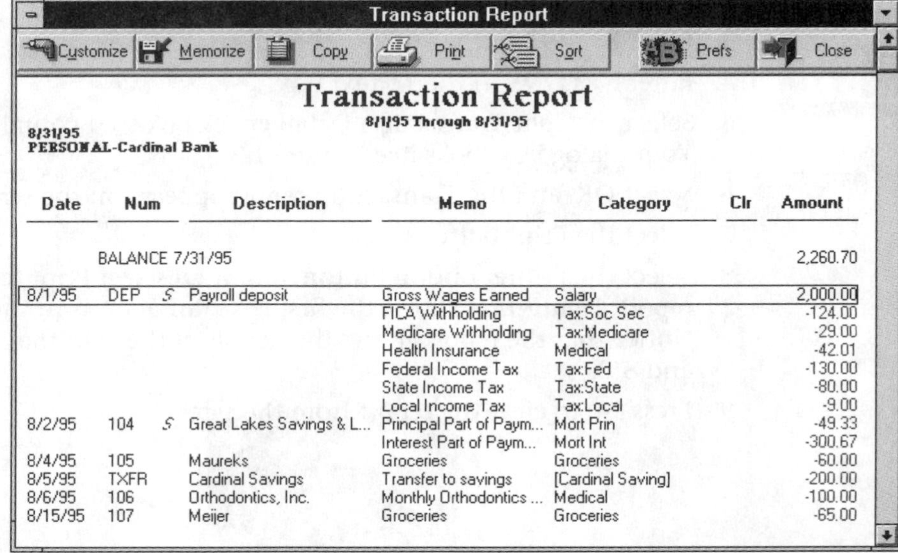

Transaction Report
8/1/95 Through 8/31/95

8/31/95
PERSONAL-Cardinal Bank

Date	Num		Description	Memo	Category	Clr	Amount
			BALANCE 7/31/95				2,260.70
8/1/95	DEP	S	Payroll deposit	Gross Wages Earned	Salary		2,000.00
				FICA Withholding	Tax:Soc Sec		-124.00
				Medicare Withholding	Tax:Medicare		-29.00
				Health Insurance	Medical		-42.01
				Federal Income Tax	Tax:Fed		-130.00
				State Income Tax	Tax:State		-80.00
				Local Income Tax	Tax:Local		-9.00
8/2/95	104	S	Great Lakes Savings & L...	Principal Part of Paym...	Mort Prin		-49.33
				Interest Part of Paym...	Mort Int		-300.67
8/4/95	105		Maureks	Groceries	Groceries		-60.00
8/5/95	TXFR		Cardinal Savings	Transfer to savings	[Cardinal Saving]		-200.00
8/6/95	106		Orthodontics, Inc.	Monthly Orthodontics ...	Medical		-100.00
8/15/95	107		Meijer	Groceries	Groceries		-65.00

A Transaction report with split transactions printed
Figure 11-4.

it also provides a subtotal of the transactions each time the selected interval occurs. For example, if you select Month, the report shows a subtotal for each month. You can also select Category, Account, Class, Payee, or Tax Schedule from this drop-down list box to have Quicken group and subtotal transactions by these entries. For example, if you select Category, Quicken will show a subtotal for each specific category of expense or income.

You can also change the Sort By setting to Amount, Category, Payee, Acct/Chk #, or Date/Acct. Quicken orders the transactions by the field you select, but does not print a subtotal for that field. For example, if you choose to sort 8/1 through 8/31 transactions by category, Quicken lists the transactions alphabetically by category and then by date within each category.

Follow these steps to create a Transaction report subtotaled by category for the Cardinal Bank account:

HomeBase

Reports | More Reports

1. Select Other from the Reports menu.
2. Select Transaction, and the Create Report dialog box appears.
3. Select Customize.
4. Enter **8/1/95** in the From text box.
5. Enter **8/31/95** in the To text box.
6. Select Category in the Subtotal By drop-down list box.
7. Clear the Cents in Amounts check box, and select OK. The Transaction report appears on your screen.
8. Select the Print button to display the Print Report dialog box.
9. Select the Printer option button, and then select Print.

You can see how the report groups and subtotals transactions by category. For example, it groups and subtotals the three transactions you've entered for the Groceries category, as you can see here:

		Groceries			
8/4/95	105	Maureks	Groceries	Groceries	-60
8/15/95	107	Meijer	Groceries	Groceries	-65
8/27/95	111	Meijer	Food	Groceries	-93
		Total Groceries			-218

This report will be essentially the same as the Itemized Categories report you created in Chapter 8 unless you choose to make additional customization changes, such as selecting accounts or filtering the information presented.

Creating a Summary Report

Summary reports can be based on categories, classes, payees, or accounts. You can use them to analyze spending patterns, prepare tax summaries, review major purchases, or look at the total charge card purchases for a given period.

Subtotaling a Summary Report by Month

Although you can choose any of the time intervals for the report subtotals, subtotaling by month is a common choice since many people budget expenses by month. This type of report shows a monthly summary of your financial transactions. Follow these steps to create a Summary Report subtotaled by month for the Cardinal Bank account register:

1. Select Other from the Reports menu.
2. Select Summary, and the Create Report dialog box appears.
3. Select Customize.
4. Enter **8/1/95** in the From text box.
5. Enter **10/31/95** in the To text box.
6. Select Month in the Column drop-down list box.
7. Clear the Cents in Amounts check box.
8. Select Cash Flow Basis in the Organization drop-down list box.

   This step instructs Quicken to prepare the report on a cash flow basis; it will be organized by cash inflows and outflows. This is the same basis used for the Monthly Budget reports prepared in Chapter 8. You will be able to compare this report to those prepared earlier, to gain additional information for assessing your budget.
9. Select Accounts.
10. Make sure that both the Cardinal Bank and the EasyCredit Card account are selected, but that the Cardinal Savings account is not.
11. Select OK, and the Summary report appears on your screen.
12. Select the Print button to display the Print Report dialog box.
13. Select the Printer option button, and select Print.

    Figure 11-5 shows a printout of this report.

The report you've created here presents a cash inflow and outflow summary by month for the period August through October. It provides additional cash flow information about the Monthly Budget reports prepared in Chapter 8. Thus, this Summary report supplements the previously prepared Monthly Budget reports.

Summary Report by Month
8/1/95 Through 10/31/95

Category Description	8/1/95	9/1/95	10/1/95	OVERALL TOTAL
INFLOWS				
Salary	2,000	2,000	2,000	6,000
FROM Cardinal Bank	450	233	957	1,640
TOTAL INFLOWS	2,450	2,233	2,957	7,640
OUTFLOWS				
Auto:				
Fuel	23	23	37	83
Total Auto	23	23	37	83
Clothing	50	50	75	175
Dining	60	60	45	165
Entertain	50	50	100	200
Furniture	217	0	550	767
Groceries	218	180	250	648
Medical	142	212	142	496
Misc	50	50	150	250
Mort Int	301	301	301	902
Mort Prin	49	49	49	148
Tax:				
Fed	130	130	130	390
Local	9	9	9	27
Medicare	29	29	29	87
Soc Sec	124	124	124	372
State	80	80	80	240
Total Tax	372	372	372	1,116
Telephone	23	29	28	80
Utilities:				
Electric	31	44	37	112
Gas	19	19	17	55
Total Utilities	50	63	54	167
TO Cardinal Saving	200	395	366	961
TO EasyCredit Card	450	233	957	1,640
TOTAL OUTFLOWS	2,255	2,067	3,476	7,798
OVERALL TOTAL	195	166	-519	-158

A Summary report subtotaled by month

Figure 11-5.

11

Filtering to See Tax-Related Categories

You can filter Quicken reports to only include tax-related categories.

Filters allow you to select the information you want to include in a report. In Chapter 4, "Quicken Reports," you used a filter to look for payee names containing "Small." Other possible selections include memo, category, or class matches. You can also choose specific categories or classes to include. You can specify tax-related items or transactions greater or less than a certain amount, and you can choose payments, deposits, unprinted checks, or all transactions. Checking the cleared status is another option; that is, you may wish to prepare a report using only transactions that have cleared the bank as part of your reconciliation process.

In the example that follows, you create a Summary report for tax-related items. Follow these steps:

1. Select Other from the Reports menu.
2. Select Summary. The Create Report dialog box appears on your screen.
3. Select Customize.
4. Enter **8/1/95** in the From text box.
5. Enter **10/31/95** in the To text box.
6. Clear the check mark in the Cents in Amounts check box.
7. Select Cash flow basis from the Organization drop-down list box.
8. Select Accounts. Make sure that only the Cardinal Bank account is selected.
9. Select Transactions.
10. Select the Tax-related Transactions Only check box. Your Customize Summary Report dialog box looks like this:

Reports | More Reports

11. Select OK, and the Summary report appears onscreen.
12. Select the Print button to display the Print Report dialog box.
13. Select the Printer option button, and select Print.
    Don't clear the report from your screen, because you'll use it in the next section.

Figure 11-6 shows the completed report with the information filtered for tax-related transactions only. This type of report can be used to monitor your tax-related activities for any part of the tax year or for the year to date. You can use this information for tax planning as well as for tax preparation.

Memorizing Reports

You have already seen how you can gain productivity by using Quicken's memorized transactions. Quicken also allows you to memorize reports. Memorized reports store your custom report definitions so that you can

Summary Report

8/1/95 Through 10/31/95

Category Description		8/1/95-10/31/95
INFLOWS		
Salary		6,000
TOTAL INFLOWS		6,000
OUTFLOWS		
Medical		496
Mort Int		902
Tax:		
Fed	390	
Local	27	
Medicare	87	
Soc Sec	372	
State	240	
Total Tax		1,116
TOTAL OUTFLOWS		2,514
OVERALL TOTAL		3,486

A filtered Summary report of tax-related transactions
Figure 11-6.

Once you customize a report, use the memorization feature to always have that format available for future use.

produce a new report instantly. This means you can enter a title or filter once and use it again by recalling the memorized report definitions.

To memorize a report, you can use the same CTRL-M Quick key used to memorize specific transactions. The only difference is that you must have a report displayed on the screen. Alternatively, you can select the Memorize button in the report window. The Memorize Report dialog box appears to allow you to enter a name for the report:

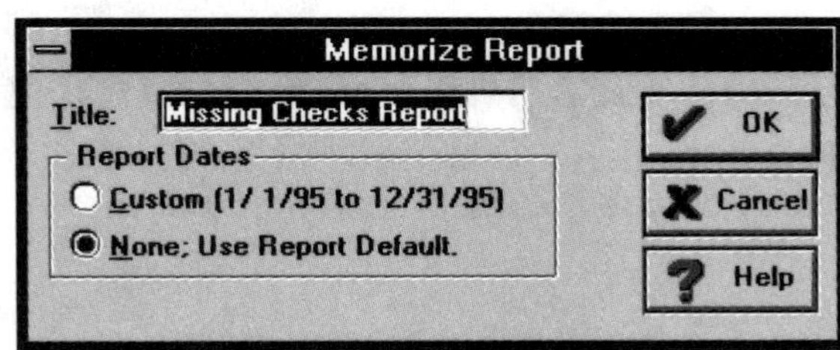

If you were memorizing the definition for the Summary report shown in Figure 11-5, you might enter the title "Tax Related Summary by Month." Make sure that each of your report names is both meaningful and unique, so that you can easily distinguish between different reports when you try to use them again later.

You can choose to memorize the report with the currently assigned dates (which would render the identical report the next time you generated it) or without them. If you memorize the report without them, the default dates will be substituted when you use the memorized report again later. This feature allows you to quickly create a periodic report, such as a monthly report used for reconciling your checking account.

To create a report from a memorized report definition, select Memorized Reports from the Reports menu. A list of memorized reports appears that looks similar to this:

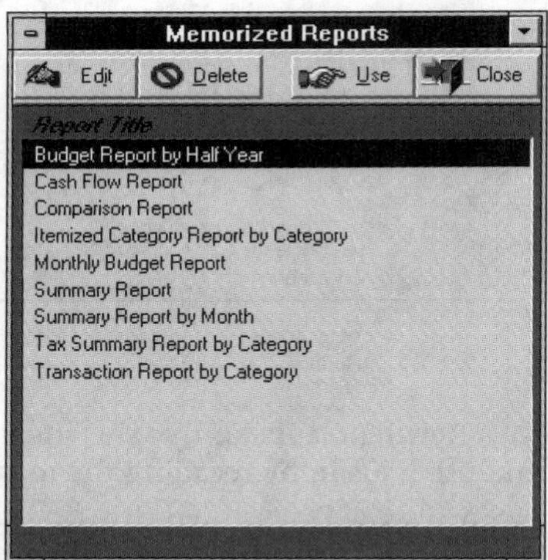

Highlight the desired report, and select Use. The report is displayed on the screen. If you select Edit, you can change the report's name. To change the settings for a report, select Use, then customize the report and memorize it again.

Using Graphs for Additional Analyses

The graphs that you created in Chapter 8 were related to your budget entries. If you activate the Graphs submenu of the Reports menu, you will see that

Graphs provide another way to help analyze your Quicken transactions.

Quicken for Windows offers many additional options for analyzing your data. Follow these steps to create a Net Worth graph:

HomeBase

Reports | More Graphs

1. Select Graphs from the Reports menu.
2. Select Net Worth Graph.
3. Type **8/95** in the From text box.
4. Type **10/95** in the To text box.
5. Select Create.

   The graph appears onscreen, as shown in Figure 11-7. The upper portion of the graph shows your assets for each of the periods designated. Your liabilities are shown in the bottom part of the graph as negative numbers. Your net worth is shown by the line connecting the assets for each of the periods. Since you have created no liability accounts, there are no liabilities included in this graph. This is not a usual financial condition.
6. Select Print from the button bar to print the graph to the default report printer.
7. Place your mouse pointer over one of the bars in the graph so that the mouse pointer becomes a magnifying glass, and double-click.

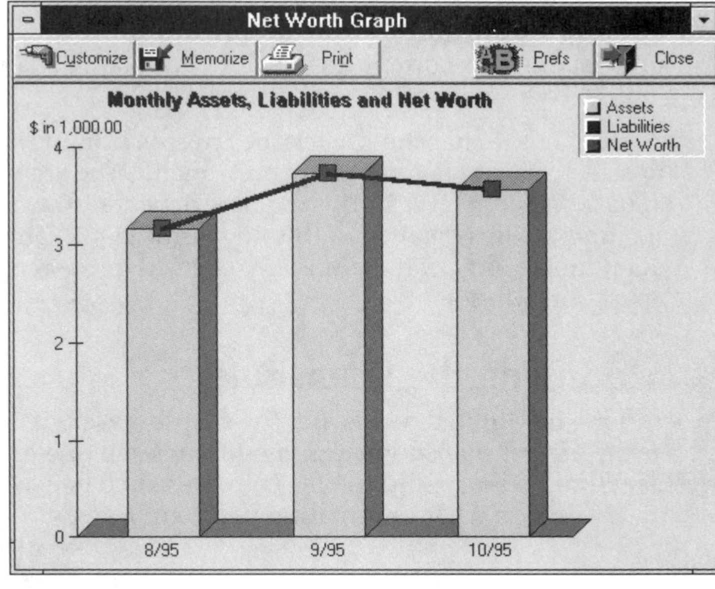

A Net Worth graph
Figure 11-7.

Quicken displays a QuickZoom Graph of your asset composition, as shown here:

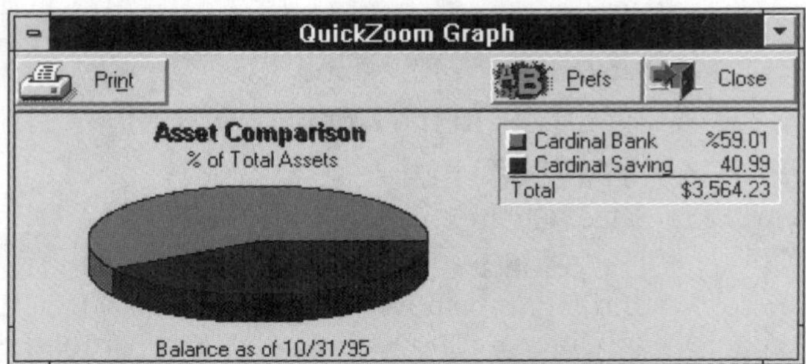

The graph you've created in this section shows the percentage composition of your two bank accounts to your total assets. You can do the same thing with your liabilities. You can also QuickZoom on the QuickZoom graph. If you click and hold down the mouse button when the magnifying glass is on the Cardinal Bank portion of the QuickZoom pie chart, the dollar amount of the account appears on your screen. When you release the mouse button, the amount disappears.

Using Quicken 4's Financial Snapshots

Use Financial Snapshots to get an overview of your financial situation.

Quicken 4 for Windows includes a new feature, Snapshots, to help you understand your current financial situation. The Snapshots provide a quick look at your current financial picture without going into a lot of detail.

To display the snapshots, click the Snpshts icon in the Quicken icon bar, or select Snapshots from the Reports menu. The Snapshots window will appear. What you see in this window depends on when you are entering the transactions detailed in this book, since Quicken uses the current date to determine which transactions are reflected in the reports and graphs in the Snapshots window.

HomeBase

Reports | Financial Snapshot

Modifying the Snapshots

You are not limited to viewing the snapshots you see originally. You can create several snapshot pages, modifying each one to show a particular set of data that you may find useful. You can switch between the different pages, depending on what information you want to see.

Create different snapshot pages for different types of information.

To create a new snapshot page:

1. Select Snapshots from the Reports menu, or click the Snpshts icon in the icon bar.
2. Select Customize in the Snapshots window, opening the Customize Snapshots dialog box shown in Figure 11-8.
3. Select New to create a new Snapshots page.
4. Enter **Expenses** in the Snapshot Page Name text box and select OK.

   Now you're ready to choose how many snapshots you want to appear on the page, and which reports and graphs you want to appear as snapshots. You're also ready to customize these reports and graphs.
5. Select the option button under Snapshots Per Page that shows three snapshots.
6. Select the first snapshot under Choose The Snapshot To Customize.
7. Select Monthly Income and Expenses in the Snapshot Type list box.
8. Select Customize Snapshot.
9. Select Include All Dates from the Date Range drop-down list box, and then select OK.
10. Select the second snapshot under Choose The Snapshot To Customize.
11. Select Monthly Income and Expenses in the Snapshot Type list box.
12. Select the Text option button.

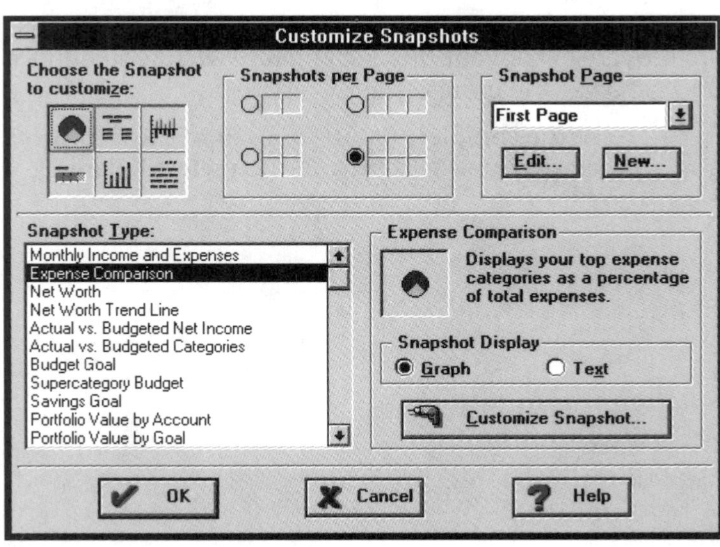

Creating a new Snapshots page
Figure 11-8.

13. Select Customize Snapshot. Then select Include all dates from the Date Range drop-down list box, and select OK.
14. Select the third snapshot under Choose The Snapshot To Customize.
15. Select Expense Comparison in the Snapshot Type list box.
16. Select Customize Snapshot. Then select Include All Dates from the Date Range drop-down list box, and select OK.
17. Select OK to display your new page. Depending on when you initially created your accounts, your page might look like this:

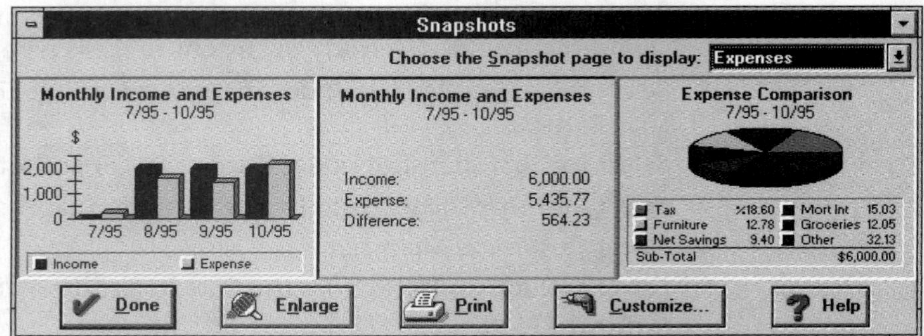

You can switch back to the default First Page by selecting it from the Choose the Snapshot Page To Display drop-down list box at the top of the Snapshot window.

You can create as many Snapshot pages as you choose, fine-tuning each of them to display information you may want to check from time to time. The financial Snapshots are easier to create than reports, and can give you a fine overview of your financial picture when you don't have time to create and analyze the more complex reports.

To see the complete report for each of the snapshots, you can double-click the snapshot, or select it and then select Enlarge.

TIPS

TIPS to KEEP YOU on TOP of YOUR PERSONAL FINANCES

The tips that follow offer many different money- and time-saving suggestions that can directly increase the funds you have available for financial goals and provide you the time you need for adequate financial planning. You'll also find tips to help you keep your financial records in order to ensure that your tax records are accurate and that you have adequate controls in your financial record keeping.

1. Look for ways to save time with the software you use. With Quicken you can use special check stock rather than writing checks manually. You can also use an online service to update your stock prices automatically.
2. Buy products like the new self-adhesive stamps. They don't cost any more and you can put your time to better use.
3. Combine exercise with tasks you need to perform. Rather than pay someone to cut your grass or dig a ditch in your yard, do the work yourself and get some exercise while you save money.
4. Keep a list of all the things you are out of to ensure that one trip to the store can restock everything.
5. Take public transportation to sporting events if possible. You are likely to be dropped off close by and can save an expensive parking fee.
6. Call ahead to see if the store you are planning to go to has the item you need to avoid a wasted trip.
7. Keep an emergency food kit in the pantry for an instant meal. If you return late from the office or airport you won't feel like cooking. Even the cost off a gourmet pasta sauce is likely to be much less than what you would spend to eat out.
8. Keep a to-do list. This way you won't forget about upcoming sales or other important events and activities.
9. Look into direct deposit options for your paycheck. There is no delay in making the deposit with this method.
10. Purchase labels with your name and address on them. Use them on all packages and letters to save the time required filling out a return address.

 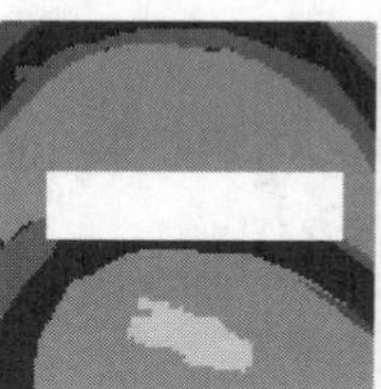  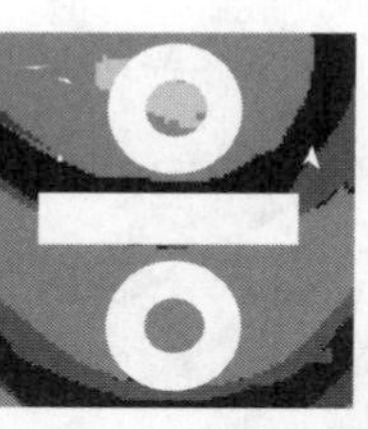

11. Find a good use for waiting time (i.e., in a doctor's office). Use it to read financial articles or crochet a gift. Doing something seems to make the wait time go faster.
12. Take a brown bag lunch to work most days. You can work through lunch at your desk and save enough to have a nice dinner out on the weekend.
13. Do your holiday shopping early in the year for the best buys.
14. File all warranties on appliances in the same place. You'll know exactly where to look when something is on the blink.
15. Make repairs while the problem is small. Things are much easier to fix before they really fall apart.
16. Cook multiple meals on the weekend. It will make weeknights much easier and you won't be tempted to spend as much eating out.
17. Take permanent press clothes with you when you travel. There will be no need to send things out for pressing.
18. Take your car to quick oil change franchises rather than the car dealership. It is much faster and will save money.
19. Trade time-saving tips and savvy financial ideas with friends.
20. Research local delivery services in your area. Some locations offer free delivery if the order is a certain size.
21. Schedule time for yourself. You won't be effective at financial planning or any other task if you are operating on the verge of exhaustion.
22. Off airport parking facilities can save you both time and money. Usually they drop you off right at the entrance. Per day fees for this parking are often less than half of those incurred in the airport facilities.

23. Keep some spare cash stashed away to avoid unnecessary trips to the bank.
24. Set a limit for long distance phone calls and stick to it.
25. Don't buy new when used will do. Garage sales, thrift shops, and newspaper ads offer the opportunity to buy usable merchandise at a fraction of the cost.
26. Consider maintenance costs when you purchase clothing. Clothes that require dry cleaning can be much more expensive over their life than an outfit that can be washed.
27. Delay purchases until you can afford to pay cash. If you wait until you have the cash for that new car or sofa you will save interest charges.
28. Be creative with decorating. Fancy sheets can become curtains or wall paper at a lower cost than alternatives.
29. Seal all exterior exposed wood with paint, stain, or sealer to prolong its life.
30. Determine the most economic quantity for items that you purchase regularly, taking into account the amount of use in a given time period, the quantity discount, storage costs, and order processing costs.
31. Tax laws are revised each year. To keep up with these changes, you are likely to need the services of a good accountant.
32. Keep in mind that the cap amount and percentage for FICA and Medicare are not necessarily the same each year.
33. A credit card purchase is treated as an expense on the date of purchase, not the date of payment, if you are planning to deduct them on your tax return.

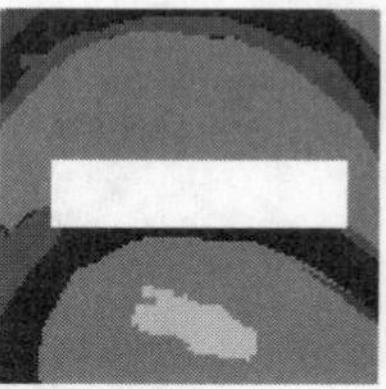

34. If you convert personal assets to business assets, the cost basis for depreciation will be either the cost or the market value, depending on which is lower.

35. Requirements for qualifying for the home office deduction are stringent; they require that a part of your residence be used exclusively for your business, and as the main place where you conduct your business.

36. You are much more likely to deduct all the expenses you are entitled to if you record these expenses in Quicken as soon as they occur.

37. Unless all of your income is from wages, you must keep accounting records that are acceptable to the IRS. All income and expenses are among the items that must be accurately documented.

38. If you obtain a filing extension, it does not grant you a tax payment extension.

39. Keep a log in your car to note business mileage right away. Otherwise, you are likely to forget to record some of it and not claim all of your allowable deduction.

40. If you purchase a few business items along with personal supplies, it is preferable to get two separate receipts. If all items are on one receipt, note immediately each item that you purchase for business.

41. Check with your company's human resource office to determine which employee benefits are taxable.

42. Utilize Quicken's budget features to put together a budget plan. A plan is essential to monitoring your financial progress.

43. Analyze budget results on a regular basis, and make decisions about bringing costs into line where necessary.

44. Always keep your personal and business accounts separate.

45. Maintain records of your daily bank balances.
46. Start organizing your tax records early.
47. Never write checks with erasable ink.
48. Return damaged goods for credit immediately.
49. Use different colored checks for different accounts.
50. Use preprinted, prenumbered business forms for control purposes.
51. If you are operating a business from your home and qualify for a home office deduction, you can allocate heat and electric costs based on square footage.
52. You must issue 1099s to all subcontractors whom you pay $600 or more.
53. Revenue earned from foreign sales is taxable in this country.
54. Interview several accountants before making your selection. You want to select one who not only has the right credentials, but with whom you feel you can communicate and work.
55. When selecting an accountant, check to ensure that he or she is a member of the state professional society and the American Institute of Certified Public Accountants. Members of these organizations have to comply with continuing education requirements.
56. Keep in mind that self-employed individuals must pay twice the Medicare and FICA on their earnings as an employee.
57. Be sure to discuss fees with your accountant up-front.
58. Enter your accounting transactions daily.
59. Prepare and distribute W-2s for all your employees by January 31.

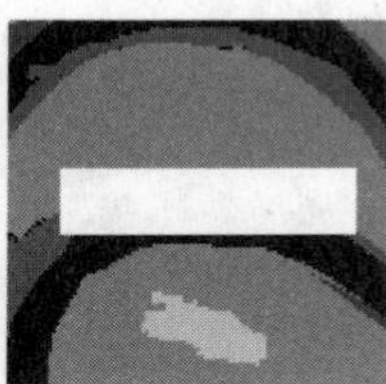

60. Depreciate part of your home if you qualify for a home office deduction.
61. If you are self-employed, remember that 50 percent of your Social Security payments in your own behalf are deductible on your tax return.
62. Consider spending one evening a month at the local library browsing through magazines rather than subscribing to so many.
63. Libraries loan more than books. Videos, books on tape, and even paintings for your walls are part of the lending materials at some libraries.
64. Joining an automobile club can save money if you do any traveling. In addition to road and tow services and free maps, many offer discount tickets to many attractions.
65. Increase the deductible on your insurance policies.
66. Change to a programmable thermostat to cut energy costs.
67. Consider using alternate transportation, such as a train or bus, during times when airfares are high.
68. Turn down your water heater if you will be away for more than a few days.
69. Check tire inflation and rotate tires periodically to extend their life.
70. Change the location of furniture exposed to light every few months.
71. Don't buy something just because it is on sale.
72. Use postcards when you want to write a quick note.
73. Have extra taxes withheld from your pay if you can't find any other way to save.

74. Sign the mailing list for your favorite stores. Often you receive special coupons and other discounts.
75. Buy greeting cards by the box rather than individually to cut costs by 75 percent or more.
76. Patch sidewalk and cement cracks before winter to keep ice from widening them.
77. Shop ethnic markets rather than gourmet shops for many of the same items at much lower prices.
78. Check the bulletin board at your store for manufacturer's rebates on products you use frequently.
79. Be willing to wait rather than use a speedy service for dry cleaning and film developing. The costs are normally much less.
80. Structure your insurance coverage to buy it all from the same company at a discount. Inquire about other homeowners discounts available for dead-bolt locks that can pay for themselves with one year's premium savings.
81. Use the flip side of used computer or calculator paper.
82. Use lower wattage bulbs in places where you don't really need the extra light to save energy costs.
83. Analyze the types of stock trades you usually do and check the costs of various discount brokers.
84. The dividends you receive from credit unions should be classified with other interest income you receive for tax purposes.
85. Carefully weigh the risks as well as the return from any investments you consider.
86. Leases are actually loans that go by another name. As you compute your net worth your lease obligations should be classified as a liability.

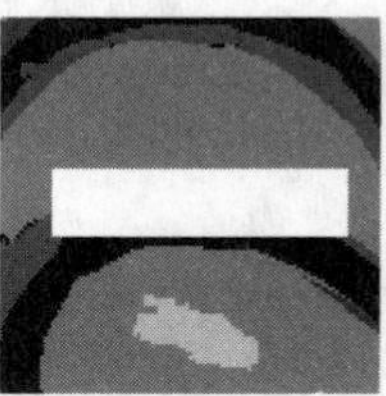

87. Apply caulking or other sealants to leaky doors and windows to prevent heat and cooling losses.

88. Know when the cheapest long distance rates are available from your long distance carrier. Check other discount plans they offer to save you additional money.

89. Have a set amount from every paycheck deposited automatically into a savings or retirement account.

90. Use household products for cleaning rather than expensive specialty cleaners. Vinegar, baking soda, and ammonia are all inexpensive and are perfect for various cleaning chores.

91. If you use reading glasses, check the variety available at your local pharmacy at much lower prices than at the optician.

92. Consider buying electronic equipment through mail order. Be sure to pay COD rather than by check with your order. The extra fee is worth the protection of not paying until you have the merchandise.

93. Keep track of the prices you pay for items you use frequently. You can then check warehouse specials to know whether it is worth buying in quantity and storing the goods for awhile.

94. Remember that buying the cheapest item isn't really cost-effective if the item is likely to break or wear out much sooner than a higher priced, higher quality alternative.

95. Ask the grocery store personnel to split a package of meat, produce, or bakery goods if you don't need the whole thing.

96. Check activities at your local parks and community centers. They are often free or low in cost.

97. Keep track of all the improvements you make to a home. They may impact the cost basis for your home when you sell it later.

98. Reduce and eliminate as much debt as possible. The interest you pay actually reduces the amount you have available for discretionary spending and investments.

99. Shop around for both banking and credit card fees. You can normally lock in rates for a year.

100. Check for rebates and free products available from credit card companies, long distance phone carriers, hotel chains, and others. Many companies have a frequent-buyer program that works a lot like airline frequent-flyer programs.

101. Audit your social security records at least once every three years. You can call your local Social Security office for a special form to be completed. You only have three years in which to dispute mistakes they've made in their records.

PART 3

BUSINESS APPLICATIONS

CHAPTER

SETTING UP QUICKEN for YOUR BUSINESS

Many small business owners find that the Quicken system of record-keeping can improve the quality of financial information used in making business decisions. You can use Quicken to record business transactions in your check register while maintaining cost and depreciation records for assets in other registers.

You can also use Quicken to budget your cash flow, track the cost of jobs in progress, monitor and record your payroll, and generate summary tax information to assist you in preparing your tax returns. If you are a building contractor, you can track the costs incurred on various jobs as they progress through construction. If you provide landscaping services, you can track the costs incurred for each job and prepare summary reports to determine the profits generated by each job. If you are an author, you can use Quicken to monitor royalties by publisher and record the costs you incurred while writing.

Although Quicken improves your ability to record and monitor your business' financial transactions, it may not eliminate the need for accounting services. There are important tax issues that affect the business transactions you record. In addition, you may want your accountant to establish the hierarchy of categories you use to record transactions. This hierarchy, used to categorize all transactions, is called a *chart of accounts*. Your accountant can help establish the structure for your chart of accounts, which will ensure the information is organized to reduce the time required for other services, such as year-end tax preparation, that the accountant will continue to supply. This is particularly important if you will be recording business expenses in both your personal and business checking accounts.

The first section of this book introduced you to Quicken's basic features. If you completed the exercises in Chapters 7 through 11, you built upon the basic skills by recording split transactions, such as mortgage payments allocated between principal and interest, and by memorizing recurring transactions. In those chapters you also used Quicken to prepare and monitor budgets, collect tax-related transactions, and prepare custom reports. In the remaining chapters you will look at some of these concepts again, from a business perspective. If you plan to use Quicken for both home and business use, you may find it beneficial to read through the earlier chapters, if you haven't done so, rather than moving directly to business transactions.

You will find many tips in the following chapters to help you avoid some of the problems encountered by small businesses. In addition, the special section "Ten Common Reasons for Business Failure" in this chapter identifies some common pitfalls, and explains how Quicken can help you avoid them.

This chapter is longer than the others since there are many decisions you need to make as you set up Quicken for your business. You also need to develop a number of basic skills to apply Quicken to all aspects of your business. The first step considers some alternatives. The next sections provide an overview of two important decisions that you must make before you use Quicken for your business. If you need additional guidance, consult with your accountant to be certain your information will be in the format you need for your entire business year.

Ten Common Reasons For Business Failure

Many of the new businesses that start each year fail. To improve your chances of success, you will want to look at some of the more common reasons for business failures and address these areas to prevent problems in your own business. Quicken can help you address some of these common problems.

Insufficient Capital

Many businesses fail because the owners don't properly plan for the capital they will need to get the business started, and don't seek outside financing, if needed, before starting. Quicken can help you put together a budget and plan your cash flow needs.

Pricing Doesn't Cover Costs

Many small business owners don't properly evaluate their costs, and set prices too low to cover all their costs. The need to pay a variety of taxes, cover depreciation expenses, and pay for expensive repairs are often overlooked when determining pricing for services and goods. Many individuals considering self-employment don't realize that their FICA and Medicare payments will be double what they were when they were working for someone else. Quicken can help you get a handle on all your costs so you can price your services appropriately.

High Fixed Costs

Fixed costs must be paid even in months when sales are low, placing a strain on a small business. Quicken can help you take a look at your fixed costs for rent, car or truck payments, other loan obligations, telephone service, utilities, and fixed salary costs. With the information Quicken can provide, you are better equipped to make decisions to help you lower fixed costs.

Inadequate Accounting Information and Controls

Shoebox record keeping will not serve you well if you are trying to keep your business afloat. Quicken's organizational capabilities make it easy to see which jobs were profitable ventures. Quicken's graph features let you get a quick picture of this information. Quicken also offers some accounting controls such as password protection.

Employee Theft

Inadequate monitoring of employee activities and lack of controls can cause a business owner to inadvertently overlook theft until it is too late. Quicken provides reports and a framework for you to implement controls to help you protect your business assets.

Poor Location

There has to be a need for your product at the location you select. If buyers are unlikely to visit the area selected, your business can be doomed to failure from the beginning. The Small Business Administration and SCORE (Service Corps of Retired Executives) can provide some help in overcoming problems with site selection.

Lack of Owner Commitment

Many new business owners don't realize that they'll have to put in more time in their own business than they did working for someone else. If family commitments and other responsibilities do not permit this, the business may be in trouble.

No Demand for Your Product

If there is no demand for your product or you can't generate the needed demand, you can't generate the revenue you need to succeed. To overcome this potential problem, you need to invest in adequate market research before starting your business. You must also realize that attempting to generate needed demand can be an expensive venture. Quicken can help you budget advertising and marketing costs.

Lack of Business Knowledge

Knowing the ropes of any business can be an important first step to success. Although you may succeed without it, your chances for success are enhanced with it. The Small Business Administration provides some low-cost seminars that can help you.

Poor Timing

Even the best conceived idea with adequate funding, a good location, and owner commitment and knowledge can fail due to bad timing. A strong economic decline just as you start your business can cause significant problems for the business. Unfortunately, this is not something which can necessarily be planned for.

You need to check some options before beginning this chapter. To do so, switch to a register window and select Options from the button bar. Select the QuickFill tab. Make sure that the Automatic Memorization Of New Transactions check box is selected and the Drop Down Lists Automatically Check Box is cleared. Then select Display and make sure the Memo Before Category check box is selected before clicking OK.

Cash Versus Accrual Accounting

The first decision you need to make is the timing of recording financial transactions. You can record a transaction as soon as you know that it will occur, or you can wait until cash actually changes hands between the parties involved in the transaction. The former alternative is accrual-basis accounting, and the latter is cash-basis accounting. (There is a third method, called modified-cash-basis accounting, which will be discussed shortly.) If your business is organized as a corporation, you must use the accrual method.

Most small businesses use the cash basis because it corresponds to their tax-reporting needs and because the financial reports prepared provide information summarizing the cash-related activities of the business. With *cash-basis* accounting, you report income when you receive cash from customers for services you provide. For example, if you are in the plumbing business, you recognize income when a customer pays for services. You might provide the services in December and not receive the customer's check until January. In this case, you record the income in January, when you receive and deposit the customer's check. Similarly, you recognize your expenses when you write your checks for the costs you incur. Thus, if you order supplies in December but don't pay the bill until January, you deduct the cost in January when you write a check to the supplier. Briefly, with a purely cash-basis accounting system, you recognize income when you receive cash and recognize expenses when you pay for expenses incurred for business purposes.

With the *accrual-basis* approach, you record your revenues and expenses when you provide services to your customers, regardless of when the cash flow occurs. Using the plumbing example from the preceding paragraph, you recognize the income from the plumbing services in December, when you provide the services to the customer, even though the cash is not received until the next year. Likewise, if you purchase supplies in December and pay for them in January, the cost of the supplies is recorded in December, not in January when you pay for them. Both methods record the same information, but at different times.

The basic difference between cash-basis and accrual-basis accounting is what accountants call *timing differences*. When a cash basis is used, the receipt of cash determines when the transaction is recorded. When the accrual basis is used, the time the services are provided determines when the revenue and expenses are recorded.

A third method of reporting business revenues and expenses is the *modified-cash-basis* approach. This method uses the cash basis as described, but modifies it to report depreciation on certain assets over a number of years. In this case, you must spread the cost of trucks, computer equipment, office furniture, and similar assets over the estimated number of years they will generate income for your business. The Internal Revenue Service has rules for determining the life of an asset. In addition, the tax laws allow you to immediately deduct the first $17,500 of the acquisition cost of certain qualified assets each year without worrying about depreciation. Once again, these are areas where your accountant can be of assistance in setting up your Quicken accounts.

Whether you use the cash, accrual, or modified cash basis in recording your transactions is determined by a number of factors. Some of the considerations are listed in the special section "Cash Versus Accrual Methods" below.

Since many small businesses use the modified cash basis of recording revenues and expenses, this method is illustrated in all the examples in Chapters 12 through 16.

Cash Versus Accrual Methods

Tax Requirements You must decide what your tax reporting obligations are and whether those requirements alone will dictate the methods you use for financial reporting. For most small businesses, tax requirements are the overriding factor to consider. For instance, if inventories are part of your business, you must use the accrual method for revenues and purchases. If inventories are not part of your business, you will probably find it best and easiest to use the cash basis of accounting.

Users of Financial Reports The people who use your financial reports can have a significant influence on your reporting decisions. For example, do you have external users such as banks or other creditors? If so, they may require special reports and other financial information that will influence how you set up your accounting and reporting system.

Size and Type of Business Activity The kind of business you have influences the type of financial reports you need to prepare and the method of accounting you will adopt. Are you in a service, retail, or manufacturing business? Manufacturing concerns should use the accrual method since they have sales that are billed and collected over weeks or even months and they carry inventories of goods. Retail stores such as small groceries should also use the accrual method of accounting, at least for sales and purchases, since they have inventories that affect the financial reports they prepare. On the other hand, a small landscaping business should probably use the cash basis since it has no inventory and the majority of the costs associated with the business are payroll and other costs generally paid close to the time the services are performed. If this business uses one or more pieces of equipment which represent a significant investment, it should use the modified cash basis to record depreciation on the property.

Establishing Your Chart of Accounts

You can use the basic set of categories that Quicken provides to categorize your business transactions, or you can create a new set. These organizational units are called categories in Quicken despite the fact that you may have been referring to them as accounts in your manual system.

You've used categories in earlier chapters. Since you've selected Business when setting up your new Quicken file, you have a wide range of business categories, such as Ads (Advertising) and Gr Sales (Gross Sales).

If you do not have an existing chart of accounts, making a few modifications to Quicken's standard categories is the best approach. Quicken's category names are suitable for most businesses. Later in this chapter, you learn to add categories of your own.

If you have an existing set of accounts, you will want to retain this structure for consistency. Many businesses assign a number to each category of income or expense—for example, a business might use 4001 as the account number for book sales. The business might use the first two digits of the number to group asset, liability, income, or expense accounts together. If you use this type of structure, you need to invest a little more time initially to establish your chart of accounts. You can delete the entries in the existing list of categories and then add new categories, or you can edit the existing categories one by one. The category names in your Category List (chart of accounts) might be numbers, such as 4001 or 5010, and the corresponding descriptions, such as 4001—Book Sales, and 5010—Freight. When you are finished, each category will contain your account number and each description will contain both the account number and some text describing the income or expense recorded in the category. You should work through all the examples in this chapter before setting up your own categories.

A Quick Look at the Business Used in the Examples

An overview of the business used for the examples in Chapters 12 through 16 will help you understand some of the selections you will make in the exercises. The business is run by an individual and is organized as a sole proprietorship. The individual running the business is married and must file a Form 1040 showing both business income and the W-2 income earned by the individual's spouse. Income categories in addition to the standard categories Quicken provides are needed for the different types of income generated. Since the company in the example offers services rather than merchandise, the income categories it makes use of must be appropriate for a service-type business. You can also use Quicken for retail or wholesale businesses that sell goods, and you can use Quicken for any organization, including sole proprietorships, partnerships, and small corporations. Look at the special section "Business Organization Options" in this chapter for a definition of these types of businesses.

The example business is based in the individual's home, which necessitates splitting some expenses, such as utilities and mortgage interest, between home and business categories. Other expenses, such as the purchase of office equipment, are business expenses. A number of expenses incurred by the business don't have appropriate entries in the Category List Quicken provides; you will have to add these categories.

Business Organization Options

You can choose from the following organization options when you set up your business:

Sole Proprietorship

A sole proprietorship provides no separation between the owner and the business. The debts of the business are the personal liabilities of the owner. The profits of the business are included on the owner's tax return since the business does not pay taxes on profits directly. This form of business organization is the simplest.

Partnership

A partnership is a business defined as a relationship between two or more parties. Each person in the partnership is taxed as an individual for his or her share of the profits. A partnership agreement defines the contributions of each member and the distribution of the profits.

Corporation

A corporation is an independent business entity. The owners of the corporation are separate from the corporation and do not personally assume the debt of the corporation. This is referred to as *limited liability*. The corporation is taxed on its profits and can distribute the remaining profits to owners as dividends. The owners are taxed on these dividends, resulting in the so-called "double tax" that occurs with the corporate structure. Unlike sole proprietorship and partnership business, corporations pay salaries to the working owners.

S Corporation

An S corporation is a special form of corporation that avoids the double tax problem of a regular corporation. A number of strict rules govern when an S corporation can be set up. Some of the limitations are that only one class of stock is permitted and that there is an upper limit of 35 shareholders.

The sample business in this book is a little more complicated than a business run from outside the home that has no transactions split between business and personal expenses. If you have a clear separation, you can simply establish a file for all your business accounts and another file for your personal transactions. The example used here includes separate checking accounts for business and personal records, but both accounts are placed in one file.

The use of separate accounts should be considered almost mandatory. All business income should be deposited into a separate account, and all expenses that are completely business related should be paid from this account. Anyone who has experienced an IRS audit can testify to the necessity of having solid documentation for business transactions. One part of that documentation is the maintenance of a business checking account and supporting receipts for your expenses and revenue. If you maintain a separate business account, your bank statement provides the supporting details for business transactions in a clear and concise manner that supports your other documentation of business activities. If your business is so small that it is not feasible to establish and maintain two checking accounts, you need to be particularly careful when recording entries in your Quicken register.

Quicken Files

When you began using Quicken, you created a file for your data. This file was named QDATA, and Quicken created other additional files on your hard disk to manage your transactions. You can use this set of files to record all your transactions if you decide to handle your business and personal financial transactions together.

In Chapters 3 through 6, you worked with only one account in QDATA. If you completed Chapters 7 through 11, you learned that it was possible to create additional accounts such as separate credit card, savings, and investment accounts. You can also create accounts for cash, assets, and liabilities. You created the PERSONAL file in Chapter 7 to organize all the personal accounts, and you created the INVEST file in Chapter 10 to hold the example investment account.

You could enter the transactions in this chapter in one of these files by setting up a new account. However, you want to set up new transactions in a separate file, so you should create a new set of files.

Adding a New File

If you completed Chapters 1 through 11, you already have the QDATA, PERSONAL, and INVEST files, which contain all the transactions entered in the first two sections of this book. If you skipped Chapters 7 through 11, you have only the QDATA file. In this section, you will learn how to create a new file and create accounts within it. If you're running short on hard disk space, you might need to delete these files. You can delete them from within Quicken or you can use the Windows File Manager to delete them when you are finished creating the new file.

You will create a file called BUSINESS and initially set up a business checking account, a personal checking account, and an asset account. The asset account will record information about equipment. In later chapters, you will establish other accounts for this file. Follow these steps to set up the new file and add the first three accounts to it:

1. Select New from the File menu.

   Quicken displays a dialog box to confirm that you want to set up a new file.
2. Select New File, and then select OK.

   Quicken opens a dialog box for creating a new file.
3. Check the location of your data files, and make changes to reference a valid drive or directory, if a change is required, by using the Drives or Directories boxes.
4. Type **BUSINESS** in the File Name text box.

   You must provide a valid filename of no more than eight characters. The filename must not include spaces or special symbols.
5. Select both the Home and Business check boxes.
6. Select OK to create the new file.

   Quicken creates five files using the name you typed in the File Name text box, and different file extensions. Although Quicken actually creates several files, they are referred to collectively as a single file because you can usually treat them as such.

   Since this is a new file, there are no accounts in it. The Create New Account dialog box shown in Figure 12-1 appears for you to set up a new account. Leave your screen as it is for a few minutes while you explore some new account options.

Adding Accounts to the New File

Quicken makes it easy to create multiple accounts. All the accounts here will be created in the same file so that you can print one report for all of them as well as print reports for individual accounts. Quicken sets up an account register for each account you create.

Selecting the new account type
Figure 12-1.

Checking, savings, investment, money market, cash, asset, liability, and credit card accounts are all possible additions. Savings, money market, and investment accounts should definitely be kept separate from your checking account since you will monitor both the growth and balance in these accounts separately. As mentioned earlier, separate business and personal checking accounts are another good idea.

You can set up Quicken accounts to conform to the needs of your business. In this section, you will add the first few accounts. In later chapters, you will establish additional accounts to monitor other business activities. From the Create New Account dialog box, follow these steps to create a new account:

1. Select the Guide Me check box if it does not already contain a check mark.
2. Select Checking for the account type.
3. Type **ANB Business** in the Account Name text box.

   "ANB" represents the bank name, and "Business" indicates that this account is the business checking account. ANB (for American National Bank) will eliminate confusion with the Cardinal Bank in earlier examples.
4. Type **Business Checking** in the Description text box, and select Next.
5. Choose Yes about having the last statement and select Next.
6. Enter **1/1/95** in the Statement Date text box by typing or using the drop-down calendar.
7. Type **4000** in the Ending Balance text box.

8. Select Done.

   The ANB Business account register appears in the Quicken window.

   Now you will establish an account for your personal checking. Using separate accounts is important to maintain accurate records.

HomeBase

Setup | Create Accounts

9. Select Create New Account from the Activities menu.

   You can also select New from the File menu, and then select New Account and OK, and continue with the following steps.
10. Select Checking.
11. Type **ANB Personal** in the Account Name text box.
12. Type **Personal Checking** in the Description text box and select Next.
13. Choose Yes about having the last statement and select Next.
14. Enter **1/1/95** in the Statement Date text box.
15. Type **2500** in the Ending Balance text box and select Done.
16. Select New from the File menu.
17. Select New Account and then select OK.
18. Select Asset.
19. Type **Equipment** in the Account Name text box.
20. Type **Capital Equipment** in the Description text box and select Next. This account will record financial transactions affecting the equipment you use in your business.
21. Choose No since you don't know the asset's worth, and then select Next. You will enter the value of these assets later in this chapter.
22. Select Next from the dialog box confirming that an asset account with a zero balance and today's date is needed.
23. Choose No since this account is not tax-deferred, and select Next.
24. Select Done without choosing the tax schedules for transfers in or out of this account.

You have now created a new file and three accounts for organizing personal and business transactions.

Changing the Active File

In the last exercise you created a new file. You can work in any file at any time, and can work with any account within a file. To change from the BUSINESS file to the QDATA file, follow these steps:

1. Select Open from the File menu.

2. Select QDATA.QDT from the File Name list box.
3. Select OK.

The QDATA file is now active. The windows that were displayed when you closed QDATA by opening a new file are now displayed again, as are any reminders that Quicken has been set to show. If you go to the register or Write Checks screen, you'll find that the 1st U.S. Bank account is active. Change back to the BUSINESS file.

Backing Up a File

It may seem a little early to be discussing backups since you haven't even entered data in this new file. However, backing up your file is important, and you'll want to get into the habit of backing up your files immediately after you create them. You should regularly back up the data managed by the Quicken system. Regular backups allow you to recover all your entries in the event of a hard disk failure since you can use your copy to restore all the entries. You need a blank formatted disk to record the backup information the first time. Subsequent backups can be made on this disk without reformatting it.

Creating Backup Files

Quicken provides a Backup and Restore feature that allows you to safeguard the investment of time you have made in entering your data. You can back up all your account files, or you can back up specific files by selecting the Backup option from the File menu. Follow these steps to back up the current file:

1. Select Backup from the File menu.
2. Place your blank formatted disk in drive A, and then select OK.

   If you want to back up another Quicken file, click the Select From List option button before selecting OK. Then select the file you want to back up, and select OK again. If you want to back up your file to a drive other than A, select that drive from the Backup Drive drop-down list box.
3. When Quicken displays the successful backup message, select OK to acknowledge the completion of the backup.
4. Select the ANB Business register window, shown in Figure 12-2.

Note: If your hard disk ever fails, you can re-create your data by selecting Restore from the File menu to copy your backup file to your directory. You should schedule backups on a regular basis to minimize the risk of data loss.

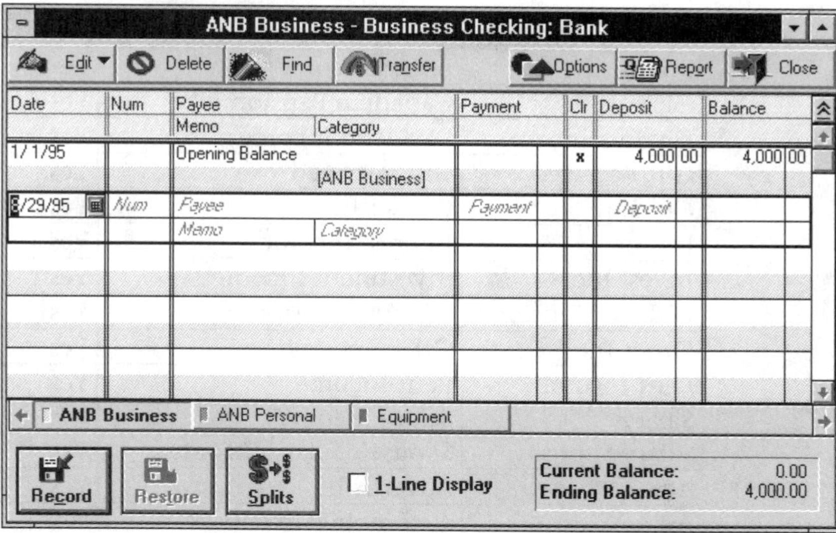

Register for a new account
Figure 12-2.

Customizing Categories

When you set up the new BUSINESS file, you selected both Home and Business as category options. This selection provides access to the more than 60 category choices shown in Table 12-1. You can see from this table that some categories are listed as expenses and others as income. Notice that some of the expense categories have more detailed subcategories beneath them. You learn how to create additional subcategories in the "Using Subcategories" section later in this chapter. Note the column in the table that shows you which categories are tax-related.

Editing the Existing Category List

You can change the name of any existing category, change its classification as income, expense, or subcategory, and change whether it is tax related. To change a category, follow these steps:

HomeBase

Setup | Category List

1. Choose Category & Transfer from the Lists menu to display the Category & Transfer List window, or press CTRL-C.
2. Move to the category you want to change.
3. Select Edit to edit the information for the category.
4. Change the settings you wish to alter.
5. Select OK to complete the changes.

Category	Description	Tax Related	Type
Bonus	Bonus Income	Yes	Income
CPP	Canadian Pension Plan	Yes	Income
Div Income	Dividend Income	Yes	Income
Gift Received	Gift Received	Yes	Income
Gr Sales	Gross Sales	Yes	Income
Int Inc	Interest Income	Yes	Income
Invest Inc	Investment Income	Yes	Income
Old Age Pension	Old Age Pension	Yes	Income
Other Inc	Other Income	Yes	Income
Rent Income	Rent Income	Yes	Income
Salary	Salary Income	Yes	Income
Salary Spouse	Spouse's Salary Income	Yes	Income
Ads	Advertising	Yes	Expense
Auto	Automobile Expenses	No	Expense
Fuel	Auto Fuel	No	Subcategory
Loan	Auto Loan Payment	No	Subcategory
Service	Auto Service	No	Subcategory
Bank Chrg	Bank Charge	No	Expense
Bus. Insurance	Insurance (not health)	Yes	Expense
Bus. Utilities	Water, Gas, Electric	Yes	Expense
Business Tax	Taxes & Licenses	Yes	Expense
Car	Car & Truck	Yes	Expense
Charity	Charitable Donations	Yes	Expense
Cash Contrib.	Cash Contributions	Yes	Subcategory
Non-Cash	Non-Cash Contributions	Yes	Subcategory
Childcare	Childcare Expense	No	Expense
Christmas	Christmas Expenses	No	Expense
Clothing	Clothing	No	Expense
Commission	Commissions	Yes	Expense
Dining	Dining Out	No	Expense
Dues	Dues	No	Expense
Education	Education	No	Expense
Entertain	Entertainment	No	Expense
Freight	Freight	Yes	Expense
Gifts	Gift Expenses	Yes	Expense
Groceries	Groceries	No	Expense
GST	Goods and Services Tax	Yes	Expense
Home Rpair	Home Repair & Maint.	No	Expense

Home and Business Category Options
Table 12-1.

Category	Description	Tax Related	Type
Household	Household Misc. Exp	No	Expense
Housing	Housing	No	Expense
Insurance	Insurance	No	Expense
Int Exp	Interest Expense	Yes	Expense
Int Paid	Interest Paid	Yes	Expense
Invest Exp	Investment Expense	Yes	Expense
L&P Fees	Legal & Prof. Fees	Yes	Expense
Late Fees	Late Payment Fees	Yes	Expense
Meals & Entertn	Meals & Entertainment	Yes	Expense
Medical	Medical Expenses	Yes	Expense
Doctor	Doctor & Dental Visits	Yes	Subcategory
Medicine	Medicine & Drugs	Yes	Subcategory
Misc	Miscellaneous	No	Expense
Mort Int	Mortgage Interest Exp	Yes	Expense
Office	Office Expenses	Yes	Expense
Other Exp	Other Expenses	Yes	Expense
PST	Provincial State Tax	Yes	Expense
Recreation	Recreation Expense	No	Expense
Rent on Equip	Rent-Vehicle,mach,equip	Yes	Expense
Rent Paid	Rent Paid	Yes	Expense
Repairs	Repairs	Yes	Expense
Returns	Returns & Allowances	Yes	Expense
RRSP	Reg Retirement Sav Plan	No	Expense
Subscriptions	Subscriptions	No	Expense
Supplies	Supplies	No	Expense
Supplies, bus.	Supplies	Yes	Expense
Tax	Taxes	Yes	Expense
Fed	Federal Tax	Yes	Subcategory
Medicare	Medicare Tax	Yes	Subcategory
Other	Misc. Taxes	Yes	Subcategory
Prop	Property Tax	Yes	Subcategory
Soc Sec	Soc Sec Tax	Yes	Subcategory
State	State Tax	Yes	Subcategory
Tax Spouse	Spouse's Taxes	Yes	Expense
Fed	Federal Tax	Yes	Subcategory
Medicare	Medicare Tax	Yes	Subcategory
Soc Sec	Soc Sec Tax	Yes	Subcategory
State	State Tax	Yes	Subcategory

Home and Business Category Options (*continued*)
Table 12-1.

Category	Description	Tax Related	Type
Telephone	Telephone Expense	No	Expense
Travel	Travel Expenses	Yes	Expense
UIC	Unemploy. Ins. Commission	Yes	Expense
Utilities	Water, Gas, Electric	No	Expense
Gas & Electric	Gas and Electricity	No	Subcategory
Water	Water	No	Subcategory
Wages	Wages & Job Credits	Yes	Expense

Home and Business Category Options (*continued*)
Table 12-1.

If you change the name of the category, Quicken changes the category's name in any transactions that are already assigned to the category.

If you need to totally restructure the categories before you begin using them, you may find it easier to delete the old categories and add new ones by following the instructions in the next section. To delete a category, follow these steps:

1. Select Category & Transfer from the Lists menu to display the Category & Transfer List window, or press CTRL-C.
2. Move to the category you want to delete.
3. Select Delete to delete the information in the category.
4. Select OK to confirm that you really want to remove the category.

You should not delete categories already assigned to transactions. If you do, you will delete the category entry in these transactions in your register. Delete categories before you start recording transactions.

Adding Categories

You can add categories to provide additional options specific to your needs. Each type of business will probably have some unique categories of income or expenses. For the example in this chapter, both income and expense category additions are needed.

The business in this example has three sources of income: consulting fees, royalties, and income earned for writing articles. It would be inappropriate to use the salary category for this income since that category should be reserved for income earned from a regular employer (reported on Form W-2 at the end of the year). You could use the Gross Sales category to record the various types of income for the business. Another solution would be to create new categories for each income source. For the examples in this chapter, you'll use three new income categories.

Many of the existing expense categories are suitable for recording business expenses, but for this example additional expense categories are needed. Equipment maintenance, computer supplies, and overnight mail service categories are needed. Although a category already exists for freight, a more specific postage category is also needed. New categories are not needed to record computer and office equipment and furniture purchases. These will be handled through an asset type account, with the specific purchase listed in the Payee field of the transaction.

You can add a new category by entering it in the Category field when you record a transaction in a register or on the Write Checks screen. If you press TAB to move to the next field, Quicken indicates that the category does not exist in the current list. You then have the choice of selecting a category already in the list or adding the new category to the list. You can choose to add it, just as you did with the category for auto loans in Chapter 7, "Expanding the Scope of Financial Entries."

If you have a number of categories to add, it is simpler to add them before starting data entry. To add the new categories needed for the exercises in this chapter, follow these steps:

1. Select Options from the Edit menu or click the Options icon in the icon bar, and then select General.
2. Make sure the Use Tax Schedules with Categories check box is selected.

   You will assign the tax-related categories you create in this example to particular lines of tax forms. This allows you to easily create reports that will help you fill out your tax forms, as discussed in Chapter 15, "Organizing Tax Information and Other Year-End Tasks."

HomeBase

Tools | Quicken Options

3. Select OK and Close.
4. Select Category & Transfer from the Lists menu to open the Category & Transfer List window.
5. Select New.

   Quicken opens this Set Up Category dialog box for you to enter a new category:

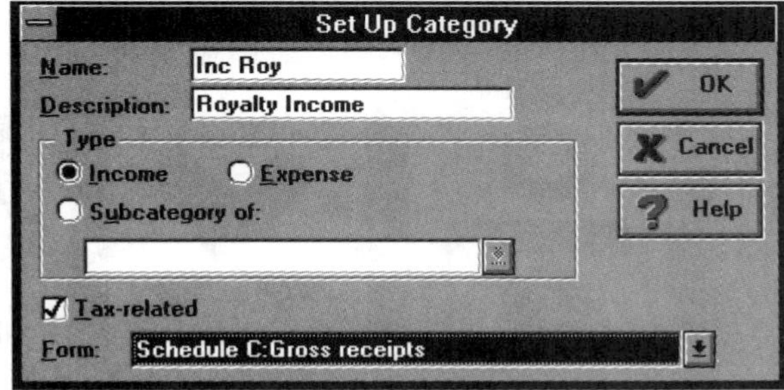

The dialog box shown here contains entries for a new royalty income category called Inc Roy. Note that the first part of the category name is Inc. If you begin all your income categories this way, you can later select all income categories by entering Inc in your report filter window. (See Chapter 4, "Quicken Reports.")

6. Type **Inc Roy** in the Name text box.
7. Type **Royalty Income** in the Description text box.
8. Select the Income option button.
9. Select the Tax-related check box.
10. Select Schedule C:Gross Receipts from the Form drop-down list box.
11. Select OK to create the category and return to the Category & Transfer List window.

    If you browse through the listed categories, you will find the one that you just added.
12. Repeat steps 5 through 11 for each of the categories that follow.

Name:	**Inc Cons**
Description:	**Consulting Income**
Type:	Income
Tax-related:	✓
Form:	Schedule C:Gross receipts

Name:	**Inc Art**
Description:	**Article Income**
Type:	Income
Tax-related:	✓
Form:	Schedule C:Gross receipts

Name:	**Equip Mnt**
Description:	**Equipment Maintenance**
Type:	Expense
Tax-related:	✓
Form:	Schedule C:Repairs and maintenance

Name:	**Supp Comp**
Description:	**Computer Supplies**
Type:	Expense
Tax-related:	✓
Form:	Schedule C:Supplies

Name:	**Postage**
Description:	**Postage Expense**
Type:	Expense
Tax-related:	✓
Form:	Schedule C:Other business expense

Name:	**Del Overngt**
Description:	**Overnight Delivery**
Type:	Expense
Tax-related:	✓
Form:	Schedule C:Other business expense

13. Select Close in the button bar to put this window away and return to the register window.

You should feel free to customize Quicken by adding any categories you need. However, be aware that the amount of available RAM (random-access memory) in your computer limits the number of categories you can create in each Category List.

Requiring Categories for All Transactions

12

You can set Quicken to remind you that a category should be entered for each transaction before it is recorded. If you attempt to record a transaction without a category when this option is active, Quicken won't complete the process until you confirm that you want the transaction added without a category.

If you want to require categories for all transactions, select Options from a register window's button bar. Select the Warn Before Recording Uncategorized Transactions check box on the Miscellaneous tab. Select OK to finalize the setting change. The next time you attempt to record a transaction without a category, Quicken stops to confirm your choice before saving.

Using Classes

Classes provide another way to organize your data.

Classes are another tool for organizing transactions. They can define the who, when, or why of a transaction. It is important to understand that although they, too, allow you to group data, classes are distinct from categories. You will continue to use categories to provide specific information about the transactions to which they are assigned. Categories tell you what kind of income or expense a specific transaction represents. You can tell at a glance which costs are for utilities and which are for entertainment. In Summary reports, you might show transactions totaled by category.

Classes allow you to slice the transaction pie in a different way. They provide a different perspective on your data. For example, you can continue to organize data in categories such as Utilities or Snow Removal yet also classify it by the rental property requiring the service. Classes were not needed in the earlier chapters of this book since categories provide all the organization you need for very basic transactions.

If you want to combine home and business transactions in one file, classes are essential for differentiating between the two types of transactions. Here, every transaction you enter will be classified as either personal or business. Business transactions will have a class entered after the category. By omitting the class entry from personal transactions, you classify them as personal. Class assignments can be used without category assignments, but in this chapter they are used in addition to categories.

Defining Classes

Quicken does not provide a standard list of classes. As with categories, you can set up what you need before you start making entries or you can add the classes you need as you enter transactions. To assign a class while entering a transaction, you type the class name in the Category field after the category name (if one is used). You must type a slash (/) before the class name.

In this example, you will create the class you need before you enter transactions. Follow these steps from the ANB Business account register to add a class for business transactions:

1. Select Class from the Lists menu to open the Class List window or press CTRL-L.
2. Select New. Quicken displays the Set Up Class dialog box, shown here:

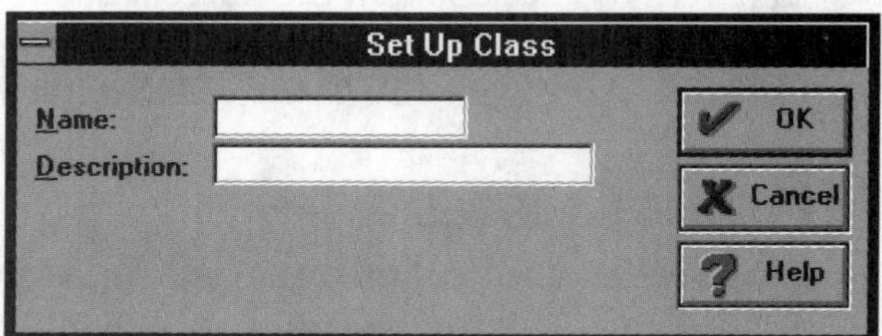

3. Type **B** in the Name text box.

   You can use a longer entry, such as Business, but Quicken has a limited amount of space to display categories, classes, and other organizational groupings, so you should keep it as short as possible.
4. Type **Business** in the Description text box, and select OK.

Quicken adds the new class to the list in the Class List window. You could create a second class for personal transactions, but it isn't really necessary. You can consider any transactions that aren't designated class B to be personal.

5. Press ESC to return to the register window.

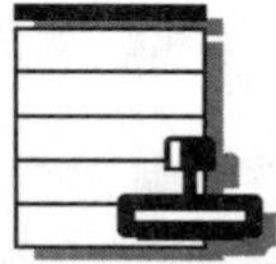

Remember: To create a class as you enter a transaction, simply type the category followed by a slash (/) and the class you want to use.

6. Highlight the opening balance transaction.
7. Tab to the Category field.
8. Type **/B**.
9. Select Record to record the changed entry.

Entering Transactions with Classes

You record the business transactions in the same manner you recorded earlier transactions. It is important that you remember to enter the class in the Category field. Follow these steps to begin entering business transactions: 12

1. Move to a blank transaction, and enter **1/2/95** in the Date field.
2. Type **Arlo, Inc.** in the Payee field.
3. Type **12500** in the Deposit field.
4. Type **Seminars conducted in 11/94** in the Memo field.
5. Type **Inc Cons/B**.

   The first part of this entry categorizes the transaction as consulting income. The slash (/) and the B classify the transaction as business related.

   When you start to record this category, Quicken uses its QuickFill feature to assist you in entering the transaction. In this case, Quicken supplies the category Inc Art. If you open the drop-down list box by pressing ALT-DOWN ARROW, you can easily move to the desired category with UP ARROW or DOWN ARROW. If your category is not on the standard list, you need to add it as you did earlier in this chapter. You can always continue to type the entire category entry without using QuickFill's suggestions. If you want the category suggested by the QuickFill feature, you can type the / and the class without typing the rest of the category name.
6. Select Record to record the transaction. Your register looks like this:

Date	Num	Payee / Memo / Category	Payment	Clr	Deposit	Balance
1/1/95		Opening Balance [ANB Business]/B		x	4,000 00	4,000 00
1/2/95		Arlo, Inc. Seminars conducted Inc Cons/B			12,500 00	16,500 00

You can record an expense transaction in the ANB Business account in a similar fashion. Follow these instructions:

1. Enter **1/2/95** in the Date field.
2. Type **101** in the Num field.
3. Type **Office All** in the Payee field.
4. Type **65** in the Payment field.
5. Type **Cartridge for copier** in the Memo field.
6. Type **Supplies** in the Category field.

   As you can see, QuickFill fills in the category as soon as you've typed enough characters for it to identify the category.
7. Type **/B**, and select Record.

   The register window looks like Figure 12-3.

The next transaction is for clothing. Since this is a personal expense paid with a personal check, it cannot be added to the current account. You must open the ANB Personal account for your entry. Follow these steps:

1. Select the Accts icon from the icon bar, or select Account from the Lists menu.

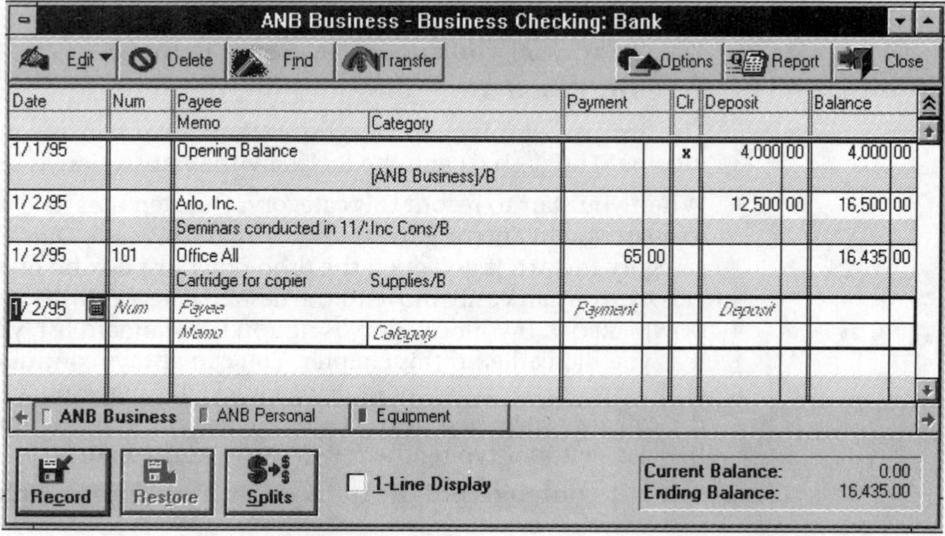

Recording business transactions in the register window
Figure 12-3.

2. Select ANB Personal.
3. Select Open.

   You can also double-click the account name in the Account List window to open its register. Another option is to click the ANB Personal account selector at the bottom of the register window.

When you enter the transaction for clothing, you will not enter a class; this indicates that the clothing transaction is a personal expense. Although you could have created another class, called P, for personal transactions, the approach used here minimizes typing; only business transactions require the extra entry. Follow these steps to add the clothing transaction:

1. Enter **1/3/95** in the Date field.
2. Type **825** in the Num field.

   This check number is not sequential with check number 101, the last business check used, since this check is from your personal account.
3. Type **Discount Coats** in the Payee field.
4. Type **120** in the Payment field.
5. Type **New winter coat** in the Memo field.
6. Enter **Clothing** in the Category field.

   Notice that no slash (/) is used since a class is not being added for personal expenses.
7. Select Record to record the transaction. Your entries should match the ones shown here:

HomeBase

Day To Day | Account List

1/ 1/95		Opening Balance				x	2,500	00	2,500	00
		[ANB Personal]								
1/ 3/95	825	Discount Coats	120	00					2,380	00
		New winter coat Clothing								

Splitting Transactions

Split transactions are transactions that affect more than one category or class. You decide how a transaction affects each of the categories or category/class combinations involved. If you split an expense transaction, you are saying that portions of the transaction should be considered as expenses in two different categories or classes. For example, a purchase at an office products store might include school supplies for your children and products for the office. You need to know exactly how much was spent for personal expenses and how much for business expenses in this transaction. Many expenses can be part business and part personal, especially if you operate a business from your home. You can allocate the amount of any transaction among different categories or classes by using the Splits window. Split transactions frequently take advantage of subcategories, which are explained in the next section.

If you select Splits in a register window, Quicken displays the Splits window. You can then enter different memos, categories, or classes for each part of the transaction. As an example, suppose you used a personal check to buy a calendar and paper for your business's laser printer. Even though the largest portion of this expense was for business, it was paid with a personal check and so must be recorded in the ANB Personal account. Follow these steps to complete an entry in the ANB Personal register for a purchase at Campus Stationery, which includes both personal and office supply expenses:

1. Enter **1/3/95** in the Date field.
2. Enter **826** in the Num field.
3. Type **Campus Stationery** in the Payee field.
4. Type **82** in the Payment field.
5. Type **Calendar and computer paper** in the Memo field.
6. Select Splits from the bottom of the register window to activate the Splits window.
7. Enter **Supp Comp/B** in the first Category field.
8. Type **Paper for laser printer** in the Memo field.

   Quicken displays the entire amount of the transaction in the Amount field.
9. Type **75.76** in the Amount field.

   Quicken subtracts this amount from $82.00 and displays the amount remaining in the Amount field for the as-yet unspecified category in the Splits window.
10. Type **Misc** in the Category field.
11. Type **New calendar for kitchen** in the Memo field.

    This completes the entries since $6.24 is the cost of the calendar. Your screen should look like Figure 12-4.

    If the total of your splits entries did not equal the transaction total that you entered in the register, there would still be something left in the Amount field in the next row. You could then select Adj. Tot. to have Quicken replace the transaction total previously recorded in the register with the total of the Splits entries. Before doing this, make sure that you haven't just entered one of the split amounts incorrectly. If the total

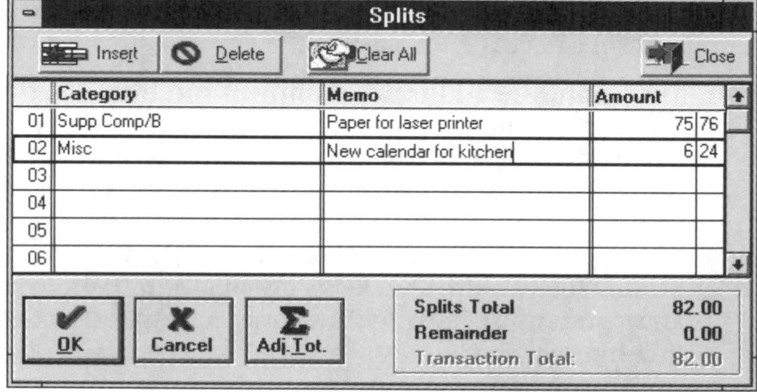

The Splits window for the Campus Stationery transaction
Figure 12-4.

splits exceed the total you entered in the Payment field, you will see a negative number in the Amount field of the next row.

12. Select OK to close the Splits window.

    Now, the Category field entry in your register displays --Splits-- to let you know that the transaction has more than one category.

13. Select Record to record the transaction.

Using Subcategories

Since you are quickly becoming proficient at basic transaction entry, you will want to see some other options for recording transactions. One option is to use subcategories to further define a category. Unlike classes, subcategories provide a detailed breakdown of the category. For instance, you could continue to allocate all your utility bills to the Utilities category, but you could create subcategories that allow you to allocate expenses to electricity, water, or gas. You can still classify these transactions as either business or personal expenses using the classes you established. You can also create reports that include all transactions from a category and its subcategories.

You can add subcategories by modifying the Category List as you add new categories, or you can create them as you enter transactions and realize the existing category entries don't provide the breakdown you need.

Entering a New Subcategory

When you enter a subcategory for a transaction, you type the category name, a colon (:), and the subcategory name. It is important that the category be specified first and the subcategory second. If a transaction has a class assigned, the class name comes third in the sequence, separated from the category and subcategory by a slash (/).

The business used in this example is run from the home of the owner, which necessitates splitting certain expenses between business and personal. Tax guidelines state that the percentage of the total square footage in the home that is used exclusively for business can determine the portion of common expenses, such as utilities, allocated to the business. The business in this example occupies 20 percent of the total square footage in the home. You can use Quicken's Calculator to perform these computations, and you can use both subcategories and split transactions in recording the first transactions.

Enter the utility bills in the new account. Follow these steps to complete the entries for the gas and electric bills, creating a subcategory under Utilities for each and allocating 20 percent of each utility bill to your business by splitting the transactions between classes:

When you need to monitor expenses closely, subcategories can help by showing a breakdown of costs at the more detailed level.

1. With the next blank transaction in the ANB Personal register highlighted, enter **1/3/95** as the date for the transaction.
2. Enter **827** in the Num field.

   Instead of typing the check number, you can type + to have Quicken enter the next check number.
3. Type **Consumer Power** in the Payee field.
4. Type **80.00** for the payment amount.
5. Type **Electric Bill** in the Memo field.
6. Select Splits to open the Splits window.
7. Type **Utilities:Electric/B** in the Category field.
   Quicken prompts you with the Set Up Category dialog box.
8. Type **Electric Utilities** in the Description text box.

   Although the description is optional, it is a good idea to enter one so that your reports will be informative. Notice that the Subcategory Of option button is selected.
9. Select the Tax-related check box.
10. Select Schedule C:Utilities in the Form drop-down list box.

    The Set Up Category dialog box shown here should match the one on your screen:

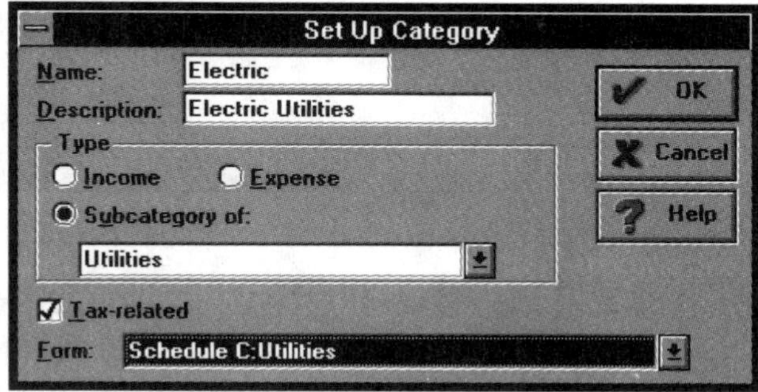

11. Select OK to close the dialog box, and move to the Memo field in the Splits window.
12. Type **Business part of electric** in the Memo field.
13. Type **20%** in the Amount field, and move to the next line.

    Quicken calculates 20 percent of your total transaction amount and enters it in the Amount field when you move to another field. The 80 percent remaining is displayed in the Amount field of the next split.
14. Type **Utilities:Electric** in the Category field.

    Note that a class was not added to the entry; Quicken will consider the entry a personal expense.
15. Type **Home part of electric** in the Memo field.

    The Splits window looks like this:

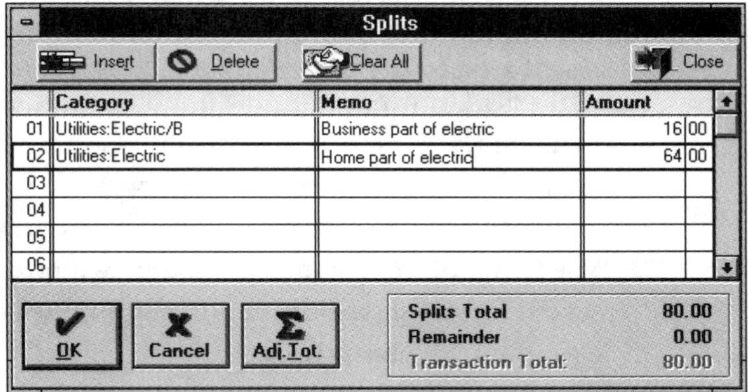

Quicken has computed the difference between $80.00 and $16.00 and displayed it in the Amount field.

16. Select OK to close the Splits window.
17. Select Record to record the transaction entry.

The transaction is displayed in the register window, as shown here:

1/ 3/95	827	Customer Power	80	00			2,218	00
		Electric Bill --Splits--						

Completing the Utility Subcategories

You have one more utility bill to enter. The bill for gas utilities also requires a new subcategory. Complete the following steps to enter the transaction and create a subcategory for the gas bill.

1. Enter the following information in each of the fields shown:

Date:	**1/7/95**
Check:	**828**
Payee:	**Western Michigan Gas**
Payment:	**40.00**
Memo:	**Gas Bill**

2. After completing the Memo field entry, select Splits to open the Splits window.

   Quicken's default categories include the subcategories Utilities:Gas & Electric and Utilities:Water. Since you already have a subcategory established for electric, you will want to narrow the Gas & Electric subcategory so that it pertains exclusively to the gas bill.
3. Select Category & Transfer from the Lists menu to display the Category & Transfer List window.
4. Highlight Gas & Electric under Utilities.
5. Select Edit to edit the current category.
6. Change the name in the Name text box to Gas.
7. Type **Gas Utilities** in the Description text box.
8. Make sure the Subcategory option button is selected.
9. Select the Tax-related check box.
10. Select Schedule C:Utilities from the Form drop-down list box.
11. Select OK.
12. Double-click this category or press ENTER to add it to the window, and then type **/B** at the end of Utilities:Gas.
13. Type **Business part of gas bill** in the Memo field.

14. Type **20%**, and move to the next line.
15. Enter **Utilities:Gas** in the Category field.
16. Type **Home part of gas bill** in the Memo field.
17. Select OK to close the Splits window.
18. Select Record to record the transaction entry.

    If you move to the top of the register, your entries will look like those in Figure 12-5.

Entering the Remaining Business Transactions

You are now acquainted with all the skills needed to enter transactions that affect a business or personal account. You should, however, complete the transactions remaining for January. Use these steps to complete the remaining entries:

HomeBase

Day To Day | Account List

1. Click the ANB Business account selector at the bottom of the register window to switch to this account.

   You can also select Account from the Lists menu or select the Accts icon to open the Account List window. Then select ANB Business, and select Open.
2. Enter **1/8/95** in the Date field.
3. Enter **102** in the Num field.
4. Type **Computer Outlet** in the Payee field.

12

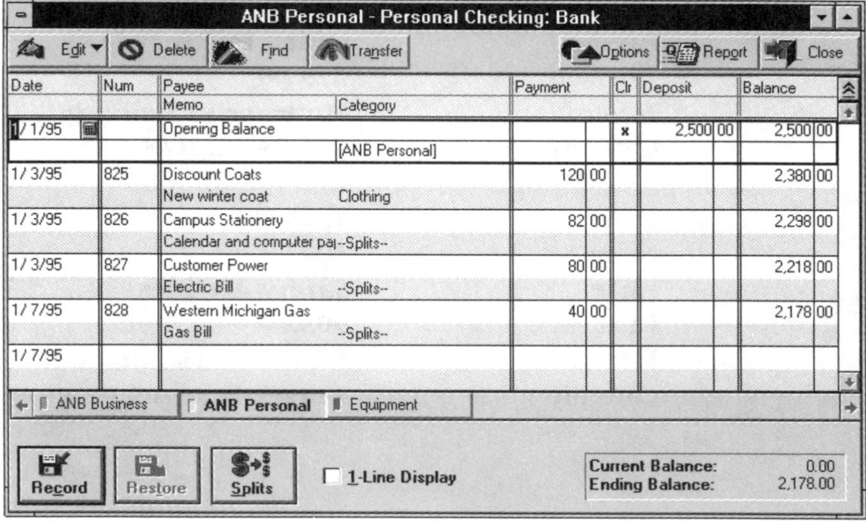

Register entries in the ANB Personal account

Figure 12-5.

5. Type **300** in the Payment field.
6. Type **Cartridges, ribbons, and disks** in the Memo field.
7. Select Splits to open the Splits window.

   This transaction will use the same category and class for each part of the split. The transaction is split to provide additional documentation for purchases.
8. Complete the entries in the Splits window as shown here:

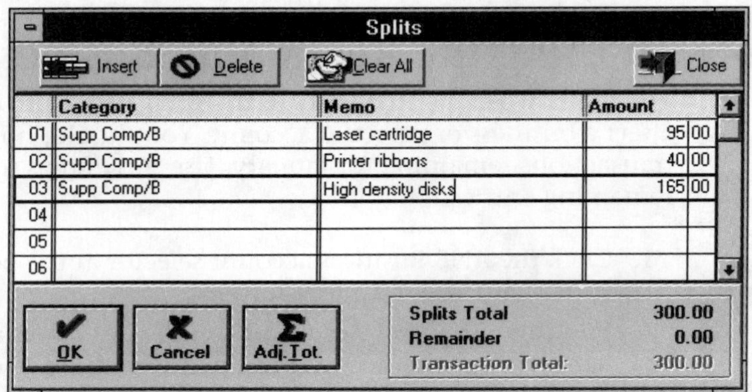

9. Select OK, and then select Record.
10. Enter the following transactions by completing the entries in the fields and selecting Record after each transaction:

Date:	**1/15/95**
Num:	**103**
Payee:	**Quick Delivery**
Payment:	**215.00**
Memo:	**Manuscript delivery**
Category:	**Del Overngt/B**

Date:	**1/15/95**
Num:	**104**
Payee:	**Safety Airlines**
Payment:	**905.00**
Memo:	**February Ticket**
Category:	**Travel/B**

Date:	**1/20/95**
Num:	**105**
Payee:	**Alltel**
Payment:	**305.00**
Memo:	**Telephone Bill**
Category:	**Telephone/B**

11. Enter the beginning of the next transaction as follows:

Date:	**1/20/95**
Num:	**106**
Payee:	**Postmaster**
Payment:	**28.25**
Memo:	**Postage for Mailing**

12. With the insertion point in the Category field, select Splits.
13. Complete the following entries in the Splits window:

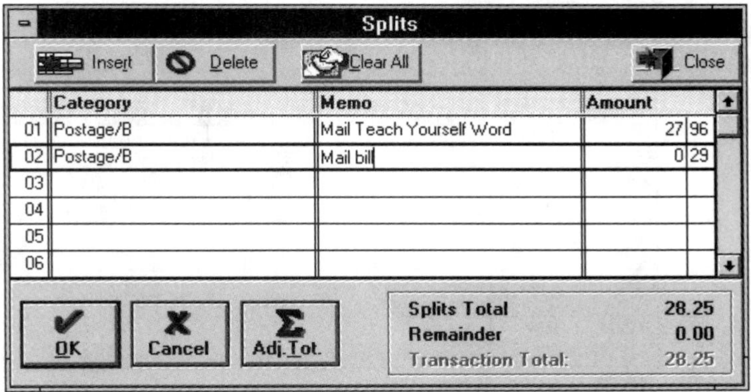

14. Select OK, and select Record.
15. Complete the next transaction to record a maintenance expense for existing equipment:

Date:	**1/20/95**
Num:	**107**
Payee:	**Fix-It-All**
Payment:	**1100.00**
Memo:	**Equipment Contract**
Category:	**Equip Mnt/B**

16. Select Record to record the transaction.

    The entries in your register should now look like Figure 12-6.

The remaining transactions for this business all relate to equipment. You will need to use the Equipment account you created earlier to handle these transactions.

Using the Asset Account

When you record asset transactions you will notice that the register fields are a little different since you are increasing or decreasing the value of the account but are not writing a check or making a deposit.

Earlier in this chapter you established an asset account called Equipment. You'll use this account to track total equipment holdings and depreciation expenses. Purchase transactions for equipment will be recorded in your business checking account register as transfers to the Equipment account. Other transactions, such as entering information about equipment purchased before you started using Quicken and a depreciation transaction, will be entered directly in the asset register. In the next section, you will look at recording transactions for existing equipment and a new purchase. In Chapter 15, "Organizing Tax Information and Other Year-End Tasks," you will learn how to record depreciation expenses as the asset ages and declines in value.

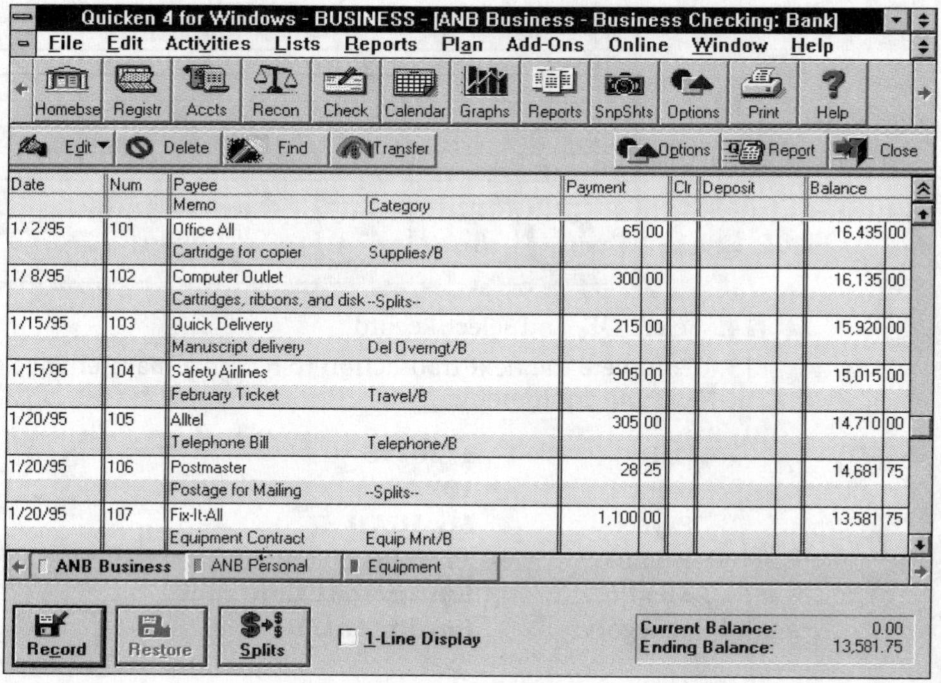

Quicken 4 for Windows - BUSINESS - [ANB Business - Business Checking: Bank]

File Edit Activities Lists Reports Plan Add-Ons Online Window Help

Homebse Registr Accts Recon Check Calendar Graphs Reports SnpShts Options Print Help

Edit Delete Find Transfer Options Report Close

Date	Num	Payee / Memo	Category	Payment	Clr	Deposit	Balance
1/ 2/95	101	Office All		65 00			16,435 00
		Cartridge for copier	Supplies/B				
1/ 8/95	102	Computer Outlet		300 00			16,135 00
		Cartridges, ribbons, and disk	--Splits--				
1/15/95	103	Quick Delivery		215 00			15,920 00
		Manuscript delivery	Del Overngt/B				
1/15/95	104	Safety Airlines		905 00			15,015 00
		February Ticket	Travel/B				
1/20/95	105	Alltel		305 00			14,710 00
		Telephone Bill	Telephone/B				
1/20/95	106	Postmaster		28 25			14,681 75
		Postage for Mailing	--Splits--				
1/20/95	107	Fix-It-All		1,100 00			13,581 75
		Equipment Contract	Equip Mnt/B				

ANB Business | ANB Personal | Equipment

Record Restore Splits 1-Line Display

Current Balance: 0.00
Ending Balance: 13,581.75

Register entries in the ANB Business account

Figure 12-6.

Recording Transactions for Existing Equipment Holdings

The existing equipment cannot be recorded as a purchase since you don't want to affect the balance in the business checking account. You need to make the transaction entry directly in the Equipment account. The fields in an asset account register are somewhat different than those in other account registers, as you can see in Figure 12-7. Follow these steps to record the equipment transactions:

HomeBase

Day to Day ¦ Account List

1. Select Account from the Lists menu, or select the Accts icon from the icon bar.
2. Select the Equipment account, and select Open.
3. Move to the Date field for the opening balance transaction.
4. Enter **1/1/95** in the Date field and select Record to modify this transaction.
5. Enter **1/1/95** in the Date field of the next transaction.
6. Type **High Tech Computer** to enter the name of the asset in the Payee field.

   You can record an inventory number as part of this entry if one is assigned.
7. Type **3000** to record the original purchase price in the Increase field.
8. Type **Original cost of equipment** in the Memo field.
9. Enter **Equipment/B** in the Category field, and select Record.

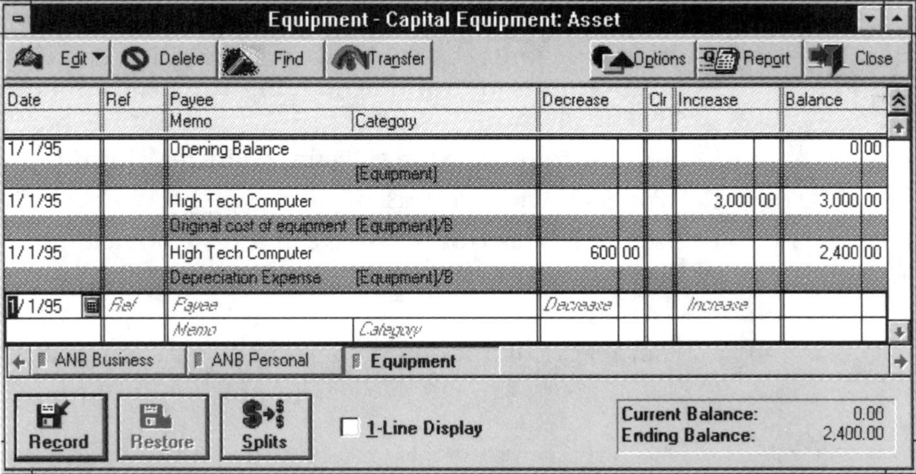

Equipment transactions
Figure 12-7.

Quicken displays the category as [Equipment] since the category is an account name. The brackets are always added when an account name is placed in the Category field. This transaction will increase the balance of that account.

To change the book value of the asset, another adjusting transaction is required. This transaction reduces the book value by the amount of the depreciation expense recognized last year and in prior years. The transaction must be recorded against the Equipment account rather than as a depreciation expense, or the amount of the depreciation for last year will appear in this year's expense reports. You do not want to record the depreciation expense in your checking account register because you are not writing a check for this expense. Follow these steps to complete the second transaction entry:

1. Enter **1/1/95** in the Date field.
2. Type **High Tech Computer** in the Payee field.

Note: It is important to use the same name in all transactions relating to a given piece of equipment.

When you typed **H**, Quicken used its QuickFill feature to complete the Payee field with "High Tech Computer." Quicken reviews all the payees in the Memorized Transaction List to make the suggestion for the payee name to use in the transaction.

You can press ALT-DOWN ARROW to open the QuickFill drop-down list box, then use UP ARROW and DOWN ARROW to review other options beyond QuickFill's first suggestion. When you find the correct payee, press TAB. Quicken records the entire previous transaction for this payee. You must edit the copy of the original transation if you want to make changes in the new entry. In this case, the following editing steps are needed:

3. Press DEL to remove the value in the Increase field.
4. Type **600** in the Decrease field.
5. Type **Depreciation Expense** in the Memo field.
6. Select Record, accepting [Equipment]/B as the category and finalizing the transaction.

Your register entries should match the ones in Figure 12-7.

Adding a New Equipment Purchase

Purchasing an asset reduces the balance in a checking account. When the asset is equipment, there must also be an entry in the Equipment account. If you list the Equipment account as the Category field in the checking account's transaction, Quicken will handle the transfer. But when entering this transaction in your checking account, you must do two unusual things: enter the name of the *asset* in the Payee field, and enter the name of the *payee* in the Memo field. This enables the information to transfer in format consistent with that of the Equipment account.

Follow these steps to record the purchase of a laser printer:

1. Click the ANB Business account selector at the bottom of the register window to switch the account displayed in this register window.
2. Enter **1/25/95** in the Date field.
3. Type + in the Num field to enter 108 as the check number.
4. Type **Laser 1** in the Payee field.
5. Type **1500** in the Payment field.
6. Type **Printer from Fran's Computer** in the Memo field.
7. Enter **Equipment/B** in the Category field.
8. Select Record to record the transaction.

   Your transaction looks like this:

1/25/95	108	Laser 1	1,500	00				12,081	75
		Printer from Fran's Computer [Equipment]							

9. Click the Equipment account selector at the bottom of the register window to show the Equipment account in this register window.

   Figure 12-8 shows the transactions in the Equipment account after the transfer transaction is recorded.
10. Click the ANB Business account selector at the bottom of the register window to return to the business checking account.

Memorized Transactions

Many of your financial transactions are likely to repeat; you pay your utility bills each month, for instance. Likewise, overnight delivery charges, phone bills, payroll, and other bills are paid about the same time each month. Cash

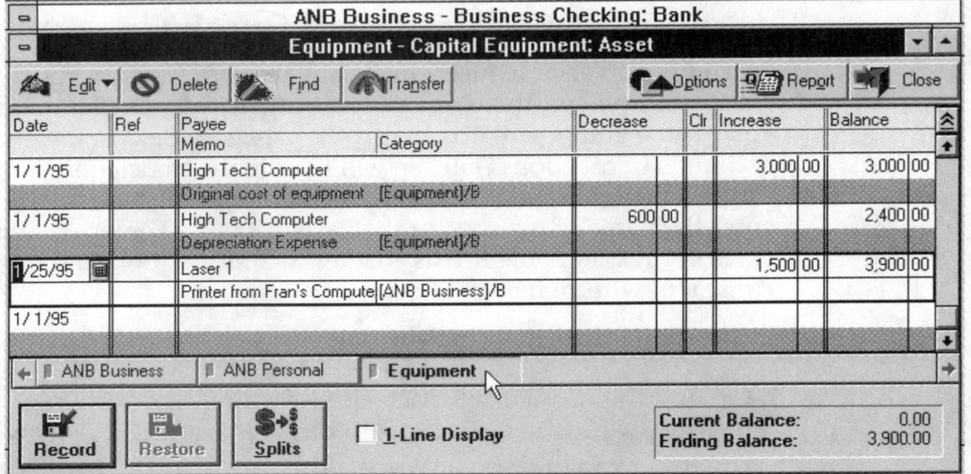

Register entries in the Equipment account after the printer purchase
Figure 12-8.

inflows for some businesses are daily, weekly, or monthly. Other payments, such as supply purchases, also repeat, but perhaps not on the same dates each month.

As discussed in Chapter 7, "Expanding the Scope of Financial Entries," Quicken memorizes transactions entered in the register or the Write Checks window, according to the Option setting. Once memorized, these transactions can generate identical transactions. Although amounts and dates may change, you can edit these fields and not have to reenter payee, memo, and category information.

Note: To make sure that your transactions are memorized, you need to select the Options button bar button from a register window and then select QuickFill. Select the Automatic Memorization Of New Transactions check box and select OK. If this option has not been selected, you cannot follow the steps in the rest of this chapter.

Editing and Deleting Memorized Transactions

To change a memorized transaction, begin by opening the Memorized Transaction List window by selecting Memorized Transaction from the Lists menu. Select the transaction you want to edit from the list, and select Edit. The Edit Memorized Transaction dialog box appears, as shown here:

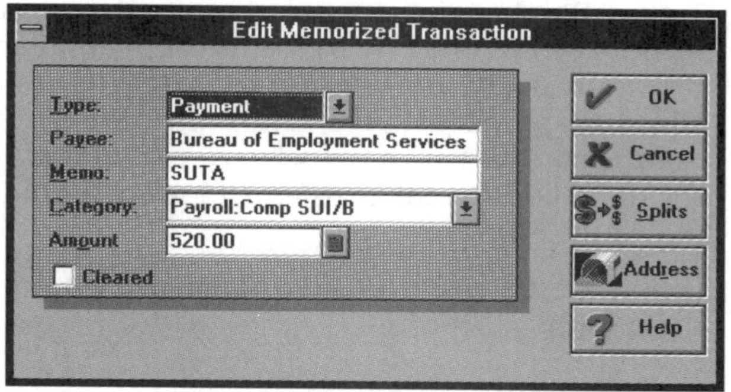

You can change the desired settings in this dialog box.

To delete a memorized transaction, open the Memorized Transaction List window. Highlight the transaction you want to delete, and then select Delete. A warning message appears, asking you to confirm the deletion. When you select OK, the transaction is no longer memorized. You can delete one-time transactions that are not likely to be often repeated. Follow these steps to delete a memorized transaction:

1. Select Memorized Transaction from the Lists menu to open the Memorized Transaction List window.
2. Highlight the Arlo Inc. transaction.

   This is a payment for a one-time service rather than an ongoing series of payments, so there is no real need to maintain this particular transaction.
3. Select Delete.
4. When Quicken prompts you to confirm the deletion, select OK.
5. Repeat steps 2 through 4 for this series of transactions:

   Campus Stationery
   High Tech Computer
   Laser 1
6. Select Close to leave the Memorized Transaction List window.

Using Memorized Transactions

To recall a memorized transaction and place it in the register, move to the next blank transaction record. (If you recall a memorized transaction while a previously recorded transaction is highlighted, the existing payee is replaced by the one in the memorized transaction.) Open the Memorized Transaction List window by selecting Memorized Transaction from the Lists menu. If you type the first letter of the payee name after you open the Memorized

Transaction List, Quicken takes you to the correct area of the list since it is in alphabetical order by payee. Select the transaction you want to add to the register by double-clicking it or pressing ENTER. When the selected transaction is added, it appears with the date of the preceding transaction in the register, not the date on which the selected transaction was last recorded. Edit the transaction in the register, and select Record when you are ready to record the entry.

Follow these steps to record a payment to Quick Delivery for later in the month:

1. Move to the end of the ANB Business register entries.
2. Select Memorized Transaction from the Lists menu.
3. Double-click the Quick Delivery transaction, or highlight it and press ENTER.
4. Quicken adds the transaction to the register.
5. Enter **1/30/95** in the Date field.
6. Enter **109** in the Num field.
7. Type **55.00** in the Payment field, and select Record to record the transaction.

   The transaction looks like this:

1/30/95	109	Quick Delivery Manuscript delivery Del Overngt/B	55 00			12,026 75

Memorizing a Check

The procedure for memorizing transactions while writing checks is identical to the procedure for memorizing register transactions. You must be in the Write Checks window when you begin, but otherwise the steps are the same. Check and register transactions for the same file will appear in the same Memorized Transaction List and can be edited, deleted, or recalled from either the Write Checks window or the account register window.

Working with Scheduled Transactions

Although you can recall memorized transactions individually as a way to reenter similar transactions, a better method is to have Quicken automatically schedule and enter transactions for you. Quicken can schedule individual transactions or groups of transactions. If you want to schedule groups of transactions, the transactions must be memorized first. You use the Financial Calendar to schedule individual transactions and transaction groups.

You can use Quicken's Financial Calendar to either prompt you to enter scheduled transactions or to enter the transactions for you at the scheduled time. You can create scheduled transaction groups, which are groups of transactions scheduled to occur together, using the Scheduled Transaction List window.

Scheduling with the Financial Calendar

The Financial Calendar shows when each of the transactions entered in your registers occurs, and it can help track your future obligations. The Financial Calendar also provides the easiest method for quickly scheduling repeated transactions.

Scheduling Transactions

You can schedule any memorized transaction in the Financial Calendar. You can schedule a transaction that will occur only a specified number of times, or you can set the transaction to recur indefinitely.

You can display the Financial Calendar by selecting Financial Calendar from the Activities menu or by selecting the Calendar icon from the icon bar. Your Financial Calendar should look like Figure 12-9.

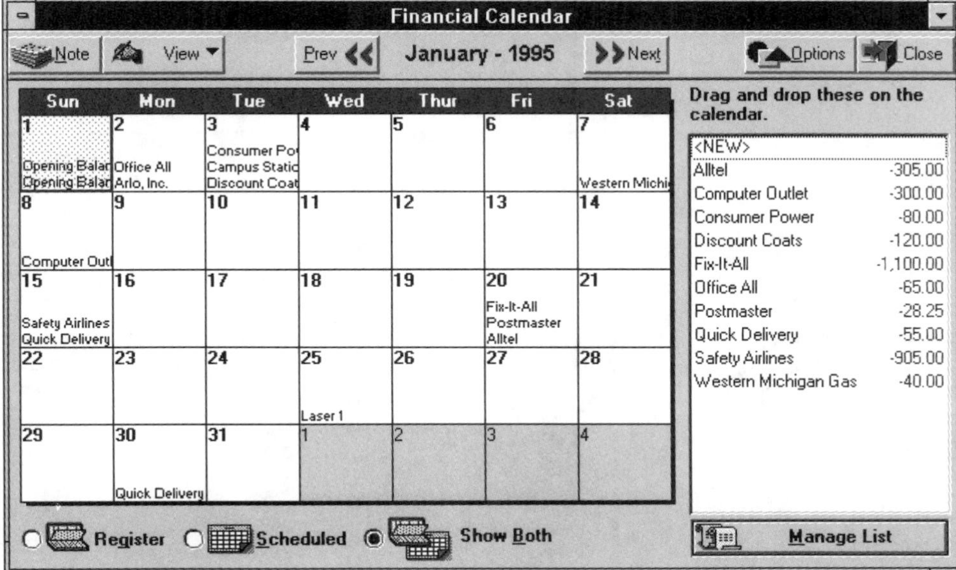

The Financial Calendar for January 1995
Figure 12-9.

Note: The Financial Calendar initially shows the current month. Since it is unlikely that you are using this book during the dates that are given for the sample transactions, you will probably have to change the month displayed by selecting the Prev or Next button at the top of the calendar to move to January 1995 to see the transactions which are entered in this file.

At the right side of the Financial Calendar window, Quicken displays a list of the memorized transactions. You can quickly schedule a transaction by using the mouse to drag one of these transactions to a day on the calendar. When you release the mouse button, Quicken displays the Drag and Drop Transaction dialog box. To schedule the regular payments for equipment maintenance, follow these steps:

HomeBase

Day to Day | Financial Calendar

1. Display the Financial Calendar by selecting Financial Calendar from the Activities menu or by selecting the Calendar icon from the icon bar.
2. Select Prev or Next to display the calendar for April 1995.
3. Drag the Fix-It-All transaction from the list box on the right side of the window to April 30, at the bottom of the calendar.
   Quicken opens the Drag and Drop Transaction dialog box like the one in Figure 12-10. This dialog box shows the transaction entries that will belong to the scheduled transaction.
4. Select Quarterly from the Frequency drop-down list box.
5. Select OK.
6. Select OK if you see the notice that Quicken will remind you to make the entry once the date arrives.

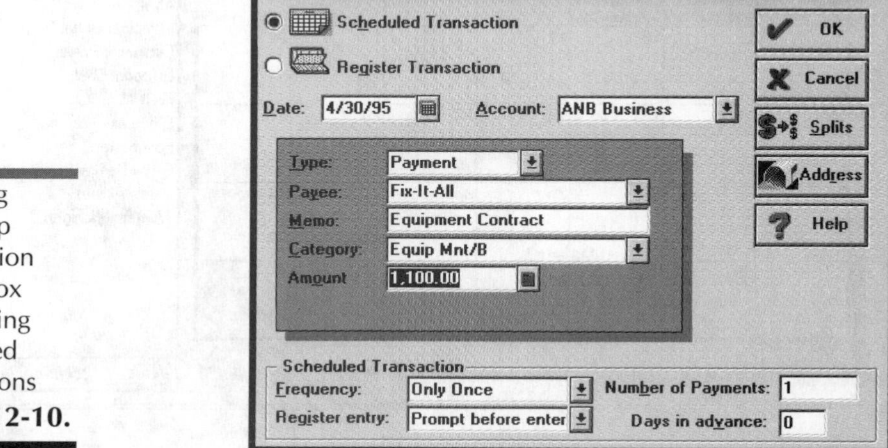

The Drag and Drop Transaction dialog box for creating scheduled transactions
Figure 12-10.

Quicken will prompt you to enter this scheduled transaction the first time you start Quicken after the scheduled date for the transaction (April 30, 1995).

Editing Scheduled Transactions

You can easily edit your scheduled transactions. For example, you can edit the transaction you just scheduled so that Quicken will enter the transaction without prompting you first. To edit the scheduled transaction, follow these steps:

1. Double-click on the day the transaction is currently entered on—in this case, 4/30/95. Quicken displays the dialog box shown here:

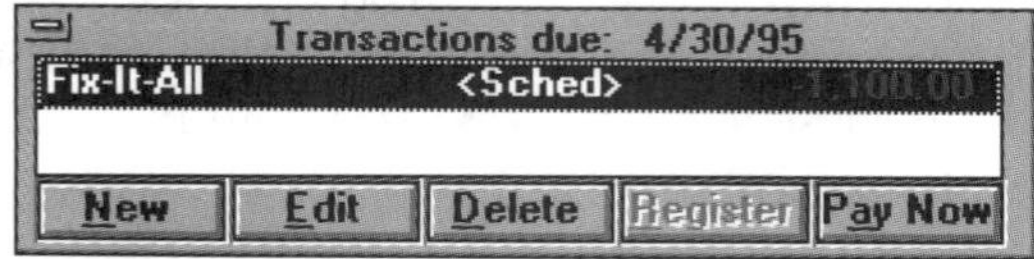

2. Select Edit. The Edit Scheduled Transaction dialog box opens to show much of the same information as the Drag and Drop Transaction dialog box shown in Figure 12-10 displays.
3. Select Automatically Enter in the Register Entry drop-down list box.

   Now Quicken will enter this quarterly maintenance expense without prompting you about it.
4. Select OK.

You may edit your transaction again when your contract changes, or if you decide you want it entered in the register a few days before it is actually due. This is useful as a reminder about bills you need to pay.

Paying a Scheduled Transaction Early

You may want to register a transaction as being paid early, either because you are going out of town or because you decided to pay the bill before the due date. To do this, click on the day containing the scheduled transaction, and then select Pay Now. Quicken prompts you to review the details of the transaction. When you select Record, the transaction is entered in the register.

Working with Scheduled Transaction Groups

Quicken can schedule both individual transactions, as just described, or groups of transactions. If you have several memorized transactions that occur at the same time, a scheduled transaction group lets you focus on other tasks while Quicken remembers to enter the transactions you need. Quicken will record the entire group for you with or without prompting you about its entries, depending on how you define the scheduled transaction group.

Defining a Scheduled Transaction Group

Quicken allows you to set up as many as twelve scheduled transaction groups. Defining a group is easy. First you have Quicken memorize all the transactions that will be placed in the group. Then you describe the group. Finally, you assign specific memorized transactions to the group. Although expense transactions are frequently used to create groups, you can also include an entry for a direct deposit payroll check that is deposited at the same time each month.

For your first transaction group, which you will title Utilities, you will group the gas and electric transactions that occur near the end of each month. Follow these steps to open the ANB Personal account and create the transaction group:

1. Select Close to close the Financial Calendar window.
2. Switch to the ANB Personal register by clicking its account selector beneath the transactions in the open register.
3. Select Scheduled Transaction from the Lists menu.

   Quicken displays the Scheduled Transaction List window:

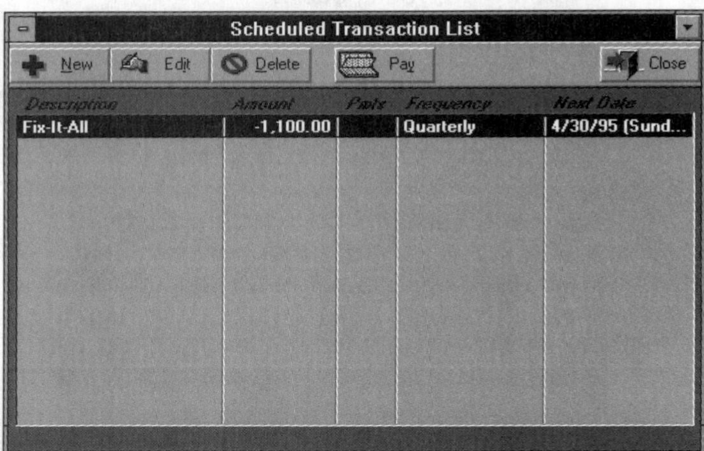

4. Select New.

   Quicken displays a dialog box so that you can define the scheduled transaction. The following dialog box contains the entries you will make in the next steps:

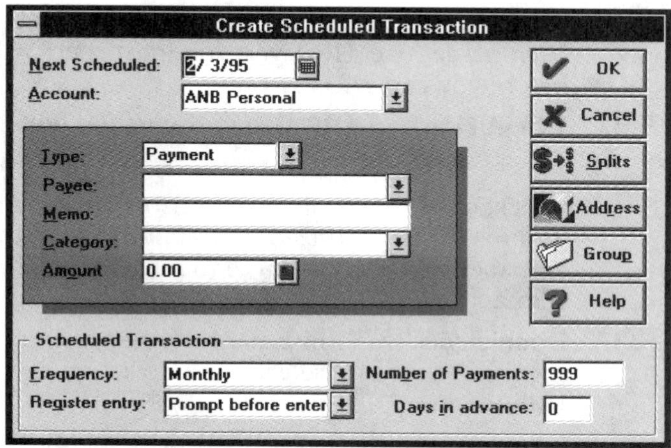

5. Type **2/3/95** in the Next Scheduled text box. Remember that you can use the drop-down calendar to select this date.

   Quicken will remind you three days in advance of this date. You can change this by changing the Reminder options.
6. Select ANB Personal from the Account drop-down list box for the account that these transactions use.
7. Select Monthly from the Frequency drop-down list box.
8. Make sure that the Number of Payments text box is still set to 999, which causes Quicken to continue entering these transactions indefinitely.
9. Make sure that the Register entry drop-down list box still shows Prompt Before Enter so that Quicken prompts you about the transactions before entering them into your account register.
10. Select Group.

    The Create Transaction Group dialog box appears, as shown here:

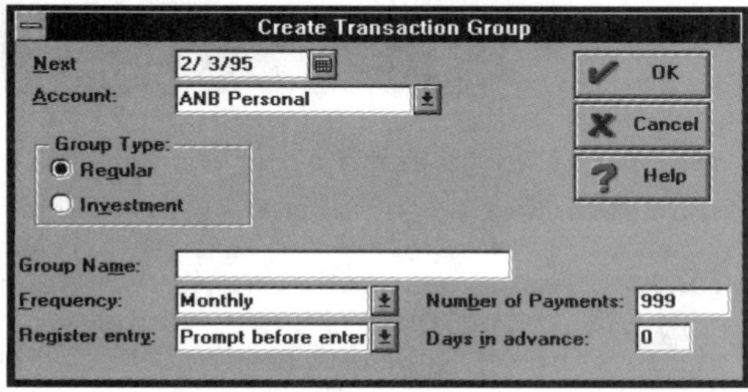

12

Many of the entries you made in the previous dialog box could have been made here. However, you must specify the account being used before you can select Group.

11. Type **Utilities** in the Group Name text box.
12. Select OK to leave the Create Transaction Group dialog box.

    Quicken displays a dialog box listing transactions you can assign to the group. Only memorized transactions are in this list. They are listed in alphabetical order by payee to make it easy to locate the desired transactions.
13. Double-click the Consumer Power transaction, or highlight it with the arrow keys and select Mark, to assign this transaction to the Utilities group.

    Note the 1 in the Grp column, which indicates that the transaction is now part of the Utilities group.
14. Select the Western Michigan Gas transaction by double-clicking it, or by highlighting it and selecting Mark.

    Quicken also marks this transaction as part of the Utilities transaction group, as shown here:

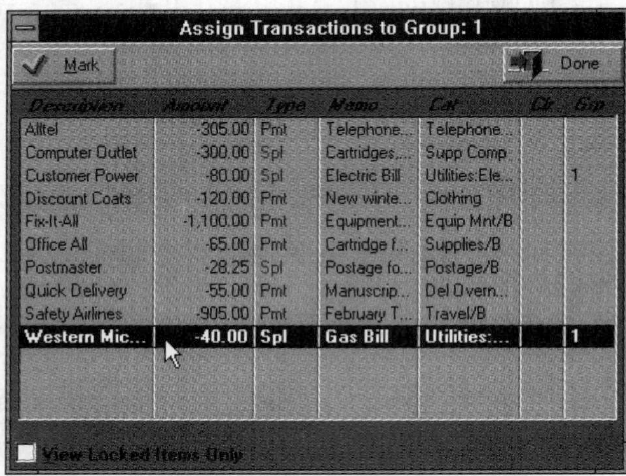

15. Select Done to indicate that you have finished selecting transactions.
16. Select Close when you are finished working with scheduled transactions.

You may want to define other transaction groups to include payroll, loan payments, and anything else that you might pay at the beginning of the month. However, you don't need to define additional groups to complete the remaining exercises in this section.

You can also create transaction groups that generate checks for you. These groups contain transactions that are memorized from the Write Checks window. The procedure is the same as that just described. You can identify these transactions in the Assign Transactions dialog box by the Chk entry in the Type field. Remember that a Pmt entry in the Type field indicates an account register transaction. Spl in this column marks split transactions that are either checks or register entries.

Changing a Transaction Group

You can add new transactions to a transaction group at any time by opening the Scheduled Transaction List window, highlighting the group, and selecting Edit. After you choose OK from the Edit Transaction Group dialog box, you can select which transactions you want to include in the group.

To make a change to the description or frequency of the reminder, use the same procedure, and make the necessary changes in the Edit Transaction Group dialog box.

To delete a transaction group, open the Scheduled Transaction List window. Highlight the group you want to delete, and select Delete. Quicken eliminates the group but does not delete the memorized transactions that are part of it. Deleting a transaction group does not affect any transactions recorded in the register by earlier executions of the transaction group.

If you want to alter a transaction that is part of a transaction group, you need to alter the memorized transaction. This means that you have to make your changes and memorize the edited transaction. Follow the procedures in the "Editing and Deleting Memorized Transactions" section earlier in this chapter.

Recording a Transaction Group

Once you define a transaction group, you do not need to wait for the reminder to record the group of transactions in your register or the Write Checks window. Since you can memorize entries for both the register and the Write Checks window, make sure you have the group correctly defined for your current needs. A group type of Chk is created in the Write Checks window and can be recorded in either the account register or the Write Checks window. Payment (Pmt) groups are recorded in the account register and can only record account register entries.

To execute a transaction group from the account register, follow these steps:

1. Select Scheduled Transaction from the Lists menu.

Quicken displays a Scheduled Transaction List window like the one shown here:

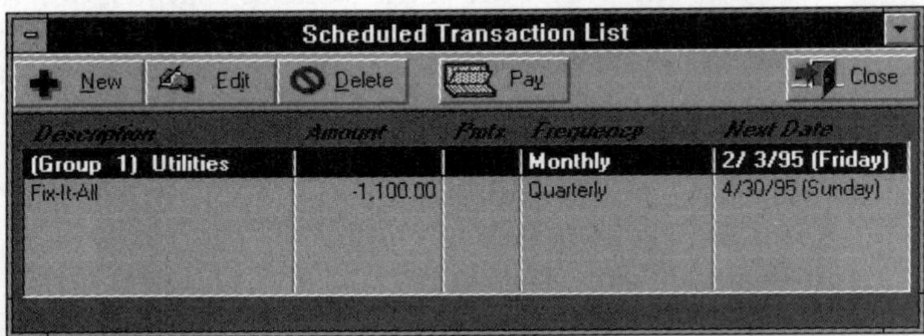

2. Highlight the Utilities group.
3. Select Pay
   Quicken displays the Record Transaction Group dialog box, as shown here:

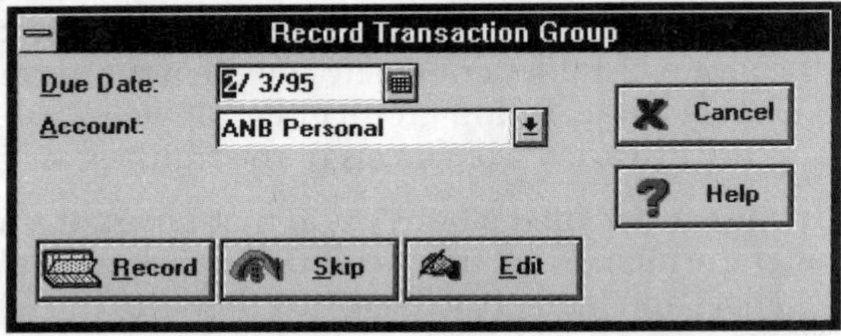

If you were actually planning to pay these bills early (as opposed to simply *record* them early), you would enter the current date in the Due Date text. Your register would then show the current date as the date you effected this transaction. In this case, you aren't going to do this.

4. Select Record to enter the transactions in the register.
5. Select Close to leave the Scheduled Transaction List window.
6. Switch to any register window and click the ANB Personal account selector to show this account.

   The new transactions are entered with the date 2/3/95, as shown here:

2/ 3/95	Sched	Customer Power		80 00			2,098 00
		Electric Bill	--Splits--				
2/ 3/95	Sched	Western Michigan Gas		40 00			2,058 00
		Gas Bill	--Splits--				

Tip: When you use a transaction group to enter transactions, make sure that you are on a blank transaction form. If you are not, the first newly inserted transaction will have an entry in the Num field that is already used for another transaction, and you will have two checks with the same number. If this occurs, Quicken displays a message to that effect.

7. Highlight the Consumer Power entry for 2/3/95.
8. Type + in the Num field to assign the next check number to this transaction.
9. Type **72.00** in the Payment field.
10. Select Record.
11. Select Allocate and Edit Splits and OK to have Quicken allocate the expenses between the categories in the split transaction.
12. Select OK, and Record again to complete the allocation and record the transaction.
13. Type + in the Num field for the West Michigan Gas transaction.
14. Type **45.00** in the Payment field of the West Michigan Gas transaction.
15. Select Record.
16. Select Allocate and Edit Splits and OK to have Quicken allocate the expenses between the categories in the split transaction.
17. Select OK, and Record again to complete the allocation and record the transaction.

Having Quicken Remind You to Record Transactions

Quicken will remind you to enter upcoming transaction group transactions. The reminder will occur either when you boot your system, when you start Windows, or when you start Quicken. You can control when Quicken's BillMinder feature reminds you to enter upcoming transaction group transactions by the selections you make when you install Quicken. If you change the way you use the computer and you need to change the BillMinder settings, select Reminders from the Activities menu. Then you can select Options to make a change.

Important Customizing Options as You Set Up Your Files

Quicken provides a number of options for customizing the software to meet your needs. These include options for the addition of passwords for accessing files, options already discussed such as requiring category entries, and other options that affect the display of information on your screen and in reports. Once you know how to access these settings, you will find that most are self-explanatory. Appendix C describes more Quicken settings you can use to customize.

Adding Passwords

To add a password, select Passwords from the File menu. Quicken presents a submenu that allows you to decide if you want to protect a file using File or protect existing transactions with Transaction. Although you can add protection with a password at both levels, you will need to select each individually.

If you select File, Quicken asks you to enter a password. Once you do so and select OK, the password is added to the active file and anyone wishing to work with the file must supply the password. Transaction is used to prevent unauthorized changes to existing transactions prior to a specified date, without the password. If you choose Transaction, you are presented with a dialog box that requires you to enter both a password and a date.

If you want to change or remove a password, you must be able to provide the password. Quicken then displays a Change Password dialog box for the entry of the old and new passwords. After you complete the entries and select OK, the new password is in effect.

CHAPTER

13

QUICKEN'S PAYROLL ASSISTANCE

For a small-business owner under the day-to-day pressure of running a business, preparing the payroll can be a time-consuming and frustrating task. The owner must be aware of annual earnings limits that affect the amount to withhold in social security taxes from employees' earnings.

You must complete withholding forms, and may need to file monthly, quarterly, and year-end reports for the federal, state, or local government.

In this chapter, you will see how Quicken can help reduce the effort it takes to prepare your payroll. Although you must still invest some time, you will find that time invested up front will substantially reduce your payroll activities once the system is running. With Quicken, you can easily prepare the payroll entry for each employee and maintain information for the Internal Revenue Service (IRS) about federal income tax withholdings, Federal Insurance Contribution Act (FICA) withholdings, and employer FICA payments. You can also maintain accounts for any state and local withholding taxes or insurance payments that must be periodically deposited. In addition to this information, you can accumulate data to help prepare W-2 forms for your employees at the end of the year. See the "Payroll Forms" section below for a list of some of the standard payroll-related payment and tax forms that Quicken can assist you in preparing.

Intuit offers a separate package, QuickPay, that contains built-in payroll tables to provide additional payroll help.

Payroll Forms

If you are thinking of hiring employees, prepare for your paperwork to increase. You must complete forms at the federal, state, and local level regarding payroll information.

Federal Payroll Forms

The following list reviews many of the payroll-related tax forms that employers must file with the Internal Revenue Service. To obtain copies of the federal forms you need, call the IRS' toll-free phone number, (800) 829-3676. If this number is not valid in your locale, check your telephone directory.

SS-4, Application for Federal Employer Identification Number The federal employer identification number identifies your business on all business-related tax forms.

Form 46-190, Federal Tax Deposit Receipt This is your record of the deposits of withholding and payroll taxes you make to a Federal Reserve bank or an authorized commercial bank.

Form 940, Employer's Annual Federal Unemployment (FUTA) Tax Return Filed annually with the IRS, this return summarizes your federal unemployment tax liability and deposits.

Form 941, Employer's Quarterly Federal Tax Return This return summarizes your quarterly FICA taxes and federal income tax withholding liability and the amounts of the deposits your business has made during the quarter.

Form 943, Employer's Annual Tax Return for Agricultural Employees Completed annually, this special form shows FICA taxes and federal income tax withholding liability for agricultural employees.

Form 1099-MISC, Statement for Recipients of Miscellaneous Income This form must be filed for all nonemployees paid $600.00 or more in the current tax year.

Form W-2, Wage and Tax Statement This six-part form (an original and five duplicates) summarizes an employee's gross earnings and tax deductions for the year. The form must be prepared annually for each employee by January 31.

Form W-3, Transmittal of Income and Tax Statements This form summarizes your business's annual payroll, related FICA taxes, and federal income tax withheld during the year. You send it with the Social Security Administration's copy of W-2 forms by February 28 of the following year.

Form W-4, Employee's Withholding Allowance Certificate Employees complete this form annually to declare the number of withholding exemptions they claim.

State and Local Government Payroll Information

These forms vary by state. The following list provides an indication of some of the forms you are likely to need to file.

- Unemployment insurance tax payments
- Workers' compensation tax payments
- State income tax withholding payments
- Local income tax withholding payments

The Quicken Payroll System

Payroll entries are processed along with your other business-related payments in your Quicken account register. To set up your system to process payroll entries, you need to establish some new categories and subcategories specifically related to payroll.

The payroll subcategories you will create are shown here:

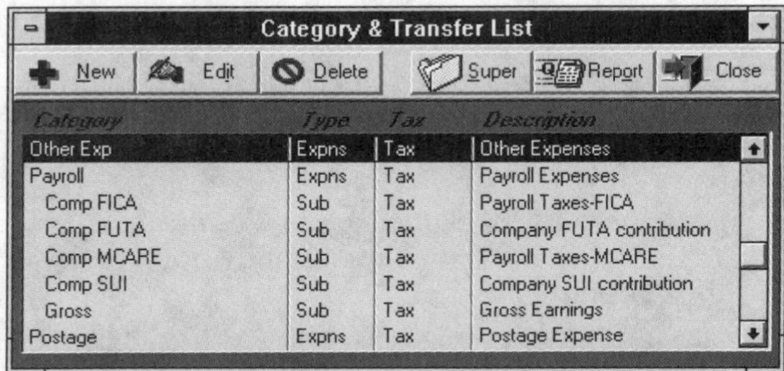

Payroll:Gross keeps track of the total wages earned by employees, and Payroll:Comp FICA keeps track of matching FICA contributions. The other payroll subcategories record contributions for federal unemployment tax, Medicare, and state unemployment tax.

Liabilities record what your business owes others.

In addition, you need to establish several *liability accounts* to maintain records of taxes withheld and employee-authorized payroll deductions for medical insurance, charitable contributions, and so on. These accounts are called liability accounts because they represent the funds withheld for payment to a third party. Here are some examples of liability accounts that you will need:

Account	Description
Payroll-FUTA	Federal unemployment taxes owed by employer
Payroll-FICA	FICA owed by employer
Payroll-FWH	Federal income tax withheld from employees' earnings
Payroll-MCARE	Medicare tax withheld from employees' earnings
Payroll-SWH	State income tax withheld from employees' earnings
Payroll-SUI	State unemployment tax owed by employer

As an employer, you are responsible for making payments to the federal, state, and local governments for employee withholdings and payroll taxes.

Notice that all of these account names begin with "Payroll." This helps Quicken prepare the Payroll report by finding all transactions that have a category title beginning with "Payroll." All the categories listed in this section start with "Payroll" and have a subcategory added—for example, Payroll:Gross. When you prepare the Payroll report later in this chapter, you will see the relationship between the category designation and the preparation of the report.

Also note that although employees must pay federal taxes as well as any state and local taxes, the employer is responsible for withholding these taxes and paying these funds to the appropriate agencies. The employer must also pay payroll taxes such as unemployment, workers' compensation, and matching FICA. These taxes are not withheld from the employee's pay, since the responsibility for payment rests with the employer. With Quicken, you can monitor your liability for these payments. With Quicken's ability to memorize payments and remind you of dates for periodic payments, you can avoid penalties and late fees that occur if you fail to file on time.

Recording Payroll Activity

To record your payroll entries for this chapter, you will use the file BUSINESS, which was established in Chapter 12, "Setting Up Quicken for Your Business." As noted in the previous section, you need to expand your category list and accounts in order to accumulate the payroll information. Once you complete the example for processing payroll that is included in this chapter, you can customize your own accounts to handle your payroll needs. For example, you might withhold medical and life insurance premiums from your employees' checks. These amounts can be recorded in other liability accounts established just for that purpose.

For the example in this chapter, it is assumed that your work force consists of salaried workers paid monthly. This means that their pay and deductions are the same month after month. John Smith is paid $2,000.00 a month, and Mary McFaul is paid $3,000.00 a month. If your employees are paid hourly and if they have a varying number of hours in each pay period, you will need to recompute their pay and deductions each period. Otherwise, the procedures shown in this chapter apply. In this example, you draw payroll checks on the last day of the month.

Establishing Payroll Liability Accounts and New Payroll Categories

The first step in recording payroll in the Quicken system is to establish the payroll liability accounts you will use throughout the year. These accounts keep track of the amounts you withhold from employees' earnings so that you can make periodic payments to various governmental agencies, health insurance companies, and pension plans. When a payment is due, you can open the liability account to determine its balance. This tells you the amount of the payment you must make.

Follow these steps to establish the payroll liability accounts you will use in this chapter:

1. Choose Open from the File menu, type **BUSINESS** in the File Name text box, and then select OK to open the BUSINESS file if it is not already open.

Setup | Create Accounts

2. Select Account from the Lists menu to show the Account List window.
3. Select New to create a new account.

   This is the same as choosing Create New Account in the Activities menu.
4. Clear the Guide Me check box.

   When this check box is cleared, all possible options are available through one dialog box rather than through several. However, you do not have all the explanations that Quicken shows when this check box is available.
5. Select Liability to set up a liability account.
6. Type **Payroll-FICA** in the Account Name text box.

   This identifies the new account as a payroll liability account in the BUSINESS file. You will accumulate all employee FICA withholdings in this account.
7. Type **0** as the opening balance in the Balance text box.

   The opening balance is 0.00 in this example since this is the first pay period for the business illustrated. When you set up your own account, enter the amount you have at the time you begin to use Quicken. If you were in business the previous year, you will probably have outstanding tax liabilities that will not be paid until January or February. The amount of these liabilities should be entered as the balance for each account.
8. Type **1/1/95** as the opening date in the text box after As Of.
9. Type **FICA Withholding** in the Description text box.
10. Select OK.
11. Select No when Quicken prompts whether you want to set up an amortized loan for this account.

    Whenever you establish a liability account, Quicken prompts you about setting up an amortized loan to associate with the account.

Note: Set up an amortization loan when creating liability accounts for loans you are paying so that you can track the money spent on interest and principal.

12. Repeat steps 3 through 11 to establish the liability accounts for the information that follows:

Account Type:	**Liability**
Account Name:	**Payroll-MCARE**
Balance:	**0**
Date:	**1/1/95**
Description:	**Medicare Withholding**

    This account will keep track of all employee Medicare withholdings during the year.

Account Type:	**Liability**
Account Name:	**Payroll-FWH**
Balance:	**0**
Date:	**1/1/95**
Description:	**Federal Withholding**

    This account will keep track of all employee federal income tax withholdings during the year.

Account Type:	**Liability**
Account Name:	**Payroll-SWH**
Balance:	**0**
Date:	**1/1/95**
Description:	**State Withholding**

    This account will keep track of all employee state income taxes withheld during the year.

Account Type:	**Liability**
Account Name:	**Payroll-FICA-Co**
Balance:	**0**
Date:	**1/1/95**
Description:	**FICA Matching**

This account will keep track of the amount of your FICA matching payment each pay period.

Account Type:	**Liability**
Account Name:	**Payroll-MCARECo**
Balance:	**0**
Date:	**1/1/95**
Description:	**Medicare Matching**

This account will keep track of the amount of your Medicare matching payment each pay period.

As a new register window opens for each account you create, close the windows to clean up your Quicken window. After adding these liability accounts, your account list will look like this:

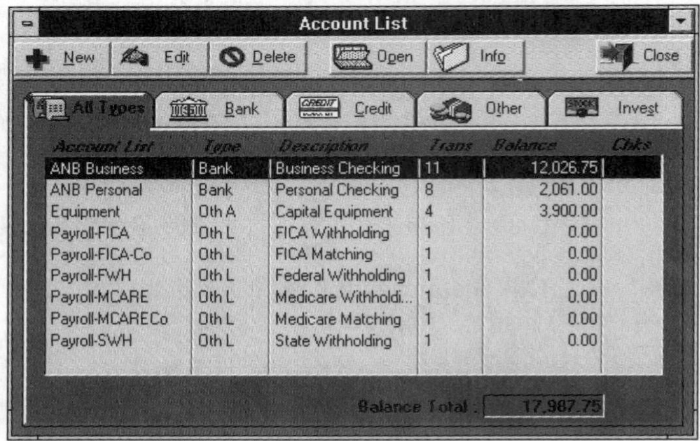

Establishing New Payroll Categories

HomeBase

Setup | Category List

You need several new categories for recording the payroll information. Follow these steps to establish Payroll as a category, with Gross as a subcategory under Payroll. You don't need to establish new categories for FICA, MCARE, and the other types of withholdings you keep track of, because you can simply select the account subnames from the Category & Transfer List. However, you will also create subcategories to track expenses for FICA, MCARE, FUTA, and SUI. The following steps will create these categories.

1. Select Category & Transfer from the Lists menu to open the Category & Transfer List window.

2. Select New.
3. Type **Payroll** in the Name text box as the category name.
4. Type **Payroll Expenses** in the Description text box as the category's description.
5. Select the Expense option button.
6. Select the Tax-related check box and Schedule C:Wages paid from the Form drop-down list box.
7. Select OK.
8. Select New.
9. Type **Gross** after Name as the category name.
10. Type **Gross Earnings** after Description as the category description.
11. Select the Subcategory Of option button and select Payroll from its drop-down list box.
12. Select the Tax-related check box and Schedule C:Wages paid from the Form drop-down list box.
13. Select OK.
14. Repeat steps 8 through 13 to create these other new Payroll subcategories:

Name:	**Comp FICA**
Description:	**Payroll Taxes-FICA**
Form:	**Schedule C:Taxes and licenses**

Name:	**Comp MCARE**
Description:	**Payroll Taxes-MCARE**
Form:	**Schedule C:Taxes and licenses**

Name:	**Comp FUTA**
Description:	**Company FUTA contribution**
Form:	**Schedule C:Taxes and licenses**

Name:	**Comp SUI**
Description:	**Company SUI contribution**
Form:	**Schedule C:Taxes and licenses**

Monthly Payroll Entries

In this section, you record paycheck entries for John Smith and Mary McFaul on January 31. Many steps are required to complete the entire entry for an individual. Once you create the first entry, however, you can memorize the transaction and repeat it for other periods, since the pay is the same each time. After you record basic information, such as the check number and the employee's name, amounts must be determined. First you establish each of the withholding amounts, and then subtract the total withholding amount from the gross pay to compute the net pay. For hourly workers, a computation is needed to determine the gross pay as well. Tax tables determine the correct withholding for federal, state, and local taxes. For figures such as FICA and net pay, you can use Quicken's Calculator to compute the amount.

Once you have determined withholding amounts and net pay, you need to enter this information. Each of the withholding amounts, such as federal income tax, FICA, and state withholdings, is entered in a Splits window. Use the following steps to record the transactions.

HomeBase

Day To Day | Use Register

1. Select Use Register from the Activities menu or click the Registr icon in the icon bar to switch to a register window.
2. Click the ANB Business account selector so the ANB Business account appears in the register window.
3. Move to the next blank transaction in the ANB Business account register.
4. Type **1/31/95** in the Date field.
5. Type **110** as the check number.
6. Type **John Smith** in the Payee field.
7. Type **1560.13** in the Payment field.

   This amount is equal to John's gross pay of $2,000.00, less federal income tax, state income tax, FICA, and Medicare withholdings.
8. Type **000-00-0001** in the Memo field.

   This is the employee's social security number. Entering it in this field can help you organize payroll reports by employee.
9. Select Splits, and the Splits window appears on your screen.

   In this Splits window, you will enter the breakdown of the total pay, withholdings, and the payroll taxes paid by the employer. When you are done, the window will look like Figure 13-1.
10. Enter **Payroll:Gross/B** in the Category field.

    You can use QuickFill for the entries throughout this chapter even though they include subcategories and classes. When you type **P**, Quicken displays "Payroll." Type : to accept "Payroll" and display the first subcategory. Type the first letter of the subcategory. When the

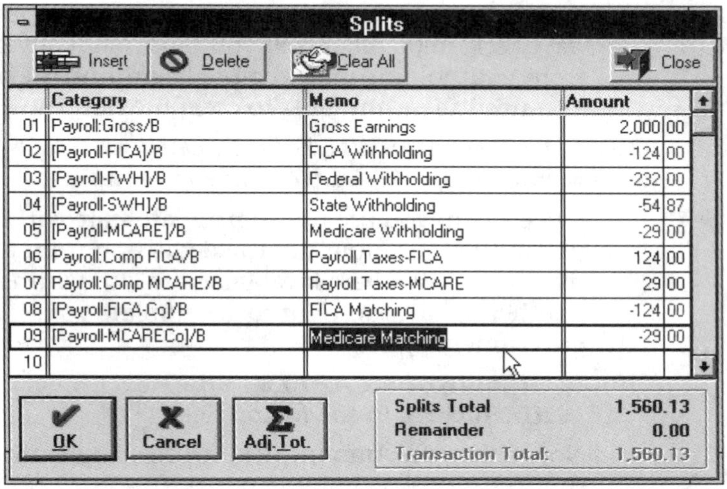

Splits

Insert | Delete | Clear All | Close

	Category	Memo	Amount
01	Payroll:Gross/B	Gross Earnings	2,000 00
02	[Payroll-FICA]/B	FICA Withholding	-124 00
03	[Payroll-FWH]/B	Federal Withholding	-232 00
04	[Payroll-SWH]/B	State Withholding	-54 87
05	[Payroll-MCARE]/B	Medicare Withholding	-29 00
06	Payroll:Comp FICA/B	Payroll Taxes-FICA	124 00
07	Payroll:Comp MCARE/B	Payroll Taxes-MCARE	29 00
08	[Payroll-FICA-Co]/B	FICA Matching	-124 00
09	[Payroll-MCARECo]/B	Medicare Matching	-29 00
10			

OK | Cancel | Adj. Tot.

Splits Total	1,560.13
Remainder	0.00
Transaction Total:	1,560.13

The Splits window, showing the complete payroll breakdown

Figure 13-1.

subcategory appears, type **/B** to accept the subcategory and mark the transaction with the Business class.

12. Type **Gross Earnings** in the Memo field.
13. Type **2000.00** as the amount.
14. Enter **Payroll-FICA/B** in the Category field.

    Quicken adds brackets around the Payroll-FICA category, as you can see in the Figure 13-1, when the transaction involves a transfer between two Quicken accounts. Here, Quicken records the liability account name in the Category field. This indicates that you are keeping track of the amount of your employee withholding in this account until you make your payment to the IRS.

15. Type **FICA Withholding** in the Memo field.
16. Type **-124.00** as the amount.

    This is the amount of FICA tax withheld from John's paycheck. The negative amount indicates that this is a deduction from the $2,000.00 gross earnings entered on the previous line. For 1994, the rate for FICA withholdings is .062 on the first $60,600 of earnings per employee. You can calculate this amount with the Calculator by typing **-2000*.062**. Although the $60,600.00 earnings limit does not affect the employees in this example, Quicken can help monitor employees' gross earnings to determine when the limit is reached.

17. Enter **Payroll-FWH/B** in the Category field, **Federal Withholding** in the Memo field, and **-232.00** as the amount.

This is the amount of federal income tax withheld from John's paycheck. Remember that you must manually determine the amounts from withholding tables before beginning the payroll transaction entry. You need these amounts to compute net pay.

18. Enter **Payroll-SWH/B** as the category, **State Withholding** in the Memo field, and **-54.87** as the amount.

    Once again, you use the appropriate state withholding tables to determine the amount of the deduction from John's paycheck. If you live in an area where local taxes are also withheld, you need to add another liability account to accumulate your liability to that government agency.

19. Enter **Payroll-MCARE/B** in the next Category field, **Medicare Withholding** in the Memo field.

    Notice that the Amount field for this line is already -29.00. For 1994, the Medicare withholding rate is .0145 so 2,000 times .0145 equals 29.00. The Remainder field at the bottom-right of the Splits window now contains 0. This indicates that the balance of the transactions entered in the Splits window now equals the amount you entered in the Payment field of the transaction.

    At this point, lines 1 through 5 record John Smith's gross earnings and the amounts withheld from his check. In the next series of steps, you record your employer payroll expenses.

20. Enter **Payroll:Comp FICA/B** in the Category field of the next line.

    As an employer, you have to match your employees' FICA contributions. This is an expense of doing business and must be recorded in your category list.

21. Type **Payroll Taxes-FICA** in the Memo field.
22. Type **124.00** in the Amount field.

    This records the amount of your matching FICA payroll expense. Notice that it is a positive amount because this is a business expense that Quicken will record in the account register.

23. Enter **Payroll:Comp MCARE/B** in the Category field, **Payroll Taxes-MCARE** in the Memo field, and **29.00** in the Amount field.
24. Enter **Payroll-FICA-Co/B** in the Category field, **FICA Matching** in the Memo field, and **-124.00** in the Amount field.
25. Enter **Payroll-MCARECo/B** in the Category field, and **Medicare Matching** in the Memo field.

    You do not need to enter an amount since Quicken correctly shows -29.00 as the amount. The complete entries match the one in Figure 13-1.

26. Select OK.
27. Select Record to record the transaction in the current register. The transaction looks like this:

1/31/95	110	John Smith	1,560	13					10,466	62
		000-00-0001 --Splits--								

You have now completed the payroll entry for John Smith for the month of January. You must now complete the recording process for Mary McFaul. Follow these steps to record the transaction in the ANB Business account register:

1. Enter **1/31/95** in the Date field.
2. Enter **111** in the Num field.
3. Type **Mary McFaul** in the Payee field.
4. Type **2284.22** in the Payment field.
5. Type **000-00-0002** in the Memo field.
6. Select Splits, and the Splits window appears on your screen.
7. Enter **Payroll:Gross/B** in the Category field, **Gross Earnings** in the Memo field, and **3000.00** in the Amount field.
8. Enter **Payroll-FICA/B** in the Category field, **FICA Withholding** in the Memo field, and **-186.00** in the Amount field.
9. Enter **Payroll-FWH/B** in the Category field, **Federal Withholding** in the Memo field, and **-382.00** in the Amount field.
10. Enter **Payroll-SWH/B** in the Category field, **State Withholding** in the Memo field, and **-104.28** in the Amount field.
11. Enter **Payroll-MCARE/B** in the Category field, **Medicare Withholding** in the Memo field, and leave -43.50 in the Amount field.
12. Enter **Payroll:Comp FICA/B** in the Category field, **Payroll Taxes-FICA** in the Memo field, and **186.00** in the Amount field.
13. Enter **Payroll:Comp MCARE/B** in the Category field, **Payroll Taxes-MCARE** in the Memo field, and **43.50** in the Amount field.
14. Enter **Payroll-FICA-Co/B** in the Category field, **FICA Matching** in the Memo field, and **-186.00** in the Amount field.
15. Enter **Payroll-MCARECo/B** in the Category field, and **Medicare Matching** in the Memo field.

    The -43.50 in the Amount field is the correct amount. Your completed entries look like Figure 13-2.

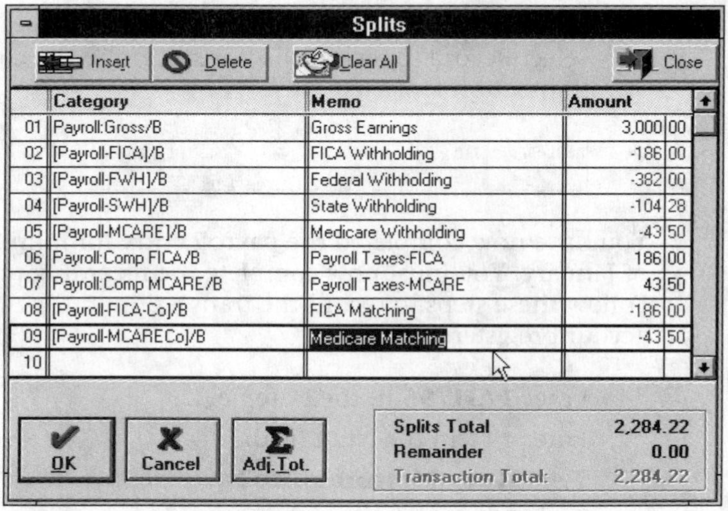

Splits

Insert | Delete | Clear All | Close

	Category	Memo	Amount	
01	Payroll:Gross/B	Gross Earnings	3,000	00
02	[Payroll-FICA]/B	FICA Withholding	-186	00
03	[Payroll-FWH]/B	Federal Withholding	-382	00
04	[Payroll-SWH]/B	State Withholding	-104	28
05	[Payroll-MCARE]/B	Medicare Withholding	-43	50
06	Payroll:Comp FICA/B	Payroll Taxes-FICA	186	00
07	Payroll:Comp MCARE/B	Payroll Taxes-MCARE	43	50
08	[Payroll-FICA-Co]/B	FICA Matching	-186	00
09	[Payroll-MCARECo]/B	Medicare Matching	-43	50
10				

OK | Cancel | Adj. Tot.

Splits Total	2,284.22
Remainder	0.00
Transaction Total:	2,284.22

Completed Splits window entries for Mary McFaul's payroll entry
Figure 13-2.

16. Select OK.
17. Select Record to record the transaction for Mary McFaul in the account register.

The paycheck transactions recorded in this section show the basic expenses and liabilities associated with the payment of wages. Your payroll entries will be more complex if you withhold medical insurance, pension contributions, and other amounts such as contributions to charities or deposits to savings accounts from employee checks. The basic format of the split transaction remains the same. You simply expand the number of categories in the split transaction and add liability accounts to cover your obligation to make payments to the parties involved. Regardless of how many withholding categories you use, the procedures you just performed can be expanded for your withholding categories and liabilities.

The Internal Revenue Service provides guidelines for making periodic payments for employee withholding and employer payroll taxes.

Recording Periodic Deposits for the Internal Revenue Service

You must periodically make deposits to the Internal Revenue Service for FICA and federal income tax withheld from employees' paychecks, as well as for your matching FICA contribution. You make your deposits to authorized banks within the Federal Reserve System. Check with your bank to be sure it can provide this service. If it can't, you must take cash or a bank check, along with the appropriate forms, to an authorized bank and make your deposit there. When you record the withholding deposit in Quicken, you designate the Internal Revenue Service as the payee.

Specific guidelines govern the timing of the payments, based on how much is owed. The fictitious company used in this example has a total tax liability for the month of $1,379. This $1,379 comes from $124 FICA from John Smith and $186 FICA from Mary McFaul and the matching amounts from the employer; $29 and $43.50 Medicare withheld from the two employees and the matching employer withholding; and $232 and $382 federal taxes withheld from these two employees. Therefore, you must make a withholding deposit for the January paychecks under the IRS's Rule 1, which is discussed in the "IRS Deposit Rules" section of this chapter. The rule states that you must make a deposit for social security taxes and withheld federal income taxes by the 15th of the following month if your total tax liability for last year was $50,000 or less. Consult your accountant or read IRS Form 941 for a full explanation of the deposit rules. Depending on the size of your payroll, you may have to make periodic payments throughout the month in order to comply with the regulations.

IRS Deposit Rules

How often you must make deposits of social security and federal income taxes depends on the amount of your liability. Effective January 1, 1993, the IRS simplified the rules that affect when you must make these deposits. Each November, the IRS reports which rule to use throughout the upcoming year. If you are not notified, use the following rules to make a determination. New employers should use Rule 1. Since the penalties for noncompliance can be steep, it is important to follow the rules strictly. Notice 931 describes the rules in detail, but a quick summary is provided here.

Rule 1 If your tax liability for the previous four quarters was $50,000 or less, file monthly.

Rule 2 If your tax liability for the previous four quarters was greater than $50,000, file every two weeks.

Rule 3 If your cumulative tax liability is $100,000 or more, you must make daily deposits.

The following example demonstrates how you would record a payment for your business's liabilities for social security taxes, Medicare, and federal withholding taxes for these two employees. You would record the transaction in the ANB Business account register.

From the ANB Business account register, record the following transaction for the required deposit:

1. Move to the Date field in the next blank transaction form.
2. Enter **2/1/95** in the Date field.
3. Enter **112** in the Num field.
4. Type **Internal Revenue Service** as the payee.
5. Type **1379.00** in the Payment field.
6. Type **Form 941 Withholding Payment** in the Memo field.
7. Select Splits to open the Splits window. After you complete the following steps, your Splits window looks like this:

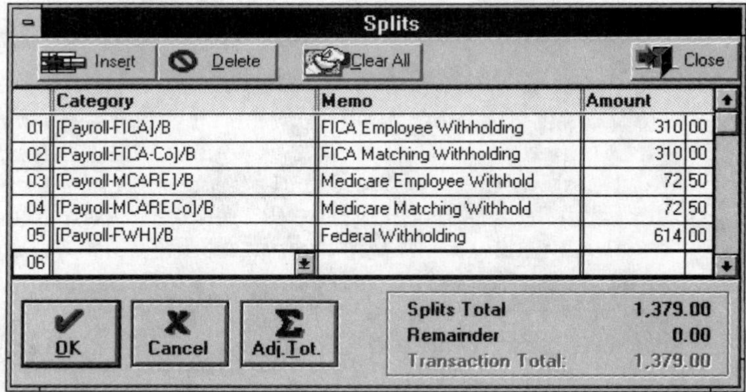

8. Enter **Payroll-FICA/B** in the Category field.
9. Type **FICA Employee Withholding** in the Memo field.
10. Type **310.00** in the Amount field.
11. Enter **Payroll-FICA-Co/B** in the Category field.
12. Type **FICA Matching Withholding** in the Memo field.
13. Type **310.00** in the Amount field.
14. Enter **Payroll-MCARE/B** in the Category field.
15. Type **Medicare Employee Withhold** in the Memo field.
16. Type **72.50** in the Amount field.

17. Enter **Payroll-MCARECo/B** in the Category field.
18. Type **Medicare Matching Withhold** in the Memo field.
19. Type **72.50** in the Amount field.
20. Enter **Payroll-FWH/B** in the Category field.
21. Type **Federal Withholding** in the Memo field.
22. Select OK to record the split.
23. Select Record to record the transaction in the account register.

You follow these same steps to record the payment of your state withholding tax liability when the payment date arrives.

Notice that no expense category was charged in the previous Splits window. This is because the deposit reduces the liability account balances that were established when payroll checks were written on 1/31/95. If you look at those transactions in your register, you can see that the gross earnings were charged to the Payroll:Gross category and that your matching FICA contribution was charged to the Payroll:Comp FICA category. Both of these categories are classified as expenses and will appear on your business Profit and Loss statement. The amounts withheld for payroll taxes, on the other hand, were charged to liability accounts that will be paid at a future date. Thus, when you pay these liabilities, as you just did, you are meeting your financial obligation to the government, not incurring additional expenses.

Other Liability Accounts

Let's look at the impact of recording the paychecks and the IRS payment on the other liability accounts. Specifically, you will see the effects of these transactions on the Payroll-FWH liability account. Follow these steps to look at the Payroll-FWH account from the ANB Business account register:

1. Select the Payroll-FWH account selector below the transactions so the register window shows this account, which you can see in Figure 13-3.

   You may need to click the arrows on either side of the account selector bar to show the selector for the account you want. This is the same as selecting Account from the Lists menu or selecting the Accts icon from the icon bar, and then choosing Payroll-FWH from the Account List window.

   Notice that the account has accumulated $614.00 as the FWH withholding liability from the January paychecks. Also notice that when you made your deposit on 2/1/95, the balance was reduced to zero. This will occur each month when you record your deposit to the IRS.

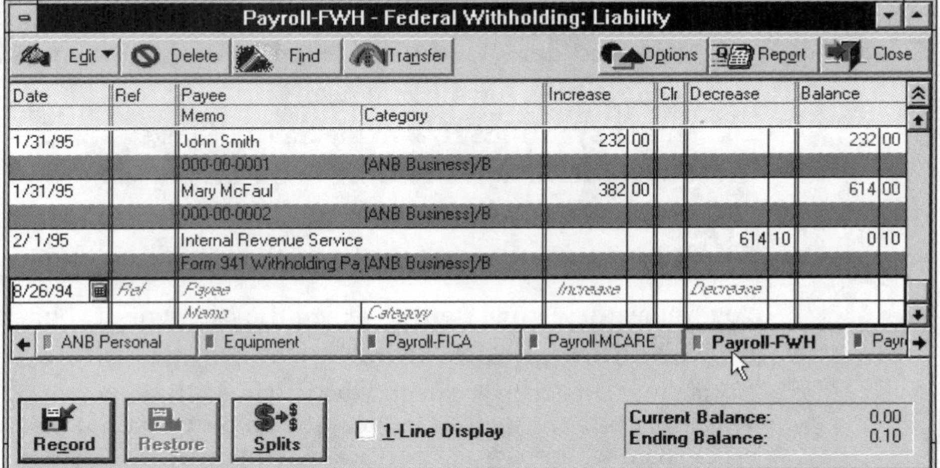

Activating the Payroll-FWH account
Figure 13-3.

2. Select the ANB Business account selector below the transactions. You are now back in the ANB Business account register.

Memorized Monthly Paycheck and Withholdings Deposit Entries

Since you will be paying your employees on a regular basis and making monthly withholdings deposits, you will want to memorize these entries to simplify recording future transactions. Since the employees in this example are all salaried, the only changes you need each month are new dates and check numbers on each transaction. All the split transaction details will be accurate. For hourly employees or employees who make more than the FICA cap amount, some pay periods will require changes to the entries in the split transaction details.

Completing the Payroll Entries

In this section, you expand your payroll transactions by adding some entries to the ANB Business account register. You add these transactions so that the examples will contain enough pay periods to generate realistic reports. You won't record check numbers for most of the remaining example transactions in this chapter, but this won't affect the reports.

Establishing Scheduled Transaction Groups

In Chapter 12, "Setting Up Quicken for Your Business," you established a transaction group for utilities payments. The object of transaction grouping is to batch together similar transactions that occur around the same time each month so that Quicken can automatically record them for you the next time they need to be made. Remember that only memorized transactions can be batched into transaction groups. From the ANB Business account register, perform the following steps to establish a transaction group for the payroll:

1. Select Scheduled Transaction from the Lists menu. The Scheduled Transaction List window appears.
2. Select New. The Create Scheduled Transaction dialog box appears.
3. Select Group, and the Create Transaction Group window appears.
4. Enter **ANB Business** in the Account text box. Remember that you can type the entry or select it from the drop-down list box.
5. Enter **2/28/95** in the Next text box.
6. Type **Payroll** in the Group Name text box.
7. Select Monthly from the Frequency drop-down list box.
8. Make sure that Prompt Before Enter is in the Register Entry drop-down list box.
9. Type **2** in the Days In Advance text box to have Quicken enter the transactions two days before the payment date.
10. Select OK, and the Assign Transactions To Group dialog box appears.
11. To include the transaction with John Smith as the payee, double-click his name, or highlight it and select Mark. Note the 2 in the Grp column, indicating that the transaction is now part of Group 2.
12. Mark the transaction with Mary McFaul as the payee to include it in the group. This transaction also becomes a part of Group 2.
13. Select Done to indicate that you are finished selecting transactions.
14. Select Close to put the Scheduled Transaction List window away and return to the register window for ANB Business.

Recording February Transactions

In this section, you add the remaining transactions to the ANB Business account register to complete the payroll entries for the month of February. Perform these steps:

1. Move to the next blank transaction.
2. Select Scheduled Transaction from the Lists menu.
   Quicken displays a list of transaction groups.
3. Move to the Payroll group, and then select Pay.
   Quicken displays the target account—ANB Business—and the date of the next scheduled entry for the group—2/28/95.
4. Select Record to confirm that this information is valid and to enter and record the group of payroll transactions in the ANB Business account register.
   If the date was not the last date of the month for payroll purposes, you could have typed the correct date in the Due Date text box before you selected Record. In this example, you don't modify the payroll amounts since they are the same from month to month. If you have employees who work on an hourly basis, you would need to select each new transaction, open the Splits window, and make the necessary modifications to the dollar amounts recorded.
5. Select Close or press ESC to remove the Scheduled Transaction List window from the screen.

Quicken has entered the scheduled transactions for the monthly payroll for February. They look like this in the account register:

2/28/95	Sched	John Smith		1,560	13			5,243	27
		000-00-0001	--Splits--						
2/28/95	Sched	Mary McFaul		2,284	22			2,959	05
		000-00-0002	--Splits--						

Notice that Quicken displays Sched in the Num field. When you write your payroll checks, you can enter the check number in this field. If you want to search your register to see if Sched still appears for any transactions, you can choose Find from the Edit menu and search for "Sched" in the Check Number field.

The payroll entries are the only February transactions that are being added to the account register at this time. Figure 13-4 shows a report of the transactions in the account register from 2/28/95 through 4/15/95, including

Register Report
2/28/95 Through 4/15/95

Date	Num	Description	Memo	Category	Clr	Amount
		BALANCE 2/27/95				6,803.40
2/28/95	Sched	John Smith	Gross Earnings	Payroll:Gross/B		-2,000.00
			FICA Withholding	[Payroll-FICA]/B		124.00
			Federal Withholding	[Payroll-FWH]/B		232.00
			State Withholding	[Payroll-SWH]/B		54.87
			Medicare Withholding	[Payroll-MCARE]/B		29.00
			Payroll Taxes-FICA	Payroll:Comp FICA/B		-124.00
			Payroll Taxes-MCARE	Payroll:Comp MCARE/B		-29.00
			FICA Matching	[Payroll-FICA-Co]/B		124.00
			Medicare Matching	[Payroll-MCARECo]/B		29.00
2/28/95	Sched	Mary McFaul	Gross Earnings	Payroll:Gross/B		-3,000.00
			FICA Withholding	[Payroll-FICA]/B		186.00
			Federal Withholding	[Payroll-FWH]/B		382.00
			State Withholding	[Payroll-SWH]/B		104.28
			Medicare Withholding	[Payroll-MCARE]/B		43.50
			Payroll Taxes-FICA	Payroll:Comp FICA/B		-186.00
			Payroll Taxes-MCARE	Payroll:Comp MCARE/B		-43.50
			FICA Matching	[Payroll-FICA-Co]/B		186.00
			Medicare Matching	[Payroll-MCARECo]/B		43.50
3/1/95		Internal Revenue Service	FICA Employee Withholding	[Payroll-FICA]/B		-310.00
			FICA Matching Withholding	[Payroll-FICA-Co]/B		-310.00
			Medicare Employee Withhold	[Payroll-MCARE]/B		-72.50
			Medicare Matching Withhold	[Payroll-MCARECo]/B		-72.50
			Federal Withholding	[Payroll-FWH]/B		-614.00
3/1/95		Tyler Corp.	Seminars conducted Jan. 95	Inc Cons/B		25,000.00
3/31/95	Sched	John Smith	Gross Earnings	Payroll:Gross/B		-2,000.00
			FICA Withholding	[Payroll-FICA]/B		124.00
			Federal Withholding	[Payroll-FWH]/B		232.00
			State Withholding	[Payroll-SWH]/B		54.87
			Medicare Withholding	[Payroll-MCARE]/B		29.00
			Payroll Taxes-FICA	Payroll:Comp FICA/B		-124.00
			Payroll Taxes-MCARE	Payroll:Comp MCARE/B		-29.00
			FICA Matching	[Payroll-FICA-Co]/B		124.00
			Medicare Matching	[Payroll-MCARECo]/B		29.00
3/31/95	Sched	Mary McFaul	Gross Earnings	Payroll:Gross/B		-3,000.00
			FICA Withholding	[Payroll-FICA]/B		186.00
			Federal Withholding	[Payroll-FWH]/B		382.00
			State Withholding	[Payroll-SWH]/B		104.28
			Medicare Withholding	[Payroll-MCARE]/B		43.50
			Payroll Taxes-FICA	Payroll:Comp FICA/B		-186.00
			Payroll Taxes-MCARE	Payroll:Comp MCARE/B		-43.50
			FICA Matching	[Payroll-FICA-Co]/B		186.00
			Medicare Matching	[Payroll-MCARECo]/B		43.50
3/31/95		Big Books	Royalties	Inc Roy/B		10,000.00
4/1/95		Internal Revenue Service	FICA Employee Withholding	[Payroll-FICA]/B		-310.00
			FICA Matching Withholding	[Payroll-FICA-Co]/B		-310.00
			Medicare Employee Withhold	[Payroll-MCARE]/B		-72.50
			Medicare Matching Withhold	[Payroll-MCARECo]/B		-72.50
			Federal Withholding	[Payroll-FWH]/B		-614.00
4/15/95		Internal Revenue Service	FUTA	Payroll:Comp FUTA/B		-104.00
4/15/95		Bureau of Employment Services	SUTA	Payroll:Comp SUI/B		-520.00
		TOTAL 2/28/95 - 4/15/95				23,929.30
		BALANCE 4/15/95				30,732.70

An account register showing additional transactions
Figure 13-4.

February's payroll entries and the remaining transactions that you will enter in this chapter.

Recording March Transactions

The March entries can be divided into three groups. The first entry is a deposit for federal social security, Medicare, and income tax withholdings in February. The second and third entries record income earned during the month from consulting and royalties. The last two entries record the payroll transactions for March.

The February Withholdings Entry

To record the deposit for taxes withheld during February, you use a memorized transaction and QuickFill. From the next blank transaction in the ANB Business account register, perform the following steps:

1. Type **3/1/95** in the Date field.
2. Type **I** in the Payee field, and press TAB.

   QuickFill finds only one memorized transaction with a Payee that starts with *I* and provides "Internal Revenue Service" to finish the field. When you press TAB, QuickFill fills in the remainder of the fields for the transaction. QuickFill doesn't fill in the other fields if you use the mouse instead of TAB to move to another field.
3. Select Record to record this transaction.

Consulting and Royalty Income Entries

In the ANB Business account register, enter the following information for the two deposit entries shown in Figure 13-4:

1. Enter **3/1/95** in the Date field.
2. Type **Tyler Corp.** in the Payee field.
3. Type **25000** in the Deposit field.
4. Type **Seminars conducted Jan. 95** in the Memo field.
5. Enter **Inc Cons/B** in the Category field.
6. Select Record. This records the Tyler Corp. revenue transaction.
7. Enter **3/31/95** in the Date field.
8. Type **Big Books** in the Payee field.
9. Type **10000** in the Deposit field.
10. Type **Royalties** in the Memo field.
11. Enter **Inc Roy/B** in the Category field.
12. Select Record.

You have now recorded both income transactions for March.

March Payroll Entries

In this section, you add the remaining transactions to the account register to complete the payroll entries for the month of March:

1. Select Scheduled Transaction from the Lists menu.
2. Highlight the Payroll group, and then select Pay. Quicken displays the date of the next scheduled entry for the group—3/28/95—and the target account—ANB Business.
3. Enter **3/31/95** in the Due Date text box, and then select Record.

   This changes the date to the last day in March and enters the group of payroll transactions in the account register.
4. Press ESC or click Close to close the Scheduled Transaction List window.

Recording April Transactions

The only transactions you will record for April are the Internal Revenue Service deposit for the March payroll and the Federal Unemployment Tax Act (FUTA) and State Unemployment Tax Act (SUTA) payments.

Complete the following steps to record the IRS transaction in the ANB Business account register. (This transaction will help you prepare several reports for the Internal Revenue Service. These reports are discussed later in this chapter.)

1. Move to the end of the register.
2. Select Memorized Transaction from the Lists menu.
3. Double-click the Internal Revenue Service transaction, or highlight it and press ENTER.
4. Enter **4/1/95** in the Date field.
5. Select Record.

In addition to your withholding tax liabilities, employers must pay unemployment taxes. This program is mandated by the federal government but administered by the individual state governments. Because of this method of administration, you must make payments to both the state and the federal government. At the time this book is being written, you must contribute .008 percent to the federal government to cover its administrative costs and up to .054 percent to the state agency that administers the program. These percentages apply to the first $7,000.00 of earnings for each employee. In some states, the salary cap on earnings may be higher; however, the example in this chapter uses a $7,000.00 limit for both federal and state employer payroll tax contributions.

You must make deposits to the federal government whenever your contribution liability reaches $100.00. You make these deposits in the same way you make FICA, Medicare, and federal income tax withholding payments, as discussed earlier in this chapter.

Your actual contributions to the state agency are based on historical rates for your business and industry classification. You may qualify for a percentage rate lower than the maximum rate allowed by law. The contribution rate for the business in this example is .04 percent.

Generally, payments to the state agency that administers the program are made quarterly. Each quarter, you are required to complete an Employer's Report of Wages form, summarizing your employees' total earnings during the quarter and the amount of your FUTA and SUTA liabilities.

From the ANB Business account register, follow these steps to make the payments for federal and state unemployment payroll taxes during the month of April:

1. Make certain you are at the next available form for recording a transaction.
2. Enter **4/15/95** in the Date field.
3. Enter **Internal Revenue Service** in the Payee field, and press TAB.

   The QuickFill feature automatically fills in the remaining fields. If you move to the Payment field by using the mouse instead of by pressing TAB, these fields are not filled in, and you can ignore steps 4, 5, and 6.
4. Click the X button after --Splits-- and select Yes to remove the split from the transaction.
5. Type **104** in the Payment field.

   Later in this chapter, you will see that Smith received $6,000.00 and McFaul received $9,000.00 in gross pay. McFaul has reached the salary limit for employer unemployment contributions for the year. The amount entered here is determined by multiplying the first $7,000.00 of McFaul's salary and all $6,000.00 of Smith's by the FUTA rate of .008.
6. Type **FUTA** in the Memo field.
7. Enter **Payroll:Comp FUTA/B** in the Category field, and then select Record.

   You have now completed the recording of the FUTA payroll tax deposit.

8. Type **Bureau of Employment Services** in the Payee field for the next transaction.
9. Type **520** in the Payment field.

   The payment amount of 520 is determined by adding $7,000.00 and $6,000.00, then multiplying the result, $13,000.00, by .04.
10. Type **SUTA** in the Memo field.
11. Enter **Payroll:Comp SUI/B**, and then select Record.

Now you have completed all the transactions that will be added to the ANB Business account register in this chapter.

Payroll Reports

Through the use of filters and customization features, you can obtain a substantial amount of the payroll-related information you need to prepare federal, state, and local payroll tax and withholding forms. However, as you will see in the following sections, you must perform some functions manually, such as totaling amounts from several Quicken reports to determine the numbers to place on some lines of tax forms.

In this section, you will learn to prepare some of the reports that you may find useful for your own business filing requirements. Although it is impossible to illustrate all the variations, preparing the reports that follow will help you become familiar with the possibilities. You can then begin to explore modifications that suit your payroll and withholding reporting needs.

From the transactions you entered for January through April, you can gather information that will assist you in preparing your quarterly reports: the FUTA form, SUTA form, workers' compensation report, and federal, state, and local withholding tax reports. Although you have not entered a full year's worth of transactions, you will see that Quicken can also help you prepare year-end W-2s, W-3s, 1099s, annual forms for federal, state, and local tax withholdings, and other annual tax forms required for unemployment and workers' compensation purposes.

Payroll Report Overview

Quicken's Payroll report summarizes all your payroll activities in any period for which you need information—that is, you can prepare the report for weekly, monthly, quarterly, or yearly payroll summary information. You can gather the information for all your employees in one report, or you can limit the report to information about one employee at a time.

Keep in mind that Quicken's Payroll report is preset to interface with only the Payroll category. All payroll-related charges are charged against the main Payroll category. Earlier in the chapter, you established subcategories such as Payroll:Gross and Payroll:Comp FICA to keep track of specific types of payroll charges. If you don't use this format, you need to select Summary from the Custom submenu of the Reports menu and customize your reports to gather the information necessary for tax-reporting purposes. For all the reports in this section, you will use the Payroll command in the Business submenu of the Reports menu.

Employer's Quarterly Federal Tax Return

In the previous sections of this chapter, you prepared entries that accumulated FICA and Medicare withholdings, the matching employer's contribution, and the federal income tax withheld from each employee's paycheck. You also recorded the required payments to the IRS, which are made to a local bank authorized to receive these funds.

Let's now examine how you can use Quicken to assist you in preparing Form 941 (shown in Figure 13-5) to meet your quarterly filing requirements. Consult Table 13-1 to find out the deadlines for filing quarterly Form 941 and annual Form 943. Starting from your ANB Business account register, complete the following steps:

HomeBase

Reports | More Reports

1. Select Business from the Reports menu, or select the Reports icon from the icon bar and then select the Business option button.
2. Select Payroll from the menu or dialog box.
3. Type **1/1/95** in the From text box.
4. Type **4/1/95** in the To text box.
5. Select OK, and the Payroll report appears on your screen.
   Although the report is for the quarter that ends on 3/31/95, you need to include the March FICA, Medicare, and income tax withholding payment entered in the register on 4/1/95.
6. Select Print, and the Print Report window appears.
7. Select Print to print the report, which will look similar to the one in Figure 13-6.
8. Select Close to close the Payroll report window.

Depending on your printer, your report may appear on several pages. If you select a smaller font or landscape mode, you can capture more of the report on each page. As a reminder, you can change the font and orientation by selecting Printer Setup from the File menu, and then selecting Report/Graph Printer Setup.

Form **941** (Rev. January 1993) Department of the Treasury Internal Revenue Service

4141

Employer's Quarterly Federal Tax Return

▶ **See separate instructions for information on completing this form.**

Please type or print.

Enter state code for state in which deposits made ▶ (see page 2 of instructions).

Name (as distinguished from trade name) — Date quarter ended

Trade name, if any — Employer identification number

Address (number and street) — City, state, and ZIP code

OMB No. 1545-0029 Expires 1-31-96

T
FF
FD
FP
I
T

If address is different from prior return, check here ▶ ☐ — IRS Use

If you do not have to file returns in the future, check here ▶ ☐ Date final wages paid ▶

If you are a seasonal employer, see **Seasonal employers** on page 1 and check here ▶ ☐

Line	Description			No.	Amount
1	Number of employees (except household) employed in the pay period that includes March 12th ▶				2
2	Total wages and tips subject to withholding, plus other compensation			2	15000
3	Total income tax withheld from wages, tips, pensions, annuities, sick pay, gambling, etc.			3	1842
4	Adjustment of withheld income tax for preceding quarters of calendar year (see instructions)			4	
5	Adjusted total of income tax withheld (line 3 as adjusted by line 4—see instructions)			5	1842
6a	Taxable social security wages	$ 15000	× 12.4% (.124) =	6a	1860
b	Taxable social security tips	$	× 12.4% (.124) =	6b	
7	Taxable Medicare wages and tips	$ 15000	× 2.9% (.029) =	7	435
8	Total social security and Medicare taxes (add lines 6a, 6b, and 7)			8	2295
9	Adjustment of social security and Medicare taxes (see instructions for required explanation)			9	
10	Adjusted total of social security and Medicare taxes (line 8 as adjusted by line 9—see instructions)			10	2295
11	Backup withholding (see instructions)			11	
12	Adjustment of backup withholding tax for preceding quarters of calendar year			12	
13	Adjusted total of backup withholding (line 11 as adjusted by line 12)			13	
14	**Total taxes** (add lines 5, 10, and 13)			14	4137
15	Advance earned income credit (EIC) payments made to employees, if any			15	
16	Net taxes (subtract line 15 from line 14). **This should equal line 20, col. (d), below or line D of Schedule B** (plus line D of Schedule A if you treated backup withholding as a separate liability)			16	4137
17	**Total deposits for quarter,** including overpayment applied from a prior quarter, from your records			17	4137
18	**Balance due** (subtract line 17 from line 16). This should be less than $500. Pay to the Internal Revenue Service			18	0

19 **Overpayment,** if line 17 is more than line 16, enter excess here ▶ $ ________ and check if to be: ☐ Applied to next return **OR** ☐ Refunded.

20 **Monthly Summary of Federal Tax Liability. If line 16 is less than $500, you need not complete line 20.** If you are a monthly depositor, summarize your monthly tax liability below. If you are a semiweekly depositor or have accumulated a tax liability of $100,000 or more on any day, attach Schedule B (Form 941) and check here (see instructions) ▶ ☐

	(a) First month	**(b)** Second month	**(c)** Third month	**(d)** Total for quarter
Liability for month				

Sign Here Under penalties of perjury, I declare that I have examined this return, including accompanying schedules and statements, and to the best of my knowledge and belief, it is true, correct, and complete.

Signature ▶ **Print Your Name and Title ▶** **Date ▶**

For Paperwork Reduction Act Notice, see page 1 of separate instructions. Cat. No. 17001Z Form **941** (Rev. 1-93)

IRS Form 941

Figure 13-5.

Payroll Report by Payee
1/1/95 Through 4/1/95

Category Description	Internal Revenue Service	John Smith	Mary McFaul	Opening Balance	OVERALL TOTAL
INCOME/EXPENSE					
EXPENSES					
Payroll:					
Comp FICA	0.00	372.00	558.00	0.00	930.00
Comp MCARE	0.00	87.00	130.50	0.00	217.50
Gross	0.00	6,000.00	9,000.00	0.00	15,000.00
Total Payroll	0.00	6,459.00	9,688.50	0.00	16,147.50
TOTAL EXPENSES	0.00	6,459.00	9,688.50	0.00	16,147.50
TOTAL INCOME/EXPENSE	0.00	-6,459.00	-9,688.50	0.00	-16,147.50
TRANSFERS					
TO Payroll-FICA	-930.00	0.00	0.00	0.00	-930.00
TO Payroll-FICA-Co	-930.00	0.00	0.00	0.00	-930.00
TO Payroll-FWH	-1,842.00	0.00	0.00	0.00	-1,842.00
TO Payroll-MCARE	-217.50	0.00	0.00	0.00	-217.50
TO Payroll-MCARECo	-217.50	0.00	0.00	0.00	-217.50
FROM Payroll-FICA	0.00	372.00	558.00	0.00	930.00
FROM Payroll-FICA-Co	0.00	372.00	558.00	0.00	930.00
FROM Payroll-FWH	0.00	696.00	1,146.00	0.00	1,842.00
FROM Payroll-MCARE	0.00	87.00	130.50	0.00	217.50
FROM Payroll-MCARECo	0.00	87.00	130.50	0.00	217.50
FROM Payroll-SWH	0.00	164.61	312.84	0.00	477.45
TOTAL TRANSFERS	-4,137.00	1,778.61	2,835.84	0.00	477.45
Balance Forward					
Payroll-FICA	0.00	0.00	0.00	0.00	0.00
Payroll-FICA-Co	0.00	0.00	0.00	0.00	0.00
Payroll-FWH	0.00	0.00	0.00	0.00	0.00
Payroll-MCARE	0.00	0.00	0.00	0.00	0.00
Payroll-MCARECo	0.00	0.00	0.00	0.00	0.00
Payroll-SWH	0.00	0.00	0.00	0.00	0.00
Total Balance Forward	0.00	0.00	0.00	0.00	0.00
OVERALL TOTAL	-4,137.00	-4,680.39	-6,852.66	0.00	-15,670.05

A Payroll report
Figure 13-6.

Using the Payroll Report to Complete Form 941

The Payroll report is shown in Figure 13-6. Let's take a look at the information gathered and discuss how you can use it to complete the appropriate lines of the Employer's Quarterly Federal Tax Return form, shown in Figure 13-5. Look at the following lines on the Employer's Quarterly Federal Tax Return form:

Line 2 This line is for the total wages subject to federal withholding. On the Payroll report, under EXPENSES, the Gross line shows that a total of $15,000.00 was earned by Smith and McFaul during the quarter.

Form 941: Employer's Quarterly Federal Tax Returns	First Quarter (Jan- Mar)	Second Quarter (Apr-Jun)	Third Quarter (Jul- Sep)	Fourth Quarter (Oct- Dec)
If deposit is required with filing:	April 30	July 31	October 31	January 31
If you deposit all taxes when due:	May 10	August 10	November 10	February 10
Form 943: Employer's Annual Tax Return for Agricultural Employees		**Calendar Year Filing**		
If deposit is required with filing:		January 31		
If you deposited all taxes when due:		February 10		

Dates for Filing Federal Payroll Tax Returns

Table 13-1.

Line 3 This line is for the total amount of income tax withheld from employee wages. On the Payroll report, under TRANSFERS, the TO Payroll-FWH line shows that the total federal income tax withheld from employees was $1,842.00. If you look at the FROM Payroll-FWH line, you can see that $696.00 was paid by Smith and $1,146.00 was paid by McFaul.

Line 6a This line is for the amount of social security taxes accumulated during the quarter. If you look at the Payroll report under TRANSFERS, you can see in the TO Payroll-FICA line that the total amount is $1,860.00. The totals in the FROM Payroll-FICA and the FROM Payroll-FICA-Co lines combine to obtain this amount. To verify the FICA tax owed, multiply the amount on line 2 of the form ($15,000.00) by .124. This should equal the total calculated in the preceding paragraph ($1,860.00), which it does. You record this amount on line 6a.

Line 7 This line is for the amount of Medicare taxes accumulated during the quarter. On the Payroll report, you get the total from the TO Payroll-MCARE line. The total is $435.00. This total comes from adding the amounts in the FROM Payroll-MCARE and FROM Payroll-MCARECo rows of the report. To verify the Medicare taxes owed, multiply $15,000 (the amount on line 2 of the form) by .029 to get the amount on line 7.

Line 17 This line is for the total deposits made to the IRS during the quarter. This amount can be obtained from the Internal Revenue Service column in the Payroll report. The OVERALL TOTAL row shows that

$4,137.00 was deposited with the Internal Revenue Service during the quarter. Note that this amount includes the 4/1/95 payment. When you complete your IRS deposit slip, you designate the quarter for which the payment applies. In this case, the payment was made for the first quarter and would thus be included in this report.

The bottom portion of Form 941 requires that you calculate your tax liabilities at specified time intervals during the deposit periods. Since you made your payments in a timely fashion during the quarter, you do not need to complete this portion. If you did need to complete this portion of the form for the example in this chapter, you could use Quicken to gather information for you. Figure 13-7 shows the Federal Tax Liability report, which captures the information for the first quarter to help you to complete the lines at the bottom of Form 941. If you pay your employees weekly, you could produce this same report for weekly periods during the quarter. If you want to reproduce Figure 13-7 with the ANB Business account register, complete the following steps:

HomeBase

Reports | More Reports

1. Select Business from the Reports menu, or select the Reports icon and the Business option button.
2. Select Payroll from the menu or dialog box.
3. Type **1/1/95** in the From text box.
4. Type **3/31/95** in the To text box.
5. Select Customize. The Customize Report dialog box appears on the screen.
6. Type **Federal Tax Liability** in the Title text box.

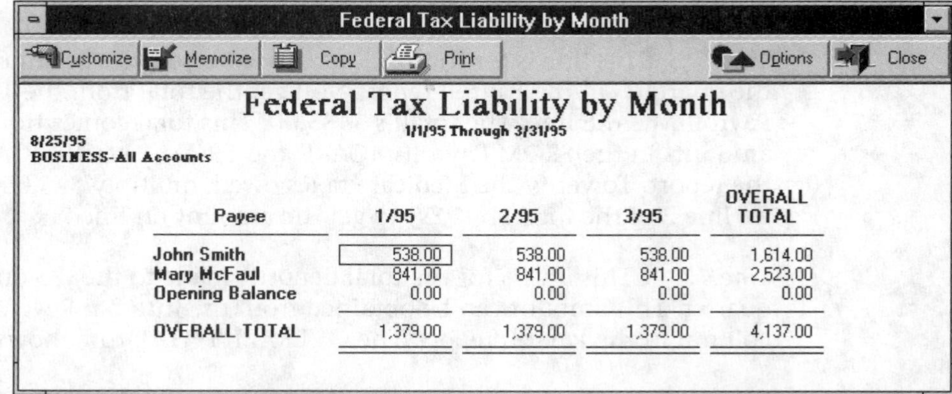

Federal Tax Liability by Month

1/1/95 Through 3/31/95

8/25/95

BUSINESS-All Accounts

Payee	1/95	2/95	3/95	OVERALL TOTAL
John Smith	538.00	538.00	538.00	1,614.00
Mary McFaul	841.00	841.00	841.00	2,523.00
Opening Balance	0.00	0.00	0.00	0.00
OVERALL TOTAL	1,379.00	1,379.00	1,379.00	4,137.00

The Tax report for employee federal tax withholding

Figure 13-7.

7. Select Payee from the Row drop-down list box.
8. Select Month from the Column drop-down list box.
9. Select the Matching option button.

   The Matching dialog box elements appear.
10. Type **~Internal Revenue Service** in the Payee Contains text box.

    A tilde (~**) in the** Payee Contains text box tells Quicken to exclude transactions with this payee from the report.
11. Enter **[Payroll..** in the Category Contains text box.

    This text box contains "PAYROLL.." by default, telling Quicken to include only transactions with a Payroll category. Adding the square bracket tells Quicken to include only transfers to Payroll liability accounts.
12. Select the Categories/Classes option button.
13. Click the liability account Payroll-SWH or highlight it and press SPACEBAR to unmark this account, as shown here:

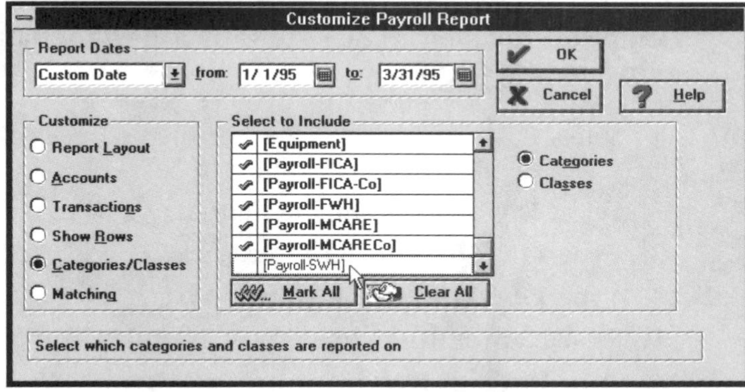

14. Select OK and the Print Report window shows the report in Figure 13-7.
15. Select Print, then select Print to print the Federal Tax Liability report.
16. Select Close to close the Payroll report window.

Preparing Other Tax Forms

In addition to the Employer's Quarterly Federal Tax Return, you will need to complete several other quarterly tax returns and reports, depending on the state where your business is located. These additional reports and tax forms may include state (SWH) and local (LWH) withholding tax reports and state unemployment tax (SUTA) reports. The Payroll report shown in Figure 13-6 provides the information needed to prepare some of these reports. For example, under TRANSFERS, the FROM Payroll-SWH line shows that $477.45 was withheld from employee wages for state taxes. You have not recorded this entry in your register; however, when the check is sent to the state taxing unit, the payment would be handled in the same manner as the payments to the IRS. You will also need to monitor individual employees' gross earnings to complete several of the other forms. Determining the total earnings for an employee for a given time period and determining your FUTA and SUTA contributions are discussed in the "Other Annual Tax Forms and Reports" section later in this chapter.

Preparing W-2 Forms

At the end of the year, you must give each employee who worked for you during the year a W-2 form. In the example developed here, assume that John Smith left your business at the end of March and received no further paychecks. The Payroll report prepared in this case is customized for John Smith and uses only the ANB Business account register, because this is the account from which you write your payroll checks. All the information concerning John Smith's earnings is included in this account.

Complete the following steps to gather the information needed to complete John Smith's W-2 form:

HomeBase

Reports | More Reports

1. Select Business from the Reports menu, or select the Reports icon and select the Business option button.
2. Select Payroll from the menu or dialog box.
3. Type **1/1/95** in the From text box.
4. Type **12/31/95** in the To text box.
5. Select Customize to open the Customize Report dialog box.
6. Type **Payroll Report-John Smith** in the Title text box.
7. Select Matching.

   The Category Contains text box contains "Payroll" by default, so Quicken limits the report to Payroll category transactions. As mentioned earlier, this feature of Quicken requires that you record all payroll activity in the Payroll category. Otherwise, Quicken's Payroll report will not gather your payroll transactions correctly. In that case, you would need to prepare your reports by using the Summary Report option.
8. Type **John Smith** in the Payee Contains text box, and then select OK.

   You have filtered the report so that it will include only the payroll information for John Smith.
9. Select Print, and the Print Report dialog box appears.

10. Select Print to print John Smith's payroll report, which appears in Figure 13-8.
11. Select Close to the close Payroll report window.

Although you have not entered the entire year's payroll transactions for Mary McFaul, the same steps will generate her W-2 information.

Using the Payroll Report to Complete a W-2

The payroll report in Figure 13-8 provides the numbers you need to complete John Smith's W-2 Wage and Tax Statement:

- Under EXPENSES, the Gross line shows the total earnings reported ($6,000.00).

Payroll Report-John Smith by Payee
1/1/95 Through 12/31/95

Category Description	John Smith	
INCOME/EXPENSE		
EXPENSES		
Payroll:		
Comp FICA	372.00	
Comp MCARE	87.00	
Gross	6,000.00	
Total Payroll		6,459.00
TOTAL EXPENSES		6,459.00
TOTAL INCOME/EXPENSE		-6,459.00
TRANSFERS		
FROM Payroll-FICA		372.00
FROM Payroll-FICA-Co		372.00
FROM Payroll-FWH		696.00
FROM Payroll-MCARE		87.00
FROM Payroll-MCARECo		87.00
FROM Payroll-SWH		164.61
TOTAL TRANSFERS		1,778.61
OVERALL TOTAL		-4,680.39

The annual Payroll report for John Smith
Figure 13-8.

- Under TRANSFERS, the FROM Payroll-FWH line shows the total federal withholding amount ($696.00).
- The FICA withholding amount ($372.00) is found in the FROM Payroll-FICA line. Notice this amount equals the company's FICA matching contribution, because the company matches employee FICA contributions dollar for dollar up to $60,600 of gross earnings.
- The Medicare withholding amount ($87.00) is shown in the FROM Payroll-MCARE line. Notice that this amount equals the company's Medicare matching contribution, because the company matches employee Medicare contributions dollar for dollar.
- The state withholding amount ($164.61) is shown in the FROM Payroll-SWH line of the report.

No local taxes have been withheld in this example. If you do business in an area where local income taxes are withheld, you need to add the appropriate liability accounts to accumulate this information.

Other Annual Tax Forms and Reports

The information provided in the preceding reports can also be used to prepare other year-end tax reports. For example, Payroll reports for the full year, similar to those shown in Figures 13-6 and 13-8, can help you complete sections of the following reports:

- Form W-3, Transmittal of Income and Tax Statements
- Form 940, Employer's Annual Federal Unemployment (FUTA) Tax Return
- Various state and local withholding and state unemployment tax (SUTA) reports

FUTA and SUTA Contributions

In the "Recording April Transactions" section of this chapter, you recorded entries on 4/15/95 for your FUTA and SUTA contributions. When completing your quarterly and annual reports, you can use Quicken's Filter option to prepare a report showing the total FUTA and SUTA contributions paid during the quarter or the year. To do this, you prepare a Payroll report using Quicken's Customize Report window, and you make the category match Payroll:Comp FUTA. Then you prepare a second report in which the category matches Payroll:Comp SUI. Figures 13-9 and 13-10 show reports prepared from your account register that have been filtered in this way. The reports show FUTA payments of $104.00 and SUTA payments of $520.00.

You can also prepare filtered reports to determine the total federal and state payments for unemployment taxes during the entire year. You can then use that information when completing your Form 940 and the corresponding state SUTA form.

Form 1099

The last payroll-related statement discussed here is Form 1099. You must provide a Form 1099 to all individuals who are not regular employees and to whom you have paid more than $600.00 during the tax year. The easiest way to record transactions for payments of this nature is to type **1099** in the Memo field when you record the transactions in your business account register during the year. You can then prepare a Transaction report for the

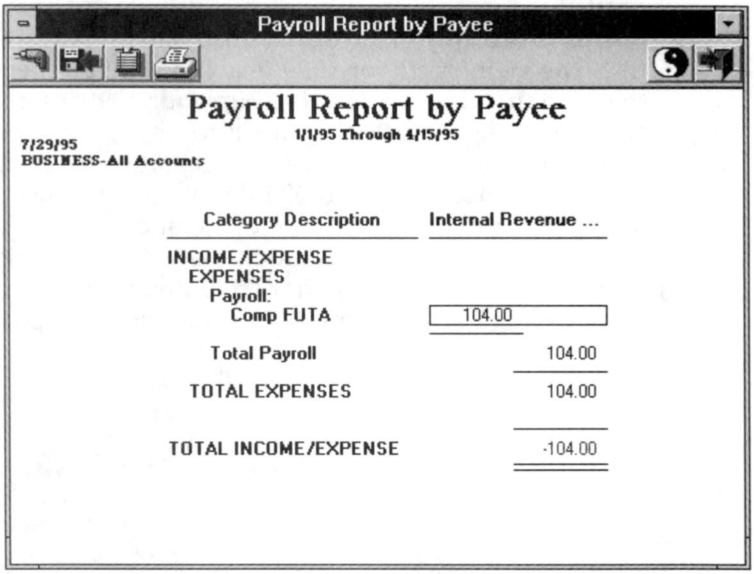

A report showing federal unemployment payments
Figure 13-9.

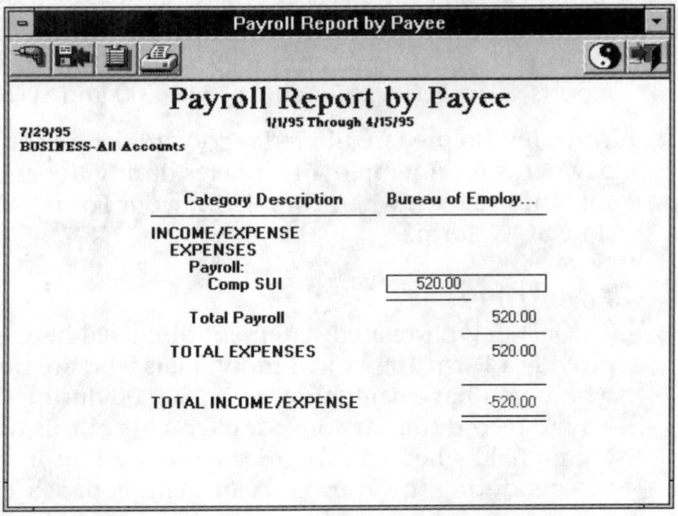

Payroll Report by Payee

Payroll Report by Payee

1/1/95 Through 4/15/95

7/29/95
BUSINESS-All Accounts

Category Description	Bureau of Employ...
INCOME/EXPENSE	
EXPENSES	
Payroll:	
Comp SUI	520.00
Total Payroll	520.00
TOTAL EXPENSES	520.00
TOTAL INCOME/EXPENSE	-520.00

A report showing state unemployment payments

Figure 13-10.

year filtered by Payee and Memo field matches to gather the information needed to prepare 1099s for each payee. If you are not certain of all the payees to whom you have paid miscellaneous income, you may want to filter the Memo field for 1099 first and print all these transactions. You can then use that information to group your 1099 information by payee. You could also assign all 1099 payments to a category (for example, Consult-1099) and filter a Summary or Transaction report by payee and category to accumulate the necessary 1099 information. Another possibility is to create a register report sorted by the Payee field and then review the payees for individuals where the total amounts are $600.00 or more. You can sort the Register report by selecting the Sort button in the report window's button bar and selecting Payee in the Sort Transactions By drop-down list box.

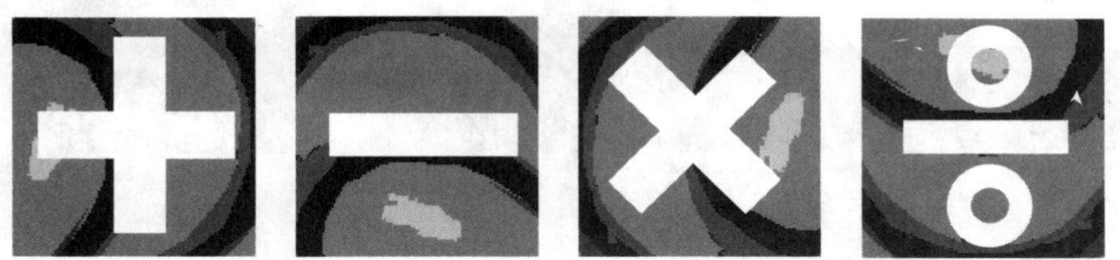

CHAPTER

PREPARING BUDGET REPORTS and CASH FLOW STATEMENTS

TO run a successful business, you need more than just a good product or service to sell to customers or clients. You also need a sound financial management program that allows your business to grow and develop. Financial management is more than just preparing the basic reports that your banker or other creditors request.

It includes a plan of action that shows your creditors you are prepared to manage your business in a changing environment. A comprehensive program to manage business finances consists of:

- A business plan
- The development of strong business relations with your banker or other creditors
- The use of budgets and cash flow statements to help in managing your financial resources

To develop a financial management program, you need a sound accounting system. Quicken can help you generate the financial information you need to make better management decisions.

Developing a Financial Management Program

Developing a sound financial management program is an important aspect of managing your business.

If you look closely at the areas of financial management, just listed, you notice that two of the three parts do not directly involve the accounting system. Let's take a more in-depth look at these components.

A business plan is a well-developed concept of where your business has been and where it is going. Keep in mind that non-financial considerations should play a major role in your business plan. That is, you need to know your product and potential market before you can begin to budget sales and costs for your business. The budget process you follow in this chapter demonstrates how budgeting and cash flow statements are prepared. More importantly, you will see that the decisions you make in estimating budget income and expenses come from non-financial considerations. In short, developing a business plan forces you to think through the finances and operations of your business. In the long run, the plan makes it easier for you to estimate the expected sales and related costs.

The importance of developing strong relations with your banker and creditors cannot be underestimated. However, a word of caution: Do not expect a bank to finance a new business for you. A good banker expects you to provide a significant part of the capital needed. From the banker's perspective, it is not good business to risk the bank's money if you are not willing to risk your own.

When you choose a banker, it's important to maintain a strong relationship for the long term. One way of doing this is to obtain a modest bank loan when your business is prospering, even though you may not need the loan now. This helps strengthen your banking relationship. Then, when you really need a loan, your banker will already be familiar with you and your business activities. This might make the difference between loan approval or rejection.

Preparing a Business Plan

If you have never prepared a business plan, determining what to include can be difficult. Your goal is to create a concise document that presents a realistic picture of your company, including its needs, assets, and products. Outside lenders will be especially interested in the financial history and resources of the firm and your sales projections. Be sure to include the following as you prepare your plan:

- A brief overview of your firm, its products, and its financing requirements. It is important to keep this short and simple.
- A brief history of the firm, including product successes and copyrights or patents held. Include a résumé of the firm's owners or partners.
- A short description of your product(s). Include information on the competition, production plans, and prices.
- A description of the market for the product(s) and your distribution plans.
- Sales and cost projections showing current capital and financing requirements.

The final part of the financial management program is budgeting and the regular monitoring of your cash flow. A budget is a plan in which you estimate the income and expenses of your business for a period of time: a week, a month, a quarter, a year, or longer. Creating a budget report requires some advance work, since you enter projected amounts for each category in the budget. Quicken guides you through the budget development process to minimize the work required. Then, you can enter your income and expenses and check the status of your actual and budgeted amounts whenever you wish. You can also use your budget figures to project the future cash flow of your business. This type of information is valuable in forecasting loans you may need and demonstrates to your banker that you are anticipating your financial needs. A budget is a sign of sound business and financial planning.

A cash flow report is related to your budget and looks at the inflow and outflow of cash for your business. This report is valuable. It can identify problems stemming from a lack of available cash, even though your business may be highly profitable at the current time. A problem with cash flow can limit your company's growth and get in the way of running your business.

Sources of Funding

Securing financing for a new business can be difficult even if you have a good product. Banks are often wary of lending money for a new venture, unless you are willing to take the high-risk position of offering your home or other assets as collateral. Other financing options to consider include:

- A commercial bank loan under the Small Business Administration Loan Guarantee Program.
- Borrowing against your life insurance policy.
- Short-term borrowing through supplier credit extensions.
- Finance companies.
- Venture capitalists—you normally give up a part of the ownership of your business with this option.
- Small business investment enterprises—you can find these by contacting your local government about agencies and programs for small business development.
- Economically disadvantaged groups and minority businesses may have other options for public or private funding. These can be located through local government or minority organizations.

In this chapter, you learn how to use Quicken to prepare a business budget. Remember the concepts discussed here as you go through the example; you are learning more than just the procedures involved. Budgeting and cash flow statement analysis can give you and your creditors important information. Quicken provides the necessary ingredients to help you prepare a financial management program that will make you a better business manager.

In the chapter's examples, you prepare budget entries for several months. Transaction groups from Chapters 12 and 13 will speed the entry process while providing enough transactions to get a sense of what Quicken can do. After making your entries, you will see how Quicken's standard Budget and Cash Flow reports can help you keep expenses in line with your budget.

Quicken's Budgeting Process

Quicken can help you manage your business finances.

A budget in Quicken contains projected income and expense levels for any supercategory, category, or subcategory. You can enter the same projection for each month of the year or change the amount allocated each month. For the business in this example, it is essential to be able to enter different budget amounts each month, especially for the projected income figures. Royalties are received at the end of each quarter, which causes some months to show a zero income in this category. Also, some other income-generating activities are seasonal and vary widely between months. These seasonal fluctuations also cause changes to each month's budgeted expenses. The timing of these expenses and income becomes important when you determine whether you have the cash flow to pay for them.

Once you have entered the budget amounts, Quicken matches your planned expenses with the actual expense entries and displays the results in a Budget report. Although you enter budget information in one window, Quicken collects the actual entries from all of your bank, cash, and credit card accounts in the current file. Therefore, if you do not pay any business expenses from your personal checking account, you may want to exclude this account from the Budget report. You can do this by selecting which accounts appear in the report. However, since in this example you have paid both personal and business expenses from the ANB Personal account, you cannot exclude this account from your budget reports. Instead, you will use the class code of B to select all business transactions when preparing reports in this chapter. You can also choose whether or not transfers between accounts should show in the budget. You can change whether transfers are shown by selecting Layout from the Budget window's button bar, then selecting or clearing the Show Transfers check box.

Although Quicken can take much of the work out of entering and managing your budget, it cannot prepare a budget without your projections. Once you have put together a plan, it is time to record your decisions in Quicken. Quicken's budgeting process will be presented in the following stages: opening the Budget window, specifying revenue amounts, moving around the Budget window, entering expense projections, and printing the report.

14

HomeBase

Planning | Budgeting

Setting Up the Budget

The Budget window is the starting place for Quicken's budget process. You can access this window in any account register. To start the budget procedure, select Budgeting from the Plan menu to open a Budget window like the one in Figure 14-1.

In Figure 14-1, the category descriptions are listed down the left side of the screen and the months of the year across the top. The layout of the

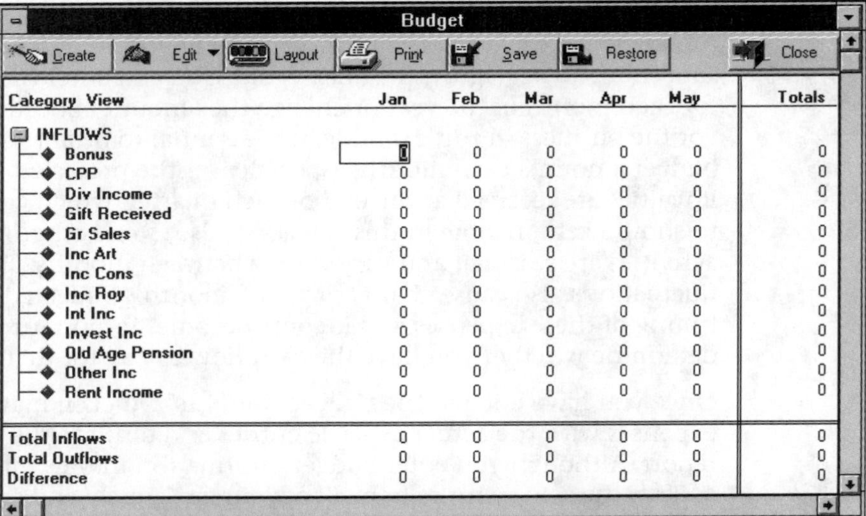

The Budget window
Figure 14-1.

information is similar to a spreadsheet in a package such as Lotus 1-2-3 or Quattro Pro.

Only a few category descriptions appear on the screen at any time. Quicken displays the total budget inflows and outflows at the bottom of the window and the total for the categories at the right. Updates to these totals occur as you make changes. The instant updating allows you to make changes to a budget amount and immediately assess the effect on budget differences.

Some categories have buttons before them that show a + or -. These symbols let you expand and contract the levels displayed. The - in front of INFLOWS means that all of its categories are shown. If you double-click this button, the - changes to a + and the INFLOWS categories do not show on screen.

You can budget for periods of months, quarters, or years using Layout on the button bar.

Entering Revenue Projections

Entering budget projections is easy. If you want the same numbers in January through December, you can enter a number for January and copy the number across to the other months. You can copy the last number entered across the row or you can copy an entire column across. After completing the copy, you can always customize entries for some of the months by typing a new number.

To set up the budget amounts for revenues, follow these steps:

Entering and changing budgeted amounts is an easy task.

1. Move to the Jan field for Inc Art category.
2. Type **50** and press RIGHT ARROW.

   To move to the next field in this current row, press TAB or RIGHT ARROW. You can also use the mouse, but it is usually quicker to use the keyboard, since you are already typing. When you move to another field, Quicken records 50 as the January amount and then waits for you to enter an amount for February.
3. Repeat step 2 twice more to record 50 for February and March, and then position the highlight for an April entry.
4. Type **3575** and press RIGHT ARROW.
5. Repeat step 4 to enter the same amount for May.
6. Type **2000** and press RIGHT ARROW.
7. Type **3575** and press RIGHT ARROW.
8. Type **2000** and select Edit, and then Fill Row Right.

   If you do not select the Edit button before finalizing the 2,000 entry, the highlight moves to another row or column.
9. Select Yes to confirm the action.

   Quicken enters 2,000 for the remaining months of the current category.
10. Move the highlight until it is on the Inc Cons field for January.
11. Type **10000**, select Edit, then Fill Row Right, and then select Yes.
12. Move to the far right of the screen; you see the 10,000 for Inc Cons in December.

    You can use the mouse, or you can press END twice.
13. Return to the January column with the mouse or by pressing HOME twice.
14. Move to the July column for Inc Cons, and type **12000**.
15. Move to the March column for Inc Roy, and type **10000**.
16. Repeat step 15 for the months of June, September, and December.

    When you look at the lower-right corner of the Budget window, you can see that the inflows total is $184,875.

Moving Around the Budget Window

Before entering additional budget data, practice moving around within the Budget window and using the keyboard. The keyboard is usually much more convenient than the mouse while in this window. After you complete the entries in the previous section, the highlight should be on the 10,000 in the Inc Roy December column. Follow these steps from that location:

1. Press HOME twice and CTRL-HOME once.

   The highlight appears at the top of the window.
2. Press END twice to move to the top field in the December column.
3. Press CTRL-END to move to the bottom of the December column.
4. Press PAGE UP to move up one window.
5. Press HOME twice and CTRL-HOME once to move to the top left of the Budget window.
6. Select Layout from the button bar to display the Layout Budgets dialog box.
7. Select Quarter under Columns, then click OK to review the data in the Budget window divided by quarters instead of months.

   Quicken has combined your monthly data so that each quarter combines three months of data. Your data is not permanently combined, so you have not lost your monthly entries.
8. Repeat steps 6 and 7 but select Year under Columns, and then select OK again to see the change in the Budget window.

   Now your budget shows the budgeted revenues combined into a single year.
9. Repeat steps 6 and 7 but select Month under Columns, and then click OK to change the time period back to the original display.

Other Budget Button Bar Options

Quicken can use last year's transactions to create a budget for you.

To select options from the button bar at the top of the window, use the mouse by clicking the button or the keyboard by pressing ALT and the underlined letter. Although you will explore many budget button bar options in more detail in the following exercises, a quick overview will help you feel comfortable with this new Quicken window.

Select Create to automatically create a budget from your existing transactions. You can select the period for the transactions in the From and To text boxes or the categories that you want to use when creating the budget by selecting Categories. You can select Use Monthly Detail or Use Average For Period. You can also choose Round Values To Nearest with options for $1, $10, or $100.

Select Edit to alter the existing budget display. Selecting 2-Week lets you create a budget for an individual category or subcategory for a two-week time period. Copy All copies the budget to the Windows Clipboard. Clear Row clears all the budgeted amounts in a specific category. Clear All Budgets clears all budget amounts. Fill Row Right fills in the same amount for a specific category in all remaining budget periods. Fill Columns fills all columns with the amounts recorded in the current column. Supercategories let you create, edit, or delete groups of budget categories at a time.

In the previous steps, you changed layout options to specify the period for the budget. Other Layout options choose whether supercategories (Show Supercategories) and transfers (Show Transfers) are shown on the budget layout. The Hide Zero Budget Categories check box hides all the budgeted category amounts that are zero.

The Print button displays the Print Report dialog box so you can print your budget report. The Save button saves a copy of your budget.

The Restore button lets you restore a previous budget if you have saved it.

The Close button closes the Budget window and saves the current budget.

Entering Expense Projections

To complete your budget picture, you need to enter projections for your expense categories. Using the information provided, complete the Budget window for the categories. Follow these steps:

1. Enter the following amounts in the January month column for the categories shown:

Category	**Budget Amount**
Del Overngt:	200
Dues:	25
Equip Mnt:	100
Freight:	20
Insurance:	50
Misc:	25
Office:	80
Payroll	
Comp FICA:	310
Comp MCARE:	73
Gross:	5,000
Postage:	10
Supp Comp:	210
Supplies:	50
Telephone:	120
Travel:	300
Utilities	
Electric:	30
Gas:	30

Some of these expenses are assigned to the category and others to subcategories. You can do both with Quicken. Remember that if you need to expand a category to show its subcategories, double-click the + button in front of the category's name. When you enter the numbers, they appear as negative numbers to indicate that they are cash outflows. Positive numbers in this window are for income amounts.

2. Move to each entry you made in the last step, and select Edit, then Fill Row Right and Yes to copy the January entries to all columns to the right.
3. Select the Layout button, then select the Hide Zero Budget Categories check box and OK.

   Now the budget shows only the categories that you have made entries. This Budget window looks like Figure 14-2.
4. Select Close, and then select Yes to close the Budget window and save the budget. Return to the ANB Business account register.

Using Budget Supercategories

Use budget super-categories to get an overview of how you

Budget supercategories are a new feature in Quicken 4 for Windows. Any category in your budget can be assigned to a supercategory. Supercategories are like the classes that you use to divide transactions into groups. Budget supercategories are used to group regular category entries. You might use them to divide categories into groups for different businesses or parts of a business. For example, in the Budget window in Figure 14-3, the

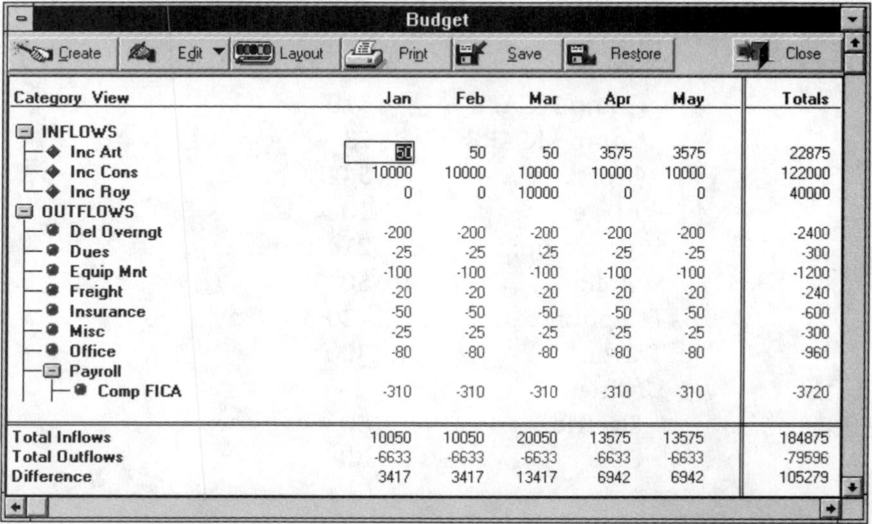

Budget
Create
Edit
Layout
Print
Save
Restore
Close
Category View Jan Feb Mar Apr May Totals
INFLOWS
Inc Art 50 50 50 3575 3575 22875
Inc Cons 10000 10000 10000 10000 10000 122000
Inc Roy 0 0 10000 0 0 40000
OUTFLOWS
Del Overngt -200 -200 -200 -200 -200 -2400
Dues -25 -25 -25 -25 -25 -300
Equip Mnt -100 -100 -100 -100 -100 -1200
Freight -20 -20 -20 -20 -20 -240
Insurance -50 -50 -50 -50 -50 -600
Misc -25 -25 -25 -25 -25 -300
Office -80 -80 -80 -80 -80 -960
Payroll
Comp FICA -310 -310 -310 -310 -310 -3720
Total Inflows 10050 10050 20050 13575 13575 184875
Total Outflows -6633 -6633 -6633 -6633 -6633 -79596
Difference 3417 3417 13417 6942 6942 105279

The Budget window after the entries are completed

Figure 14-2.

supercategories include Income, Division 1, Division 2, and Head Office/Overhead. You can assign categories to any budget supercategory, creating your own supercategories if you prefer. You can then use these supercategories in reports and the Budget window to better monitor your budget.

Quicken assigns the original categories to supercategories. When you create new ones, Quicken does not assign them to any of the default supercategories. To assign categories to a supercategory, follow these steps:

1. In the Budget window, select Edit from the button bar.
2. Select Supercategories, opening the Manage Supercategories dialog box. This dialog box lists the categories and their supercategory assignments as well as the available supercategories.
3. Select a category in the Category Name list box.
4. Select a supercategory in the Supercategory Name list box.
5. Select Assign.
6. Repeat steps 3 through 5 to assign other categories to a supercategory.
7. Select OK when you are finished reassigning categories.

Note: You can create custom supercategories by selecting New in the Managing Supercategories dialog box.

14

Supercategories to divide the budget categories into groups
Figure 14-3.

Budget

Create | Edit | Layout | Print | Save | Restore | Close

Supercategory View	Jan	Feb	Mar	Apr	May	Totals
INFLOWS						
Income						
Gr Sales - 1	25000	25000	25000	25000	25000	300000
Gr Sales - 2	30000	30000	30000	30000	30000	360000
OUTFLOWS						
Division 1						
Payroll - 1	-10000	-10000	-10000	-10000	-10000	-120000
Supplies - 1	-5000	-5000	-5000	-5000	-5000	-60000
Utilities - 1	-250	-250	-250	-250	-250	-3000
Division 2						
Payroll - 2	-8500	-8500	-8500	-8500	-8500	-102000
Supplies - 2	-16000	-16000	-16000	-16000	-16000	-192000
Utilities - 2	-200	-200	-200	-200	-200	-2400
Head Office/Overhead						
Total Inflows	55000	55000	55000	55000	55000	660000
Total Outflows	-53715	-52465	-52765	-52465	-52465	-632030
Difference	1285	2535	2235	2535	2535	27970

To display your supercategories in the Budget window, as Figure 14-3 shows, just select Layout from the window's button bar, then select the Show Supercategories check box and OK. Quicken displays the supercategories with categories beneath them. You can double-click the icons in front of the supercategories to display or hide the categories beneath them.

Printing the Budget Report

HomeBase

Reports | More Reports

After entering your budget data, you can print your report by following these steps:

1. Select Other on the Reports menu, or select the Reports icon and select the Other option button.
2. Select Budget from the menu or dialog box.
3. Select Customize.

   The Customize Budget Report dialog box, as you will complete it, is shown here:

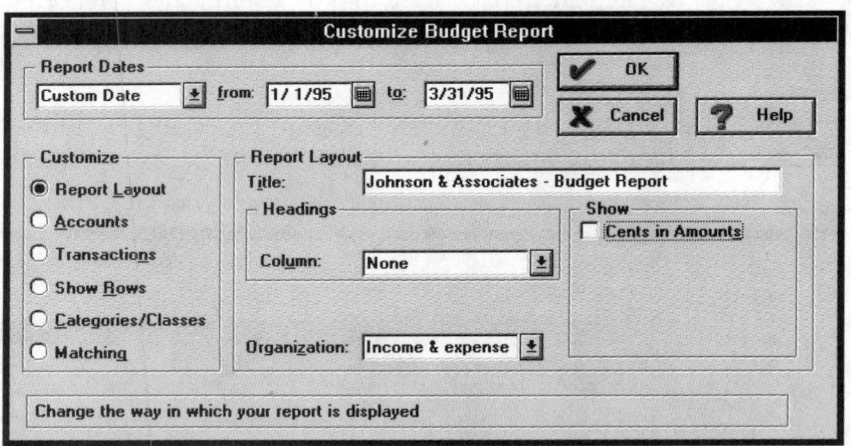

4. Enter **1/1/95** in the From text box.
5. Enter **3/31/95** in the To text box.
6. Type **Johnson & Associates - Budget Report** in the Title text box.
7. Clear the Cents in Amounts check box.
8. Select the Accounts option button.
9. Select Mark All, if all accounts are not already marked to be included in the report.

10. Select the Matching option button and enter **B** in the Class Contains text box to limit the transactions to the business ones.
11. Click OK to display the budget report in a window.
12. Select the Options button in the button bar to display the Report Options dialog box.

    This dialog box has more advanced settings for changing how the report appears. The Account Display and Category Display sections let you choose whether the report shows the names or longer descriptions for the accounts and categories.
13. Select the Description and the Description option buttons, and then select OK so the report shows the longer account and category descriptions.

    Some of the expense categories are in a different order since they are now alphabetized according to their descriptions rather than names.
14. Select the Print button from the report window button bar, and then select Print. The report prints as shown in Figure 14-4.
15. Select the Options button in the button bar to display the Report Options dialog box.
16. Select the Name and the Name option buttons, and then click OK to return the report to showing the account and category names instead of descriptions.

You can also use the Customize Report dialog box to tell Quicken which categories you want in your report. Select the Show Rows option button, and then select from the Categories drop-down list box. If you select Include All, Quicken will show the entire category list even if many of the categories were not used for budgeting purposes (for example, Old Age Pension). You could also select Non-Zero Actual/Budgeted or Budgeted Only to display. The default option is Budgeted Only, where Quicken only displays the accounts for which budget information was entered.

If you need to change printer settings, refer to Chapter 4. You might want to use smaller fonts when printing wide reports to capture more of your report on each page. For example, if you print the budget report using months for the column heading, your report will print across two pages unless you use a font smaller than the default.

Report Discussion

Let's take a look at the report shown in Figure 14-4. The report compares the actual expenditures made during the quarter with those you budgeted. An analysis of the income section shows you received more income than you budgeted during the period. This was due to receiving more in consulting

Johnson & Associates - Budget Report
1/1/95 Through 3/31/95

Category Description	1/1/95 Actual	Budget	3/31/95 Diff
INCOME/EXPENSE			
INCOME			
Article Income	0	150	-150
Consulting Income	37,500	30,000	7,500
Royalty Income	10,000	10,000	0
TOTAL INCOME	47,500	40,150	7,350
EXPENSES			
Computer Supplies	376	630	254
Dues	0	75	75
Equipment Maintenance	1,100	300	-800
Freight	0	60	60
Insurance	0	150	150
Miscellaneous	0	75	75
Office Expenses	0	240	240
Overnight Delivery	270	600	330
Payroll Expenses:			
Gross Earnings	15,000	15,000	0
Payroll Taxes-FICA	930	930	0
Payroll Taxes-MCARE	218	219	2
Total Payroll Expenses	16,148	16,149	2
Postage Expense	28	30	2
Supplies	65	150	85
Telephone Expense	305	360	55
Travel Expenses	905	900	-5
Water, Gas, Electric:			
Electric Utilities	30	90	60
Gas Utilities	17	90	73
Total Water, Gas, Electric	47	180	133
TOTAL EXPENSES	19,244	19,899	655
TOTAL INCOME/EXPENSE	28,256	20,251	8,005

A Budget report for the first quarter of 1995
Figure 14-4.

income than anticipated, although you received no income from articles. You can then check the cause of these differences. Perhaps you didn't project all the consulting activities you were involved in during the quarter, or a client paid you earlier than you had anticipated.

The expense portion of the report shows the actual and budgeted expenses for the period. An analysis of individual categories is not worthwhile because the data you entered did not include expense entries for all the months in the report. However, you can see that the report compares budgeted with actual expenses during the period and shows the differences in the Diff column. In general, you are concerned with all the differences shown in this report, but

Comparing budgeted revenues and expenses with actual amounts is an important aspect of managing your business finances.

you will probably only want to spend your time investigating the large dollar differences between budgeted and actual amounts. For example, you might decide to investigate in detail only those budget differences that exceed $300.00. For these categories, you might want to examine the underlying transactions in more depth. A quick way to look at the detail behind a number in the Actual column is to double-click the number or highlight it and press ENTER. Quicken creates a QuickZoom report. For example, the -800 difference for equipment maintenance is large. You can see where the $1,100 comes from by double-clicking it or highlighting it, and then pressing ENTER to show the report in Figure 14-5.

The essence of budgeting is to determine where potential problems exist in your business and detect them early. Quicken's budget reporting capabilities can help you in making these business decisions.

Modifying the Budget Report

In the early stages of budgeting, it generally takes several months to develop sound estimates for all your expense categories. You can change your projections at any time by selecting Budgeting from the Plan menu. You can also modify the report you just created to show different time periods or a selected group of accounts. Follow these steps to look at a monthly budget report for the same time period:

1. Switch back to the Johnson & Associates - Budget Report window if you are looking at another one.

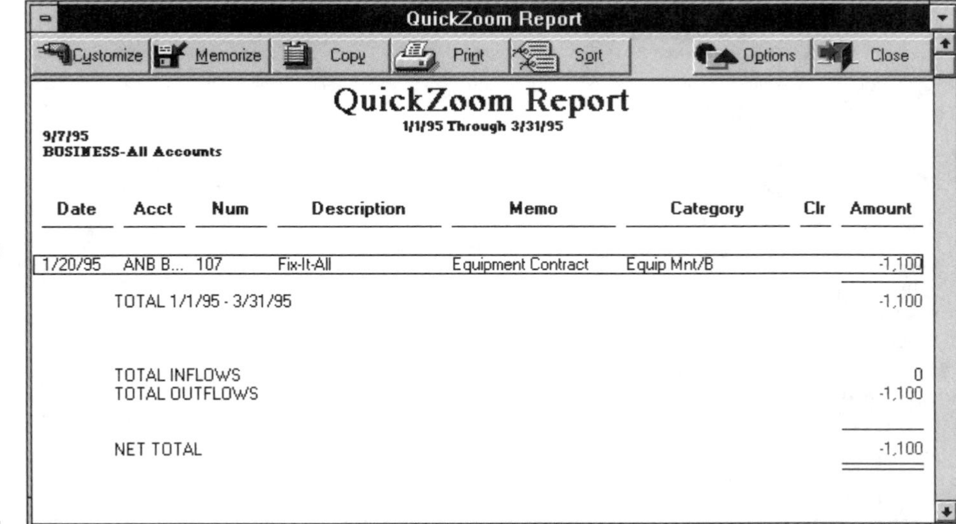

A QuickZoom report showing the transactions behind the Actual column of a budget
Figure 14-5.

2. Select Customize from the button bar.
3. Change the entry in the Title text box to **Johnson & Associates - Budget**.

   A title can only contain up to 39 characters. After you perform the next step, Quicken adds "By Month" to the report title, which causes the beginning text of longer titles to be dropped.
4. Select Month from the Column drop-down list box, telling Quicken you want the budget broken out into months.
5. click OK.
6. Select Print, and the Print Report dialog box opens. To print the report, select Printer and then select Print. Since this report is too wide to fit on one page, Figure 14-6 is split over two pages.

So far, the budgets you have looked at focused on the first quarter of 1995. For your own situation, you need to extend the budget over a longer period. It is impractical to enter all of the transactions for a year at this time, but

Johnson & Associates - Budget by Month

1/1/95 Through 3/31/95

9/7/95 Page 1

BUSINESS-All Accounts

Category Description	1/1/95 Actual	- Budget	1/31/95 Diff	2/1/95 Actual	- Budget	2/28/95 Diff	3/1/95 Actual	- Budget
INCOME/EXPENSE								
INCOME								
Inc Art	0	50	-50	0	50	-50	0	50
Inc Cons	12,500	10,000	2,500	0	10,000	-10,000	25,000	10,000
Inc Roy	0	0	0	0	0	0	10,000	10,000
TOTAL INCOME	12,500	10,050	2,450	0	10,050	-10,050	35,000	20,050
EXPENSES								
Del Overngt	270	200	-70	0	200	200	0	200
Dues	0	25	25	0	25	25	0	25
Equip Mnt	1,100	100	-1,000	0	100	100	0	100
Freight	0	20	20	0	20	20	0	20
Insurance	0	50	50	0	50	50	0	50
Misc	0	25	25	0	25	25	0	25
Office	0	80	80	0	80	80	0	80
Payroll:								
Comp FICA	310	310	0	310	310	0	310	310
Comp MCARE	73	73	1	73	73	1	73	73
Gross	5,000	5,000	0	5,000	5,000	0	5,000	5,000
Total Payroll	5,383	5,383	1	5,383	5,383	1	5,383	5,383
Postage	28	10	-18	0	10	10	0	10
Supp Comp	376	210	-166	0	210	210	0	210
Supplies	65	50	-15	0	50	50	0	50
Telephone	305	120	-185	0	120	120	0	120
Travel	905	300	-605	0	300	300	0	300
Utilities:								
Electric	16	30	14	14	30	16	0	30
Gas	8	30	22	9	30	21	0	30
Total Utilities	24	60	36	23	60	37	0	60
TOTAL EXPENSES	8,456	6,633	-1,823	5,406	6,633	1,227	5,383	6,633
TOTAL INCOME/EXPENSE	4,044	3,417	627	-5,406	3,417	-8,823	29,618	13,417

A Budget Report by Month for the first quarter of 1995

Figure 14-6.

Johnson & Associates - Budget by Month
1/1/95 Through 3/31/95

9/7/95 Page 2
BUSINESS-All Accounts

Category Description	3/31/95 Diff	1/1/95 Actual	- Budget	3/31/95 Diff
INCOME/EXPENSE				
INCOME				
Inc Art	-50	0	150	-150
Inc Cons	15,000	37,500	30,000	7,500
Inc Roy	0	10,000	10,000	0
TOTAL INCOME	14,950	47,500	40,150	7,350
EXPENSES				
Del Overngt	200	270	600	330
Dues	25	0	75	75
Equip Mnt	100	1,100	300	-800
Freight	20	0	60	60
Insurance	50	0	150	150
Misc	25	0	75	75
Office	80	0	240	240
Payroll:				
Comp FICA	0	930	930	0
Comp MCARE	1	218	219	2
Gross	0	15,000	15,000	0
Total Payroll	1	16,148	16,149	2
Postage	10	28	30	2
Supp Comp	210	376	630	254
Supplies	50	65	150	85
Telephone	120	305	360	55
Travel	300	905	900	-5
Utilities:				
Electric	30	30	90	60
Gas	30	17	90	73
Total Utilities	60	47	180	133
TOTAL EXPENSES	1,251	19,244	19,899	655
TOTAL INCOME/EXPENSE	16,201	28,256	20,251	8,005

A Budget Report by Month for the first quarter of 1995 (*continued*)
Figure 14-6.

you can still look at a report for a year, with budget and actual amounts shown monthly. To practice working with a larger report, follow these steps:

1. Switch to the Johnson & Associates - Budget By Month window if another window is on top.
2. Select Customize.
3. Enter **12/31/95** in the To text box.
4. Click OK.

   The budget for the entire year appears. Although there are no actual figures beyond the first few months, the instructions in the next section will show you how to look at a wide report like this on screen.

Wide-Screen Reports

You can use shortcuts to move around wide-screen reports.

The Monthly Budget report just generated is wider than the Quicken window. However, as you will see, Quicken makes it easy to move around through the report. Remember, you can use the mouse to scroll by using the scroll bars. The instructions given here are for using the keyboard, which is less intuitive than using the mouse.

Use TAB, SHIFT-TAB, PAGE UP, PAGE DOWN, HOME, and END to navigate. Pressing HOME twice returns you to the left side of the wide-screen report; pressing END twice takes you to the right side of the report. TAB moves you right one column, and SHIFT-TAB moves you left one column. PAGE UP moves you up, and PAGE DOWN down, by one screen. CTRL-HOME moves you to the first category in the same column, and CTRL-END moves you to the last category in the same column. CTRL-LEFT ARROW moves you one screen to the left and CTRL-RIGHT ARROW moves you one screen to the right.

Budget reports can be combined with Cash Flow reports to project your future cash needs.

You can use a small font to print wide reports. This significantly increases the amount of material you can print on a page. When you print wide-screen reports, Quicken numbers the pages of the report so you can more easily follow on hard copy. As a reminder, you can change the font by selecting Printer Setup from the File menu and then selecting Report/Graph Printer Setup.

Preparing a Cash Flow Report

Quicken's Cash Flow report organizes your account information by cash inflow and outflow. In this example, the results presented are the same as the amounts in the budget. Chapter 15 introduces you to depreciation expense, which is shown on the budget report but not on the Cash Flow report. This is because this expense does not require a cash outlay. Prepare a Cash Flow report for the first quarter by following these steps:

HomeBase

Reports | More Reports

1. Open the Reports menu or select the Reports icon.
2. Select Business, then Cash Flow from the menu or dialog box.
3. Select Customize.
4. Enter **1/1/95** in the From text box.
5. Enter **3/31/95** in the To text box.
6. Clear the Cents in Amounts check box.

   Notice that Cash Flow Basis is selected for the Organization drop-down list box.
7. Select the Show Rows option button.

   Exclude Internal is selected in the Transfers drop-down list box so the Cash Flow report only includes transfers to accounts outside this report. Quicken selected these options by default when you selected the Cash Flow report.
8. Select Matching.

9. Enter **B** in the Class Contains text box to restrict the report to business transactions.

   This step is essential; you need to include both ANB Personal and ANB Business in this report because business expenses were paid from both accounts. If you did not restrict the class to business, all of the personal expenses included in ANB Personal would appear on the report as well.

10. Select the Accounts option button.
11. Check that the Equipment account is unmarked and that the payroll liability accounts are marked (you have six of them). To mark or unmark an account, highlight it and press SPACEBAR, or click it. The list box looks like the one shown here:

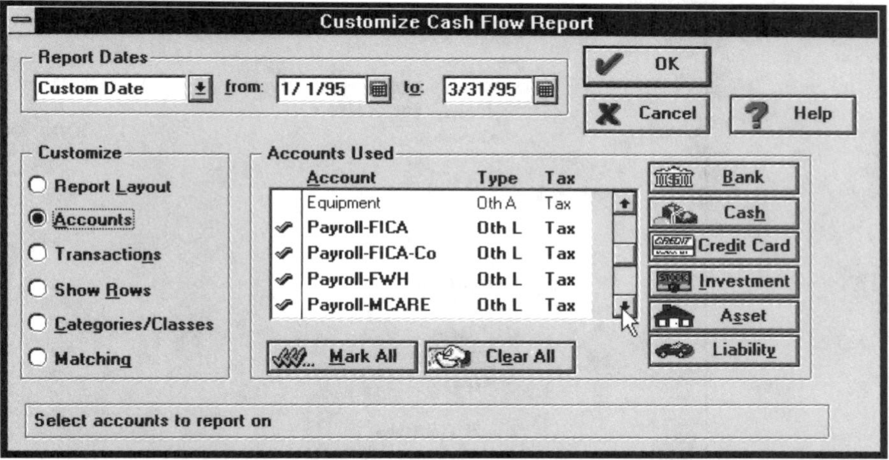

   Equipment is excluded because Quicken does not show transfers between accounts included in the Cash Flow report. However, since the purchase of equipment involved the use of cash funds, that amount should be shown as a cash outflow. Quicken will show this as an outflow to the Equipment account on this report. The payroll liability accounts are included because you want the Cash Flow report to show the total difference of the transfers to and from these liability accounts. 14

12. Select OK to create the Cash Flow report. Quicken displays the report shown in Figure 14-7.

Notice that this report shows the entire amount of gross earnings ($15,000) as a cash outflow, even though you have not paid the entire amount of federal and state withholding to the governmental agencies at the end of the period. If you want to account for these amounts from the report, you can re-create the report with only the ANB Personal and ANB Business accounts

Cash Flow Report
1/1/95 Through 3/31/95

Category Description		1/1/95- 3/31/95
INFLOWS		
Inc Cons		37,500
Inc Roy		10,000
TOTAL INFLOWS		47,500
OUTFLOWS		
Del Overngt		270
Equip Mnt		1,100
Payroll:		
Comp FICA	930	
Comp MCARE	218	
Gross	15,000	
Total Payroll		16,148
Postage		28
Supp Comp		376
Supplies		65
Telephone		305
Travel		905
Utilities:		
Electric	30	
Gas	17	
Total Utilities		47
TO Equipment		1,500
TOTAL OUTFLOWS		20,744
OVERALL TOTAL		26,756

A Cash Flow report of the first quarter of 1995

Figure 14-7.

included. However, since the liability exists for the withheld amounts, the Cash Flow report shown in Figure 14-7 is a conservative approach to presenting the cash flow. Also, the Cash Flow report matches the Actual amount in the budget report in Figure 14-4 with one exception. The cash flow includes the equipment purchase of $1,500 that is missing from the budget. Equipment didn't appear in the budget because zero was budgeted for this account. You can include this account and other accounts that have a balance even when they were not budgeted. To customize the budget report, select Show Rows in the Customize Report dialog box, select Non-Zero Actual/Budgeted from the Categories drop-down list box, and then select OK.

Creating a Budget Variance Graph

Graphs can provide a much better overview of your data than a report that displays all the numbers. Quicken provides a budget variance graph that lets you visually compare budgeted versus actual numbers in a bar graph format. You can zoom in for a closer look at any part of the graph. In the example that follows, the graph is created for a quarter. Then a bar in the graph is selected for a closer look, and a graph showing a breakdown by month is displayed with the QuickZoom feature. A bar in the QuickZoom graph is selected and the data is displayed in a report. To look at a budget variance graph for 1/95 through 3/95, follow these steps:

HomeBase

Reports | More Graphs

1. Select Graphs from the Reports menu or click the Graphs icon in the icon bar.
2. Select Budget Variance from the menu or Budget Variance Graph from the Create Graph dialog box.
3. Type **1/95** in the From text box.
4. Type **3/95** in the To text box.
5. Select Create to display the graph like the one shown in Figure 14-8.

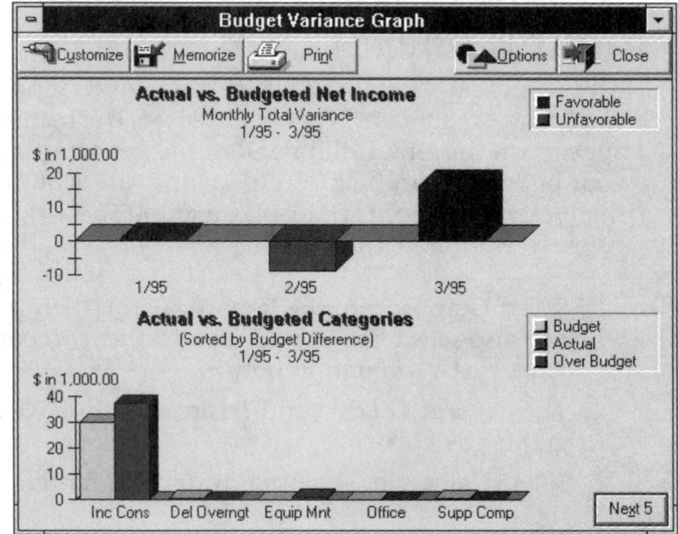

An Actual Versus Budgeted graph
Figure 14-8.

14

6. Select Next 5 three times to display additional data.
7. Select Print in the button bar to print the graph.
8. Select Next 5 until you see Inc Cons again.
9. Move the mouse to the Inc Cons bars. When you do, the mouse pointer displays as a magnifying glass with a *Z* for QuickZoom.
10. Double-click the mouse, and you will see this close-up display:

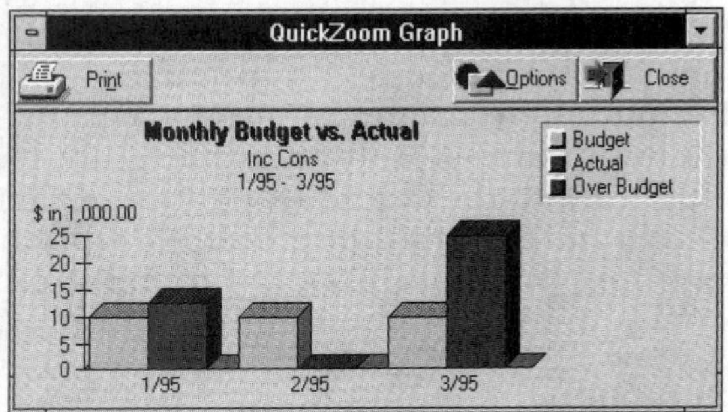

If you need to look even closer, you can double-click one of the QuickZoom graph bars and see the actual transactions in a report format.

11. Select the Close button from the QuickZoom Graph window and the Budget Variance Graph window to put these windows away.

Graphs that Show Where You Spend Your Money

One way to see where your business spends its money is to see what percentage you spend on different types of expenses. The Income and Expense graph that appears on the Graph submenu of the Reports menu is a tool for monitoring your budget. It can help you to identify areas of major costs and see if any of them can be reduced. To display a graph showing expense composition on your screen, follow these steps:

HomeBase

Reports | Income/Expense Graph

1. Select Graphs from the Reports menu, then Income and Expense. You can also select the Graphs icon in the icon bar, then the Income and Expense Graph option button.

   The dates after From and To are already 1/95 and 3/95 from the last graph you created.
2. Select Categories since you want the graph to omit all income categories.

3. Unmark all income categories in the list box, and then click OK. The income categories all have Inc in the Type column.
4. Select Classes, unmark the Not Classified class, and then click OK.
5. Select Create.

   Quicken displays the graph shown in Figure 14-9. The window actually displays two graphs. The first one, the bar graph at the top of the window, shows the income and expenses for each month. Since you excluded the income categories, the Income bars all equal zero. The pie graph at the bottom of the window displays what percentage of the total expenses that each category constituted. If you had more than ten categories of expenses, you could select Next 10 at the bottom of the window to display a pie graph of the next ten categories. Also, with more than ten categories, the categories not listed separately are combined in an "Other" category. You can see that Payroll is by far the largest expense.
6. Select the Close button in the Income And Expense Graph window to close the windows.

Note: Some buttons that display lists can display different symbols at different times. This includes the Accounts, Categories, and Classes buttons in the Create Graph dialog box. These different symbols describe whether all, some, or none of the items in the list are selected.

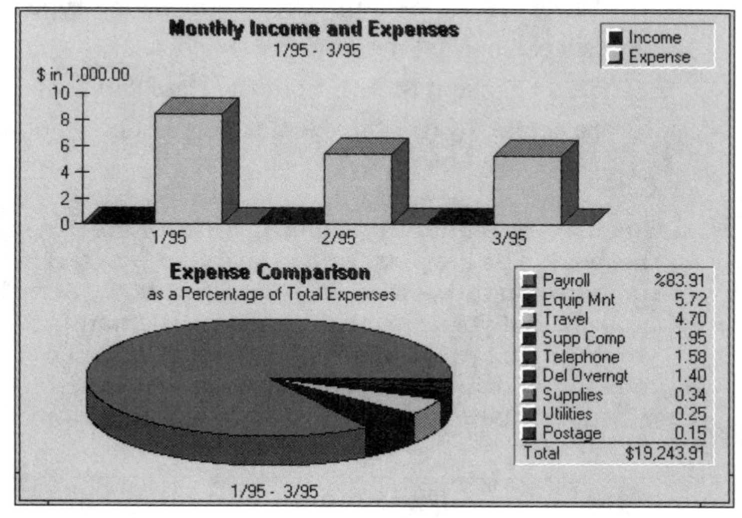

An Income and Expense graph
Figure 14-9.

14

Using the Progress Bar

Quicken 4 for Windows offers a new feature that helps you track your progress on individual budgeting goals: the Progress Bar. To set up and display the Progress Bar, follow these steps:

1. Select Progress Bar from the Plan menu. Quicken displays a blank Progress Bar at the bottom of your Quicken window.
2. Select Cust at the right end of the Progress Bar to display this dialog box:

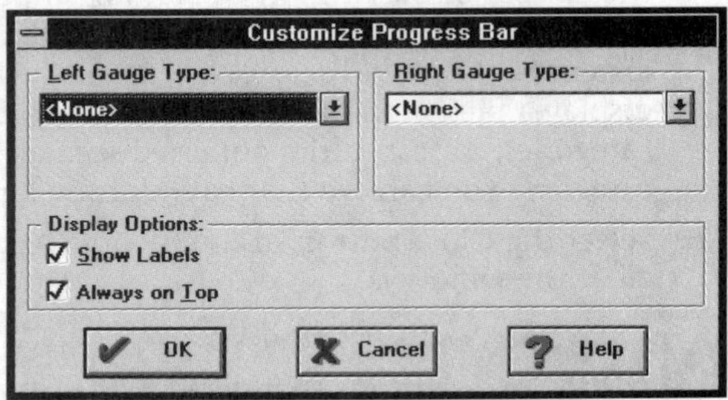

3. Select Budget Goal from the Left Gauge Type drop-down list box.
4. Select Choose Category.
5. Select Current Month from the Date Range drop-down list box.
6. Select Misc from the Category list box, and then OK to have the left half monitor actual spending versus the budget for the Miscellaneous category.
7. Select Budget Goal from the Right Gauge Type drop-down list box.
8. Select Choose Category.
9. Select Current Month from the Date Range drop-down list box.
10. Select Inc Cons from the Category list box, and then OK.
11. Select OK.

You may encounter a problem, because of the dates used for transactions in this book. The Progress Bar displays your progress in this budget category for the *current* month, based on your computer's internal clock. Since it is unlikely that you are actually entering the transactions in this book in January 1995, your Progress Bar probably shows nothing because the transaction dates won't match your system date. However, if your computer system's date were 1/20/95, your Progress Bar would look like this:

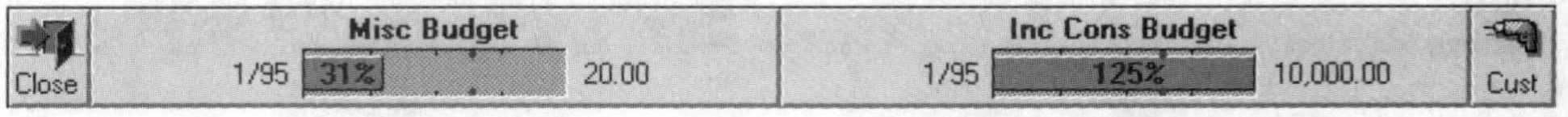

To remove the progress bar, select the Close button on the left.

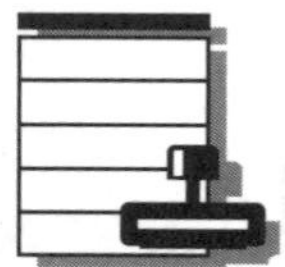

Remember: You won't have this problem of conflicting dates when you enter your own data, because you'll be entering it on a timely basis. This book has to use specific dates, however, to let you get consistent reports that you can compare against the reports shown in the book.

Creating Savings Goals

Quicken 4 for Windows includes a new budgeting tool called *savings goals*. When you transfer money between accounts in Quicken, you record an actual banking transaction. However, if you're contemplating a future purchase such as a new computer, you may not want to transfer money from your checking account to a new savings account. With savings goals, you can set aside and build funds for a future purpose, without opening a new account or transferring funds. This money remains in your original account, but it is marked as unavailable. You are essentially hiding money from yourself. You can view the progress of your earmarked savings in a separate Quicken register or with the Progress Bar.

Creating a Savings Goal

HomeBase

Planning | Savings Goals

To create a savings goal for a project, such as new furniture for redecorating your office, follow these steps:

1. Select Savings Goals from the Plan menu to open the Savings Goals window.

   Figure 14-10 shows a Savings Goals window after creating a goal and setting some money aside for this goal.
2. Select New.
3. Type **New Furniture** in the Goal Name text box.
4. Type **5000** in the Goal Amount text box.
5. Enter **10/1/95** in the Finish Date text box, and then select OK.

   Now the savings goal appears in the Savings Goals window. Also, Quicken calculated the projected amount you need to contribute each month between now and the finish date.

Transferring Money to a Savings Goal

Now that you've created the savings goal, you need to indicate the money you are setting aside. To do so:

1. Select Contribute to open this dialog box that shows the completed entries you need to make:

2. Select ANB Business in the From Account drop-down list box.
3. Enter **4/15/95** in the Date text box.
4. Type **1000** in the text box after the $, and then select OK.
5. Select the Registr button in the icon bar and the ANB Business selector button to show the ANB Business checking account.
6. Move to the last transaction, which looks like this:

4/15/95		Contribution towards goal	1,000	00				29,732	70
		[New Furniture]							

Quicken deducts the $1,000 you've contributed to the New Furniture savings goal just as if you'd written a check to a savings account at your

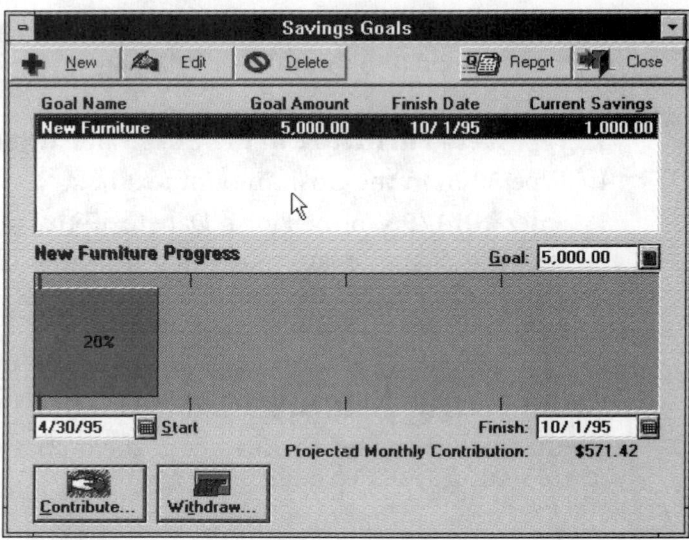

The Savings Goals window that records your savings goal
Figure 14-10.

bank. However, you haven't actually removed any money from your checking account; you've just hidden it. You'll notice the new Hide Sav. Goal. check box at the bottom of the register window.

7. Select the Hide Sav. Goal check box that now appears at the bottom of the register window.

   The transfer to the New Furniture account disappears. Your register now shows only those transactions that the bank reports on its statement.

8. Select the New Furniture account selector just beneath the transactions in your register window.

   You will need to click the right arrow at the end of the selector buttons several times since the account is at the end of the list. This account shows the $1,000 that you've set aside.

9. Select Savings Goals from the Plan menu again.

   Quicken displays a "gas-gauge" of your progress to the current date. However, this gauge, like the Progress Bar, uses the current date on your computer. Therefore, this gauge remains at 0% until your computer's date is after the date of the transactions. Figure 14-10 shows this window when the system date is 4/16/95, one day after the transaction you entered. Since you didn't plan to start saving until 4/30/95, you are ahead of the plan for reaching your savings goal.

Spending Savings Goal Money

Since your savings goal account isn't a real one, you can't spend money directly from it. After all, how would you write a check from an account the bank knew nothing about? To spend the money you have saved, you need to enter a transaction transferring the money back to the account in which it's really stored. Then you can write a check from that account and delete the savings goal account.

For example, on October 10, 1995, you receive the bill of $4,583 for the new office furniture. You can delete the savings goal account, and then write the check. To delete the savings goal:

1. Highlight the New Furniture goal in the list box, and then select Delete. Quicken displays the Delete Savings Goal dialog box.
2. Select No.

   Quicken deletes the goal, the account, and all transactions between the goal's account and the ANB Business account. It's as if the savings goal never existed. Now, you can write the check for the furniture knowing that the account has sufficient funds.

3. Select Close to remove this Savings Goals window.

Forecasting Your Budget

Quicken 4 for Windows includes two features for budget forecasting. The Financial Calendar is a simple way to see the total effects of your current and scheduled transactions. You can use this feature to get a feel for whether your current or planned rate of expenditure is feasible. Quicken 4 for Windows also offers the more sophisticated Forecasting feature. This feature predicts a future budget based on estimated incomes or expenses, scheduled transactions, and historical averages. You can add information to this forecast to create several different scenarios to judge the effect of different choices.

Forecasting with the Financial Calendar

HomeBase

Day to Day | Financial Calendar

Chapter 12 introduced the Financial Calendar for scheduling transactions. This calendar shows all your transactions. The calendar can also forecast how well you comply with your budget and how your financial planning is progressing. Follow these steps to view a Financial Calendar graph that can help with your financial planning:

1. Select the Calendar icon from the icon bar, or select Financial Calendar from the Activities menu to open the Financial Calendar window.
2. Select View from the Calendar's button bar.
3. Select Show Memorized Txns.
4. Select View, and then Show Account Graph.

   The calendar raises from the bottom of the window to make room for the graph that shows account balances.
5. Click Next or Prev in the button bar until the calendar displays January 1995. The bottom of the Financial Calendar now shows a graph like this:

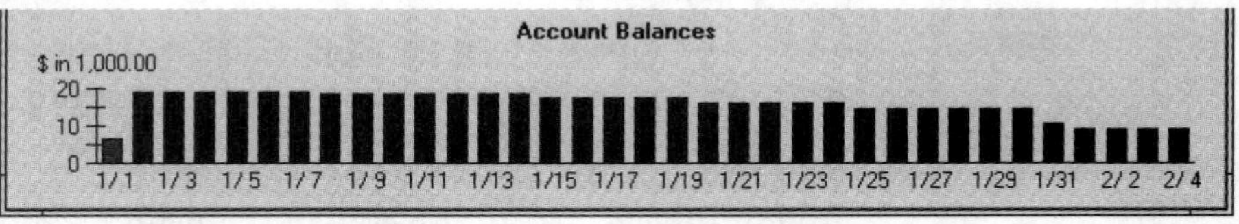

This graph shows the total account balances for all your accounts on each day of the month. The graph uses your actual transactions, scheduled transactions, and transaction groups to calculate these balances.

Note: You can click a bar in the graph to select the bar. Hold down the mouse on this bar and Quicken displays the amount of the account balances. The account balances included in the total are the ones selected when you choose the Options button in the button bar and select the Accounts tab.

Predicting Your Financial Future

Quicken 4 for Windows has a new Forecasting feature. The Forecasting feature graphs a projection of your finances based on your actual and budgeted data. This graph can help you do "what-if" planning for your budget. In this graph, you can add or remove income or expenses to find out what would happen to your financial picture if a specific element changed. For example, the Forecasting feature can calculate the affect of moving to a more or less expensive apartment.

The Forecasting feature uses three sources of information to predict your financial picture into the future:

- Your income and expenses to date, taken from your registers or budget
- Scheduled transactions that you can see in your Financial Calendar
- Amounts you enter to affect the forecast

Creating a Forecasting Scenario

You'll want to create your forecasting graph to see how current expenditures will affect your future financial picture. At this point, however, because of the way that the Forecasting feature works, you are going to need to change the system date on your computer. This is not something you normally do when creating forecasting graphs with your own data. However, if you want the forecasting graph you create for this example to match the ones shown here, you need to change the date to match the example. To change your system date:

1. Open the Windows Control Panel by double-clicking its program icon in the Program Manager. This program icon is normally found in the Main program group window.
2. Double-click the Date/Time icon in the Control Panel.
3. Change the Date to 4/1/95.
4. Click OK and switch back to Quicken.

Caution: As soon as you finish with this exercise, change the date on your computer system back to the current date.

To create a forecasting scenario, follow these steps:

HomeBase

Planning | Forecasting

1. Select Forecasting from the Plan menu. Quicken opens the Forecasting window and opens the Automatically Create Forecast dialog box, shown here:

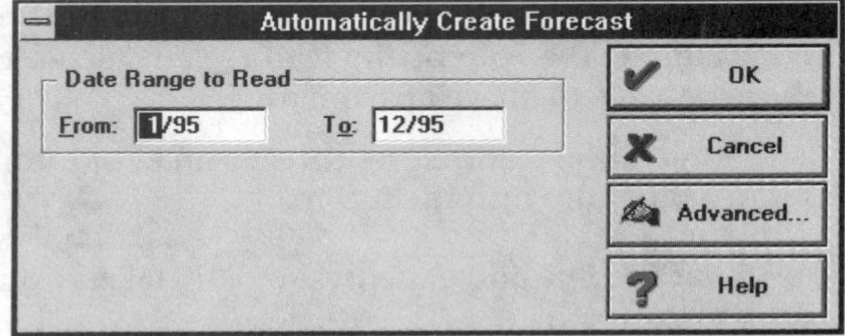

2. Type **1/95** in the From text box.
3. Type **3/95** in the To text box, and then click OK.

   The Forecast window opens looking like Figure 14-11.

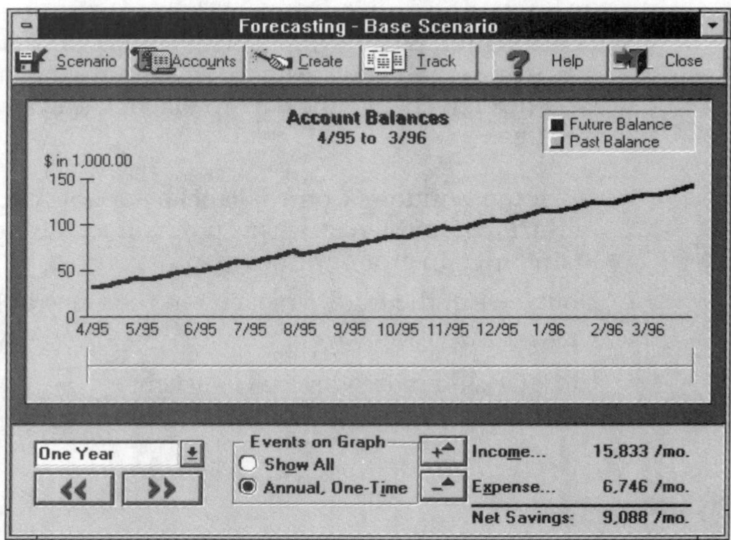

The default Forecast graph
Figure 14-11.

4. Select the Expense button in the lower-right corner of the window, opening the Forecast Expense Items dialog box shown in Figure 14-12. The known items are your scheduled transactions such as payroll. You also have estimated items that are based on your past transactions. You can also add items.
5. Select New.
6. Type **Unemployment Taxes** in the Description text box.
7. Type **640** in the Amount text box.
8. Select Quarterly in the Frequency drop-down list box.
9. Enter **12/31/95** in the Next Scheduled Date text box, and then select OK.
10. Select the Income Items option button at the top of the dialog box. Now the list box displays your known and estimated income.
11. Now that you've added the items that you want to include in the forecast, select Done.
12. Click the >> button in the lower-left corner of the Forecasting window to see how these new expenses will change your budget for the next year.

You have now created a new planning scenario. You can save this specific scenario for future reference or to compare to other scenarios. Then you can make changes to the forecasted income and expenses knowing that you can return to the saved one. To save the scenario, follow these steps:

1. Select Scenario from the window's button bar.

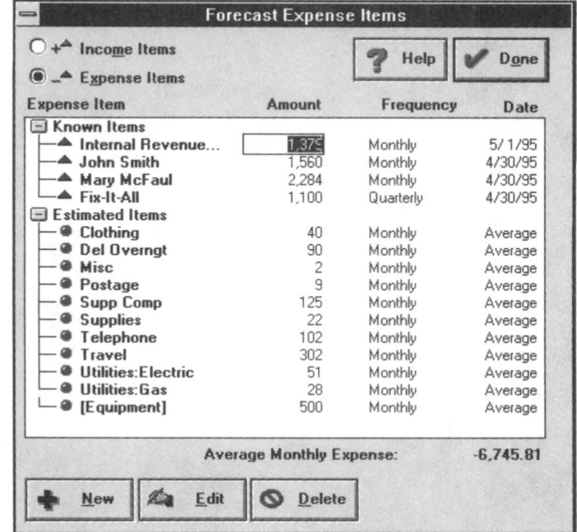

The Forecast Income/Expense Items dialog box
Figure 14-12.

2. Select New under the Scenario Data drop-down list box.
3. Type **Basic Scenario** in the Scenario Name text box, and then click OK.
4. Select Done. You've now saved the scenario.

In the future, you can recall this scenario to look at your forecast. To compare two scenarios, save one scenario. Then open the Manage Forecast Scenarios dialog box by choosing Scenario from the button bar. Choose a scenario from the Compare Current Scenario With drop-down list box. Quicken displays the line of the chosen scenario along with the current scenario. This lets you compare the effects of two different situations.

Caution: You must now reset your computer's date to the current date. If you don't, you will encounter problems with some programs and in correctly identifying your files or working with your own Quicken files.

Take some time to experiment with the Forecasting feature. Nothing you enter in the forecasting feature will affect your scheduled transactions, budget, or register entries. By developing many alternative forecasts, you can take a variety of situations into account. For example, you can use this feature to determine how changing your mix of business income affects your bottom line or how your company is affected if you add or lose employees.

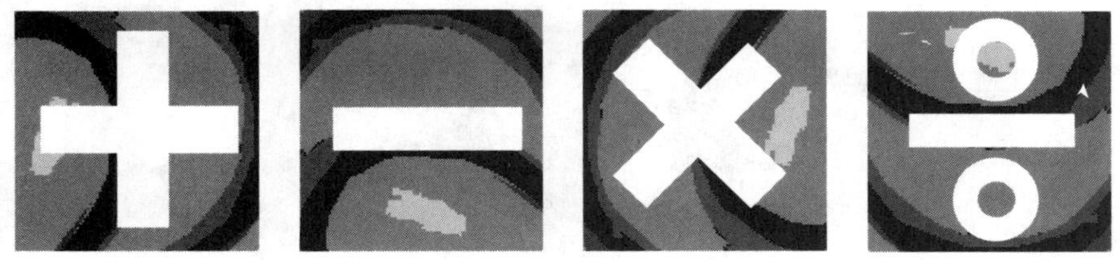

CHAPTER

15

ORGANIZING TAX INFORMATION and OTHER YEAR-END TASKS

For the small-business owner, tax time may seem like an endless round of activity. If it's not time to file a payroll tax form, it's practically time to file quarterly tax estimates or year-end tax returns. You saw in Chapter 13 how Quicken can help you prepare payroll tax forms. As you will learn in this chapter, it can also save you significant time and effort as you prepare income tax returns.

Although Quicken can provide all the information you need to complete your tax returns, you may want to spend a little time studying tax requirements, unless you have a CPA do everything for you. The "Free Tax Information" box lists just some of the free forms that you can get from the U.S. government.

Free Tax Information

Tax regulations can be complex. To help you determine filing options, due dates, payment methods, and estimated tax, the Department of the Treasury provides several free tax publications, listed in Table 15-1, that describe how to fill out the necessary returns. You can order these publications by calling the IRS toll-free number, (800) 829-3676.

Publication Number	Publication Name
334	*Tax Guide for Small Business*
463	*Travel, Entertainment, and Gift Expenses*
510	*Excise Taxes*
515	*Withholding of Tax on Non-Resident Aliens*
533	*Self-Employment Tax*
534	*Depreciation*
535	*Business Expenses*
538	*Accounting Periods and Methods*
541	*Tax Information on Partnerships*
542	*Tax Information on Corporations*
544	*Sales and Other Dispositions of Assets*
551	*Basis of Assets*
560	*Retirement Plans for the Self-Employed*
587	*Business Use of Your Home*
589	*Tax Information for S Corporations*
686	*Certification for Reduced Tax Rates in Tax Treaty Countries*
911	*Tax Information for Direct Sellers*
917	*Business Use of a Car*
937	*Business Reporting*
946	*How to Begin Depreciating Your Property*

Free Tax Publications Available to the Public
Table 15-1.

In this chapter, you see how Quicken can gather information to complete the tax forms for your business-related activities. You are introduced to the concept of depreciation and how it affects business profits. You learn how to use Quicken to prepare your Schedule C, Profit or Loss from Business statements, shown in Figure 15-1. You can also use Quicken features to help you prepare for recording the following year's transactions. Quicken can help you complete your tax forms through the Tax Planner. The Tax Planner consolidates the numbers that you use to complete your forms, breaking them down by line number. The Tax Planner is designed for individual tax returns, not corporate returns. The Tax Planner features described later in the chapter are of special interest for business owners filing 1040s.

Depreciation

Depreciation expense is not a cash expenditure in the current year.

Depreciation is an expense recorded at the end of the tax year (or any accounting period). The concept of depreciation can be confusing, since it does not follow the same rules as other expenses. Depreciation does not require a cash expenditure in the current year; you are recognizing a part of a cash outflow that occurred in a prior year when you record depreciation expense. Tax rules do not allow you to recognize the full cost of some purchases as expenses in the earlier tax year because the resource is used in business for many tax years. For example, resources such as a truck or piece of machinery are not expensed in the year purchased since they benefit the business over a number of years. Purchases such as paper, on the other hand, are consumed in the year purchased, and their entire cost is recognized in that tax year.

In simple terms, depreciation is a portion of an asset's original cost, charged as an expense to a tax period. For the example developed in this section, suppose you purchase computer hardware for your business. You may think its cost should apply to your business in the year you paid for it, just as other cash expenses would apply to the year paid. This seems fair, since the purchase involved a significant cash outflow for the year. However, from an accounting or tax perspective, your acquisition will affect your business operations over a number of years. For this reason, accountants and the Internal Revenue Service require you to apply the concept of depreciation when you prepare your Schedule C, Profit or Loss from Business statements. Often, the cost of the asset must be expensed over the years that it is expected to generate business revenues. The "Section 179 Property" section later in this chapter tells you about one important exception to the requirement that you depreciate your long-lived assets.

You can depreciate only assets that lose their productivity as you use them in your business activity. For example, you cannot record depreciation on the land where your building stands. Even though you may feel your land

SCHEDULE C (Form 1040)

Department of the Treasury Internal Revenue Service (O)

Profit or Loss From Business

(Sole Proprietorship)

▶ Partnerships, joint ventures, etc., must file Form 1065.

▶ Attach to Form 1040 or Form 1041. ▶ See Instructions for Schedule C (Form 1040).

OMB No. 1545-0074

1993

Attachment Sequence No. **09**

Name of proprietor | **Social security number (SSN)**

A Principal business or profession, including product or service (see page C-1) | **B Enter principal business code** (see page C-6) ▶

C Business name. If no separate business name, leave blank. | **D Employer ID number (EIN), if any**

E Business address (including suite or room no.) ▶

City, town or post office, state, and ZIP code

F Accounting method: (1) ☐ Cash (2) ☐ Accrual (3) ☐ Other (specify) ▶

G Method(s) used to value closing inventory: (1) ☐ Cost (2) ☐ Lower of cost or market (3) ☐ Other (attach explanation) (4) ☐ Does not apply (if checked, skip line H) | **Yes** | **No**

H Was there any change in determining quantities, costs, or valuations between opening and closing inventory? If "Yes," attach explanation

I Did you "materially participate" in the operation of this business during 1993? If "No," see page C-2 for limit on losses.

J If you started or acquired this business during 1993, check here ▶ ☐

Part I Income

1	Gross receipts or sales. **Caution:** *If this income was reported to you on Form W-2 and the "Statutory employee" box on that form was checked, see page C-2 and check here* ▶ ☐	1	47500
2	Returns and allowances	2	
3	Subtract line 2 from line 1	3	
4	Cost of goods sold (from line 40 on page 2)	4	
5	**Gross profit.** Subtract line 4 from line 3	5	
6	Other income, including Federal and state gasoline or fuel tax credit or refund (see page C-2)	6	
7	**Gross income.** Add lines 5 and 6 ▶	7	47500

Part II Expenses. Caution: *Do not enter expenses for business use of your home on lines 8–27. Instead, see line 30.*

Line	Description	Amount	Line	Description	Amount
8	Advertising		19	Pension and profit-sharing plans	
9	Bad debts from sales or services (see page C-3)		20	Rent or lease (see page C-4):	
			a	Vehicles, machinery, and equipment	
10	Car and truck expenses (see page C-3)		b	Other business property	
			21	Repairs and maintenance	1100 00
11	Commissions and fees		22	Supplies (not included in Part III)	440 76
12	Depletion		23	Taxes and licenses	1771 50
13	Depreciation and section 179 expense deduction (not included in Part III) (see page C-3)	275 00	24	Travel, meals, and entertainment:	
			a	Travel	905
14	Employee benefit programs (other than on line 19)		b	Meals and entertainment	
15	Insurance (other than health)		c	Enter 20% of line 24b subject to limitations (see page C-4)	
16	Interest:				
a	Mortgage (paid to banks, etc.)		d	Subtract line 24c from line 24b	
b	Other		25	Utilities	352 40
17	Legal and professional services		26	Wages (less jobs credit)	15000 00
18	Office expense		27	Other expenses (from line 46 on page 2)	298 25

28	**Total expenses** before expenses for business use of home. Add lines 8 through 27 in columns ▶	28	20142 91
29	Tentative profit (loss). Subtract line 28 from line 7	29	27357 09
30	Expenses for business use of your home. Attach **Form 8829**	30	
31	**Net profit or (loss).** Subtract line 30 from line 29. • If a profit, enter on **Form 1040, line 12,** and ALSO on **Schedule SE, line 2** (statutory employees, see page C-5). Fiduciaries, enter on Form 1041, line 3. • If a loss, you MUST go on to line 32.	31	27357 09

32 If you have a loss, check the box that describes your investment in this activity (see page C-5).

- If you checked 32a, enter the loss on **Form 1040, line 12,** and ALSO on **Schedule SE, line 2** (statutory employees, see page C-5). Fiduciaries, enter on Form 1041, line 3.
- If you checked 32b, you MUST attach **Form 6198.**

32a ☐ All investment is at risk.

32b ☐ Some investment is not at risk.

For Paperwork Reduction Act Notice, see Form 1040 instructions. Cat. No. 11334P **Schedule C (Form 1040) 1993**

Schedule C

Figure 15-1.

has lost value in recent years, you cannot recognize this decline until you sell the land. On the other hand, a *depreciable asset* is an asset that has a life longer than one year and benefits business operations in several accounting periods. Equipment is a depreciable asset; land is not.

Depreciation Terminology

Let's review several terms pertaining to depreciation in more depth. First, you must always depreciate the original cost of an asset. *Original cost* is the total cost of the asset. For example, if you purchased a piece of machinery and paid shipping charges and sales tax, these additional costs are considered to be associated with getting the asset into an income-producing condition. Therefore they are part of the original cost. Figure 15-2 shows the Equipment account register after recording the transactions in Chapter 12. The first transaction recorded in the register shows $3,000.00, the original cost of the High Tech Computer. The printer purchase on 1/25/95 is recorded at its original cost of $1,500.00.

In Chapter 10, you learned to revalue personal assets to market value. You cannot do this with business assets. If your asset increases in value, you

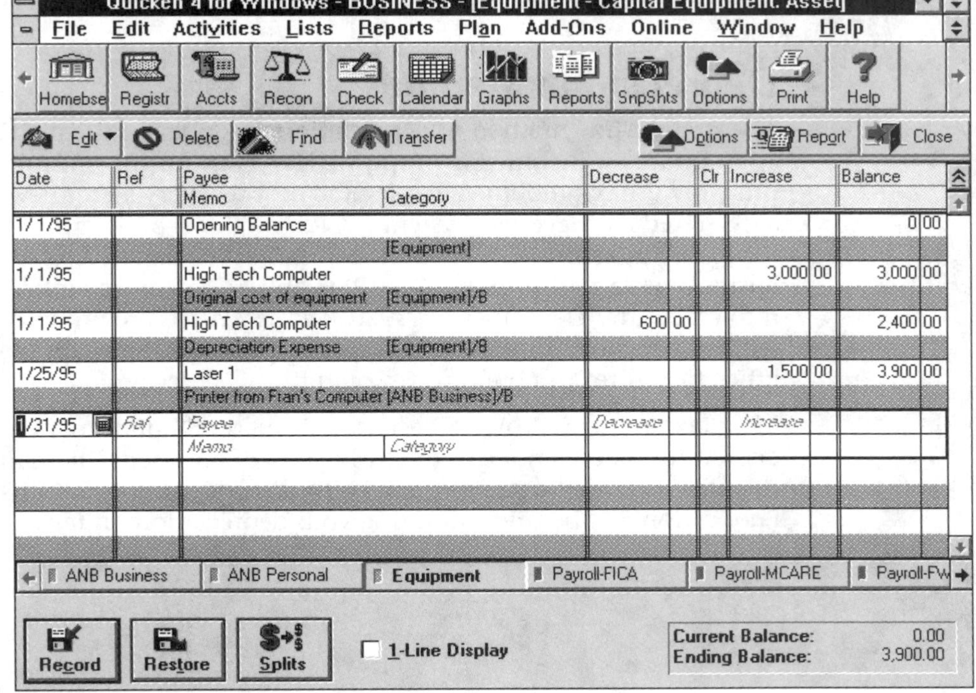

The Equipment account register window
Figure 15-2.

cannot recognize this increase in your Quicken system. You must always carry (show on your business accounting records) your business assets at their original cost.

Another important term is *accumulated depreciation*. This is the amount of depreciation you have recorded for an asset in all previous years. Your assets will always appear on the balance sheet at its original cost minus accumulated depreciation. For example, for the $3,000.00 High Tech Computer asset, you recorded depreciation expense of $600.00 in the previous year. Because you have an accumulated depreciation of $600.00 from the previous year, your asset carrying value is $2,400.00 before recording this year's depreciation.

Establishing Accounts for Assets

You probably will establish another asset account for each major type of depreciable asset your business uses. You follow the same procedures used in Chapter 12 to set up the Equipment account. If you have equipment, office furniture, and buildings that you use in your business, including the portion of your home used exclusively for business purposes, you will depreciate the original cost of each of these assets. If you have few depreciable assets, you may decide to establish a separate account for each asset. You can only create 64 accounts in your Quicken file. Later in this chapter you will learn how to depreciate more than one asset in an account.

Depreciation Methods

The straight-line method of depreciation described in the next section is appropriate for income tax purposes. However, for the most part, you will probably use the modified accelerated cost recovery system (MACRS) and the accelerated cost recovery system (ACRS) methods of determining your depreciation amounts. Generally, MACRS covers tangible assets put into business use after December 31, 1986, and ACRS covers tangible assets put into place after December 31, 1980. *Tangible assets* are property that can be felt and touched. All the assets mentioned in our discussion (equipment, office furniture, and buildings) would fit this description.

Most taxpayers use MACRS because this method builds in a higher level of depreciation deductions in the early years of an asset's life than would be calculated using the straight-line method of depreciation. Consult IRS Publication 534 before computing your depreciation on tangible assets.

Straight-Line Depreciation Method

The Internal Revenue Service has established guidelines for depreciation assets. Consult IRS publication 534 for details.

In this example, you use the straight-line method to record depreciation on an asset. *Straight-line depreciation* expenses the cost of the asset evenly over the life of the asset. For example, the High Tech Computer has a useful life of five years, and you recorded depreciation expense at $600.00 in 1994. Since this method does not attempt to recognize more depreciation in the early years of an asset's life, it is always acceptable to the IRS. Many other depreciation methods can be used and may be more favorable since they recognize greater depreciation in the early years of the asset's life. IRS Publication 534 lists the many rules that apply to the selection of a depreciation method. One of the considerations that determine the depreciation method chosen is the year in which you placed the asset in service. Once you select a method of depreciation for an asset, you cannot change to another depreciation method. Table 15-2 lists some of the other depreciation methods. You will need to check with your accountant or check IRS Publication 534 for specific rules on which methods you can use.

Method	Description
ACRS	The Accelerated Cost Recovery System is an accelerated depreciation method that can be used for assets placed in service after December 31, 1980, and before December 31, 1986.
Declining-balance	This method allows the deduction of depreciation expense at a faster rate than the straight-line method. There are several different percentages used in computing this type of depreciation. One acceptable option is 140 percent of straight-line depreciation.
MACRS	The Modified Accelerated Cost Recovery System is an accelerated depreciation method used for assets placed in service after December 31, 1986.
Straight-line	This method is the easiest to compute since the cost of the asset is depreciated evenly over the life of the asset. It is also the least advantageous to the business owner since it does not accelerate depreciation expense in the early years of the asset's life.

Depreciation Methods
Table 15-2.

When using the straight-line method of depreciating an asset, use the following formula:

$$\frac{\text{original cost-salvage value}}{\text{useful life of asset}}$$

The original cost of depreciable assets has already been discussed; however, "salvage value" is a new term. *Salvage value* is the amount of cash you expect to recover when you dispose of your depreciable asset. This is, obviously, always an estimate and in the case of a computer not easily estimated due to rapid changes in the computer field. For this reason, many accountants assign a salvage value of zero to this type of asset, stating in effect that it will have no value at the end of its estimated life. This is also the assumption made in the entries recorded here. When you record salvage values for your assets, you can use the history of similar assets to estimate salvage values. If equipment that is five years old typically sells for 20 percent of its original cost, that would be a good estimate for the salvage value of equipment bought today with an estimated five-year life.

Depreciation Calculation

The amounts used in the depreciation entries in this chapter are determined by the calculations shown here:

High Tech Computer:

$$\frac{\$3000.00 \text{ (original cost)} - 0 \text{ (salvage value)}}{5 \text{ years (useful life)}} = \$600.00 \text{ depreciation per year}$$

Laser Printer:

$$\frac{\$1500.00 \text{ (original cost)} - 0 \text{ (salvage value)}}{3 \text{ years (useful life)}} = \$500.00 \text{ depreciation per year}$$

Depreciation is generally recorded only once, at the end of the year, unless you need financial statements prepared for a bank or other third party during the year. The amounts calculated in this example are the annual depreciation expenses for the computer and printer—the amounts you would use to record depreciation for the year ending 12/31/95. (Note that even though the printer was acquired at the end of January, it is acceptable to record a full year's depreciation on the asset. This is because the difference between 11 and 12 months' worth of depreciation is so small that it would not be considered to have a material effect.)

In the examples developed in Chapters 12 and 14, the account register transactions have been limited to the first quarter of the year. (Recall that in Chapter 13, you completed several April 1995 entries in order to see the complete process of payroll accounting.) Since there is not a full year of expense entries, you can compute the depreciation on the computer and printer for just the first quarter of 1995. This is accomplished by dividing both annual amounts of depreciation by four. Thus, here are the first quarter's depreciation charges that you will record:

High Tech Computer:

$$\frac{\$600.00 \text{ (annual depreciation)}}{4 \text{ (quarters)}} = \$150.00 \text{ depreciation for first quarter, 1995}$$

Laser Printer:

$$\frac{\$500.00 \text{ (annual depreciation)}}{4 \text{ (quarters)}} = \$125.00 \text{ depreciation for first quarter, 1995}$$

Now you are familiar with the method used to record depreciation in the example and how the amounts you will record were determined. It's time to record the depreciation entry in your account register.

Establishing Depreciation Categories

Before recording the depreciation entries in this chapter, you establish a Depreciation expense category with Computer and Printer subcategories in your category list. Select the Equipment account in the BUSINESS file, open the account register, and follow these steps:

HomeBase

Setup | Category List

1. Select Category & Transfer from the Lists menu to open the Category & Transfer List window.
2. Select New to open the Set Up Category dialog box.
3. Type **Depreciation** in the Name text box.
4. Type **Depreciation Expense** in the Description text box.
5. Select the Expense option button.
6. Select the Tax-related check box.

   Remember that before you can assign categories to tax schedules, you need to set your options. If you do not have a Form drop-down list box, select Cancel, then select Options from the Edit menu, then General, and check the Use Tax Schedules With Categories box. Select OK, and then Close to leave those dialog boxes and perform the first six steps again.
7. Select Schedule C:Other business expense.

8. Select OK.
9. Select New.
10. Type **Computer** in the Name text box.
11. Type **Depreciation-Computer** in the Description text box.
12. Select the Subcategory of option button.
13. Select Depreciation from the drop-down list box.
14. Select the Tax-related check box.
15. Select Schedule C:Other business expense.
16. Select OK.
17. Select New.
18. Type **Printer** in the Name text box.
19. Type **Depreciation-Printer** in the Description text box.
20. Select the Subcategory of option button.
21. Select Depreciation from the drop-down list box.
22. Select the Tax-Related check box.
23. Select Schedule C:Other business expense.
24. Select OK.
25. Press ESC to close the Category & Transfer List window.

You can now begin recording your depreciation expense transactions.

Depreciation Expense Transactions

Let's record the depreciation on the assets in your Quicken account. Starting in the BUSINESS file:

1. Choose Use Register from the Activities menu, or click the Registr icon on the icon bar, to switch to the register window if this window is not on top.
2. Click the Equipment account selector button below the transaction entries if the register window shows a different account, so you can see transactions like the ones in Figure 15-2.
3. Enter **3/31/95** in the Date field of the next empty transaction.
   Notice that no check numbers are recorded in this register since all checks are written against the business checking account.
4. Type **High Tech Computer** in the Payee field.
5. Type **150** in the Decrease field.

6. Type **Depreciation-1995** in the Memo field.
7. Type **Depreciation:Computer/B** in the Category field and select Record.

   You have just recorded the depreciation expense on the computer for the months January through March of 1995. The remaining steps record depreciation on the laser printer you acquired in January.
8. Enter **3/31/95** in the Date field.
9. Type **Laser 1** in the Payee field.
10. Type **125** in the Decrease field.
11. Type **Depreciation-1995** in the Memo field.
12. Type **Depreciation:Printer/B** in the Category field and select Record.

These register entries show how your depreciation transactions will appear after you record both of them:

3/31/95		High Tech Computer		150 00				3,750 00
		Depreciation-1995	Depreciation:Computer/B					
3/31/95		Laser 1		125 00				3,625 00
		Depreciation-1995	Depreciation:Printer/B					

This completes the depreciation transaction entry for the first quarter of 1995. Remember, depreciation is normally recorded only at the year's end. However, for purposes of this example, we have prepared the entries at the end of the first quarter.

Customized Equipment Report

After recording the depreciation transactions in the Equipment account, you will want to look at a customized Equipment report. This report, which you will prepare shortly, summarizes all the activity in the account. Figure 15-3 shows the Equipment report for your business since 1/1/95. Notice that the report shows the depreciation expense taken during the first quarter for both the computer and the printer, as well as the total for the category. You can also see that there was a $1,500.00 transfer from business checking for the purchase of the printer in January.

Finally, you can see that the balance forward amount of $2,400.00 is the $3,000.00 original cost of the asset minus the $600.00 accumulated depreciation taken in the prior year. Thus, when you prepare a balance sheet in Chapter 16, the equipment asset will total $3,625.00.

To produce the Equipment report, follow these steps, starting from the Equipment account register:

1. Select Other from the Reports menu.
2. Select Summary, and the Create Report window appears.
3. Select Customize, and the Customize Summary Report window appears.
4. Enter **1/1/95** in the From field.
5. Enter **3/31/95** in the To field.
6. Type **Equipment Report** in the Title text box, and then select OK.
7. Select Print, and the Print Report dialog box appears.
8. Select Print to create the report in Figure 15-3.
9. Select Close to put this report window away.

Equipment Report
1/1/95 Through 3/31/95

Category Description		1/1/95- 3/31/95
INCOME/EXPENSE		
EXPENSES		
Depreciation:		
Computer	150.00	
Printer	125.00	
Total Depreciation		275.00
TOTAL EXPENSES		275.00
TOTAL INCOME/EXPENSE		-275.00
TRANSFERS		
FROM ANB Business		1,500.00
TOTAL TRANSFERS		1,500.00
Balance Forward		
Equipment		2,400.00
Total Balance Forward		2,400.00
OVERALL TOTAL		3,625.00

The Equipment report
Figure 15-3.

Depreciation and the IRS

The transactions in this chapter record depreciation using the straight-line method to determine the amounts for the entries. This method was demonstrated to cover the recording process without going into too much detail about IRS rules for determining depreciation expense for tax purposes. When you enter your own depreciation expense, you will need to review IRS publications that include tables of percentages for the amount you depreciate each year. However, we need to briefly discuss one additional aspect of deducting the cost of long-lived assets for IRS purposes: section 179 property. Be sure to obtain IRS Publication 534 (free upon request) before making decisions concerning the amount of depreciation you will charge against income on your tax return.

Section 179 Property

Section 179 property eases keeping track of depreciable property by letting you expense some of it in one year.

Many small businesses will be interested in the type of property called *section 179 property*. Here, certain capital expenditures are treated as deductions in the current year rather than depreciating the cost of the asset over its life. Buildings, air conditioning units, and structural components of a building do not qualify as section 179 property, though a computer or office furniture would. For a complete list of qualified property and the specific rules that apply, consult IRS Publication 534.

Under section 179 of the Internal Revenue Service code, you can deduct up to $17,500 of the cost of property in the current tax year at the time of this writing. For this sample business, you can deduct the entire cost of the laser printer this year against your business income and not depreciate the asset in future years.

Schedule C, Profit or Loss from Business

Schedule C is the tax form sole proprietorships use when reporting business income and expenses during the year. Quicken can provide the information you need to complete your form. If you examine Schedule C (Figure 15-1), you see that it is a business profit and loss statement. This statement can be prepared from the Quicken Reports menu. Quicken can also prepare a tax report of your business transactions just like the ones you create when you use Quicken for personal transactions. Not only that, Quicken's Tax Planner can consolidate the numbers for you.

Creating a Profit and Loss Statement

Quicken's Profit and Loss statement summarizes the expenses and revenue for your business. Starting from the ANB Business account register in the BUSINESS account group, complete the following steps:

HomeBase

Reports | More Reports

1. Select Business from the Reports menu or click the Reports button on the icon bar and select the Business option button.
2. Select P&L Statement.
3. Select Customize so the Customize Profit & Loss Statement dialog box appears.
4. Enter **1/1/95** in the From field.
5. Enter **4/15/95** in the To field.
6. Select Matching.
7. Select B in the Class Contains drop-down list box.
8. Click OK, and the Profit and Loss Statement window appears. This report even includes the first quarter's payroll taxes, paid on April 15th.
9. Select Print and the Print Report dialog box appears.
10. Select Print to print the Profit and Loss statement shown in Figure 15-4.
11. Select Close to leave the Report window.

Using the Tax Planner to Generate Tax Numbers

Before the Tax Planner can generate the numbers for your tax forms, you need to make sure that the tax-related categories are marked as such. The categories also need the correct tax form assignments, for accurate reporting. To check the tax form lines that your categories use:

1. Select Category & Transfer from the Lists menu to see the list of available categories.
2. Move to the Inc Art category.
3. Select Edit.
4. Check that the Tax-related check box is selected and that Schedule C:Gross receipts is in the Form drop-down list box.

Profit & Loss Statement
1/1/95 Through 4/15/95

Category Description		1/1/95- 4/15/95
INCOME/EXPENSE		
INCOME		
Inc Cons		37,500.00
Inc Roy		10,000.00
TOTAL INCOME		47,500.00
EXPENSES		
Del Overngt		270.00
Depreciation:		
Computer	150.00	
Printer	125.00	
Total Depreciation		275.00
Equip Mnt		1,100.00
Payroll:		
Comp FICA	930.00	
Comp FUTA	104.00	
Comp MCARE	217.50	
Comp SUI	520.00	
Gross	15,000.00	
Total Payroll		16,771.50
Postage		28.25
Supp Comp		375.76
Supplies		65.00
Telephone		305.00
Travel		905.00
Utilities:		
Electric	30.40	
Gas	17.00	
Total Utilities		47.40
TOTAL EXPENSES		20,142.91
TOTAL INCOME/EXPENSE		27,357.09

A Profit and Loss statement
Figure 15-4.

15

5. Click OK.
6. Repeat steps 3 through 5 for each of the categories listed in Table 15-3, replacing Schedule C:Gross receipts in step 4 with the form entry in the second column of this table.
7. Click Close in the button bar to put this window away.

Category	Form
Inc Cons	Schedule C:Gross receipts
Inc Roy	Schedule C:Gross receipts
Del Overngt	Schedule C:Other business expense
Equip Mnt	Schedule C:Repairs and maintenance
Payroll	Schedule C:Wages
Payroll:Comp FICA	Schedule C:Taxes and licenses
Payroll:Comp FUTA	Schedule C:Taxes and licenses
Payroll:Comp MCARE	Schedule C:Taxes and licenses
Payroll:Comp SUI	Schedule C:Taxes and licenses
Payroll:Gross	Schedule C:Wages
Postage	Schedule C:Other business expense
Supp Comp	Schedule C:Supplies
Supplies	Schedule C:Supplies
Telephone	Schedule C:Utilities
Travel	Schedule C:Travel
Utilities:Electric	Schedule C:Utilities
Utilities:Gas	Schedule C:Utilities

Categories for Schedule C and the Form Drop-Down List Box Setting
Table 15-3.

Now that Quicken knows the form entries for your business expenses and income, you can see how easily the Tax Planner can generate the numbers for Schedule C. To have Quicken show numbers for Schedule C, follow these steps:

1. Select Tax Planner from the Plan menu.
2. Select 1995 in the Year drop-down list box.
3. Choose Quicken Data from the button bar to take the data from your Quicken transactions.

   Quicken breaks down the transactions according to the lines in tax forms, as shown in Figure 15-5. The Quicken Amount column shows total transactions from 1/1/95 to 3/31/95. The Amount column shows what the totals would be if the amounts remain the same for the remaining nine months.

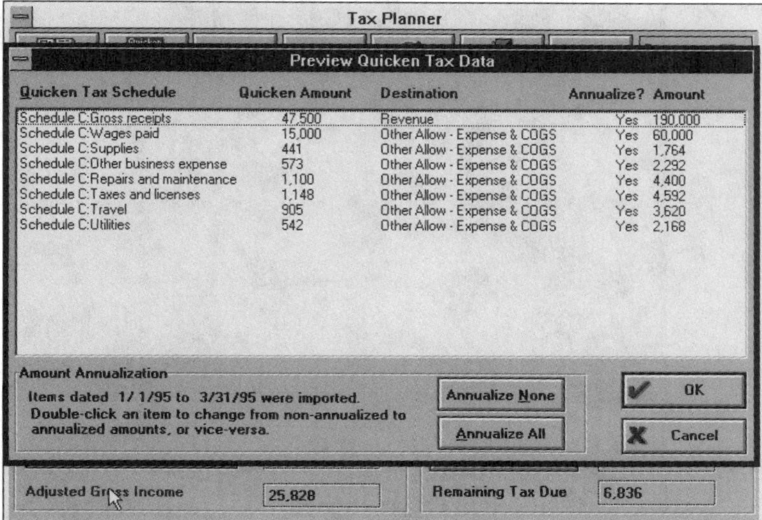

The Tax Planner totaling amounts for tax schedules
Figure 15-5.

This breakdown of expenses for Schedule C has a $190 discrepancy between the Tax Planner and the Profit and Loss statement. $68 of this amount is for gas and $122 is for electric, representing the home use of these utilities. If you plan to use the Tax Planner more extensively, you will want to create separate categories to hold your business and home portions of expenses that now share the same category. Remember, you've been separating the business part of these expenses using the B class since Chapter 12.

4. Click Annualize None if Yes appears anywhere in the Annualize column so the Amount column contains the same number in the Quicken Amount column.
5. Select OK to return to the Tax Planner dialog box, and then select Business Income.

   Quicken has summarized the Schedule C information and entered it into this dialog box. However, you know that the Other Allowable Expenses number is too high, so you can change this to adjust the final Schedule C information that you include in your tax plan.
6. Type **19519** in the Other Allowable Expenses text box and press TAB so your summarized Schedule C income looks like that shown in Figure 15-6.
7. Click OK, and then select Close to close the Tax Planner dialog box.

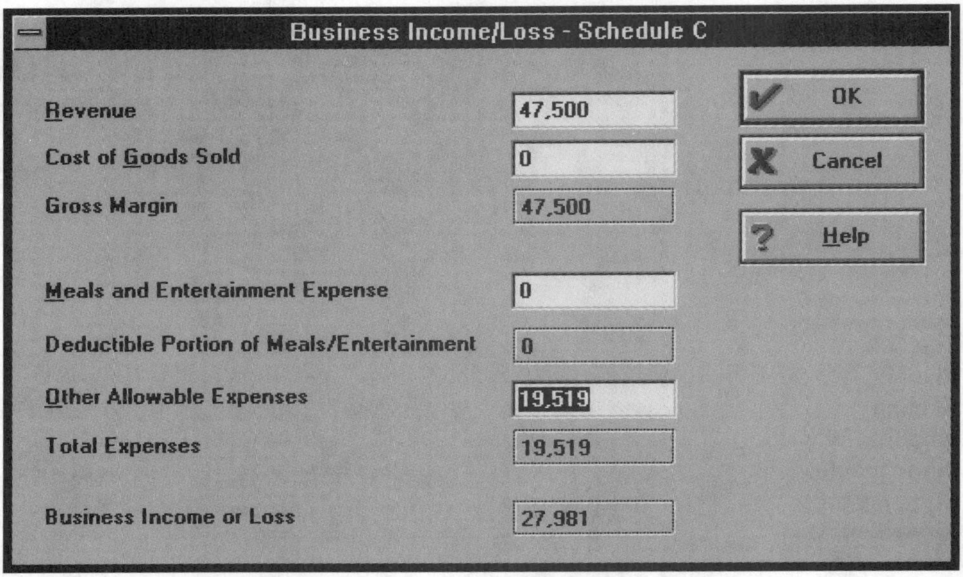

Business Income/Loss - Schedule C

Revenue	47,500
Cost of Goods Sold	0
Gross Margin	47,500
Meals and Entertainment Expense	0
Deductible Portion of Meals/Entertainment	0
Other Allowable Expenses	19,519
Total Expenses	19,519
Business Income or Loss	27,981

OK
Cancel
Help

Summarized Schedule C information for the Tax Planner
Figure 15-6.

Completing Schedule C

With Quicken's Profit and Loss statement, you can now complete the appropriate lines of the federal tax form Schedule C. Because Schedule C is basically a profit and loss statement, many of the entries can be obtained directly from your Quicken report. The following is a list of line numbers and how you can complete them in Schedule C. When you use separate categories for home and business use, you can get these amounts directly from the Tax Planner's dialog box shown in Figure 15-5.

Line 1 This line shows gross sales. The total income shown on your report, $47,500.00, would be placed on this line.

Line 13 This section shows depreciation and section 179 deduction from Form 4562, Depreciation and Amortization. The Total Depreciation Expense, $275.00, would be entered here.

Line 21 This line shows repairs. The amount you show for Equip Mnt, $1,100.00, would be entered here.

Line 22 This line shows the total of all your business supplies. You would use the Calculator to add $375.76 and $65.00, the amounts shown for Computer Supplies and Supplies, and then enter the total, $440.76, here.

Line 23 This line shows taxes. You would add the amounts that are shown as Payroll:Comp FICA, Payroll:Comp FUTA, Payroll:Comp MCARE, and Payroll:SUI. Enter the total, $1,771.50, here.

Line 24 This line shows the total amount of your business travel. The amount of Travel Expense, $905.00, would be entered here. This assumes that all these expenses are associated with travel and not meals or entertainment. You can establish separate categories for these items in your Quicken Category and Transfer list.

Line 25 The total for utilities and telephone is placed on this line. You would use the Calculator to add the amounts shown for Telephone Expense and Total Utilities, $305.00 and $47.40, and record the total expense as $352.40.

Line 26 This line shows the total wages paid. You would enter $15,000.00, the amount shown as Payroll:Gross.

Line 27a This line shows your other business expenses. You would add the amounts shown for Postage and Del Overngt, $28.25 and $270.00, and show the total, $298.25, as Misc Exp in this section.

Line 28 This line shows your total deductions. This is the amount of Total Expense, $20,142.91.

Line 29 This line shows your net profit or loss. Here you would enter the net profit, $27,357.09, from your Profit and Loss report.

Note: You can round the cents to the nearest dollar when completing your tax forms. The Tax Planner does this automatically.

After completing this exercise, you see how establishing classes helps gather your tax information. Remember, one of the constraints faced in this example was that you recorded business expenses in both personal and business checking accounts. Also, the utility categories combined the home and business portion of these expenses. If you had separate categories, you could use the numbers directly from the Tax Planner.

Other Business-Related Tax Forms

When you completed line 13, Depreciation, you used the Total Depreciation Expense amount from your Profit and Loss statement. This information must be included on Form 4562, Depreciation and Amortization. After reading through Publication 534, you would have entered the appropriate amounts for section 179 property and ACRS or MACRS depreciation. This results in a total of $275.00, shown on line 20 of Form 4562 and transferred to line 13 on Schedule C.

As a sole proprietor, you also need to complete Schedule SE, Social Security Self-Employment Tax. The net profit from your Schedule C, $27,357.09, would be carried to line 2 of that form, and the rest of the form can be easily completed. The Tax Planner can even calculate these taxes for you. The Tax Planner calculates Self-Employment tax from the business income in the Business Income/Loss - Schedule C dialog box like the one in Figure 15-6. You can see the amount calculated when you select Other Tax, Credits from the Tax Planner dialog box. See Table 15-4 for a list of important tax forms for the small-business owner.

Business Classification	Form	Name
Sole Proprietorship	Schedule C (Form 1040)	*Profit or Loss from Business*
	Form 4562	*Depreciation and Amortization*
	Schedule SE (Form 1040)	*Social Security Self-Employment Tax*
	Form 1040ES	*Estimated Tax for Individuals*
Partnership	Form 1065	*U.S. Partnership Return of Income*
	Schedule D (Form 1065)	*Capital Gains and Losses*
	Schedule K-1 (Form 1065)	*Partner's Share of Income, Credits, Deductions, Etc.*
Corporation	Form 1120-A	*U.S. Corporation Short-Form*
	Form 1120	*U.S. Corporation Income Tax Return*
	Form 1120S	*U.S. Income Tax Return for an S Corporation*
	Schedule K-1 (Form 1120S)	*Credits, Deductions, Etc.*

Year-End Business Tax Forms
Table 15-4.

Year-End Activities

You are not required to take any special actions at the end of the year in order to continue using Quicken. The package allows you to select transactions by date if you want to purge some of the older transactions from your file. Unless you need the disk space or begin to notice sluggish response time from your system, plan to keep at least three years of historical information in your file. You may find it convenient to be able to print historical reports for comparison with this year's results.

To copy accounts, categories, classes, and other information to a new file, you use the Year-End Copy command from the File menu. You can then decide whether the file that you continue to work with will contain the older transactions.

The following steps explain how to copy the BUSINESS file you have been using since Chapter 12. Complete these steps:

1. Select Year-End Copy from the File menu.
2. Select Archive and OK to display the Archive File dialog box:

3. Type **BUSINE95** in the Archive Old Quicken Data To text box for the name of the new file if it is not already there.
4. Type a new directory location or press TAB to accept the existing location.
5. Type **12/31/95** in the Archive Transactions Prior To And Including text box.

   This tells Quicken that you want to transfer all the transactions before and on 12/31/95 to the new file.

6. Select OK to create the file.

   After Quicken creates the archive file, you can use the archive version (BUSINE95) or the current version (BUSINESS). BUSINE95 contains transactions up to 12/31/95. BUSINESS contains transactions up to and beyond 12/31/95.

7. Select Use current file, and then select OK.

Another option for copying information at the end of the year is to use the Start New Year option instead of Archive. This option removes uncleared transactions from the current file while putting the entire version into a new file. The difference is that when you are done, the only transactions before 12/31/95 that the current file contains are uncleared transactions. This means that this file contains only checks that have yet to clear your bank, so that you can reconcile your bank account. The same is true for uncleared credit card and other banking transactions.

CHAPTER

16 MONITORING FINANCIAL CONDITIONS

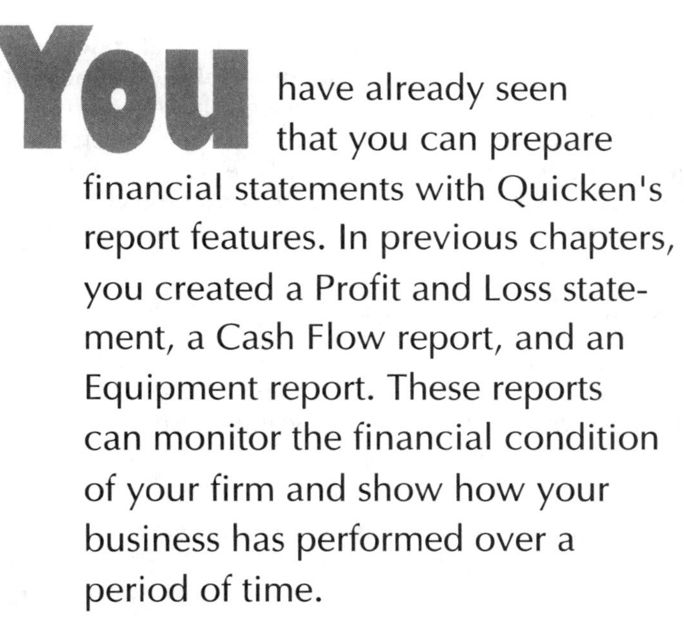

You have already seen that you can prepare financial statements with Quicken's report features. In previous chapters, you created a Profit and Loss statement, a Cash Flow report, and an Equipment report. These reports can monitor the financial condition of your firm and show how your business has performed over a period of time.

These reports not only help you assess the success you've had in managing the business, but they can also be used by outsiders for the same purpose. Bankers and other creditors review your financial statements to determine whether to make loans to your business. Quicken can prove a valuable tool in preparing loan applications or, as you saw in earlier chapters, in providing information to others who use financial statements, such as the Internal Revenue Service.

This chapter presents another major financial statement: the Balance Sheet. The Balance Sheet provides a snapshot of the financial resources and obligations of your business. Although the Profit and Loss statement, the Cash Flow report, and the Balance Sheet have been introduced separately, they are interrelated. Bankers and other readers will review these statements as a package when assessing the past and projecting the future success of your business.

The Balance Sheet

The Profit and Loss statement helps explain the changes that occur between two Balance Sheets.

The Balance Sheet shows your business assets, liabilities, and equity or investment at a specific date. Remember that *assets* are things of value that your business uses to generate revenue. Cash, for example, is an asset that is used to acquire other assets, such as supplies and labor, which are then used to generate revenue.

Liabilities are the obligations incurred as part of your business operations. Borrowing from the bank is a financial obligation. The money owed to the IRS for payroll expenses is another. These obligations are shown as liabilities on your Balance Sheet.

Owner's equity is the amount of personal resources you have invested in the business. In the example you've been working on in the preceding chapters, you opened your business checking account with a $4,000 deposit. You put $2,400 of equipment in the Equipment account ($3,000 original cost - $600 of accumulated depreciation). This $6,400 is the amount of your personal assets invested in the business and is your owner's equity at the beginning of the year. Bankers and other creditors are interested in your equity in the business. If you ask for a loan, they will want to know how much of your own financial resources you are risking. This is measured by your equity in your business, as well as by any other personal assets you may be willing to offer as collateral.

Before you prepare a Balance Sheet, it's important to know two concepts. First, the Balance Sheet is prepared at a specific date. When you create a Balance Sheet, Quicken asks you to define the date that you want to use in preparing your Balance Sheet. For example, you will define the date as 3/31/95 for a Balance Sheet later in this chapter. This tells Quicken to prepare the

Balance Sheet that shows the balances in your business accounts on 3/31/95. The only time you need more than one date for a Balance Sheet is when you create a comparative Balance Sheet that shows the account balances for two separate dates.

The second important concept is that the Profit and Loss statement and the Balance Sheet are related. The Balance Sheet shows your assets, liabilities, and equity at a specific date, and the Profit and Loss statement details the changes in your assets, liabilities, and equity between two Balance Sheets. The Profit and Loss statement represents how you used your assets to generate more income, the liabilities you incurred, and whether your equity in the business increased or decreased.

Remember these two concepts as you prepare the Balance Sheets in this chapter: the Balance Sheet is prepared at a specific date. The Profit and Loss statement helps explain how assets, liabilities, and equity change between two Balance Sheet dates. In the examples that follow, you see how the Profit and Loss statement demonstrates how changes in owner's equity occurred between 1/1/95 and 3/31/95.

The Balance Sheet is prepared as of a specific date. Each transaction you enter in Quicken will change your Balance Sheet amounts.

Creating a Balance Sheet

In this section, you prepare a Balance Sheet as of 3/31/95 from the transactions you entered in the BUSINESS file in previous chapters. This report shows the assets, liabilities, and owner's equity of the business at the end of the quarter. Starting from the ANB Business account register in the BUSINESS file, follow these steps:

HomeBase

Reports | More Reports

1. Select Business from the Reports menu, or click the Reports icon on the icon bar and select the Business option button.
2. Select Balance Sheet from the menu or list box.

   The date prompt at the top of the dialog box has changed because you only need to enter one date for the Balance Sheet.
3. Enter **3/31/95** in the Report Balance as of text box.
4. Select Customize to open the Customize Balance Sheet dialog box.
5. Select Matching.
6. Enter **B** from the Class Contains drop-down list box, and then click OK.
7. Select Print, and the Print Report dialog box appears.
8. Select Print. Your Balance Sheet looks like Figure 16-1.

Balance Sheet
As of 3/31/95

Acct	3/31/95 Balance
ASSETS	
Cash and Bank Accounts	
ANB Business	32,735.70
ANB Personal	-123.16
Total Cash and Bank Accounts	32,612.54
Other Assets	
Equipment	3,625.00
Total Other Assets	3,625.00
TOTAL ASSETS	36,237.54
LIABILITIES & EQUITY	
LIABILITIES	
Other Liabilities	
Payroll-FICA	310.00
Payroll-FICA-Co	310.00
Payroll-FWH	614.00
Payroll-MCARE	72.50
Payroll-MCARECo	72.50
Payroll-SWH	477.45
Total Other Liabilities	1,856.45
TOTAL LIABILITIES	1,856.45
EQUITY	34,381.09
TOTAL LIABILITIES & EQUITY	36,237.54

The Balance Sheet as of 3/31/95
Figure 16-1.

Using the Balance Sheet

You can see from the Balance Sheet that the total of the Cash and Bank accounts is $32,612.54. This is the amount shown in your ANB Business checking account on 3/31/95 ($32,735.70) less $123.16. The deduction is the cash used from your personal checking account to cover business expenses. (Remember that you wrote several personal checks and charged a portion of the cost to business by using the /B class entry.) These amounts appear in the Profit and Loss statement prepared in the previous chapter and in the Cash Flow report prepared in Chapter 14, "Preparing Budget Reports and Cash Flow Statements." Thus, Quicken adjusts your business assets by the amount of expenses paid from your personal accounts. The importance of this adjustment is discussed shortly.

You can also see that the equipment is carried at a balance of $3,625. The carrying value of depreciable assets is discussed in Chapter 15, "Organizing Tax Information and Other Year-End Tasks." The Equipment report produced there shows the underlying transactions that explain the carrying value on the Balance Sheet.

Your total assets are the resources available to your business on the date of the report. These resources are used to generate future income.

The amounts you withhold from employee wages are liabilities of your business.

The liabilities shown are all related to the payroll prepared on 3/31/95. You owe the federal and state governments $1,856.45 for withholding and social security tax payments. On 4/1/95, you made a deposit with your bank for all the federal government payroll liabilities. However, this doesn't affect the Balance Sheet prepared on 3/31/95. The payroll taxes are liabilities on the date the statement is prepared, even though the deposit on 4/1/95 reduces your total liabilities by $1,379. Likewise, the state withholding liability will remain on the Balance Sheet until you make a deposit to the state.

The difference between the total assets of the business and its total liabilities is the owner's equity in the business. In this case, you have $34,381.09 of your equity invested in the business. Thus, the Balance Sheet shows that most of the business's assets were contributed by you, with only $1,856.45 outstanding to creditors.

Creating a Comparative Balance Sheet

In this section, you will see how Quicken's Profit and Loss statement helps explain the changes that occur between two Balance Sheets. First, you will prepare a comparative Balance Sheet; then the Balance Sheet's relationship with the Profit and Loss statement will be discussed. Starting from the Balance Sheet window that is open from creating the balance sheet in Figure 16-1, follow these steps:

1. Select Customize to open the Customize Balance Sheet dialog box.
2. Enter **1/1/95** in the From text box.

   3/31/95 is already entered in the To text box. This time you need two dates because you will show the balance sheet amounts for two dates.
3. Select Quarter for the Interval under Headings and select OK.
4. Select Print, and the Print Report dialog box appears.
5. Select Print. Your report will resemble the one in Figure 16-2.

Using the Comparative Balance Sheet

Understanding the underlying reasons for changes between two Balance Sheets will help you better manage your business.

The comparative Balance Sheet prepared in this section shows the balances of the business on 1/1/95 and 3/31/95 side by side. You can see that the assets of the business on 1/1/95 consisted of the $4,000.00 initial deposit made to the business checking account and the $2,400.00 carrying value ($3,000.00 - $600.00) of the High Tech computer recorded in the Equipment account on 1/1/95. Thus, the total assets were $6,400.00. There were no liabilities at that time, so the owner's equity is the $6,400.00 shown as the overall total.

The question you should be asking now is, "What caused the changes in assets, liabilities, and equity between these two Balance Sheet dates?"

The best way to understand how the changes occurred is to create a Cash Flow report and a Profit and Loss statement. You have already created these reports in Chapters 14 and 15. If you wish to create these statements again, follow these steps.

HomeBase

Reports | More Reports

1. Open the Reports menu or select the Reports icon.
2. Select Business, and then select Cash Flow from the menu or dialog box.
3. Select Customize.
4. Enter **1/1/95** in the From text box.
5. Enter **3/31/95** in the To text box.
6. Select Matching.
7. Enter **B** in the Class Contains text box to restrict the report to business transactions.
8. Select the Accounts option button.
9. Check that the Equipment account and the six payroll liability accounts are unmarked. To mark or unmark an account, highlight it and press SPACEBAR, or click it.
10. Select OK to create the Cash Flow report.

Balance Sheet by Quarter

As of 3/31/95

Acct	1/1/95 Balance	3/31/95 Balance
ASSETS		
Cash and Bank Accounts		
ANB Business	4,000.00	32,735.70
ANB Personal	0.00	-123.16
Total Cash and Bank Accounts	4,000.00	32,612.54
Other Assets		
Equipment	2,400.00	3,625.00
Total Other Assets	2,400.00	3,625.00
TOTAL ASSETS	6,400.00	36,237.54
LIABILITIES & EQUITY		
LIABILITIES		
Other Liabilities		
Payroll-FICA	0.00	310.00
Payroll-FICA-Co	0.00	310.00
Payroll-FWH	0.00	614.00
Payroll-MCARE	0.00	72.50
Payroll-MCARECo	0.00	72.50
Payroll-SWH	0.00	477.45
Total Other Liabilities	0.00	1,856.45
TOTAL LIABILITIES	0.00	1,856.45
EQUITY	6,400.00	34,381.09
TOTAL LIABILITIES & EQUITY	6,400.00	36,237.54

The comparative Balance Sheet as of 3/31/95

Figure 16-2.

11. Select Print and Print to print the Cash Flow statement shown in Figure 16-3.
12. Select Close to leave the Report window.

The biggest change in assets is the $28,612.54 increase in checking accounts. This is explained in the Cash Flow report. This report shows $28,612.54 more inflows than outflows between 1/1/95 and 3/31/95.

You can examine the Equipment report prepared in Chapter 15 to explain the increase in the Equipment account. You can see from the comparative Balance Sheet that the changes in your liabilities are clearly related to the payroll withholdings you owe on 3/31/95.

The owner's equity (investment) in a business is the difference between the total assets and total liabilities of the business. As just noted, the owner's equity on 1/1/95 was $6,400.00, whereas the owner's equity on 3/31/95 is $34,381.09. This $27,981.09 change can be explained by examining the Profit and Loss statement. To create this statement, follow these steps:

HomeBase

Reports | More Reports

1. Select Business from the Reports menu or click the Reports icon on the icon bar and select the Business option button.
2. Select P&L Statement.
3. Select Customize so the Customize Profit & Loss Statement dialog box appears.
4. Enter **1/1/95** in the From field.
5. Enter **3/31/95** in the To field.
6. Select Matching.
7. Enter **B** in the Class Contains field.
8. Click OK, and the Profit and Loss Statement window appears.
9. Select Print and Print to print a Profit and Loss statement resembling the one shown in Figure 16-4.
10. Select Close to leave the Report window.

A Profit and Loss statement covers a specific time period—in this example, the first quarter of 1995. You can see that the net profit (total income - total expenses) is $27,981.09. This amount is equal to the change in the owner's equity between the two Balance Sheet dates. Thus, the net profit or loss of a business helps explain changes that occur between Balance Sheets from the beginning and from the end of the profit and loss period.

One final point to note about the Balance Sheet is the amount -123.16 shown on the 3/31/95 Balance Sheet. This number appears because you entered business expense transactions in your personal checking account. Although this is not recommended, it is not uncommon for small-business owners to

Cash Flow Report

1/1/95 Through 3/31/95

Category Description		1/1/95- 3/31/95
INFLOWS		
Inc Cons		37,500.00
Inc Roy		10,000.00
FROM Payroll-FICA		930.00
FROM Payroll-FICA-Co		930.00
FROM Payroll-FWH		1,842.00
FROM Payroll-MCARE		217.50
FROM Payroll-MCARECo		217.50
FROM Payroll-SWH		477.45
TOTAL INFLOWS		52,114.45
OUTFLOWS		
Del Overngt		270.00
Equip Mnt		1,100.00
Payroll:		
Comp FICA	930.00	
Comp MCARE	217.50	
Gross	15,000.00	
Total Payroll		16,147.50
Postage		28.25
Supp Comp		375.76
Supplies		65.00
Telephone		305.00
Travel		905.00
Utilities:		
Electric	30.40	
Gas	17.00	
Total Utilities		47.40
TO Equipment		1,500.00
TO Payroll-FICA		620.00
TO Payroll-FICA-Co		620.00
TO Payroll-FWH		1,228.00
TO Payroll-MCARE		145.00
TO Payroll-MCARECo		145.00
TOTAL OUTFLOWS		23,501.91
OVERALL TOTAL		28,612.54

The Cash Flow report

Figure 16-3.

Profit & Loss Statement

1/1/95 Through 3/31/95

Category Description		1/1/95- 3/31/95
INCOME/EXPENSE		
INCOME		
Inc Cons		37,500.00
Inc Roy		10,000.00
TOTAL INCOME		47,500.00
EXPENSES		
Del Overngt		270.00
Depreciation:		
Computer	150.00	
Printer	125.00	
Total Depreciation		275.00
Equip Mnt		1,100.00
Payroll:		
Comp FICA	930.00	
Comp MCARE	217.50	
Gross	15,000.00	
Total Payroll		16,147.50
Postage		28.25
Supp Comp		375.76
Supplies		65.00
Telephone		305.00
Travel		905.00
Utilities:		
Electric	30.40	
Gas	17.00	
Total Utilities		47.40
TOTAL EXPENSES		19,518.91
TOTAL INCOME/EXPENSE		27,981.09

A Profit and Loss statement for the period ending 3/31/95

Figure 16-4.

make this sort of transaction. You must rememberthe $123.16 is included in the Profit and Loss statement as a business expense; thus, the reported net profit is reduced by that amount. Since you paid for this expense from your personal checking account, Quicken is telling you that using your personal funds for business expenses reduces your total business assets. Problems like this occur when you are running a very small business in which office supplies and personal supplies may be purchased at the same time and with the same payment.

Note: Although Quicken can handle paying business expenses out of both business and personal checking accounts, it is better to limit business expense payments to your business checking account. If the nature of your business necessitates the payment of expenses with cash rather than with a check, establish a Quicken Cash account for your business. Use this account in combination with your business checking account to record business expenses paid with cash.

Sole Proprietor Withdrawals from the Business

Withdrawals made by sole proprietors are not business expenses. They are reductions in owner equity.

So far in the examples developed in this book, you have not spent any of the cash generated from your business for personal use. In accounting, it is called a *withdrawal,* or simply *draw,* when sole proprietors take cash or other assets out of their businesses for personal use. Obviously, these are not business expenses, so the Profit and Loss statement is not affected. On the other hand, when you transfer cash out of your business you reduce the assets of your business.

In this section, you see how owner withdrawals affect the Balance Sheet of a business. Starting from the ANB Business account register, follow these steps to record your withdrawal of cash from the business checking account:

1. Select Use Register from the Activities menu or click the Registr icon on the icon bar.
2. Click the ANB Business account selector.
3. Move to the next empty transaction at the end of the account register.
4. Enter **3/31/95** in the Date field.

   The cash withdrawal is handled as a transfer between your business and personal checking accounts. Just as it is not good practice to pay business expenses from a personal checking account, neither should you use business checks to pay for personal expenditures.
5. Type **Mr. Johnson** in the Payee field.

Since the transaction is a withdrawal, the payee name matches the name of the business owner.

6. Type **5000** in the Payment field.
7. Type **Transfer - Withdraw** in the Memo field.
8. Enter **ANB Personal** in the Category field.
9. Type **/B** after [ANB Personal] in the Category field, and then select Record.

   The class designation indicates to Quicken that this is a business transaction. This transaction now appears in your ANB Business account register, as shown here:

3/31/95		Mr. Johnson Transfer - Withdraw [ANB Personal]/B	5,000	00				27,735 70

10. Highlight the transaction you just entered, and press CTRL-X to view the transaction in the ANB Personal register.

    Pressing CTRL-X is the same as selecting Go To Transfer in the Edit menu.
11. Move to the Memo field.
12. Type **Withdraw from business**, and then select Record.

    This is an important step in recording the transaction. This memo will describe all withdrawals from the business, so the memo can later be a filter when you prepare the Balance Sheet. Here is how this transaction appears in your ANB Personal account register:

3/31/95		Mr. Johnson Withdraw from business [ANB Business]/B				5,000	00	7,061 00

13. With this transaction highlighted, press CTRL-X to return to the ANB Business register.

The Balance Sheet After an Owner's Withdrawal of Capital

Now that you have recorded your owner's withdrawal, let's take a look at the business's Balance Sheet. From the main menu of the ANB Business account, follow these steps:

1. Open the Reports menu.

HomeBase

Reports | More Reports

2. Select Business.
3. Select Balance Sheet.
4. Select Customize to open the Customize Balance Sheet dialog box.
5. Enter **1/1/95** in the From text box.
6. Enter **3/31/95** in the To text box.
7. Select Quarter from the Interval drop-down list box. This causes Quicken to create a comparative Balance Sheet that shows balances for the beginning and the end of the quarter.
8. Select Matching.
9. Type **~Withdraw..** in the Memo Contains text box.

   This entry filters to exclude transactions that start with Withdraw. The ~ represents "Not", indicating a search for whatever *does not* match what appears after this symbol. The .. matches anything.
10. Select B from the Class Contains drop-down list box. The Customize Balance Sheet dialog box now looks like this:

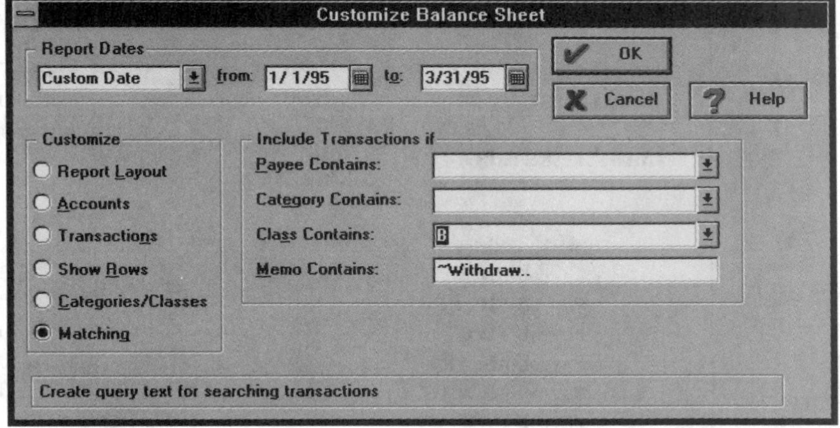

11. Click OK to create this report.
12. Select Print, and the Print Report dialog box appears.
13. Select Print. Your Balance Sheet looks like Figure 16-5.

Effects of the Owner's Withdrawal

The Balance Sheet now shows your total equity as $29,381.09, which is $5,000.00 less than the equity shown on the previous Balance Sheet (see Figure 16-2). You can see that the owner's equity in a business is affected

Balance Sheet by Quarter

As of 3/31/95

Acct	1/1/95 Balance	3/31/95 Balance
ASSETS		
Cash and Bank Accounts		
ANB Business	4,000.00	27,735.70
ANB Personal	0.00	-123.16
Total Cash and Bank Accounts	4,000.00	27,612.54
Other Assets		
Equipment	2,400.00	3,625.00
Total Other Assets	2,400.00	3,625.00
TOTAL ASSETS	6,400.00	31,237.54
LIABILITIES & EQUITY		
LIABILITIES		
Other Liabilities		
Payroll-FICA	0.00	310.00
Payroll-FICA-Co	0.00	310.00
Payroll-FWH	0.00	614.00
Payroll-MCARE	0.00	72.50
Payroll-MCARECo	0.00	72.50
Payroll-SWH	0.00	477.45
Total Other Liabilities	0.00	1,856.45
TOTAL LIABILITIES	0.00	1,856.45
EQUITY	6,400.00	29,381.09
TOTAL LIABILITIES & EQUITY	6,400.00	31,237.54

The Comparative Balance Sheet after the owner's withdrawal is recorded

Figure 16-5.

not only by net profits and losses, but also by owner withdrawals of equity. You also know that an investment of additional cash or assets in a business increases the owner's equity. This occurred on 1/1/95 when you invested cash and equipment to set up the business. Thus, you account for the owner's equity change between the two Balance Sheets by adding the net profits for the period to the beginning owner's equity and then reducing it by withdrawals ($6,400.00 + $27,981.09 - $5,000.00 = $29,381.09).

Quicken Graphs

Now that you have prepared reports for your business data, you can use Quicken to create graphs of your income and expenses, budget variances, net worth, and investments. In this section, you will prepare an asset comparison pie graph. Follow these steps:

HomeBase

Reports | More Graphs

1. Select Graphs from the Reports menu, or click the Graphs icon on the icon bar
2. Select Net Worth Graph.
3. Type **1/95** in the From text box and **3/95** in the To text box.

   Notice the buttons at the bottom of the dialog box that allow you to filter the data used in the graph.
4. Select Create, and Quicken displays the Monthly Assets, Liabilities, and Net Worth graph shown in Figure 16-6.

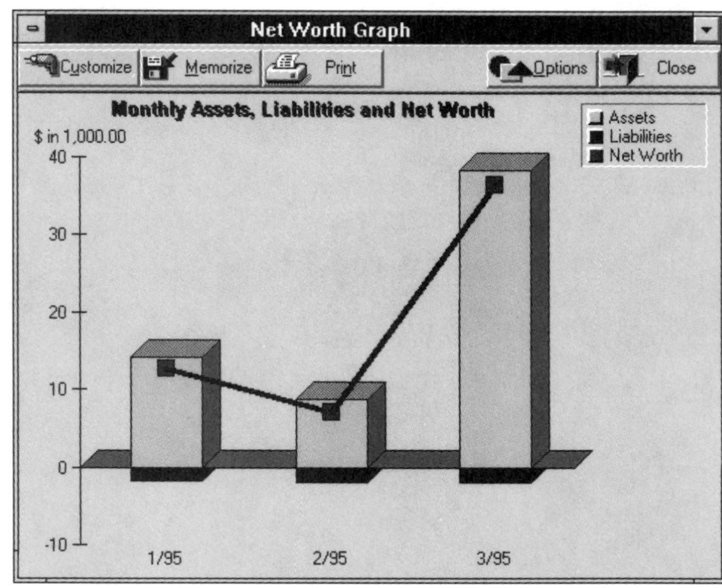

A Monthly Assets, Liabilities, and Net Worth graph
Figure 16-6.

5. Double-click on the column indicating assets for 3/95.

   When you point at the graph column, your mouse pointer becomes the QuickZoom magnifying glass pointer. When you double-click, you display a graph that provides more detailed information about the data represented by the graph column. In this case, you display the asset comparison graph shown here:

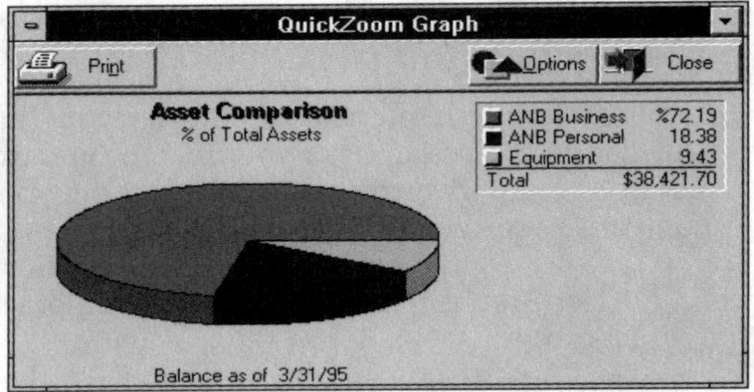

   This graph shows that your business bank account constitutes approximately 72 percent of your total assets, your personal bank account 18 percent, and your business equipment 9 percent.

6. Select the Print button from the window's button bar to print the graph.

TIPS

TIPS to KEEP YOU on TOP of YOUR BUSINESS FINANCES

The tips that follow offer many different cost saving suggestions that can directly increase the resources that you have available for business financial goals. You'll also find tips to help you keep your financial records in order to ensure that you have the tax records you need as well as adequate controls in your financial record keeping.

1. Consider self-insuring your equipment, rather than paying extra for maintenance agreements. The charges for these agreements can add up quickly.
2. Shop for the lowest cost on office items. You might buy supplies in bulk at warehouse clubs and other outlets. Also, consider purchasing used office furniture and equipment.
3. Consider hiring an intern from a local college for the summer. He or she might even work part-time during the school year. Students today are very anxious for experience and if you can offer them a learning experience that they can add to their resume, they may even accept volunteer-type opportunities.
4. Use temps rather than adding a new position until you are sure you will need the position permanently.
5. Contract out for services that you need only occasionally.
6. Look for non-computer products that can substitute for more expensive computer products. A travel case for your notebook computer and disk mailers are two examples where good substitutes might be much cheaper.
7. Don't let key employees get so overworked and stressed out that they get sick. If necessary, enroll employees in stress management programs if the work environment is hectic.
8. Leave the printer off until the first time you need it each day.
9. Keep a record of the discounts available through memberships such as AAA and other associations, and use them.
10. Make sure you take advantage of frequent-flyer miles by flying on one airline as much as possible.
11. Look for other promotions that allow you to increase your frequent-flyer miles such as car rentals, hotel stays, and so on.

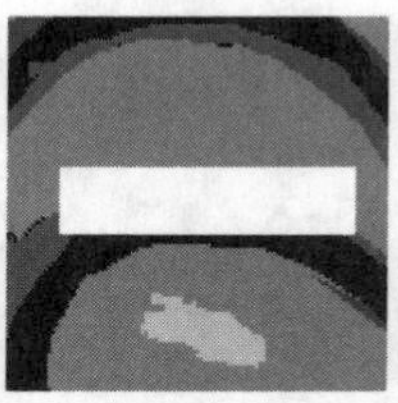

12. Watch the dates for payroll deposits closely, as the fees for late payments can be very high.
13. Be sure to pay your invoices within the discount period.
14. Look for a bank that bases checking account charges on an average monthly balance rather than minimum monthly balance.
15. Utilize all mailings for multiple purposes. If you are mailing a bill, enclose a flyer on new goods and services or send a special promotional notice of an upcoming sale.
16. Plan your business calls to utilize rate savings. If you are on EST, wait until evening to call the West Coast; they will still have several working hours left.
17. Reward employees for cost-saving suggestions.
18. Utilize employee recommendations to fill new positions. You can give them a small cash bonus for employees hired who stay at least six months. They are more likely than a head hunter to choose an employee that fits with the corporate culture.
19. Consider paying overtime for a period rather than hiring a new employee. This way you can avoid paying all the overhead costs until you are certain that your business has grown enough to require permanent extra help.
20. Base raises strictly on performance. There is no need to reward mediocre results with even a small raise.
21. Implement profit-sharing plans that let employees share in increased profits and cost savings they help to achieve.
22. Check into postal costs for different-sized mailings to make sure that the size you choose qualifies for the type of mailing you want to do.

23. Make sure that the packing materials you are using are not adding to the weight of the package. New featherweight options offer protection and reduced mailing costs.

24. Don't ignore problem employees. If you do not take action, the morale and productivity of all employees will be adversely affected.

25. As an employer, you can provide a per diem allowance to employees that is non-taxable as long as it is not in excess of the rate the federal government allows its own employees. This rate is to include lodging, meals, and incidentals. In 1993, the rate ranged from $67 to $174, with rates set individually for over 500 localities.

26. If your business receives cash, you must record the amount immediately. Encourage customers to report incorrect receipts by offering free goods or services if the receipt is not correct.

27. Consider hiring a shopping service to check on employees if you suspect that all sales are not being recorded.

28. Have an employee receiving goods verify that the shipment is complete before he or she authorizes a cash disbursement.

29. If you establish a petty cash fund for convenience, use a petty cash voucher for each disbursement, and require that a bill or receipt be submitted along with it.

30. Assets may be written down ahead of schedule if they have become obsolete and if you must replace them to remain competitive. Take the item's accumulated depreciation into account when determining the write-off value.

31. A sole proprietorship is not taxed as a business; instead, its profits appear on the owner's tax return.

32. An S corporation does not pay a corporate tax. It operates much like a partnership from a tax standpoint.

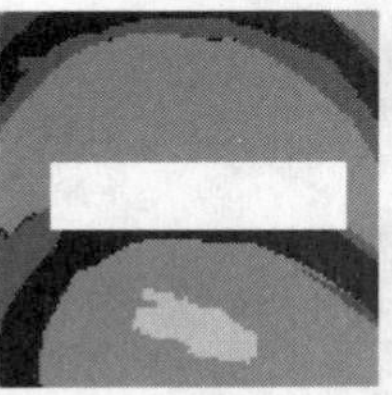

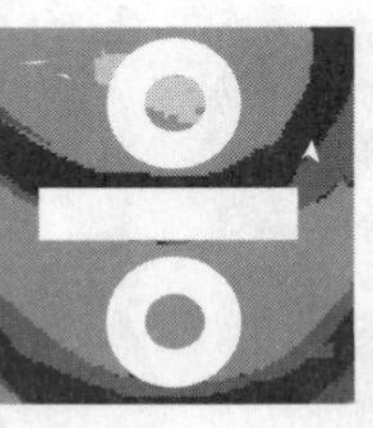

33. Accrual accounting methods are required for C Corporations and partnerships.
34. Your accountant can help you establish some quick ratios to monitor the liquidity of your business and look at other measures of risk or success.
35. Involve employees in budget planning and performance monitoring.
36. Instituting a voucher system for disbursements and requiring several signatures can help control disbursements.
37. Reconcile all bank and credit card accounts monthly so that you will spot problems immediately.
38. Entertainment expenses for business that meet all qualifying rules are only 50 percent deductible.
39. A credit card purchase is treated as an expense on the date of purchase, not the date of payment, even if you maintain your business books on a cash basis.
40. If you keep accurate records of business mileage you can deduct 28 cents per mile. This is likely to be much better than tallying gasoline and toll expenses because the IRS includes vehicle depreciation in their rate.
41. In order to deduct business mileage, you must be able to provide a record showing the date and purpose of each business trip and the mileage traveled, as well as the total mileage for the vehicle during the year.
42. You may deduct business gifts to clients in full if their cost does not exceed $25 per recipient per year.
43. The following information is needed to substantiate a business gift: the recipient, the cost, the date given, the purpose of the gift, and a description of the gift.

44. IRS publication 463 will provide valuable information on travel, entertainment, and gifts. It is available by calling the IRS at (800) 829-3676.
45. Business startup expenses are those expenses incurred before the business is actually established and producing income. These costs can be amortized over a five-year period.
46. Advertising expenses are deductible as long as they promote your business products, services, or name.
47. Travel expense restrictions are stricter for foreign travel. If you spend extra days sightseeing, you will need to allocate your travel expense based on the number of business and personal days included on the trip.
48. If you switch between calendar and fiscal year reporting, you must file a separate, special return for the period that is less than a full year long.
49. Both voluntary and involuntary business losses may be deductible.
50. If you recover a business debt that you have written off, you must increase your income by the amount of this recovery.
51. If you are uncertain whether to treat an individual as an employee or an independent contractor, submit FORM SS-8 to the IRS to get a ruling.
52. Inventory is typically valued either at cost, or at the lower of cost or market value.
53. If you own multiple businesses, it may be possible to use cash basis accounting for one business and accrual basis accounting for the other.
54. Unless all of your income comes from wages, you must keep accounting records that are acceptable to the IRS. All income and expenses are among the items that must be accurately documented.

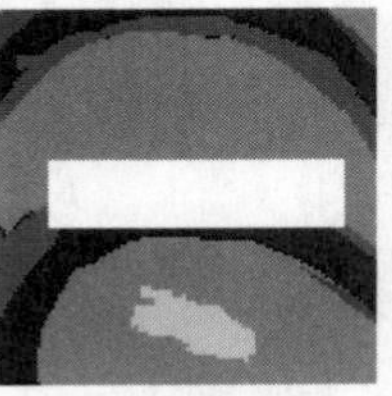

55. In most cases, you can deduct inventory donated to charity at cost.
56. Accounts receivable, cash, securities, and equipment are not considered inventory.
57. Wages paid for overtime and bonus awards are subject to withholding.
58. If you want to find out more about business report requirements for the IRS, call (800) 829-3676 and ask for publication 937, "Business Reporting."
59. Income taxes withheld must be paid to a Federal Reserve Bank, and submitted with Form 8109 or your own personalized forms.
60. You must report the amount of tips your employees report to you on their W-2 forms.
61. You may have a Taxpayer Identification Number for personal use and an Employer Identification Number for business use.
62. If you obtain a filing extension, it does not grant you a tax payment extension.
63. A corporation conforming to a calendar year must file a return by March 15 of the following year.
64. Before writing off a bad debt, make sure you have documented collection efforts.
65. Utilize Quicken's budget features to put together a budget plan. A plan is essential to monitoring your progress.
66. Analyze budget results on a regular basis, and make decisions about bringing costs into line where necessary.
67. Engage in tax planning to control the timing of revenues and expenses, when possible.

68. Consult with your accountant to make decisions about your fiscal or calendar year, cash versus accrual accounting basis, and your inventory valuation method.

69. Carefully evaluate a business location as well as the business before buying. Your business can fail just by being in the wrong location.

70. Take collection action on slow payers at least weekly.

71. Check to see how the profitability of your business compares with that of similar businesses.

72. Maintain all of your business records for a minimum of three years.

73. In general, it is necessary that during the year you pay the smaller of: 90 percent of the tax shown on your previous year's tax return, or 110 percent of the tax for the year before that. See Form 1040.ES [OCR] for complete details.

74. Inspect shipments as they are received, and establish reorder points for inventory to avoid shortages.

75. Cross-train employees who handle critical financial functions. You can have periodic duty rotations to prevent fraudulent behavior and maintain some measure of protection if you lose one of your employees.

76. Start organizing your tax records early.

77. If you are on a fiscal-year reporting basis, schedule the end of your year during a slow time.

78. Try to have inventories at their lowest possible level at year's end to lower the cost of taking a physical inventory.

79. The IRS has special tax publications for specific types of business, such as farms. Call (800) 829-3676 to see if they have anything specific to your needs.

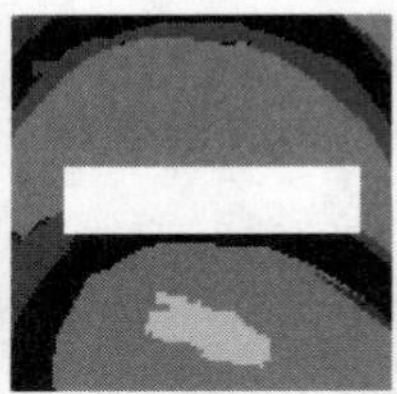

80. Use a copier key, and require employees to log the purpose of copy work. Also keep a log of all long distance calls.
81. Consider using a separate checking account for payroll; this will help you increase control over one of your major expenditures.
82. Consider writing payroll checks yourself to oversee this task closely. If you do not have time to attend to payroll yourself, consider using a payroll service.
83. Deposit cash receipts daily.
84. Check with your accountant to see if any of your equipment purchases qualifies for a section 179 direct deduction.
85. Require that your personnel take annual vacations.
86. Use preprinted, prenumbered business forms for control purposes.
87. Improve your controls by having one person write checks and another reconcile the checking account statement.
88. Revenue earned from foreign sales is taxable in this country.
89. You must withhold federal and state tax, as well as FICA and Medicare, from part-time employees.
90. Keep in mind that self-employed individuals must pay twice the Medicare and FICA on their earnings as an employee.
91. Enter your accounting transactions daily.
92. Prepare and distribute W-2s for all your employees by January 31.
93. Check with your state and local authorities to see if you are required to collect sales tax on goods and services sold.
94. If you are planning to claim a car as a business expense, consult IRS publication 917, "Business Use of a Car."

95. If you are self-employed, remember that 50 percent of your Social Security payments in your own behalf are deductible on your tax return.
96. If you are confused about depreciation, call the IRS at (800) 829-3676 and order publications 534, "Depreciation," and 946, "How to Begin Depreciating Your Property."
97. There are some attractive retirement plan options for the self-employed. Consult IRS publication 560, "Retirement Plans for the Self-Employed," for more information.
98. If you currently handle your business taxes yourself, research different tax software packages that might make your job easier. If you are a sole proprietor, you are likely to find that the TurboTax product will meet all of your needs, including Schedule C.
99. Obtain a vendor's license before attempting to sell merchandise.
100. Consult IRS publication 544 for help with the disposition of assets.
101. Enroll in a time management class or read a good book on time management. Time is definitely money, so you should quickly recoup what you spend on these items.

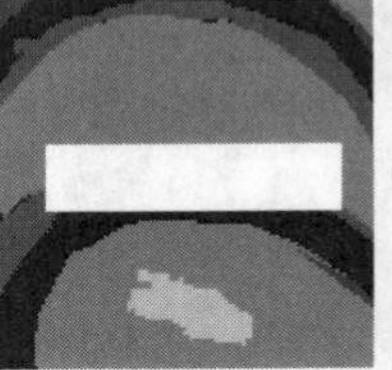

PART

APPENDIXES

APPENDIX

SPECIAL QUICKEN and WINDOWS TASKS

If you have the right equipment, Quicken is easy to install. The package handles most of the installation work for you.

To install and use the Windows version of Quicken discussed in this book, you need an IBM 386 or higher or a 100% compatible computer.

You must have at least 2 MB of RAM, 7 MB of available hard disk space, and a monitor with a graphics card. You also need Windows 3.1 or later to install and run Quicken 4 for Windows.

Installing Quicken

Quicken is very easy to install. All you need to do is put the first installation disk in drive A, select Run from the Program Manager's File menu, type **A:INSTALL**, and select OK. You can also install from drive B. Quicken offers four ways in which you can customize the installation procedure: it lets you change which drive you are installing from, which directory and hard drive you are installing to, which program group to add the program icons to (by default, a new Quicken program group in Windows), and how BillMinder works. The installation will also prompt you when to insert the other installation disks.

Starting Quicken

To start the Quicken program, open the program group containing the Quicken program icon and highlight it. Then double-click on the program icon or press ENTER. Alternatively, you can select Run from the Program Manager's File menu, type **C:\QUICKENW\QW**, and select OK. Quicken will help you set up your first file and account as described in Chapter 3.

Upgrading from an Earlier Release

You can use any files created with Quicken 1, 2, or 3 for Windows with Quicken 4 for Windows without complications. If you have been using Quicken 5, 6, 7, or 8 for DOS, Quicken 4 for Windows can read your files. You can use all the new features with your existing data immediately. You can even go back to your older Quicken release and still read the files after you have worked with them in Quicken 4 for Windows. However, this is not recommended, since you will not get the full use of some of the new features.

If you are upgrading from Quicken 3 or 4 for DOS, Quicken 4 for Windows will convert the files the first time you open them. However, you will be unable to use them with the earlier release of Quicken after this conversion. You might want to create a backup copy of the files before opening them in Quicken 4 for Windows, in case you ever need to use them with the older release again.

Working with Windows in Quicken

If you are new to the Windows operating environment, you will find that there are many differences from working with DOS. One of the differences that can be very confusing is that everything appears within a window. Your Quicken data appears in document windows within the bigger Quicken window. You can have any number of document windows open. You may soon find that your Quicken window is as crowded as a messy desk, showing your investment forms, a report, category or account lists, and a register or two, just as you might keep paper copies of all of these documents on your desktop. You can see in Figure A-1 just how confusing this can be.

Remember, you can close windows you are not using by pressing ESC or by double-clicking your mouse on the control menu box which appears in the upper-left corner of the window next to the title bar. You can also size and move windows.

The easiest way to size or move windows is to use your mouse. To move a window, point your mouse at the title bar of a window, press the left mouse button, drag the window to a new location, and release the mouse button. To size a window using your mouse, move the mouse pointer to one of the window's borders. The mouse pointer will change to a double-headed arrow.

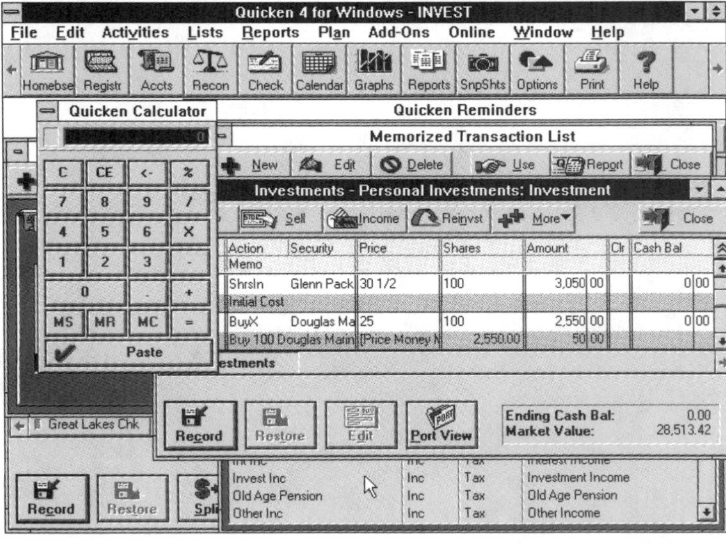

A messy Quicken desktop makes it hard to work

Figure A-1.

Drag the border in or out to change the size of the window. An easier way is to click one of the buttons in the upper-right corner of the window, next to the title bar. Click on an up arrow button to make the window as large as possible. Click on a down arrow button to reduce the window to a small graphic icon. To restore the maximized window to its previous size, click the button with two arrows.

Moving and sizing windows with the keyboard is a little more complicated. First, you need to open the control menu box by pressing ALT-- (hyphen). Select Move from this menu, and then use the arrow keys to position the window. When you press ENTER, the window moves to the location you've specified. To size the window, open the control menu again and select Size. Use the arrow keys again. The first arrow key you press determines which side of the window you are moving, and the rest you press move that side in the given direction. You can maximize the size of the window by selecting Maximize, or reduce it to an icon by selecting Minimize from this menu.

You can also use Quicken to arrange the windows. Select Cascade from the Window menu to arrange the windows so that they are stacked on top of each other, with only the title bar of each showing. You can then click the title bar of the window you want to activate.

APPENDIX B

GLOSSARY

In order to understand how Quicken supports your financial activities, you will need to be familiar with a number of basic financial terms. For your convenience, this appendix presents brief definitions of the terms used throughout this book.

Accelerated Depreciation A method of depreciation in which more expense is recognized in the early years of an asset's life.

Account A Quicken document where personal and/or business transactions are recorded that increase or decrease the total balance. Examples include bank, cash, credit card, other assets, and other liabilities accounts. Several accounts can exist in a single file.

Account Balance The amount of money in an account.

Accounts Payable Money owed to suppliers for goods or services.

Accounts Receivable Money owed to you by customers or clients.

Accrual Basis An accounting method in which income is recorded when services are provided rather than when cash is received. Expenses are treated similarly.

Accumulated Depreciation The total amount of depreciation expense taken on an asset since the time it was placed in service.

ASCII (American Standard Code for Information Interchange) This is a standard set of codes used for storing information. When you write information to disk with Quicken, the data is stored in ASCII format. This makes it easy to transfer the data to a word processing package or any other application that reads ASCII data.

Asset Any item of value that a business or individual owns.

Average Annual Total Return The average annual percent return on your investment. Interest, dividends, capital gains distributions, and unrealized gains/losses are used in computing this return on your investment.

Average Cost The total cost of all shares divided by the total number of shares.

Balance Sheet A financial statement that summarizes a business's assets, liabilities, and owner's equity at a specific time.

Book Value The cost of an asset less the amount of depreciation expensed to date.

Brokerage Account An account with a firm that buys and sells shares of stocks and other investments on your behalf.

Budget A plan indicating projected income and expenses. Budget also refers to a comparison between the projections and actual amounts for each income or expense category.

Cash Money or currency.

Cash Basis A method of accounting used for business or tax purposes. Income is recorded when cash is received, and expenses are charged when cash is paid.

Cash Flows The inflow and outflow of cash during a specific time period.

Category Identifies the exact nature of income and expenses, such as salary income, dividend income, interest income, or wage expense. Categories are distinct from classes.

Chart of Accounts A list of the categories used to classify transactions.

Class Allows you to define the time period, location, or type of activity for a transaction. Classes are distinct from categories. For example, you could use classes to distinguish between salary income from two jobs.

Cleared Item An item that has been processed by the bank.

Corporation A form of business organization that limits the liability of the shareholders.

Cost Basis Total cost of stock bought or sold plus commission.

Current Balance The present balance in an account. This does not include postdated items.

Deductions Amounts that reduce the gross pay to cover taxes and other commitments, such as health insurance premiums.

Deposit An amount of funds added to an account. A deposit is sometimes referred to as a "credit" to the account.

Depreciable Base The cost of an asset that will be expensed over its useful life.

Depreciation The portion of the cost of an asset that is expensed each year on a profit and loss statement.

Dividends Cash payments made to the shareholders of a corporation from current or past earnings.

Double Entry System An accounting method that requires two accounts to be used when recording a transaction. For example, when supplies are purchased, both the cash and supplies accounts are affected.

Equity The amount of the owner's investment in the business. For individuals, this is the money invested in a property or other asset.

Expense The cost of an item or service purchased or consumed.

FICA Social security tax paid by employers and employees.

File A group of related accounts, such as a personal checking account, a savings account, and an asset account for your home.

Financial Obligations Commitments to pay cash or other assets in return for receiving something of value—for example, a bank loan for equipment or an automobile.

Financial Resources Objects or property of value owned by a person or business that is expected to increase future earnings.

Financial Statements Periodic reports prepared by businesses to show the financial condition of the firm. Major financial statements include balance sheets, profit and loss statements (income statements), and cash flow reports.

FUTA Federal unemployment tax.

Future Value An expected value at some future point, given that today's investments appreciate at the expected rate.

FWH Federal income tax withheld from employees' earnings.

Gross Earnings Total earnings of an employee before deductions are subtracted.

Income The money earned by an individual or business. On a cash basis, it is the amount of cash received for goods or services provided. On an accrual basis, it is the amount of income recognized and recorded during the year for services provided.

Income Statement A summary of the income and expenses of a business.

IRA Individual Retirement Account. Depending upon your income level, you may experience tax benefits from setting up an IRA.

Job/Project Report A method of reporting revenues and expenses on a job or project basis.

Liability The money you owe to a vendor, creditor, or any other party.

Life of an Asset The number of years that the asset is expected to last.

Liquidity A measure of how easy it is to convert an asset to cash.

Memorized Transaction A transaction that you have asked Quicken to remember and recall at a later time.

Menu A related list of commands presented for selection. Menus are frequently used in Windows applications as a means of offering features to choose from.

Money Market Account An account held with a bank or other institution used to preserve capital from risk. Most provide limited checking account privileges.

Mutual Fund An investment vehicle that allows you to purchase shares in the fund; the proceeds are used by the fund to buy shares in a variety of stocks or bonds.

Net Pay The amount of pay received after deductions.

Net Worth An amount determined by subtracting the value of financial obligations from financial resources.

P & L Statement An abbreviation for profit and loss statement; it shows the profit or loss generated during a period.

Partnership A form of business organization where two or more individuals share in the profits and losses of the business.

Payment The amount paid to a vendor, creditor, or other party.

Payroll SDI State disability insurance payments, often referred to as Workers' Compensation.

Payroll Taxes The taxes a business pays on employee earnings—for example, matching FICA contributions, federal and state unemployment taxes, and workers' compensation payments.

Point in Time A specific time when some activity is occurring.

Postdated Transaction A check dated after the current date.

Present Value A value in today's dollars for a sum that will not be received until a later time.

Reconciliation The process of comparing a copy of the bank's records for your account with your own records. Any differences should be explained in this process.

Revenue The money or income generated.

Salvage The worth of an asset at the end of its useful life.

Security An investment such as a stock, bond, or mutual fund.

Service Charge A fee the bank adds for maintaining your account. This fee can be part of the difference in reconciling a bank statement.

Single Entry System An accounting method in which one account is used to record a transaction. When supplies are purchased, only the cash (or checking) account is affected.

Sole Proprietorship The simplest form of small-business organization. There is no separation between the owner and the company.

Straight-line Depreciation A method of expensing the cost of an asset evenly over its life.

Supercategory A grouping of categories that can be used for budgeting. This can eliminate the need for many detail entries.

SUTA State unemployment tax. (Also known as SUI.)

SWH State income taxes withheld from employee gross earnings.

Transaction Group A group of memorized transactions that can be scheduled whenever you need them.

Transfer A transaction that affects the balance in two accounts at the same time by moving funds between them.

Unrealized Gain/Loss A gain or loss estimated on the basis of current market value.

Valuation The current value of an asset.

APPENDIX

CUSTOMIZING QUICKEN

You can customize many features in Quicken, changing settings to affect how Quicken functions and how it looks. By customizing Quicken to suit the way you use the application, you will make your work with Quicken more productive.

To use Quicken's customization features, select Options from the Edit menu, opening the Options dialog box, or click the Options icon in the icon bar. You can select any of the six buttons in this dialog box to open dialog boxes in which you can set different options.

The six buttons found in this dialog box are: General, Checks, Register, Reports, Reminders, and Iconbar. In this appendix, an explanation of the options is presented as well as details on changing the icon bar and some options located on different menus.

General Options

These options let you change how Quicken works in some general ways.

Use Quicken's Custom Colors When this check box is selected, Quicken uses a gray background in all windows, regardless of the color setting in Windows.

Confirm Investment Transactions from Forms When this check box is selected, Quicken prompts you to confirm transactions entered in an investment form before recording them in the register.

Save Price History in DOS Quicken Format When this check box is selected, Quicken saves price histories for securities in the format used for Quicken for DOS.

Use Tax Schedules with Categories When this check box is selected, you can assign categories to lines of tax schedules, so that you can easily create reports that will be helpful when filling those forms out.

Calendar Year/Fiscal Year You can select one of these two option buttons under Working Calendar to specify which type of year you are using. If you select Fiscal Year you will also need to specify a month in the Starting Month text box.

Checks Options

These options are organized onto three sheets that you can access from the Checks, Miscellaneous, and QuickFill tabs that appear in the dialog box.

Checks Options

These options let you change the appearance of the checks you create in Quicken.

Printed Date Style Select one of the four date style buttons to choose how dates will be printed on your checks.

Allow Entry of Extra Message on Check When this check box is selected, an extra field appears on checks in which you can enter short messages.

Print Categories on Voucher Checks When this check box is selected, categories assigned to the transaction are printed on voucher checks.

Warn if a Check Number is Re-used When this check box is selected, Quicken warns you when you attempt to print a check with the same number as one printed previously.

Change Date of Checks to Date When Printed When this check box is selected, checks are printed with the date they are printed, not the date you originally entered the check into Quicken.

Artwork on Check Entry Screen You can use this check box to indicate that you want artwork to appear, then select the desired artwork image from the drop-down list.

Miscellaneous Options

These options affect a variety of Quicken features.

Date Style You can select either the MM/DD/YY or DD/MM/YY option buttons to determine the format used for dates in Quicken. The first is standard in the United States, while the second is standard in Canada and European countries.

Enter Key Moves Between Fields When this check box is selected, pressing ENTER moves between fields, instead of recording the transaction.

Beep When Recording and Memorizing When this check box is selected, Quicken beeps when you record a transaction or memorize a transaction or report.

Warn Before Recording Uncategorized Transactions When this check box is selected, Quicken warns you when you attempt to record a transaction which is not assigned a category.

Request Confirmation Before Changes When this check box is selected, Quicken prompts for confirmation before recording a changed transaction.

QuickFill Options

These options let you change how the QuickFill feature works.

Automatic Memorization of New Transactions When this check box is selected, Quicken automatically adds all newly recorded transactions to the Memorized Transactions list.

Automatic Completion of Fields When this check box is selected, Quicken automatically completes entries as you type based on the QuickFill information.

Automatic Recall of Transactions When this check box is selected, Quicken automatically fills in the remaining fields in a transaction when you use TAB to leave the Payee field, and your Payee field entry has a match in QuickFill.

Drop Down Lists Automatically When this check box is selected, Quicken automatically displays the drop-down list in a QuickFill field when you move to the field.

Buttons in Quickfill Fields When this check box is selected, Quicken displays arrows for activating drop-down lists in fields that can be filled using QuickFill.

Auto Memorize to the Calendar List When this check box is selected, automatically memorized transactions are automatically added to the Financial Calendar's transactions list.

Register Options

These options are organized onto three sheets that you can access from the Display, Miscellaneous, and QuickFill tabs that appear in the dialog box.

Display Options

You can make changes to the display with the options in this window. Each of the options toggles the feature on or off:

- Show Account Selector
- Show Description Bar
- Date In First Column

- Memo before Category
- Color Shading

Choosing the Register Font

You can use these options to select how your register entries are displayed on the screen after selecting the Fonts button.

Font Select the typeface for the register font from this list box.

Size Select the size of the register font from this list box.

Bold Select this check box to have the register font boldfaced.

Reset Select this button to return to the default font for the register.

Choosing the Register Colors

You can use these options to select the colors used in the transactions in your registers' screen displays after selecting the Colors button.

Account Type Select the type of account you want to change by choosing Bank, Cash, Credit Card, Asset, Liability, or Investment.

Color Select the color you want to use with the selected account type from the list box.

Reset Select this button to have all register colors return to the default.

Miscellaneous Options

Most of these options are identical to the ones listed under Checks Options. Only the new additions are listed.

Use a Single Check Register Window This option determines whether additional registers are placed in the same window or new ones.

Warn When Recording Out of Date Transactions You use this option to have Quicken warn you when you enter a transaction for a different year.

QuickFill Options

These options are identical to the ones listed under Checks Options.

Reports Options

These options let you change the appearance of your reports and set defaults to make report creation faster.

Account Display Select one of the three option buttons to set how account names are displayed in reports. You can display the account name, the account description, or both.

Category Display Select one of the three option buttons to set how categories are displayed in reports. You can display the category name, the category description, or both.

Default Report Date Range Set the default time period used for your reports by selecting a time period from this drop-down list box, or by entering specific dates in the two text boxes.

Default Comparison Report Date Range Set the default second time period used in comparison reports by selecting a time period from this drop-down list box, or by entering specific dates in the two text boxes.

Skip Create Report Prompt Select this check box to have Quicken create reports without first displaying the Create Report dialog box.

QuickZoom to Investment Forms Select this check box to have Quicken display an investment form rather than a transaction in an investment register when you use QuickZoom in an investment report.

Use Color in Report When this check box is selected, Quicken displays negative amounts and report headings in color on the screen.

Reminders Options

These options let you change how Quicken reminds you of upcoming transactions.

Turn on BillMinder Select this check box to activate the BillMinder feature.

Days in Advance When you want an advance reminder of upcoming transactions, enter in this text box the number of days in advance you want the reminder to first appear.

Show Reminders on Startup When this check box is selected, Quicken displays a special reminder box for upcoming transactions when you first start Windows.

Show Calendar Notes Lets you determine whether to display the calendar notes you've created.

Icon Bar Options

The icon bar provides shortcuts for carrying out various Quicken activities. You can either use the default Quicken icon bar or you can customize the icon bar to suit yourself. You can change the appearance of the current icon bar, add new icons, or delete or edit existing ones. The icon bar stays the same as you open or close files.

Changing the Appearance of the Icon Bar

Each icon that appears on the icon bar has two visual elements. One is the picture that represents the action, and the second is the word that appears below this icon. You can customize the icon bar so that it displays both the graphic image and the text, only the text, only the graphic image, or neither of them. To change the appearance of the icon bar, follow these steps:

C

1. Select the Iconbar icon or select Options from the Edit menu, then select Iconbar, opening the Customize Iconbar dialog box, shown here:

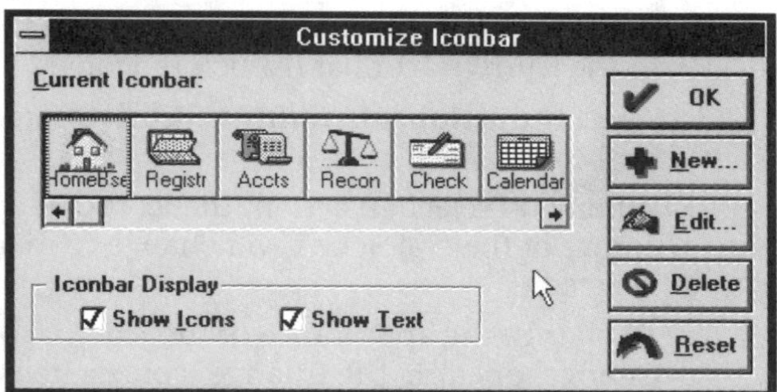

2. Select the Show Icons check box to display the graphic images, or clear it to remove them. The change in the icon bar will appear as soon as you select or clear this check box, before you select OK to exit the dialog box.
3. Select the Show Text check box to display the text, or clear it to remove the text. Again, the change in the icon bar appears immediately.
4. Select OK to exit the dialog box.

Deleting an Icon

You can remove icons from the icon bar, either to make room for icons more useful to you or to trim the icon bar down to those icons you use constantly. Follow these steps to delete an icon from the icon bar:

1. Select the Iconbar icon or select Options from the Edit menu, then select Iconbar, opening the Customize Iconbar dialog box.
2. Highlight the icon in the Current Iconbar list box of icons.
3. Select Delete.
4. Select OK to confirm that you want to delete the icon.

Adding or Editing an Icon

When you add a new icon, you can select the activity that the icon represents, the graphic image and the text that appear on the icon, and a speed key combination that selects the icon from the keyboard. When you edit an icon, you can change any of these properties of the icon.

To add or edit an icon, follow these steps:

1. Select the Iconbar icon or select Options from the Edit menu, then select Iconbar, opening the Customize Iconbar dialog box.
2. Select New to add an icon or Edit to edit the one currently highlighted in the Current Iconbar list box of icons.
3. Select the action you want the icon to carry out in the Icon Action list box.

   When you select an action, the icon that appears in the lower-right corner of the dialog box will change to match the action you have selected.
4. To change the appearance of the icon or to assign a Quick key, select Change, opening the Change Iconbar Item dialog box.
5. Select a graphic image in the Graphic list box of images.
6. Type the text to use with the icon in the Icon Text text box.
7. Enter a key such as **a** or **d** in the Speed key text box if you want to be able to activate the icon with a key combination. You will press ALT, SHIFT, and the key you enter together to activate the icon. For example, if you used **a**, you would press ALT-SHIFT-A.
8. When you have finished making these changes, select OK twice to return to the Customize Iconbar dialog box. Then select OK to close this dialog box.

When you assign actions to an icon, you do not provide all the information that the icon needs to have in order to work. The first time you select the icon, another dialog box will appear requiring further information, such as the account to be used.

Qcard Options

These options let you turn on or off the Qcards which can guide you through some Quicken tasks. The change is made through the Help menu as you toggle Show Qcards on and off.

Saving the Desktop Arrangement

You can tell Quicken to save the arrangement of windows so you can return to the same place each time you start Quicken. You will choose Save Desktop from the File menu, then specify your preference.

Save Desktop on Exit Select this option button to have Quicken save the arrangement of all open windows each time you exit, so that the exact same display is shown when you restart the program.

Save Current Desktop Select this option button to save the current desktop arrangement to a file.

INDEX

Special Characters

A

D

E

F

N

O

P

Q

R

S

U

W

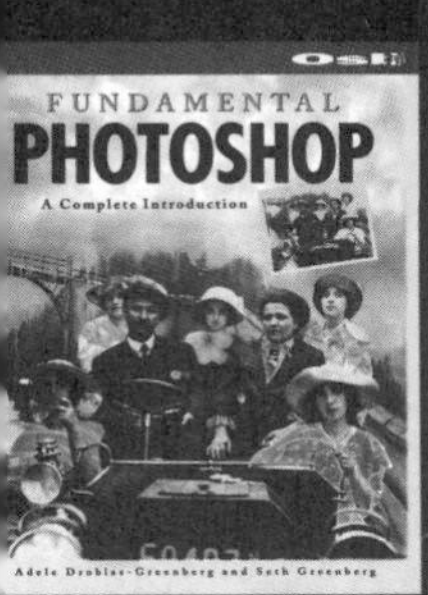

undamental Photoshop: Complete Introduction
Adele Droblas-Greenberg
Seth Greenberg
7.95 ISBN: 0-07-881994-6

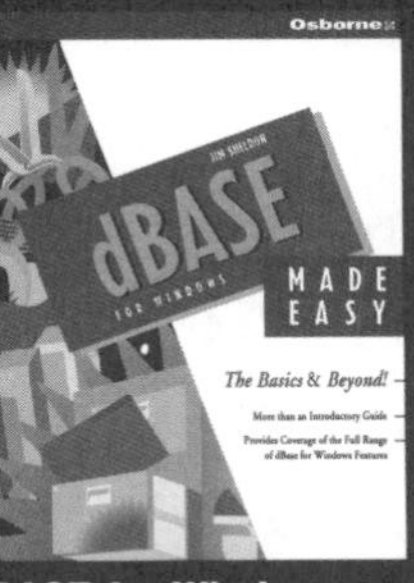

BASE for Windows lade Easy
y Jim Sheldon
6.95 ISBN: 0-07-881792-7

he Best Guide To usiness Shareware
y Judy Heim, John Haib
nd Mike Callahan
ncludes Two 3.5-Inch Disks
34.95 ISBN: 0-07-882076-6

The Visual C++ Handbook
by Chris H. Pappas and
William H. Murray, III
34.95 ISBN: 0-07-882056-1

GET WHAT YOU WANT...

Expert Advice & Support 24 Hours A Day

Do you need help with your software?

Why pay up to $25.00 for a single tech support call!

Now, in conjunction with **Corporate Software Inc.**, one of the world's largest providers of tech support (they field more than 200,000 calls a month), Osborne delivers the most authoritative new series of answer books — **The Certified Tech Support** series.

- These books will bail you out of practically any pitfall.
- Find answers to the most frequently asked end-user questions, from the simple to the arcane.
- **Lotus Notes Answers: Certified Tech Support** is the next best thing to having an expert beside your computer.
- Watch for other books in the series.

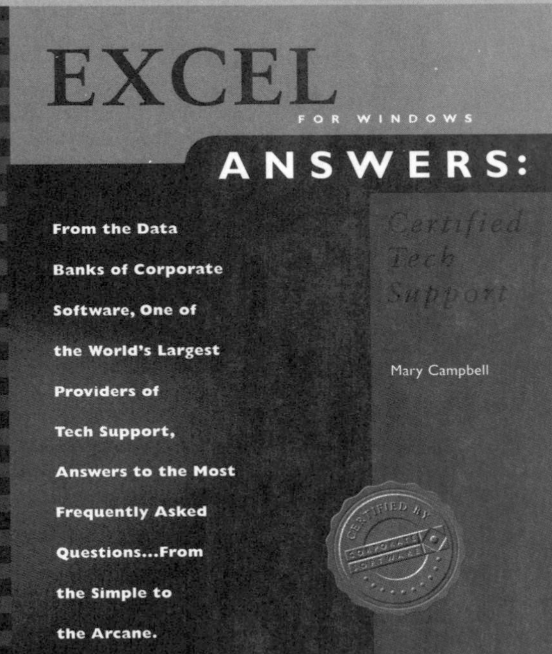

Excel for Windows Answers: Certified Tech Support
by Mary Campbell
$16.95
ISBN: 0-07-882054-5

Order Today!

BC640SL

Think Fast PASSING LANE AHEAD

What's the quickest route to tech support? Osborne's new Certified Tech Support series. Developed in conjunction with Corporate Software Inc., one of the largest providers of tech support fielding more than 200,000 calls a month, Osborne delivers the most authoritative question and answer books available anywhere. Speed up your computing and stay in the lead with answers to the most frequently asked end-user questions—from the simple to the arcane. And watch for more books in the series.

Lotus Notes Answers: Certified Tech Support
by Polly Russell Kornblith
$16.95 U.S.A.
ISBN: 0-07-882055-3

YELLOW PAGES

The Internet Yellow Pages
by Harley Hahn and Rick Stout
$27.95 U.S.A.
ISBN: 0-07-882023-5

Sound Blaster: The Official Book, Second Edition
by Peter M. Ridge, David Golden, Ivan Luk, Scott Sindorf, and Richard Heimlich
Includes One 3.5-Inch Disk
$34.95 U.S.A.
ISBN: 0-07-882000-6

Osborne Windows Programming Series
by Herbert Schildt, Chris H. Pappas, and William H. Murray, III
Vol. 1 - Programming Fundamentals
$39.95 U.S.A.
ISBN: 0-07-881990-3
Vol. 2 - General Purpose API Functions
$49.95 U.S.A.
ISBN: 0-07-881991-1
Vol. 3 - Special Purpose API Functions
$49.95 U.S.A.
ISBN: 0-07-881992-X

The Microsoft Access Handbook
by Mary Campbell
$27.95 U.S.A.
ISBN: 0-07-882014-6

BC640SL

Revolutionary Information on the Information REVOLUTION

Alluring opportunities abound for the global investor. But avoiding investment land mines can be tricky business. The first release in the Business Week Library of Computing lets you master all the winning strategies. Everything is here—from analyzing and selecting the best companies, to tax planning, using investment software tools, and more. Disks include MetaStock, Windows On WallStreet, and Telescan, the leading investment analysis software.

The Business Week Guide to Global Investments Using Electronic Tools
by Robert Schwabach
Includes Three 3.5-Inch Disks
$39.95 U.S.A. ISBN: 0-07-882055-3

The Business Week Guide to Multimedia Presentations Create Dynamic Presentations That Inspire
by Robert Lindstrom
Includes One CD-ROM
$39.95 U.S.A.
ISBN: 0-07-882057-X

The Internet Yellow Pages
by Harley Hahn and Rick Stout
$27.95 U.S.A.
ISBN: 0-07-882023-5

BYTE's Mac Programmer's Cookbook
by Rob Terrell
Includes
One 3.5-Inch Disk
$29.95 U.S.A.
ISBN: 0-07-882062-6

Multimedia: Making It Work, Second Edition
by Tay Vaughan
Includes
One CD-ROM
$34.95 U.S.A.
ISBN: 0-07-882035-9

BC640SL

The Internet Yellow Pages
by Harley Hahn and Rick Stout
$27.95 U.S.A.
ISBN: 0-07-882098-7

The Internet Complete Reference
by Harley Hahn and Rick Stout
$29.95 U.S.A.
ISBN: 0-07-881980-6

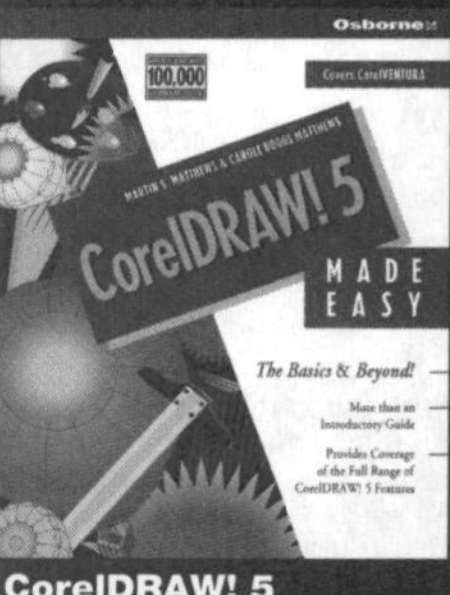

CorelDRAW! 5 Made Easy
by Martin S. Matthews and Carole Boggs Matthews
$29.95 U.S.A.
ISBN: 0-07-882066-9

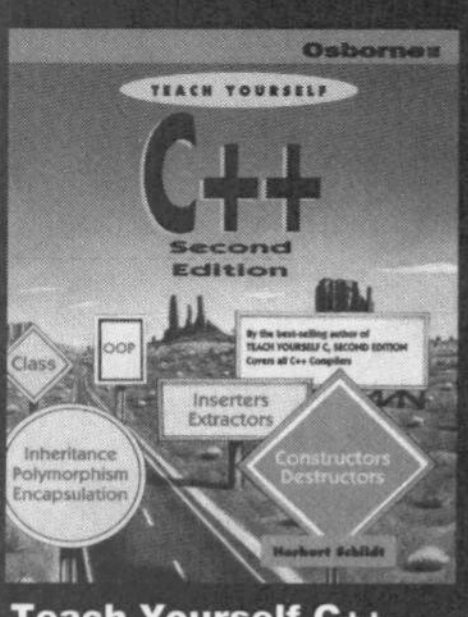

Teach Yourself C++, Second Edition
by Herbert Schildt
$24.95 U.S.A.
ISBN: 0-07-882025-1

When It Comes to CD-ROM

We Wrote the Book

Everything You Always Wanted to Know About CD-ROMs and More!

This Exclusive Book/CD-ROM Package Includes

- Sound and Clip Art
- Samples of CD-ROM Applications
- Multimedia Authoring Tools

Part buyer's guide, part standards guide, and part troubleshooter, the **BYTE Guide to CD-ROM** discusses all aspects of this proliferatin technology so you can take full advantage.

BYTE Guide to CD-ROM
by
Michael Nadeau,
BYTE Senior Edit
Includes CD-RO
$39.95 U.S.A.
ISBN: 0-07-88198

Osborne
Get Answers—Get Osborne
For Accuracy, Quality and Value

BC640SL

Secret Recipes FOR THE SERIOUS CODE CHEF

No longer underground...the best-kept secrets and profound programming tips have been liberated! You'll find them all in the new BYTE Programmer's Cookbook series – the hottest hacks, facts, and tricks for veterans and rookies alike. These books are accompanied by a CD-ROM or disk packed with code from the books plus utilities and plenty of other software tools you'll relish.

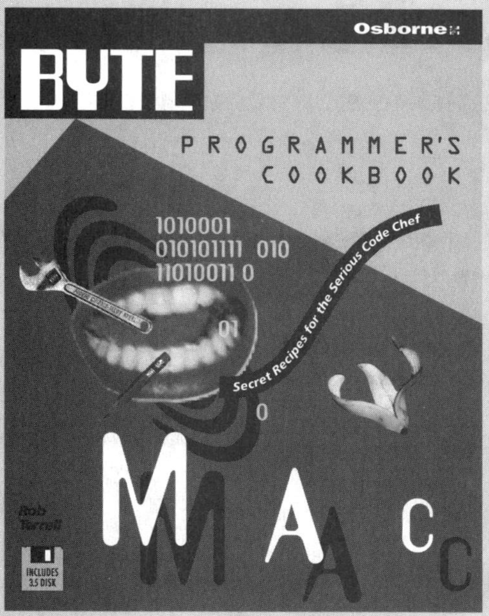

BYTE's Mac Programmer's Cookbook
by Rob Terrell
Includes One 3.5-Inch Disk
$29.95 U.S.A., ISBN: 0-07-882062-6

BYTE's Windows Programmer's Cookbook
by L. John Ribar
Includes
One CD-ROM
$34.95 U.S.A.
ISBN: 0-07-882037-5

BYTE's DOS Programmer's Cookbook
by Craig Menefee, Lenny Bailes, and Nick Anis
Includes
One CD-ROM
$34.95 U.S.A.
ISBN: 0-07-882048-0

BYTE's OS/2 Programmer's Cookbook
by Kathy Ivens and Bruce Hallberg
Includes
One CD-ROM
$34.95 U.S.A.
ISBN: 0-07-882039-1

BYTE Guide to CD-ROM
by Michael Nadeau
Includes
One CD-ROM
$39.95 U.S.A.
ISBN: 0-07-881982-2

BC640SL

Yo Unix!

INNOVATIVE BOOKS FROM OPEN COMPUTING AND OSBORNE/MCGRAW-HILL

OPEN COMPUTING'S GUIDE TO THE BEST FREE UNIX UTILITIES
BY JIM KEOUGH AND REMON LAPID
INCLUDES ONE CD-ROM
$34.95 U.S.A.
ISBN: 0-07-882046-4
AVAILABLE NOW

OPEN COMPUTING'S BEST UNIX TIPS EVER
BY KENNETH H. ROSEN, RICHARD P. ROSINSKI, AND DOUGLAS A. HOST
$29.95 U.S.A.
ISBN: 0-07-881924-5
AVAILABLE NOW

OPEN COMPUTING'S UNIX UNBOUND
BY HARLEY HAHN
$27.95 U.S.A.
ISBN: 0-07-882050-2

OPEN COMPUTING'S STANDARD UNIX API FUNCTIONS
BY GARRETT LONG
$39.95 U.S.A.
ISBN: 0-07-882051-0

BC640SL